理解句法学

第四版

UNDERSTANDING SYNTAX

Fourth Edition

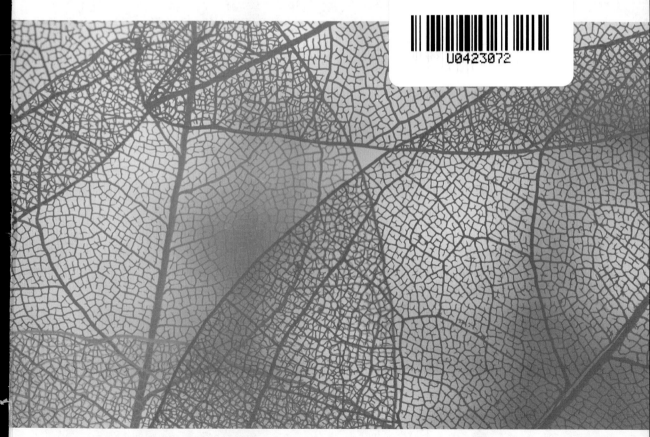

[英] 麦基·陶乐曼 著　崔 刚 注

清华大学出版社
北京

Maggie Tallerman: Understanding Syntax (Fourth Edition)

ISBN 978-0-415-74698-4

All Rights Reserved.

Copyright © 1998, 2005, 2011, 2015 Maggie Tallerman

Authorised edition from English language edition published by Routledge, a member of the Taylor & Francis Group.

本书中文简体注释改编版授权由清华大学出版社独家出版并仅限在中华人民共和国境内（不包括中国香港、澳门特别行政区和台湾地区）销售。未经出版者书面许可，不得以任何方式复制或发行本书的任何部分。

本书封面贴有Taylor & Francis公司防伪标签，无标签者不得销售。

北京市版权局著作权合同登记号　图字：01-2016-9795

版权所有，侵权必究。举报：010-62782989，beiqinquan@tup.tsinghua.edu.cn。

图书在版编目（CIP）数据

理解句法学＝第四版/（英）麦基·陶乐曼（Maggie Tallerman）著；崔刚注.—北京：清华大学出版社，2020.5（2022.9重印）

书名原文：Understanding Syntax（Fourth Edition）

ISBN 978-7-302-54475-3

Ⅰ.①理…　Ⅱ.①麦…②崔…　Ⅲ.①句法—研究　Ⅳ.①H043

中国版本图书馆CIP数据核字（2019）第264784号

责任编辑：曹诗悦
封面设计：子　一
责任校对：王凤芝
责任印制：杨　艳

出版发行：清华大学出版社
　　网　　址：http://www.tup.com.cn, http://www.wqbook.com
　　地　　址：北京清华大学学研大厦A座　邮　　编：100084
　　社 总 机：010-83470000　邮　　购：010-62786544
　　投稿与读者服务：010-62776969, c-service@tup.tsinghua.edu.cn
　　质量反馈：010-62772015, zhiliang@tup.tsinghua.edu.cn

印 装 者：三河市科茂嘉荣印务有限公司

经　　销：全国新华书店

开　　本：180mm×250mm　印　张：23.75　字　数：360千字

版　　次：2020年5月第1版　印　次：2022年9月第2次印刷

定　　价：109.00元

产品编号：068169-02

全书导读

一、什么是句法学

语言学是对人类语言的科学研究。语言本身是由多种成分构成的一个复杂的系统，其中包括语音、词汇、语义、句子和语篇等层次；语言作为人类区别于动物的标志性特征，它又与神经、心理、社会等具有密切的联系。因此，我们可以从微观与宏观两个角度去研究语言。所谓微观，就是只针对语言本身，是对语言材料所进行的语言本体的研究与分析。微观语言学包括语音学、音位学、形态学、语义学、句法学、语篇分析等。而所谓宏观，就是从更广的角度去研究语言，对它进行外围性的研究，进而探讨语言与其他相关事物之间的关系。宏观语言学包括心理语言学（研究语言和心理之间的关系，探讨语言习得、语言理解和语言产出的心理机制）、神经语言学（研究语言和大脑之间的关系）、社会语言学（研究语言和社会之间的关系），等等。从宏观语言学和微观语言学的划分来看，句法学属于微观语言学的范畴，同时也是其核心的分支学科之一。

句法学在英语中是 syntax，该词来自于古希腊语 syntaxis 一词，意思是"安排，排列，组合在一起"。由此我们可以看出，句法学研究语言中句子的结构特征以及构造规律，换言之，句法学研究不同的词是如何组合在一起构成句子的，其中内在的规律是什么，不同的句子构成要素以及不同句子之间的相互关系又是什么。关于句子的结构特征有两个问题最为核心：一是它的线性特征；二是它的层级特征。所谓线性特征是指句子中词的排列顺序。虽然我们说出或者写出一个句子时，其中的词都是按照顺序一个接一个出现的，但是它们的出现不是随意的，都隐含着一定的句法规则。这些规则决定着词的具体位置，或者词的先后顺序，还决定着句子的不同要素之间的语法关系以及它们的句法功能。但是，句子的结构并不仅仅局限于词的线性顺序上，它还表现在句子的层级特征上。句子是由层级性的结构组成的，一个句子可以被进一步分为更小的成分，换言之，不同层次的小成分可以结合起来形成更大的单位。

二、句法学研究的历史回顾

句法学研究经历了长期的发展过程。在 17 和 18 世纪，关注句子结构的学者主要是哲学家，而不是语言学家。他们把句法视为思想和逻辑的反映，把语言视为一种能够反映推理过程的抽象系统，而不是像今天这样从实际使用的角度把语言视为交际的工具，也不会以实际出现的语料为基础对它们进行实证性的分析与研究。到了 18 世纪末期，学者们对语言研究的重点更多地集中到语言的多样性上，当时的语言类型学所关注的重点也集中在形态学上。但是，这一阶段研究者的思想对于今天的句法学研究具有重要的影响，其中最为突出的是德国语言学家洪堡特（W. von Humboldt）。在他看来，语言和思维是密不可分的，语言不仅仅代表着思维，还在思维形成的过程中发挥着根本的作用。每种语言都有其特定的认知形式，即内部构造（inner structure），而句法的某些现象最能够揭示语言的内部构造。

在 19 世纪，众多描述性和历史性语法论著出版，这些著作一般只包括关于音位学和形态学的章节，而句法更多地作为形态学的附属部分被加以讨论。到了 19 世纪末期，一些新语法学派[1]的研究者才开始转向句法学，并且进行了广泛的研究。这些早期的句法分析与研究仍然更多地借助哲学理论。与此同时，心理学理论也对当时的句法学研究产生了重要的影响，其中影响最大的当属冯特（W. Wundt）。冯特是德国著名的心理学家和哲学家，他于 1879 年在莱比锡大学创立世界上第一个心理学实验室，成功地把心理学从哲学中分离出来，使之成为一门独立的科学，冯特因此也被公认为实验心理学之父。冯特认为，心理学研究的对象是人的直接经验，而直接经验存在于经验者的主观世界之中，因此内省法是心理学研究的特有方法。但是，他认为传统的内省法并不科学，必须和实验法结合起来，借助于实验进行内省和自我观察。在众多的语言学研究者之中，叶斯柏森（O. Jespersen）是值得关注的。

---

1 新语法学派是由德国莱比锡大学布鲁格曼（K. Brugmann）、奥斯特霍夫（H. Osthoff）、德尔布吕克（B. Delbrück）等人在 19 世纪 70 年代创立的，该学派强调语音规律的普遍性，认为语音的演变规律没有例外，还提倡分析活的方言。它总结了 19 世纪比较语言学和历史语言学的成果，预示了 20 世纪初结构主义语言学的诞生。

叶斯柏森是丹麦著名的语言学家，他的研究范围涵盖了普通语言学、语音学、语法学、语言史、外语教学、符号系统、语言哲学、国际辅助语等众多的领域，其中对普通语言学和语法学的贡献最为突出，影响了后来包括布龙菲尔德（L. Bloomfield）、乔姆斯基（N. Chomsky）和韩礼德（M. A. K. Halliday）在内的许多学者。在《英语语法精要》一书中，他认为研究句法要从意义到形式，而研究词法则要从形式到意义。在《分析句法》中，他使用符号研究了英语的内在句法结构。《语法哲学》被认为是叶斯柏森最为重要的著作之一。[2] 在该书中，他讨论了逻辑范畴、语法范畴以及它们之间的相互关系。他认为语言理论应是概括语言事实的工具，而不是让语言事实去迁就语法的教条。这对一般语法理论的探索具有很重要的意义，是传统的规范语法向现代的描写语法转变的重要一步。他指出，在任何一个表示事物或人的词组中，总可以发现其中一个词最重要，而其他的词则结合在一起从属于这个词。基于这一观点，叶斯柏森提出了著名的"三品说"：根据词在句子中的作用与地位，把它们分为"首品"（primary）、"次品"（secondary）和"末品"（tertiary），其中"首品"大致等于名词，"次品"大致等于形容词和动词，"末品"大致等于副词。另外，他还在书中创造了大量新的术语，如"组连式"（nexus）、"附连式"（junction）、"存在句"（existential sentence）等，并对这些术语作了阐述。这些概念对后来的句法分析都产生了重要的影响。例如，"组连式"的概念被认为是现代"依附"（dependency）和"管辖"（government）的雏形。此外，他最先使用SVO三个字母代表"主谓宾"的结构。

到了20世纪，以索绪尔（F. de Saussure）的《普通语言学教程》的出版为标志，语言学研究进入了一个新的阶段。索绪尔被称为现代语言学之父，其主要原因在于他所做的三种区分对于后来的语言学研究产生了重要影响。第一，他把语言分成语言和言语。语言是指语言的系统，是一套符号系统；言语是实际运用的话语，即以语言系统为基础的言语行为。语言学家的任务就是研究语言，即语言的系统。这一区分与后来乔姆斯基所做的关于语言能力（competence）和语言运用（performance）的区分具有异曲同工之处。

---

[2] 叶斯柏森的另一部重要作品是《语言：性质、发展和起源》，它与索绪尔的《普通语言学教程》、布龙菲尔德的《语言论》等同属西方语言学的经典名著。

第二，索绪尔区分了共时语言学和历时语言学。第三，索绪尔区分了组合关系和联想关系。组合关系是指在文字或口语的线性结构中一个语言成分与其他语言成分之间的关系。组合关系就是共现关系，也就是整体与部分和部分与整体的关系。联想关系是语言成分之间的关系；这种关系的产生不是由于几个成分同时出现于一个结构，而是由于它们同属一种语言，而且由于它们在意义上的相似或区别而发生联系。现在，这种关系通常被称为聚合关系。这一区分对于后来的句法学研究产生了重要的影响。

紧随索绪尔之后发展起来的是欧洲功能主义语言学，其中布拉格学派[3]的研究最为显著。除了对语音学和音位学的贡献之外，该学派还从功能语言观出发对句子进行了分析。马泰修斯（V. Mathesius）从所传递信息的角度观察句子，他发现，句子有三种成分：主位（theme）、过渡（transition）和述位（rheme）。主位是话语的出发点，是所谈论的对象，是从上下文已经知道的事实或设想的已知信息，这一部分不增加待传的新信息。述位是话语的核心，是说话人对主位要讲的话，它包含待传的全部新信息，并可增加听话人的知识。这种区分可以用来对比语言变体和不同语言的句子结构。马泰修斯比较了英语、捷克语和德语，发现英语的明显倾向是用主语表达主位，有些"主语—谓语"次序正好符合"主位—述位"序列。布拉格学派还研究了控制信息分布的规则。他们提出"交际力"的概念，来测量信息分布情况。一个语言成分的交际力就是它推动交际向前发展的程度。

在欧洲功能主义语言学不断发展的同时，美国结构主义语言学也应运而生，其中的代表性人物是布龙菲尔德，他把欧洲的语言学传统与美国的语言学实践相结合，影响了一代语言学家，其中包括威尔斯（R. Wells）和哈利斯（Z. Harris）等。他们认为语言是个具有不同层次和组成部分的结构，语言学的一个重要目标就是建立一套可以用于语言分析的"发现程序"，从而确保获得准确客观的关于语音和语法的描述。美国结构主义语言学对句法学研究最为突出的贡献在于直接成分（immediate constituents，IC）分析

---

[3] 布拉格学派成立于1926年，其主要成员有马泰修斯（V. Mathesius）、特鲁别茨考依（N. S. Trubetzkoy）、雅各布逊（R. Jakobson）、卡采夫斯基（S. Karcevski）、哈兰尼克（B. Havranek）。这些语言学家的作品都被收录在《布拉格小组论丛》中出版。到1939年，该《论丛》共出版八辑，他们的观点得以被其他国家所了解。布拉格学派于1950年停止集体活动。后来，有些捷克语言学家又成立了新布拉格学派，既研究语言学，又研究语文学。

法。直接成分这一概念最早是由布龙菲尔德在其 1933 年出版的《语言论》中首先提出，他说，"任何一个说英语的人，如果他有意来分析语言形式，一定会告诉我们：Poor John ran away 的直接成分是 poor John 和 ran away 这两个形式；而这两个形式又分别是个复合形式，ran away 的直接成分是 ran 和 away，poor John 的直接成分是 poor 和 John"（p. 161）。由此可见，直接成分就是直接位于一个结构体层面之下的成分，这个结构体可以是一个句子，也可以是一个短语。而直接成分分析法就是对句法结构组织形式的层次性分析，它把句子不断地一分为二，直到不能再分为止。

美国结构主义语言学以归纳实证主义和行为主义心理学为基础，主张对语言现象的解释必须要以可观察的现象为基础，要按照数学和逻辑的原则进行。在布龙菲尔德的影响下，该学派的学者大都反对对语言进行心灵主义的（mentalistic）和认知的解释。到了 20 世纪 50 年代，美国结构主义语言学似乎解决了语言分析中的许多基本问题。哈利斯[4]的研究，尤其是他写的《结构主义语言学方法论》，使结构主义思想对方法论的重视发展到一个新的高度，其中的句法方法尤其受到学者的好评。哈利斯认为，语言结构分析有两个基本的任务：一是把话语里的单位切分出来；二是把有关的单位归类。在分析时，要根据语言单位的分布特征，用替换的方法来进行鉴别，这种方法也被称为"分布主义"，该方法对后来的句法分析，尤其是语言单位范畴的鉴别具有重要的影响。在该书前言的末尾，哈利斯对乔姆斯基的帮助表示感谢。结果，几年之后，恰恰是乔姆斯基推翻了结构主义的所谓科学方法，在语言学界引起了一场"革命"。

当时，许多语言学家认为，一旦找到了语法的发现程序，语言描写的问题就基本解决了，剩下的工作通过计算机即可完成。可是，信息论的发展和心理语言学的诞生为语言学研究开辟了广阔的前景，而结构主义的方法论过于僵化，不允许研究观察不到的东西，从而大大限制了语言学的新

---

4 哈利斯是继布龙菲尔德之后的美国结构主义的主要语言学家之一。他的主要著作《结构主义语言学方法论》是对形式描写方法（即发现程序）的最全面的总结和最精辟的论述。发现程序是一系列的详细规则，说明如何从话语的语音记录，通过音位和语素分析，实现对句法类型的描写。哈利斯意识到发现程序的局限性，于是开始探讨如何用转换关系来解释句子之间的关系，称之为"语符串分析"。哈利斯在结构主义语言学中之所以占有举足轻重的地位，是因为他试图描写句法关系。布龙菲尔德语法的分析基础是成分的出现位置，而哈利斯的分析基础是语素类。哈利斯是从语素开始，通过替换把它们归为更大的类别。

探索。当时，结构主义者仍然专心致志地罗列可观察的语言事实，仍用机械的程序去进行语言描写。他们对音位学和形态学的贡献较大，相比之下，对句法研究不甚突出。不过，当时哈利斯已经开始寻找描写句际关系的程序，初步探讨了对语篇的描写。他认为，句子之间的关系要用转换来解释。乔姆斯基是哈利斯的学生，他很可能从转换思想中得到启发，加之他对发现程序的枯竭无力十分不满，这就构成了他创立转换生成语法的思想基础。

1957 年，乔姆斯基出版了《句法结构》一书，从而开启了人们所说的"乔姆斯基革命"。在此书中，乔姆斯基不再讨论什么描写方法，而是试图建立一种语言学理论。从此以后，整个语言学的研究方向发生了变化，语法不再是什么等待发现的东西，而成了一种语言学说，是一系列的公理，用来生成无限句子，每个句子有相应的结构描写。语法的优劣要看它能否处理语言素材，即能否解释本族语者的语言直感。既然本族语者可以创造出无限多句子，这种语言必须是生成性的。乔姆斯基认为，最有解释力的生成语法是转换生成语法，其中包括短语结构规则、句法转换规则和语素音位规则三大部分。

《句法结构》问世之初，只有寥寥几篇肯定性的评论，并没有很多人响应，到了 20 世纪 60 年代初期才有几个支持者。乔姆斯基继续提炼自己的看法，支持者也开始阐述自己的意见。例如，李斯（R. B. Lees）写了《英语名词化语法》，从转换的角度解释英语中的名词化问题，指出了许多派生现象。凯茨（J. J. Katz）和福特（J. Fodor）写了《语义理论结构》，讨论了转换生成语法中的语义问题，尤其是语义与句法的关系，还探讨了语义结构的普遍性和先天性。凯茨和波斯特尔（P. Postal）又撰写了《语言描写的统一理论》，讨论了转换如何影响意义。他们认为，语义解释所需要的一切信息都能在基础句法结构中找到。这一观点后来被称为"凯茨—波斯特尔假说"。在这一时期，转换生成语法中许多没有讲清楚的问题有了比较清楚的解释。例如，语法的充分性应有几种，应该如何定义；什么是形式普遍现象和实体普遍现象。此外，他们还区分了语言能力（competence）（即语言知识）和语言行为（performance）（即语言运用）。

这些新的见解大都汇集到乔姆斯基的第二部著作《句法理论中的若干问题》之中。此书的观点后来被称为转换语法的"标准理论"。乔姆斯基总结了几年的辩论成果，提出了更为全面的普遍语言理论。同时，他站在唯理主义和心灵主义立场上，反对结构语言学的经验主义和行为主义的观点。他从哲学和心理学的角度，详细阐述了为什么语法要包括三大部分：生成性的句法部分、解释性的语义部分和音位部分。他还详细解释了这三大部分的构成和功能。句法部分又叫基础部分，其中包括一个词汇库和范畴部分和一个转换部分。范畴和词汇部分可生成有限的带有结构描写的基础语符列，这些语符列则是深层结构的基本成分。转换部分负责把深层结构改写为表层结构。深层结构的输出决定着每个句子的语义解释，也就构成了语义部分的输入。音位部分决定着表层结构所产生句子的发音情况。这种模式把句法作为中心环节，把语法的生成潜力放在句法部分。

到了 20 世纪 60 年代后期，无论是在美国还是在其他国家，关于转换生成语法的辩论主要在支持者内部进行，非支持者并没有参与。辩论的主要内容是句法结构的抽象程度。当然，语法结构都是抽象的，但是对生成语法学家来说，必须弄清深层结构和表层结构之间到底有多大距离，到底深层结构具有哪些特点。费尔默（C. J. Fillmore）写了几篇文章，提出另一种语法模式——"格语法"。他认为，在句法结构的最深层次，句子只有两种成分：一是情态；二是命题。命题就是动词与名词之间各种格的关系。费尔默指出，"标准理论"难以区分范畴信息和功能信息，所以无法区分介词短语和状语。他认为，乔姆斯基的深层结构没有必要，这个深层结构实际上是表达格的关系的语义结构。费尔默的格语法理论对后来的句法学研究产生了深远的影响。其他学者对深层结构的地位和特征也有异议，如拉克夫（G. Lakoff）、罗斯（J. R. Ross）、波斯特尔、麦科利（J. D. McCawley）等，他们质疑深层结构与语义解释之间，到底是什么关系。拉克夫和罗斯在《深层结构有必要吗？》一文中，首次提出应该放弃深层结构。他们认为，深层结构与语义解释不能分开，语义本身就有生成性。他们的思想后来发展成"生成语义学"，在 20 世纪 60 年代末和 70 年代初十分盛行。

这场争论给语言学研究提出了许多有趣的问题，例如，语迹问题、筛选问题、词项分析问题、言语行为分析、语言的使用特征问题等。其实，大部分转换生成语法学家认为，在某种表达层次上，句子一定具有一种类似符号逻辑的形式。关于对深层结构的批评，乔姆斯基最初的回答是，可用词项化假设来解释，即排除改变范畴的转换规则。他在《论名词化》一文中指出，必须假设深层结构的存在，否则不能对句子结构作出有意义的概括。在这篇论文中，他还首次提出了 X 阶的概念。在《深层结构、表层结构、语义解释》一文中，乔姆斯基又有新的阐述，承认表层结构的特征对语义解释也有一定的作用。到这时，乔姆斯基及其支持者的立场被称为"解释主义"，就是说，语义解释规则也适用于句子结构。

经过几年的发展，乔姆斯基一派的理论又发展为"扩充式标准理论"，后来又变成"修正的扩充式标准理论"。这个时期的句法研究集中到规则的作用问题上，尤其是转换规则的作用。起初，乔姆斯基等人普遍认为，转换不许改变句子的意义，后来开始讨论如何保持结构也不发生变化。于是，转换规则和基础规则的应用都有了限制。所以，这个时期的基本特点是对句法规则作用的约束。1973 年，乔姆斯基写了《论转换条件》一文，他重申，在扩充式标准理论的研究中，已经对基础结构、转换规则和语义解释规则等作了限制。他探讨了应用转换规则的条件，并对表层结构作了某些限制。

20 世纪 70 年代末，乔姆斯基和他的同事（如赖斯尼克 H. Lasnik）开始研究筛选问题，发展了管辖和约束理论。1978 年，乔姆斯基写了《约束论》，提出"核心语法"的概念，详细讨论了非自由变量（如代词）的问题，并对逻辑式作了某些限制。逻辑式是"谓语演算"的另一种形式，大致相当于语义解释。在《规则与表达》一书中，乔姆斯基讨论了语言学、哲学等多方面的问题。此书比较通俗易懂，其重要内容之一是关于"普遍语法"的特性。

1981 年，乔姆斯基出版了《管辖与约束讲稿》，继续探索对语法系统的抽象限制条件。他首先详尽讨论了"核心语法"的结构和地位，然后重申了《约束论》中的观点，但又发现概念上的缺欠和实际分析中的困难，所以改变了原先的看法，又把"管辖"理论放在首要地位。由此，他提出了"管辖-约束"论；在此基础上，乔姆斯基又提出了"原则-参数理论"。按照这一理论，语言的语法规则系统由词库（lexicon）和句法通过转换而生成语音表现形式（phonetic form, PF）和逻辑式（logical form, LF）。但是这并不是转换生成语言学的顶峰，乔姆斯基一直在不断地发展自己的理论，又陆续发表了一系列的研究成果，主要包括《语言理论的最简方案》《最简方案》和《最简方案探究框架》等。最简方案代表着转换生成语言学的最新进展。

  最简方案依然保持了乔姆斯基的内在主义语言观。乔姆斯基认为，语言是由生物遗传而来的语言机能所呈现出的语言状态。语言机能的组成成分是一个生成程序，也就是内在化语言（internalized language），这个程序叫运算推导（computation and derivation）。内在化语言生成结构描写 SD（structure description），即语言的表达式。内在化语言内嵌在应用系统之中，应用系统把语言所生成的表达式应用于与语言有关的活动之中。结构描写被视为对这些应用系统所发出的指令。与内在化语言相关的应用系统分为两个：一个是发声感知系统（articulatory-perceptual system，A-P）；一个是概念意向系统（conceptual-intentional system，C-I）。每个运算生成的语言表达式都包含着给予这些系统的指令。语言与这两个系统形成的界面是 A-P 和 C-I，它们分别给发声感知系统和概念意向系统提供指令。A-P 界面一般被认为是语音表现形式，C-I 界面一般被认为是逻辑式。从语言理论构建的必要性考虑，最简方案中的语言设计只需要 A-P 和 C-I 这两个界面就可以了，这一理念符合我们对于语言的形式主要由语音和意义组合而成的认识。最简方案也进一步发展了乔姆斯基关于派生的经济性和表达的经济性的思想。根据派生的经济性原则，词的移位（或转换）只有在为了使可解释的特征与不可解释的特征相匹配的情况下才发生。例如，在英语中，规则名词的复数形式 dogs 一词，它只能用来指"几条狗"，那么它的屈折变化对于意义就产生了影响，因此是可以解释的。而英语中的动词为了保持与其主语在数上的一致，有时也需要有屈折变化（例如，Dogs bite 和 The dog bites），而在这种情况下，屈折变化只是复制了主语中已经具备的关于数的信息，因此是不可解释的。根据表达的经济性原则，语法结构的存在都是有目的的，也就是说，句子的结构只要能满足语法性的限制即可。最简方案还主张句法结构的派生应该是统一的，句法规则不应该仅仅应用于派生过程的一些点上，而是整个的派生过程。最简方案采用无标短语结构取代了 X 阶标理论，去掉了原来的 S-结构和 D-结构，保留了语音和意义的接口层次。

  尽管乔姆斯基一直不断地发展自己的理论，提出新的学说，但是他的基本语言观并没有改变。乔姆斯基在语言研究中发现，有许多现象是结构主义语法和行为主义心理学所无法解释的。一个五六岁的儿童就可以掌握母语,而这个年龄段的儿童的智力还很不发达,学习其他知识还相当困难,而学习语言却这么容易。儿童在学习其他知识方面都表现出天赋方面的差别,有人善于学习数学,有人善于学习音乐,另外,儿童的生活环境也千差万别,但是这些差异都不影响母语的习得。儿童学习母语就像学走路一样,似乎根本不用学。这些现象,用行为主义的"刺激—反应"论是解释不通的。因此,乔姆斯基认为,儿童天生就有一种学习语言的能力,有一个语言习得机制(language acquisition device, LAD),它能使所有正常的儿童,只要接触语言材料,就能在几年内习得母语。语言习得机制中包含一系列人脑的初始状态,而这一初始状态应该包括人类一切语言共同具有的特点,可称为普遍语法(universal grammar)或者语言普遍现象(linguistic universals)。简单地说,普遍语法就是构成语言学习中的初始状态的一组特性、条件和其他东西,是一切人类语言必须具有的原则、条件和规则系统。

乔姆斯基被认为是"天赋说"(innateness hypothesis)的主张者,但是他并不否认后天经验的重要性。他认为,人的语言知识可分为两种:一种是我们大脑中与生俱来的、固有的、具有程序性或指令性的普遍语法,这是无法从经验中获得的,具有"不可学得性"(unlearnability);另一种是我们讲的具体语言,这是靠后天经验获得的,具有可学得性(learnability)。儿童大脑中的语言官能(language faculty)需要与周围环境中的语言输入相接触,才能开始工作,并由普遍语法发展为个别语法(particular grammar)。个别语法就是儿童接触语言材料之后内化了的语言规则,是潜意识的语言知识,乔姆斯基称之为语言能力(competence),以区别于语言应用。语言能力是指在最理想的条件下说话人/听话人所掌握的语言知识,语言运用是对这种知识在适当场合下的具体使用。乔姆斯基主张语言学研究的对象是语言能力,而不是语言运用。

乔姆斯基认为,研究语言能力就是为了建立一种反映语言能力的生成语法。生成语法不是说话过程的模式,而是语言能力的模式,是对语言能力作出的形式化的描述,用一套公式将其内容表达出来。生成语法不局限于对个别语言的研究,而是要揭示个别语法与普遍语法的统一性,换言之,它不以具体语言的描述为归宿,而是以具体语言为出发点,探索出语言的普遍规律，最终弄清人的认知系统、思维规律和人的本质属性。为了达到这个目标，乔姆斯基提出了三个不同的层面来评价语法。能够对原始语言材料做出正确解释的语法，就算达到了观察的充分性（observational adequacy），但是达到这一要求的语法不能模拟说话人和听话人的语言知识，因此，语法应该达到另一个高的层面，即描写充分性（descriptive adequacy），在这一平面上，语法不仅能正确解释原始语言材料，而且要正确解释说话人和听话人的内在语言能力，也就是他们的语言知识。但是，仅仅达到描写充分性也还是不够的，一种语言可能同时存在几种描写充分的语法，所以还需要达到更高的层面，即解释充分性（explanatory adequacy）。如果在几种都已达到描写充分性的语法之间，还能建立一些基本原则来做出选择，那就已达到解释充分性。[5]

并不是所有的转换生成语法学者都一直追随乔姆斯基的理论。许多学者在乔姆斯基转换生成语法的基础上，又提出了自己的句法理论，其中影响较大的有"关系语法""词汇功能语法""角色参照语法"和"中心语驱动短语结构语法"等。关系语法（Relational Grammar）由美国语言学家波斯特尔和波尔马特（D. Perlmutter）在 20 世纪 70 年代创建。该理论抛弃了传统生成语法对次序的描写，把语法关系（例如，主语和宾语）视为句子结构的原始成分，认为解决语法关系在句法上的转换问题才具有普遍意义，因此，它对句子结构的描述主要通过对语法关系作多层次的分析来进行。一个句子的语法关系可以在几个层次中表现出来，第一层次的语法关系和语义紧密相关，而最后一个层次的语法关系则主要决定表层句法词序、格等问题。[6]

词汇功能语法（Lexical Functional Grammar）产生于 20 世纪 80 年代初，由美国语言学家布雷斯楠（J. Bresnan）和坎普兰（R. Kaplan）创立。布雷斯楠是乔姆斯基的学生，他的早期研究都是在转换生成语法的框架内进行的。坎普兰是一位心理语言学家和计算语言学家，在用计算机模拟人脑的语言

---

[5] 上述三段内容的撰写主要参照了刘润清教授编著的《西方语言学流派》（外语教学与研究出版社，2013）中的相关部分内容，特此致谢。

[6] 关于关系语法，读者可以进一步阅读由金顺德以及姚岚、马玉蕾分别撰写的名为《关系语法述评》的两篇文章，前者刊登于《外语教学与研究》1988 年第 2 期，后者刊登于《外语学刊》2003 年第 2 期。

处理机制方面做了大量的工作，两人共同提出的词汇功能语法借鉴了生成语法理论中关于表层结构和深层结构的划分，提出了成分结构（constituent structure，C-structure）和功能结构（functional structure，F-structure）的概念。前者以 X 阶理论为基础，采用短语结构树形图的形式对句子的外部结构进行描述，它代表着句子成分的先后次序，而后者则带有非成分信息，表示各语法成分之间的关系（如主语和宾语）以及各种语法特征（例如，时态、数、人称等）。词汇功能语法突出了词汇在语法理论中的作用，其中尤以谓词（predicate）最为重要。英语中的动词、一部分名词和形容词在句子的语法结构中发挥着相当于数理逻辑中的谓词的作用，谓词的语义决定了它的主目结构（argument structure）。词汇功能语法主要由词库、句法和语义解释机制三部分组成，词库中的谓词决定了它的主目结构，而主目结构通过词汇编码分配到语法功能，语法再将句子的语义映射到句法之上。句子在句法层面有成分结构和功能结构两个表达层次。[7]

角色参照语法（Role and Reference Grammar）也是在转换生成语法的基础上发展起来的，开始于 20 世纪 70 年代的中后期，以佛雷（W. Foley）和万林（R. Valin）等学者为代表。该理论的提出起源于有关学者对于拉霍它语（Lakota）、塔加禄语（Tagalog）和迪尔巴尔语（Dyirbal）的研究。与英语等欧洲语言相比，这些不属于印欧语系的语言在语言结构上具有自己显著的特点。因此，有学者就提出疑问，如果转换生成语法不是以英语为基础，而是以其他的语言为基础，它会是什么样子？鉴于对这一问题的思考，学者们就提出了角色参照语法，并力图让该理论不仅能够描述和分析英语等印欧语言，而且能够适用于更多的、尤其是那些少数人群的语言，以便解释各种语言的结构系统中句法、语义和语用之间的相互关系和相互作用。该理论把语言看作是一种社会交际的行为系统，认为语法分析要从语言基本单位在系统中的功能角色入手，然后分析它们的形式和结构特征。角色参照语法吸收生成语法理论的诸多长处，但是没有像它那样的派生转换，并不从抽象的基础形式派生出相关的句子，

---

[7] 关于词汇功能语法，读者可以进一步阅读由赵军撰写的《词汇功能语法》（刊登于《语言文字应用》1996 年第 4 期）和由高明乐和方立撰写的《词汇功能语法解析》（刊登于《语文学刊》2009 年第 1 期）。

而是采用小句分层结构的模型（layered structure of the clause，LSC）。这个小句模型由三个层次组成：（1）核心谓词（nucleus）；（2）由核心谓词及其主目语构成的小句中心（core）；（3）由附属小句中心的时间、地点等修饰语所构成的小句外缘（periphery）。上述三个层次都由一个或者一个以上的功能元（operator）管辖，管辖核心谓词的功能元一般是"体"，管辖小句中心的功能元一般是"情态"，而小句外缘关系中最常见的功能元是"时态"与"言外之意"。因此，功能元不仅包括了时态、体、情态等语法范畴，还包括了"言外之意"等语义和语用范畴。[8]

中心语驱动短语结构语法（Head-driven Phrase Structure Grammar，HPSG）是由美国俄亥俄州立大学的普拉德（C. Pollard）和斯坦福大学的萨格（I. G. Sag）于20世纪80年代末所创立的一种形式语法理论。该理论借鉴了转换生成语法、关系语法和词汇功能语法等众多的句法理论，是在中心词语法（Head Grammar）和广义短语结构语法（Generalized Phrase Structure Grammar）的基础上发展而来的。HPSG的所有语言单位均由被索绪尔称为"符号"的特征结构（feature structure）来表征，它们含有为语音、句法和语义信息作代码的特征。语法以特征结构的形式来表征，特征值之间的连接决定着语音和语义之间的语法对应关系。该理论是一种高度词汇化的、基于约束的词汇主义理论。[9]

上述句法理论都可以被笼统地归于形式句法的范畴，除此之外，还有以系统功能语法（Systemic Functional Grammar）为代表的功能主义学派，因为它们与本书的内容关系不大，在此我们不再赘述。

三、关于本书

本书的作者陶乐曼（M. Tallerman）于1979年毕业于英国赫尔大学（University of Hull），获得学士学位，并于1987年从该校获得博士学位。从1983年到2004年，她任教于杜伦大学（University of Durham），先后任

---

[8] 关于角色参照语法，读者可以进一步阅读由潘永梁撰写的《角色参照语法述评》（刊登于《当代语言学》2000年第3期）。

[9] 关于HPSG，读者可以进一步阅读由方立和吴平以及由尤爱莉分别撰写的《中心语短语结构语法评介》两篇同名论文，前者刊登于《语言教学与研究》2003年第5期，后者刊登于《外语学刊》2000年第2期。

讲师和高级讲师，其后到纽卡斯尔大学（Newcastle University）担任语言学教授至今。她长期从事凯尔特语语言学、语言的起源与进化、语言类型学、形态学和句法学等领域的研究工作。本书是国际上被广泛采用的句法学教材之一，第一版出版于 1998 年，其后又经三次修订，分别于 2005 年和 2011 年出版了第二版和第三版，现在我们所使用的是第四版，于 2015 年出版。

经过几百年的发展，尤其是在 20 世纪 50 年代之后，句法学已经成为语言学里的第一学科，在整个语言学理论中占据核心的地位。句法学研究不仅极大地推动了语言学理论的发展，还影响了心理语言学、二语习得研究、神经语言学、社会语言学等众多的学科。更为重要的是，有关的理论还被广泛地应用于自然语言处理、人机对话、机器翻译、人工智能等领域，这极大地提高了语言学研究的地位。掌握句法学的研究方法以及主要的理论应该是对语言学专业学生的基本要求，但是对于我国的许多外国语言学及应用语言学学科的研究生来说，他们对于句法学的了解还远远不够。在许多学校，句法学只是作为普通语言学中的一个部分被简单地介绍，这在很大程度上影响了我国语言学专业研究生的质量，也影响了我国语言学研究的发展。造成这种状况的原因是多方面的，其中的一个原因在于目前以形式语言学为主导的句法学理论往往比较抽象，其中借用了许多哲学和数学等相关学科的概念，还包含着众多的推理和推导过程，这令许多仅具有文科背景的外语专业的学生望而生畏。而本书的出版将会对这一问题的解决有所帮助。

从第一版到现在，本书历经多次修订，充分吸收了多方面的意见，在内容的选取与编排、练习的设计等各个方面日趋合理，是一本难得的句法学入门教材，或者说是一本句法分析的训练教材。在阅读完本书之后，读者可以掌握句法学的基本概念和理论，并且具备初步的进行句法分析和研究的能力。从整体上来看，本书具有以下几个特点：（1）语言朴素，通俗易懂。从内容来看，本书更多地基于转换生成语法的理论和思想，这也符合目前句法学教材的主流，但是本书的读者并不需要具备专门的句法学知识，而且书中的内容并不涉及句法研究中有争论的前沿问题，读者只要认真阅读就能够理解书中的内容。对于一些重要的概念，作者都用大写字母表示，并且在书中反复提及。更为重要的是，作者对于这些概念的解释是有层次性的，她会根据具体的情况不断地由浅入深、从具体到抽象进行论述，非常有助于读者的理解。（2）语言实例丰富。对于句法学基本概念和基本理论的阐述，作者都列举了大量的语言句子实例，把抽象的理论融于具体的语言实例之中，使得理论的讲解和句法的分析生动具体。这些句子来自于一百多种不同的语言（其中包括许多少数民族的语言），这在同类教材之中是少见的，因此也是本书的一大特色。读者通过阅读这些实例，一方面可以增加自己对于世界上不同种类语言的认识，另一方面也可以掌握对于不同语言的句法分析方法。（3）内容全面，结构安排合理，非常适合读者深入学习与思考。本书全面地涵盖了句法学研究的核心内容，内容的安排层层递进。当讲解达到一定阶段后，作者设置了一些思考题，读者可以通过对这些问题的思考，一方面检查对前面内容的理解程度，另一方面也会为后面的阅读奠定基础，很好地起到了承上启下的作用。在每个章节结束时，作者还以问题的形式对整个章节的要点进行了总结，通过对这些问题的思考，读者可以很好地把握整个章节的核心内容。另外，在每个章节的最后都有丰富的练习题目，都与本章节的内容密切结合，它们不仅可以帮助读者复习、巩固本章节的内容，还可以训练他们分析问题和解决问题的能力。

四、学习建议

对于句法学的学习以及本书的阅读，有以下几条建议供大家参考：

1. 端正态度，克服浮躁的心理。如上文所述，句法学是语言学的核心分支，近几十年语言学研究的主要理论进展很大一部分都和句法研究有关，因此，掌握句法学的基本理论和基本方法是每个语言学研究者的核心素养，即使是对于不专门从事句法学研究的人来说，句法学也是必不可少的。例如，如果你对儿童语言习得感兴趣，句法学理论可以使你对儿童语言习得过程做出准确的描述，并且有助于解释语言习得内在的过程与原因。如果你对社会语言学感兴趣，句法学理论可以帮助你描述与分析不同语言变体之间的异同以及语言的变化。另外，它对语言教学以及计算机自然语言处理等领域也具有特殊的价值。但是，现代句法学理论更多地受到以转换生成语法为代表的形式句法的影响，而生成语法使用数学符号和公式来规定概念、表达规则，这在很大程度上增加了这门学科的难度，又加之目前社会大环境的影响，人们普遍较浮躁，很多人不愿意静下心来进行认真的阅读和思考，从而使得句法学成为一门让许多人感到枯燥的学科。尽管本书的语言平实、实例丰富，但是要想读懂并深入地理解其中的内容，还需要读者具有一定的耐心，这也是一个学者所必备的素养。

2. 认真通读全书，完成书中的各项任务要求。在与研究生们接触的过程中，笔者发现他们许多人都存在着浅尝辄止的问题，很少能够完整地读完一个学科的一本书。这对学生知识结构的建立是非常不利的。当我们学习一个学科时，首先要选取一本好的教材，认真地通读全书，这样就可以全面地把握这一学科的基础知识、基本理论和研究方法，在此之后再去读其他的同类著作或论文就会容易很多。对于句法学的学习也是如此，希望读者能够通读全书，并且能够认真地思考作者提出的问题以及章节之后的练习题。相信大家在完成本书的学习之后一定会大有收获。

3. 认真阅读本书的导读和注释。在每一章之前我们都为本章撰写了导读，梳理了全章的核心内容。建议读者在阅读正文之前先阅读一遍章节导读，这样可以对全章的内容具有一个轮廓性的认识。在阅读完全章之后，建议大家再把本章的导读阅读一遍，这样可以帮助你梳理整个章节的内容，而且还可以强化大家对句法学的核心概念和理论的认识与记忆，增强学习的效果。另外，在正文中我们也对其中的内容进行了注释，这些内容包括一些重要的概念和句法学理论，也有我们对于某个段落的整体评价和认识，还有一些希望大家思考的问题，希望它们能够对大家的阅读起到一定的帮助作用。

4. 结合汉语的情况进行必要的思考。对于语言学专业的中国学生来说，研究汉语具有重要的意义。一方面，我们生活在汉语环境中，能够获得最为丰富的语言材料和研究对象；另一方面，汉语作为世界上使用人口最多的语言，对于它的研究具有特别重要的价值。但是，对于许多外国语言学和应用语言学专业的学生来说，虽然汉语是他们的母语，但是他们对汉语的认识并不充分，对汉语的句法分析工作也进行得很少。这不能不说是一大遗憾。因此，我们建议读者在阅读本书时，经常自问：针对作者讨论的某个句法现象，汉语的具体情况如何？这样可以充分发挥阅读的价值，并且为自己今后的学习和研究打下良好的基础。

5. 手头准备两到三本参考书。虽然本书的语言比较平实，而且我们也对其中的一些重要概念做了必要的注释，但是仅靠这些还是不够的。我们建议读者在阅读时，手头上准备几本相关的参考书，在遇到一些重要的概念或者理论时，进行必要的查阅，以确保自己阅读的效果。在此我们向大家推荐以下几本书：

（1）Crystal, D. (2008). *A Dictionary of Linguistics and Phonetics*. Oxford: Blackwell.[10]

（2）Luraghi, S. & Parodi, C. (2008). *Key Terms in Syntax and Syntactic Theory*. New York: Continuum.

（3）戴炜华，2007.《新编英汉语言学词典》，上海：上海外语教育出版社．

（4）劳允栋，2004.《英汉语言学词典》，北京：商务印书馆．

（5）刘润清，2013.《西方语言学流派》，北京：外语教学与研究出版社．

（6）温宾利，2002.《当代句法学导论》，北京：外语教学与研究出版社．

（7）张伯江，2013.《什么是句法学》，上海：上海外语教育出版社．

崔　刚

2019 年 10 月于清华园

---

10 这是本书的第六版，本书的第四版已由沈家煊先生翻译成中文，并于 2011 年由商务印书馆出版发行。

For my dear family

Contents

Note to the instructor	xxvi
Note to the student	xxvii
Acknowledgements	xxix
Abbreviations used in examples	xxx
Tables and figures	xxxi
1 What is syntax?	**1**
章节导读	1
1.1 Some concepts and misconceptions	2
1.1.1 What is the study of syntax about?	2
1.1.2 Language change	9
1.2 Use of linguistic examples	13
1.2.1 Why not just use examples from English?	13
1.2.2 How to read linguistic examples	14
1.3 Why do languages have syntax?	20
1.3.1 Word order	21
1.3.2 Promotion and demotion processes	23
1.3.3 All languages have structure	25
Further reading	28
Exercises	29
Notes	34
2 Words belong to different classes	**35**
章节导读	35
2.1 Identifying word classes	37
2.1.1 How can we tell that words belong to different classes?	37
2.1.2 Starting to identify nouns, adjectives and verbs	38
2.1.3 An illustration: How do speakers of a language identify word classes?	41
2.2 Verbs	44
2.2.1 An introduction to verb classes	44
2.2.2 Verbs and their grammatical categories	47

2.3	Nouns	51
	2.3.1 Semantic roles for noun phrases	51
	2.3.2 Syntactic roles for noun phrases	52
	2.3.3 Nouns and their grammatical categories	56
	2.3.4 Nouns, definiteness and determiners	59
2.4	Adjectives	61
	2.4.1 Positions and functions of adjectives	61
	2.4.2 Adjectives and intensifiers	63
	2.4.3 Adjectives and their grammatical categories	63
	2.4.4 Are adjectives essential?	64
2.5	Adverbs	67
	2.5.1 Adverbs and adjectives	67
	2.5.2 The adjunct function	68
2.6	Prepositions	69
	2.6.1 Identifying prepositions in English	69
	2.6.2 Postpositions	71
	2.6.3 Grammatical categories for adpositions	71
2.7	Conclusion	72
	Further reading	73
	Exercises	73

3 Looking inside sentences — 81

章节导读 — 81

3.1 Finiteness and auxiliaries — 82
   3.1.1 Independent clauses — 82
   3.1.2 Finiteness — 84
   3.1.3 Main verbs and verbal auxiliaries — 85
   3.1.4 Ways to express the grammatical categories for verbs — 88
   3.1.5 Non-finite verbs — 89
   3.1.6 Co-ordination of clauses — 93
   3.1.7 Summary — 93

3.2 Introduction to subordination — 94
   3.2.1 Complement clauses — 94
   3.2.2 Adjunct or adverbial clauses — 98
   3.2.3 Identifying subordinate clauses — 98
   3.2.4 Special properties of root clauses — 100
   3.2.5 Some cross-linguistic variation in subordination — 103
   3.2.6 Summary: Properties of subordinate clauses and root clauses — 104

3.3 Major cross-linguistic variations — 105
   3.3.1 The co-ordination strategy — 105
   3.3.2 Nominalization — 106

	3.3.3 Serial verbs	107
	3.3.4 Summary	110
Further reading		111
Exercises		111

4 Heads and their dependents — 120

章节导读 — 120

4.1 Heads and their dependents — 121
- 4.1.1 What is a head? — 121
- 4.1.2 The influence of heads on their dependents — 123
- 4.1.3 Summary: The properties of heads — 124
- 4.1.4 More about dependents: Adjuncts and complements — 125
- 4.1.5 More about verb classes: Verbs and their complements — 127
- 4.1.6 Other heads and their complements — 130
- 4.1.7 Summary: The main properties of complements vs. adjuncts — 131
- 4.1.8 Is the noun phrase really a determiner phrase? — 132
- 4.1.9 Phrases within phrases — 133

4.2 Where does the head occur in a phrase? Head-initial and head-final languages — 133
- 4.2.1 Head-initial languages — 134
- 4.2.2 Head-final languages — 135
- 4.2.3 An exercise on head-initial and head-final constructions — 136

4.3 Head-marking and dependent-marking languages — 137
- 4.3.1 Definitions and illustrations: Syntactic relationships between heads and dependents — 137
- 4.3.2 Head adposition and its NP object — 138
- 4.3.3 The clause: A head verb and the arguments of the verb — 140
- 4.3.4 Head noun and dependent possessor NP — 143
- 4.3.5 Head noun and dependent AP — 144
- 4.3.6 An exercise on head-marking and dependent-marking — 145
- 4.3.7 Some typological distinctions between languages — 146
- 4.3.8 Summary — 149

Further reading — 149
Exercises — 150

5 How do we identify constituents? — 158

章节导读 — 158

5.1 Discovering the structure of sentences — 159
- 5.1.1 Evidence of structure in sentences — 159
- 5.1.2 Some syntactic tests for constituent structure — 161

	5.1.3 Introduction to constituent structure trees	167
	5.1.4 Summary	172
5.2	Relationships within the tree	172
5.3	Developing detailed tree diagrams and tests for constituent structure	175
	5.3.1 Verb classes and constituent structure tests	175
	5.3.2 The co-ordination test for constituency	182
	5.3.3 Do all languages have the same constituents?	184
	5.3.4 An introduction to the bar notation	185
5.4	Summary	189
Further reading		189
Exercises		190
Note		195

6 Relationships within the clause — 196

章节导读 — 196

6.1	Indicating grammatical relations in the clause	197
6.2	Order of phrases within the clause	199
	6.2.1 Basic and marked orders	199
	6.2.2 Statistical patterns	200
6.3	Case systems	203
	6.3.1 Ways of dividing core arguments	203
	6.3.2 Nominative/accusative systems	205
	6.3.3 Ergative/absolutive systems	206
	6.3.4 Split systems I	208
	6.3.5 Marked and unmarked forms	210
6.4	Agreement and cross-referencing	211
	6.4.1 What does verb agreement involve?	211
	6.4.2 Nominative/accusative agreement systems	212
	6.4.3 Ergative/absolutive agreement systems	215
	6.4.4 Split systems II	216
6.5	Grammatical relations	217
	6.5.1 Investigating core grammatical relations	217
	6.5.2 Subjects: Typical cross-linguistic properties	217
	6.5.3 An examination of subjects in specific languages	219
	6.5.4 Objects	226
6.6	Free word order: A case study	228
6.7	Summary	231
Further reading		232
Exercises		233

7	**Processes that change grammatical relations**	**241**
	章节导读	241
	7.1 Passives and impersonals	242
	7.1.1 The passive construction and transitive verbs	242
	7.1.2 The impersonal construction	248
	7.2 The antipassive	249
	7.2.1 Basic facts	249
	7.2.2 Primary grammatical relations and grammatical pivot	251
	7.3 The applicative construction	257
	7.4 The causative construction	261
	7.5 Summary	266
	Further reading	266
	Exercises	266
	Notes	276
8	***Wh*-constructions: Questions and relative clauses**	**277**
	章节导读	277
	8.1 *Wh*-questions	278
	8.1.1 Languages with *wh*-movement	278
	8.1.2 Languages with *wh*-in-situ *wh*-questions	282
	8.1.3 Multiple *wh*-questions	284
	8.2 Relative clauses	286
	8.2.1 Relative clauses in English	286
	8.2.2 Cross-linguistic variation in relative clauses	289
	8.3 Focus movements and scrambling	295
	8.4 Some conclusions	297
	Further reading	298
	Exercises	298
	Note	308
9	**Asking questions about syntax**	**309**
	章节导读	309
	9.1 Syntactic description: What questions to investigate	310
	9.2 A case study: Grammatical sketch of Colloquial Welsh	313
	9.3 Some questions concerning syntax	320
	9.4 Last words: More syntax ahead	324
Sources of data used in examples		**326**
Glossary		**329**
References		**334**

Note to the instructor

Changes to the fourth edition

If you have used this textbook before, you will find that this new edition contains essentially the same material as the third edition, but that every chapter has been revised. I hope to have improved the clarity of discussion and level of explanation for all the most complex concepts that are introduced, and I have attempted to anticipate more precisely the needs of the beginning student with no background whatever in language studies. One new development is strategically placed checklists of material covered, typically at the end of a major section or at the end of a chapter. A number of new exercises have also been added, and some of the old ones removed, in cases where I felt that they didn't work too well. Please let me know if you find the changes helpful.

As always, I'd be glad to hear from any instructors about the success or otherwise of any of the changes I've made, and I'm also happy to receive data corrections and suggestions for further improvements.

Maggie Tallerman
Newcastle
February 2014

Note to the student

This book is an introduction to the major concepts and categories associated with the branch of linguistics known as syntax. No prior knowledge is assumed, although it is assumed that you will learn from each chapter, and assimilate much of the information in a chapter, before reading further. However, I generally don't expect you to learn what something means from a single discussion—instead, you will meet the same terms and concepts on several different occasions throughout the book. The first mention of some concept might be quite informal, with examples just from English, and then later I will give the discussion a broader perspective with illustrations from other languages. I use SMALL CAPITALS to introduce technical terms and concepts: these can be found in the subject index at the back. I also use small capitals to indicate any particularly important discussion or illustration of a term or concept that you've already met earlier. It will probably help to look up in the index all the previous mentions of this item, especially if you're finding it hard to grasp.

Many of the example sentences used in the text are given as a phonetic transcription, for instance when the language under discussion does not have a written form. Although you don't need to know how to pronounce the examples in order to understand the point being made, you may well be interested in their pronunciation. If you'd like further information about the various symbols used, I recommend that you consult the *Phonetic symbol guide* (Pullum and Ladusaw 1996), for comprehensive details of phonetic symbols and their pronunciation, or Davenport and Hannahs (2010) for general information on phonetics and phonology.

You are invited to tackle exercises within the body of the text in each chapter, and these are separated from the running text by rows of arrows that mark out the start:

and finish:

of the exercise. The answers to these problems are discussed in the text itself. If you attempt these exercises as you go along, they will certainly help you to check that you've understood the section you've just finished reading. If you don't get the right answer, I recommend re-reading that section before reading further. There are also checklists in each chapter that remind you of the main material covered. If you don't feel that you've taken the topics on board, you are recommended to revise them before moving on.

Additionally, there are exercises at the end of each chapter, for which I don't provide answers. If you are having real problems with the text, or want to discuss the exercises, please email me and I will try to help by suggesting a strategy, but I won't tell you the answers unless I can be sure that I'm not giving away the answers to a set assignment! For that reason, students should ask their instructors to email. My email address is: maggie.tallerman@ncl.ac.uk.

I will also be happy to receive corrections to data or to claims I make about any language, or further illustrations, or suggestions for new exercises.

Maggie Tallerman
Newcastle
February 2014

Acknowledgements

Over the sixteen years or so since the first edition of this book was published, I have been overwhelmed by the interest shown in the material it presents, and by the kindness of very many people from around the world. I have received dozens of emails, often from complete strangers, volunteering corrections to data, offering new data, suggesting ways in which the book could be improved, discussing fine linguistic points at great length, offering to read drafts of new material, and generally providing constructive criticism. Doubtless, I have overlooked some of you in the list that follows; for this, I heartily apologize, and I stress my genuine gratitude to all who helped make this fourth edition a better text. Many thanks, then, to the following colleagues, friends and students whose real and virtual presence has helped so much in the writing of all the editions of this textbook: Muteb Alqarni, Abdelrahman Altakhaineh, Clayton Ashton, Seiki Ayano, Ute Bohnacker, Bob Borsley, Siobhan Casson, Zedric Dimalanta, Joe Emonds, Tom Ernst, Abdelkader Fassl Fehri, Stuart Forbes, Don Frantz, Anders Holmberg, Chris Johns, Andreas Kathol, Jagdish Kaur, Daniela Kolbe, Lan Yin Kong, Nedzad Leko, Joan Maling, Anna Margetts, Jenny Marjoribanks, Roger Maylor, Sadat Peyambar, Tenzin Rigzin, Caroline Gray Robinson, Stuart Payton Robinson, the late Anna Siewierska, the late Carlota S. Smith, Rex Sprouse, Siti Hamin Stapa, Maite Taboada, Höski Thráinsson, Graham Thurgood, Antoine Trux, Ian Turner, Robert D. Van Valin, Nigel Vincent, Emiel Visser, Stephen M. Wechsler, Ian Woo, Wim van der Wurff and Monaliza Sarbini Zin. None of the above should be held responsible for any remaining errors.

I also owe a great debt of thanks to the series editors, Bernard Comrie and Grev Corbett, who improved this work in immeasurable ways. I hope that this new edition will be of credit to both these linguists, because their own work has inspired me throughout. Of course, full credit for any shortcomings remains with the author.

Finally, especial thanks to my husband, S. J. Hannahs, for massive support, both practical and moral, for reading and commenting on drafts, and for generally putting up with me during the preparation of this edition. This fourth edition is dedicated to my wonderful family: S. J., Lillian, Maggie and Caitlin.

Abbreviations used in examples

1	first person	PN	proper noun marker
2	second person	POSS	possessive marker
3	third person	PRED	predicate marker
ABS	absolutive	PRES	present tense
ACC	accusative	PROG	progressive
APPLIC	applicative	PRT	particle
AUX	auxiliary	QU	question marker
CAUS	causative	RM	relative marker
COMP	complementizer	SEQ	sequential
CONJ	conjunction	SG	singular
CONT	continuous	SJTV	subjunctive (mood)
DEF	definite	SM	subject marker
DEF ART	definite article	SU	subject (or subject marker)
DEM	demonstrative	TRANS	transitive marker
ERG	ergative		
EXC	exclusive		
F, FEM	feminine		
FUT	future tense		
GEN	genitive		
IMPER	imperative		
IMPF	imperfect (tense/aspect)		
INC	inclusive		
INDEF	indefinite		
INDIC	indicative mood		
INFIN	infinitive		
INTRANS	intransitive		
M, MASC	masculine		
NEG	negative		
NOM	nominative		
NONPAST	nonpast tense		
OBJ	object (or object marker)		
OBL	oblique (case)		
PAST	past tense		
PERF	perfect (tense/aspect)		
PERFCTV	perfective (tense/aspect)		
PL	plural		

Tables and figures

Tables

1.1	Present tense of French *parler* 'to speak'	18
1.2	Glosses for person and number	20
4.1	Syntactic relationships between a head and dependent	137
6.1	The core arguments	203
6.2	The major case systems	205
7.1	Accusative and ergative alignment systems	246
7.2	Primary grammatical relations	252
9.1	Inflectional paradigm for the Welsh preposition *wrth* 'at'	315
9.2	Inflectional paradigm for the past tense of the Welsh verb *gweld* 'see'	317

Figures

6.1	The nominative/accusative grouping	204
6.2	The ergative/absolutive grouping	205

1

What is syntax?

章节导读

　　句法学是研究句子结构，也就是词是如何构成短语和句子的科学。语法（grammar）一词经常和句法一起出现，在语言学界，有的学者把语法和句法等同起来，但有更多的学者认为，语法的涵义要比句法更广，语法既包括组词造句的规律，也包括语音的组织规律、词的结构规律，甚至也包括语义在内。因此，句法只是语法的一个组成部分。但是现在很多的语法理论（例如关系语法、角色参照语法等）都以句法为核心，因此它们一般被认为是句法学理论，这也反映了句法学在语言学中的核心地位。

　　句法学研究语言中的句子，但是语言本身也是不同的，我们可以区分两种不同的语言：一种是我们在现实生活的不同情景之中使用的语言；另一种是人们大脑中的语言知识系统。前者被称为外表化语言（externalized language, E-language），这是描述语法的研究对象，相当于乔姆斯基在早期所说的"语言运用"（performance）；后者被称为内在化语言（internalized language, I-language），相当于乔姆斯基早期所提出的"语言能力"（competence）。生成语法认为，语言研究的对象应该是内在化语言，语言理论应该是关于语言知识的理论，而且必须能解释母语习得现象。

　　对于所有正常的儿童来说，不论他们的天赋如何，也不论他们的生活环境是多么不同，他们都能像学走路一样在差不多同样的年龄习得自己的母语，但即使是让最高级的动物学会人类的语言也是根本办不到的事情。乔姆斯基认为，儿童天生就有一种学习语言的能力（language faculty[1]），也就是一种特定的官能或心智模块，为他们母语语法的发展提供了一套程序，这也被称为"语言习得机制"（language acquisition device, LAD）。对于语

---

[1] 也被翻译成语言器官、语言能力、语言天赋、语言官能等。

言习得机制的内容，乔姆斯基推论说，人脑的初始状态应该包括人类一切语言共同具有的特点，可以称为"普遍语法"（universal grammar）或语言普遍现象（linguistic universals），简单地说，"普遍语法就是构成语言学习者的'初始状态'的一组特性、条件和其他东西，所以是语言知识发展的基础（Chomsky, 2005: 69）。"[2] 更具体地讲，"普遍语法是一切人类语言必须具有的原则、条件和规则系统，代表了人类语言最基本的东西（Chomsky, 1975: 29）。"[3] 普遍语法是语言学理论，尤其是句法学理论研究的核心内容。

世界上的语言为数众多，有的语言使用人数众多，达到几亿甚至几十亿人，还有的语言使用人数极少，只有几千甚至几百人。同一种语言还会有不同的变体或者方言。从社会的角度来看，不同的语言有"国际"和"地方"之分，不同的方言有"标准"和"非标准"之分，但是从句法研究来看，所有的语言或者语言变体的地位都是相同的，它们都有句法。人类的语言尽管千差万别，但是这些差异之后都隐含着共同的规律，即语言普遍现象。要研究普遍语法，就要研究世界上各种不同的语言或者语言变体。但是对于研究者来说，每个人能懂的语言都是有限的，他们在分析句法时所使用的句子实例很可能是同行所不懂的语言，这就要求研究者在进行句法分析或是进行例证时严格按照通用的规范。目前国际上一般采用的是三行表达式，第一行是源语言，第二行是直译，其中标注具体每个词的意义以及语法特征（例如，人称、数等），第三行是意译。句法学的学习者不仅要学会使用这些规范的方法，还要学会读懂其中所包含的信息。

1.1 SOME CONCEPTS AND MISCONCEPTIONS

1.1.1 What is the study of syntax about?

This book is about the property of human language known as syntax. 'Syntax' means 'sentence construction': how words group together to make phrases and sentences. Some people also use the term GRAMMAR to mean the same as syntax, although most linguists follow the more recent practice whereby the grammar of a language includes all of its organizing principles: information about the sound system, about

---

2 N. Chomsky. (2005). *Rules and Representations*. New York: Columbia University Press.
3 N. Chomsky. (1975). *Reflections on Language*. New York: Pantheon.

the form of words, how we adjust language according to context, and so on; syntax is only one part of this grammar.

The term 'syntax' is also used to mean the *study* of the syntactic properties of languages. In this sense it's used in the same way as we use '**stylistics**' to mean the study of literary style. We're going to be studying how languages organize their syntax, so the scope of our study includes the classification of words, the order of words in phrases and sentences, the structure of phrases and sentences, and the different sentence constructions that languages use. We'll be looking at examples of sentence structure from many different languages in this book, some related to English and others not. All languages have syntax, though that syntax may look radically different from that of English. My aim is to help you understand the way syntax works in languages, and to introduce the most important syntactic concepts and technical terms which you'll need in order to see how syntax works in the world's languages. We'll encounter many grammatical terms, including 'noun', 'verb', 'preposition', 'relative clause', 'subject', 'nominative', 'agreement' and 'passive'. I don't expect you to know the meanings of any of these in advance. Often, terms are not formally defined when they are used for the first time, but they are illustrated so you can understand the concept, in preparation for a fuller discussion later on. More complex terms and concepts (such as 'case' and 'agreement') are discussed more than once, and a picture of their meaning is built up over several chapters. A glossary at the end of the book provides definitions of important grammatical terms.

To help you understand what the study of syntax is about, we first need to discuss some things it isn't about. When you read that 'syntax' is part of 'grammar', you may have certain impressions which differ from the aims of this book. So first, although we will be talking about grammar, this is not a **descriptive grammar** of English or any other language. Such books are certainly available, but they usually aim to catalogue the regularities and peculiarities of one language rather than looking at the organizing principles of language in general. Second, I won't be trying to improve your 'grammar' of English. A PRESCRIPTIVE GRAMMAR (one that prescribes how the author thinks you should speak) might aim to teach you where to use *who* and *whom*; or when to say *me and Kim* and when to say *Kim and I*; it might tell you not to say *different than* or *different to*, or tell you to avoid split infinitives such as *to boldly go*. These things aren't on our agenda, because they're essentially a matter of taste—they are social, not linguistic matters.

In fact, as a linguist, my view is that if you're a native speaker of English, no matter what your dialect, then you already know English grammar perfectly. And if you're a native speaker of a different language, then you know the grammar of that language perfectly. By this, I don't mean that you know (consciously) a few prescriptive rules, such as those mentioned in the last paragraph, but that you know (unconsciously) the much more impressive mental grammar of your own language—as do all its native speakers. Although we've all learnt this grammar, we can think of it as knowledge that we've never been taught, and it's also knowledge that we can't take out and examine. By the age of around seven, children have a fairly complete knowledge of the grammar of their native languages, and much of

Stylistics，文体学，指对文本体裁的特征、本质及其规律的研究。句法学和文体学一样都属于语言学的一个分支，但是两者在语言学中的地位是不一样的，句法学属于微观语言学的一部分，而文体学则属于宏观语言学的一部分。

这反映了作者的用心之处，要深入准确地理解一个概念是什么，我们可以先从它的反面去理解它不是什么。

Descriptive grammar，描述语法，与规定语法相对，后者试图建立正确用法的规则，告诉人们应该如何用语言才是正确的，而描述语法则重在描述人们实际运用语言的方式，关注语言是如何被人们使用的。

母语习得是一种自然的、本能性的过程，不需要专门的教授。儿童出生后，只要置身于一个正常的语言环境之中，他就会自然地获得自己母语的心理语法，其中的知识大多是内隐性的，是无法通过语言来表达的。

what happens after that age is learning more vocabulary. We can think of this as parallel to 'learning' how to walk. Children can't be taught to walk; we all do it naturally when we're ready, and we can't say how we do it. Even if we come to understand exactly what muscle movements are required, and what brain circuitry is involved, we still don't 'know' how we walk. Learning our native language is just the same: it happens without outside intervention and the resulting knowledge is inaccessible to us.

Here, you may object that you *were* taught the grammar of your native language. Perhaps you think that your parents set about teaching you it, or that you learnt it at school. But this is a misconception. All normally developing children in every culture learn their native language or languages to perfection without any formal teaching. Nothing more is required than the simple exposure to ordinary, live, human language within a society. To test whether this is true, we just need to ask if all cultures teach their children 'grammar'. Since the answer is a resounding 'no', we can be sure that all children must be capable of constructing a mental grammar of their native languages without any formal instruction. Most linguists now believe that, in order to do this, human infants are born pre-programmed to learn language, in much the same way as we are pre-programmed to walk upright. All that's needed for language to emerge is appropriate input data—hearing language (or seeing it; sign languages are full languages too) and taking part in interactions within the home and the wider society.

So if you weren't taught the grammar of your native language, what was it you were being taught when your parents tried to get you not to say things like *I ain't done nowt wrong*, or *He's more happier than what I am*, or when your school teachers tried to stop you from using a preposition to end a sentence with? (Like the sentence I just wrote.) Again, consider learning to walk. Although children learn to do this perfectly without any parental instruction, their parents might not like the way the child slouches along, or scuffs the toes of their shoes on the ground. They may tell the child to stand up straight, or to stop wearing out their shoes. It's not that the child's way doesn't function properly, it just doesn't conform to someone's idea of what is aesthetic, or classy. In just the same way, some people have the idea that certain forms of language are more beautiful, or classier, or are simply 'correct'. But the belief that some forms of language are better than others has no linguistic basis. Since we often make social judgements about people based on their accent or dialect, we tend to transfer these judgements to their form of language. We may then think that some forms are undesirable, that some are 'good' and some 'bad'. For a linguist, though, dialectal forms of a language don't equate to 'bad grammar'.

Again, you may object here that examples of NON-STANDARD **English**, such as those italicized in the last paragraph, or things like *We done it well good*, are sloppy speech, or perhaps illogical. This appeal to logic and precision makes prescriptive grammar seem to be on a higher plane than if it's all down to social prejudice. So let's examine the logic argument more closely, and see if it bears scrutiny. Many speakers of English are taught that 'two negatives make a positive', so that forms like (1) 'really' mean *I did something wrong*:

Non-standard English, 非标准英语，对于标准和非标准语言的划分主要是社会性的，更多地与一个言语社团相关的社会因素有关，而对于句法学研究来说，所有的语言和语言变体都是平等的。

(1) I didn't do nothing wrong.

Of course, this isn't true. First, a speaker who uses a sentence like (1) doesn't *intend* it to mean *I did something wrong*. Neither would any of their addressees, however much they despise the double negative, understand (1) to mean *I did something wrong*. Second, there are languages such as French and Breton which use a double negative as STANDARD, not a dialectal form, as (2) illustrates:¹

(2) Je **ne** mange **jamais** de viande.   (French)
    I negative eat never of meat
    'I never eat meat.'

Example (2) shows that in standard French the negative has two parts: in addition to the little negative word *ne* there's another negative word *jamais*, 'never'. Middle English (the English of roughly 1100 to 1500) also had a double negative. Ironically for the 'logic' argument, the variety of French that has the double negative is the most formal and prestigious variety, whereas colloquial French typically drops the initial negative word.

Another non-standard feature of certain English dialects which doesn't conform to prescriptive notions is illustrated in (3), from a northern (British) English dialect:

(3) I aren't going with you.

Here, the logic argument runs like this: you can't say *I are not (the star or asterisk is a convention used in linguistics to indicate an impossible sentence), so the contracted form *I aren't* must be wrong too. It's true that speakers who accept (3) don't ever say *I are not*. But the argument is flawed: standard English is just as illogical. Look how the statement in (4a) is turned into a question in (4b):

(4) a. **I'm not** going with you.
    b. **Aren't I** going with you?

Example (4) does not conform to the usual rules of English grammar, which form questions by inverting the word order in *I can't* to give *can't I*, and *I should* to give *should I*, and so on. Given these rules, the 'logically' expected form in (4b) would be *amn't I* (and in fact this form is found in some dialects). If the standard English in (4) fails to follow the usual rules, then we can hardly criticize (3) for lack of logic. And since *aren't I* is OK, there's no logical reason for dismissing *I aren't*. The dialects that allow either *I aren't* or *amn't I* could actually be considered more logical than standard English, since they follow the general rule, whilst the standard dialect, in (4), has an irregularity.

It's clear, then, that socially stigmatized forms of language are potentially just as 'logical' as standard English. Speakers of non-standard dialects are, of course, following a set of mental rules, in just the same way that speakers of the most prestigious dialects are. The various dialects of a language in fact share the majority

各种方言看似不同，实则共同之处众多，而各种语言也是如此。以任何一种语言或者方言为母语的人都具有完整的心理语法体系。

of their rules, and diverge in very few areas, but the extent of the differences tends to be exaggerated because they arouse such strong feelings. In sum, speakers of prestige dialects may feel that only their variety of English is 'grammatically correct', but these views cannot be defended on either logical or linguistic grounds.

If, on the other hand, a speaker of English produced examples like (5), then we could justifiably claim that they were speaking ungrammatically:

(5)   *I do didn't wrong anything.
       *Do wrong didn't anything I.

这句话反映了现代形式句法对于句法学研究方法的一个基本观点。句法学研究可以采用内省的方法，即通过本族语者的直觉判断来决定句子是否合乎语法。

此句对应了前文中关于句法学和规定语法、教学语法以及描述语法差异的讨论。

Such examples completely contravene the mental rules of all dialects of English. We all agree on this, yet speakers of English haven't been taught that the sentences in (5) are bad. Our judgements must therefore be part of the shared mental grammar of English.

Most of the rules of this mental grammar are never dealt with by prescriptive or teaching grammars. So no grammar of English would ever explain that although we can say both (6a) and (6b), we can't have questions like (7) (the gap ___ indicates an understood but 'missing' element, represented by the question word *what*):

(6)   a.   They're eating eggs and chips.
       b.   What are they eating ___?

(7)   *What are they eating eggs and ___?

The rules that make (7) impossible are so immutable and fundamental that they hardly seem to count as a subject for discussion: native speakers never stop to wonder why (7) is not possible. Not only are examples like (7) ungrammatical in English (i.e. they sound impossible to native speakers), they are ungrammatical in Welsh, as in (8):

(8)   *Beth   maen   nhw   yn   bwyta   wyau   a   ___?   (Welsh)
        what   are   they   in   eat   eggs   and
       *'What are they eating eggs and ___ ?'

许多句法学研究者，尤其是形式句法学者，都相信人类语言能力是一样的，世界上各种看似差异很大的语言在深层次上都存在着共同的普遍规律。

In fact, the equivalents to (7) and (8) are generally ungrammatical in the world's languages. It seems likely, then, that many of the unconsciously 'known' rules of individual languages like English or Welsh are actually universal—common to all languages.

Before reading further, note that English does have a way of expressing what (7) would mean if it were grammatical—in other words, a way of expressing the question you would ask if you wanted to know what it was that they were eating with their eggs. How is this question formed?

You could ask: *They are eating eggs and **what**?* (with heavy emphasis on the *what*).

The fact that certain organizing rules and principles in language are universal leads many linguists to conclude that human beings have an INNATE LANGUAGE FACULTY—that is, one we are born with. We can't examine this directly, and we still know relatively little about what brain circuitry is involved, but we do know that there must be something unique to humans in this regard. All normal children learn at least one language, but no other animals have anything like language as a natural communication system, nor are they able to learn a human language, even under intense instruction. To try and understand the **language faculty**, we examine its output—namely the structures of natural languages. So by looking at syntax we hope to discover the common properties between languages, and maybe even ultimately to discover something about the workings of the human brain.

As well as looking for absolutely universal principles, linguists are interested in discovering what types of construction are possible (and impossible) in the world's languages. We look for recurring patterns, and often find that amazingly similar constructions appear in unrelated languages. In the next paragraph I give an example of this type which compares Indonesian and English. You don't have to know anything about Indonesian to get the point being made, but if the idea of looking closely at exotic languages seems too daunting at this stage, come back to the examples after you've read Section 1.2. The notation >—→—→ marks the start of a section of the text in which the reader is invited to work something out, as in the example just above; ←—←—< marks the end of that section, and where necessary, the exercise is followed by a suggested answer. Here, the task is simply to examine all the sentences, and try to follow the argument.

Language faculty，语言能力，也被翻译成语言天赋。许多语言学者相信人的语言能力（尤其是句法能力）是与生俱来的，儿童生来就具有一种语言习得机制，这一机制遵循所有语言的共同规则，即普遍语法。

In English we can say either (9a) or (9b)—they alternate freely. In (9b) *Hasan* appears before *the letter*, and the word *to* has disappeared; let's say that in (9b) *Hasan* has been PROMOTED in the sentence:

(9) a. Ali sent the letter to Hasan.
    b. Ali sent Hasan the letter.

In Indonesian, we find the same alternation, shown in (10). If you're reading this before the discussion on the use of linguistic examples in Section 1.2, please remember to concentrate particularly on the second line of each example: the literal translation. The main 'foreign' feature in (10) is *surat itu* 'letter the' where English has the word order 'the letter'; otherwise, the word order in the two Indonesian examples is the same as that of the two English examples in (9):

(10) a. Ali meng-kirim surat itu kepada Hasan. (Indonesian)
　　　Ali send　　　letter the　to　　Hasan
　　　'Ali sent the letter to Hasan.'
　　b. Ali meng-kirim-**kan** Hasan surat itu.
　　　Ali send　　　　　Hasan letter the
　　　'Ali sent Hasan the letter.'

In (10b) we find an ending *-kan* on the word for 'send': this ending indicates in Indonesian that the word *Hasan* has been promoted. English has no equivalent to *-kan*.

Now look again at the English in (9). When *Hasan* is in the promoted position in (9b), we can promote it further in the sentence, giving (11). We indicate the position that *Hasan* is understood to have moved from with the gap ___. In (11) there is also a change from *sent* to *was sent*, which signals this further promotion of *Hasan*. To understand why a language would need to indicate the promotion of some part of the sentence, think about the difference in meaning between *Hasan sent the letter* and *Hasan was sent the letter*.

(11) Hasan was sent ___ the letter by Ali.

If we start with (9a), however, where *Hasan* is not in a promoted position, then trying to promote it from there *directly* to the very highest position in the sentence would give (12): again, I show the position the word *Hasan* has moved from with the gap. But (12) is not a possible sentence of English (as indicated by the **asterisk**):

(12) *Hasan was sent the letter to ___ by Ali.

So if the word *Hasan* is already promoted, as in (9b), then it can move again, giving (11). Otherwise, promotion of *Hasan* is impossible, as (12) shows. In fact, it seems like the promotion has to occur in stages, rather than in one single jump straight to the beginning of the sentence. Perhaps you're thinking, maybe it's just a question of getting rid of the *to* in (12), then it'd be fine. But if we look at (13) and (14), the Indonesian equivalents to (11) and (12), we get some strong clues that this is not the case. Note that the change from *meng-kirim* in (10) to *di-kirim* in (13) and (14) is equivalent to the change in English from *sent* to *was sent*:

(13) Hasan di-kirim-**kan** surat itu oleh Ali.
　　　Hasan was-sent　　letter the　by　 Ali
　　　'Hasan was sent the letter by Ali.'

(14) *Hasan di-kirim surat itu (kepada) oleh Ali.
　　　Hasan was-sent letter the (to)　 by　 Ali
　　　*'Hasan was sent the letter to by Ali.'

Asterisk，星号，它在句法学研究中具有特殊的地位，用来表示不合乎语法的句子。有人说乔姆斯基对句法学研究最大的贡献就是这个"星号"，因为这反映了转换生成语法与以往句法理论的一个最大不同，即好的句法理论不仅能够描述语言的语法系统，还要能够预测什么是合乎语法的句子，什么是不合乎语法的句子。

Just as in English, one construction is fine, the other impossible. What makes the difference? In the Indonesian we can tell that it can't be anything to do with the word for 'to' (*kepada*), because (14) is impossible with or without that word—the parentheses (...) mean that whether or not *kepada* is included makes no difference to the acceptability of the sentence. The reason only (13) is acceptable is that we have to start off with (10b) to get there—the version in which *Hasan* has already been promoted once. And we know that (13) does indeed come via (10b) because the word which means 'was sent', *di-kirim-kan*, has that ending *-kan* which shows that *Hasan* has been promoted—whereas *di-kirim* in (14) doesn't. So we could hypothesize that English probably works in the same way. Although there's nothing in English to mark the first promotion of *Hasan* in (9b), it's likely that just as in Indonesian, it's the promotion that's the distinguishing factor between the grammatical example in (11) and the ungrammatical one in (12).

At this stage, I hope to have shown that two totally unrelated languages can display some remarkably similar syntactic behaviour. Finally, please note that although this section was rather technical, you should be able to understand it if you read it through more than once, stopping to work out each stage as you go. This tip will also be helpful throughout the book.

从表面上来看，不同的语言在句子结构上具有明显的不同，但是经过仔细的分析，我们会发现，它们的内在结构具有许多的共同之处。

1.1.2 Language change

Speakers of established languages such as English often dislike changes occurring within their own language, believing that change equates with declining standards. In fact, though, the grammar of all languages changes over time, and no amount of intervention by prescriptive grammarians or language academies can prevent this. In this section I look at some examples from the history of English, and then at more recent changes. The examples of **Middle English** in (15) are from the prologue to Chaucer's *Wife of Bath's Tale*, written in the fourteenth century:

(15)   a.   I sey **nat** this by wyves that been wyse   (Middle English)
                'I **do not** say this for wives that are wise.'
       b.   But Crist ... bat **nat** every wight he sholde go selle al that he hadde
                'But Christ **did not** bid every one to go (and) sell all that he had.'

The major change here is in the negation of verbs such as *say* and *bid* (Chaucer's *bat* is modern *bade*). In Chaucer's English any verb can be negated by putting *not* directly after it: *I sey nat*; *Crist bat nat*. In Modern English, we don't negate verbs directly in this way: **I say not this*, **Christ bade not everyone* aren't possible. Instead, to give the negative we use a form of *do* which doesn't add any meaning of its own, but is there purely to support *not*, as in: *I do not/don't say this*. Chaucer's English doesn't have this '*do*-support' rule, as it is sometimes known.

本书作者是研究语言演变与进化的专家，因此从语言变化的角度来讨论句法学的定义可以说是发挥了她的特长，这在其他同类教材中是不多见的。

Middle English，中古英语，指诺曼征服（1066）之后到15世纪后期这段时间的英语。与在此之前的古英语相比，中古英语的语法在形态变化方面发生了简化。例如，名词逐渐失去了古英语复杂的数和格的变化，简化成了单数和复数两种形式。

Before reading further, think of at least five words other than forms of *do* that can be directly negated by a following *not* in Modern English: find words that fit into the gap in a sentence such as: *I ___ not/n't leave*.

This gap can be filled by *may, might, must, can, could, will, would, shall, should* as well as *dare* and *need*. By changing *leave* to *left* or *leaving* we can also add *have* and *be* to the list of words that can fit the gap, as in *I have not left, I am not leaving*. In Modern English only words of a certain class, a verb-like word known as an AUXILIARY, can be directly negated by *not*. Where there is no other auxiliary in the sentence, *do* is used as a kind of 'dummy' auxiliary.

Auxiliary, 助词，指本身没有词汇意义和独立的功能意义，而只能和其他词结合在一起使用的词。

Apart from its role in negation, *do*-support has another major role in Modern English. Try to think of some examples of this.

Do is also used to form 'yes/no' (or POLAR) QUESTIONS, where there's no other auxiliary. So although we can say *Might/can/will you leave?*, using one of the auxiliaries listed above, as well as *Are you leaving?* and *Have you left?*, an ordinary verb can't be used in question formation: **Left you yesterday?*. Once again, Middle English did allow this construction:

Polar question, 极性疑问句，又称是/非疑问句（yes/no question），是指可以用 yes 或者 no 回答的疑问句。

(16) a. Sey you no?
 'Do you say no?'
 b. Why hydestow (i.e. *hidest thou*) the keyes ... ?
 'Why do you hide the keys?'

So these are two ways in which MAIN verbs in Middle English (verbs that aren't auxiliaries) behave differently than in Modern English. You may also have noticed that '*do*-support' is used in Modern English for emphasis too. We had an example just above: *Middle English **did** allow this construction*.

Main verb, 主动词，在英语中又称 full verb, principal verb, 与助动词相对。另外，请思考，中古英语和现代英语中主动词的使用有哪两方面的不同？

Although you may not be surprised that changes like this occurred over a period of several hundred years (with *do*-support becoming standard by around 1700), it may be less obvious that English changed in the twentieth century, and indeed, is still changing constantly in the twenty-first. In fact there are plenty of syntactic changes in progress right now. At the moment, these are restricted to certain dialects or to non-standard British English, but all the examples of change discussed below are spreading, and some may eventually become standard English. First, consider TAG QUESTIONS such as those in bold in (17):

Tag question, 附加疑问句。

(17) a. It is a hot day, **isn't it**?
    b. I can come, **can't I**?
    c. We still lost in the end, **didn't we**?

These questions 'tagged onto' the end of a statement are formed by specific rules in standard English which match the tag to the statement. A positive statement like *It is ...* gets a negative tag, *isn't it*. Most importantly, an auxiliary used in the statement must be used in the tag (*I can* and *can't I*) and the pronoun (such as *it*, *I*, *we*) in the statement is also in the tag. In (17c) there's no auxiliary: main verbs like *lose* can't occur in tags (**lost we*) so *do*-support occurs, as in other questions. But in some dialects of British English, a single tag question *innit* is used in each of the contexts shown in (17). Example (18) illustrates. The tag *innit* is a reduced form of *isn't it*, a form which in standard English is only possible if the statement contains *is*. In *innit* dialects, though, this has become an invariant tag, so that as well as the grammatically standard *It's a hot day, innit?*, we find:

(18) a. I can come, **innit**?
    b. We still lost in the end, **innit**?

Some other varieties of English, such as Indian English, already have an invariant *isn't it* tag. And in some languages, an invariant tag is completely standard, as in French: *n'est-ce pas* (literally, 'isn't it?') occurs whatever the form of the statement:

(19) a. Il   va   arriver   demain,   n'est-ce pas?   (French)
        he   goes arrive   tomorrow   TAG
        'He will arrive tomorrow, won't he?'
    b. Nous n'   avons   pas   de   pain,   n'est-ce pas?
        we   NEG   have   NEG   of   bread   TAG
        'We haven't got any bread, have we?'

Perhaps standard British English will also have an invariant tag one day too.

A second example of ongoing change is illustrated by the differences between (20) and (21). Example (20) illustrates standard English, but in a very common, though technically non-standard variant, (20b) is replaced by (21):

(20) a. less difficulty; less wheat; less boredom; less milk
    b. fewer students; fewer sheep; fewer people; fewer difficulties

(21) less students; less sheep; less people; less difficulties

Look first at (20) and work out what it is that conditions the use of *less* versus *fewer* in standard English: in other words, what distinct contexts is each word used in? Then describe how the non-standard variety in (21) differs. If you don't have the

grammatical terminology, give as accurate a description as you can of the properties involved.

In standard English, *less* is used only with MASS or NON-COUNT nouns—words like *difficulty*, *wheat*, *boredom* and *milk*. These are inherently singular; we can't say **three boredoms*. COUNT nouns on the other hand have a plural form, such as *students*, *sheep*, *people* and *difficulties*, and in standard English these occur with *fewer*. (Note that although *sheep* doesn't take the regular plural *-s*, one way we can tell that it can be a plural word is exactly by the fact that it can occur after *fewer*.) Some nouns can in fact be either mass or count, like *difficulty*. Example (21) reflects a widespread non-standard usage in which *less* is used before any noun, including plural count nouns.

Our final example of language change in progress comes from the non-standard use of *they*, illustrated by the attested (= real-life) examples in (22).

(22) a. If **any candidate** hasn't got a form, **they** need to get one from the office.
 b. I remember **one student** who said **they** couldn't write the answers because **they**'d lost **their** one and only pen.
 c. Our cat food gives **your cat** the nutrients **they** need.

The pronouns *they* and *their* are always plural in standard English, so can only be used to refer to a plural noun phrase, such as *the candidates*. But in (22) these pronouns refer back to a noun phrase which is singular in form: *any candidate*, *one student*, *your cat*. This is actually not a new usage—similar uses of *they* occur even as far back as Middle English. In modern standard British English, though, still reflected in the speech of some older speakers, a singular pronoun *he* or *she* is required in each of these contexts. This gives examples like *If anyone needs to leave he should raise his hand*, whereas most speakers nowadays would say *If anyone needs to leave they should raise their hand*. Note that there's no plural intended in the use of *they* in (22): it's used not as a plural pronoun, but rather as a gender-neutral singular pronoun. This is clear in (22a), where *any candidate* was addressed to a group of males and females; but *they* can also be used as in (22b), where the speaker must know the actual sex of the person referred to. (I can confirm that this is the case for (22b), since I was that speaker, and heard myself say this!).

Interestingly, this development seems to have occurred independently of any desire to use non-sexist language; British English has not, for example, adopted such forms as *waitperson*, often used in American English.

To summarize, I argued in Section 1.1 that all native speakers of a language share an internal grammar, though they have never been taught its rules. Evidence for this is that we largely agree about what is and what is not a possible sentence of our language, though speakers are likely to differ over their acceptance of certain non-standard or dialectal variants. What is more, languages which are unrelated share many common properties and constructions, suggesting that human beings have an innate language faculty. Finally, we saw that language changes through time, and I gave some examples of ongoing changes. I now demonstrate how to make use of examples from other languages.

1.2 USE OF LINGUISTIC EXAMPLES

1.2.1 Why not just use examples from English?

This book contains examples from a wide variety of languages, including English. At first you may find it difficult to study examples from unfamiliar languages, and perhaps you wonder why we don't just use examples from English. There are two main reasons for using foreign-language examples: to learn about the differences between languages, and to learn about the similarities between them.

First, then, languages don't all look the same, and examining just our own language and its immediate relatives doesn't show how much languages can differ. Imagine that you've met only two languages, English and German, two closely related Germanic languages from northern Europe. Example (23), from German, is a word-for-word translation of the English.

(23) der schöne Wasserfall (German)
      the pretty waterfall

You might imagine that the translation of this phrase would look the same in any language: first a word for 'the', then a word for 'pretty' or 'beautiful', then a word for 'waterfall'. But this is not so. In Spanish, for instance, we'd get (24):

(24) la cascada hermosa (Spanish)
      the waterfall beautiful
      'the beautiful waterfall'

Here, the word order is different in one respect: the word for 'beautiful' follows 'waterfall'. Otherwise, the Spanish is not too different from the English: it has just the same three words, and a word for 'the' in the same position. This isn't too surprising, as Spanish is also related to English, although more distantly than German. But in certain other languages, the equivalent to 'the' comes at the end of the phrase, as in Indonesian *surat itu* 'letter the' illustrated in (10), or else there may be no word for 'the' at all, as in Japanese and Chinese; what's more, in some languages there isn't even a direct translation of the adjective *beautiful*.

The world's languages have many interesting and important syntactic features that I'd like you to know about. English has some but not all of these features, so if we only looked at English you'd miss out on the rest. In (25) we see one example, from Spanish:

(25) Es   nuevo.   (Spanish)
     is   new
     'It's new.'

Example (25) has no word for 'it'; it literally means 'Is new'—an impossible sentence in English. Spanish typically drops the subject pronoun meaning 'it' in such examples; for this reason, it's known as a PRO-DROP **language**. Many languages have examples parallel to this, but confining the discussion to English would never reveal that. In yet other languages, such as Arabic and Indonesian, the three-word English sentence *It is new* translates as 'It new' (this is illustrated in Chapter 2, page 52). These simple examples show that we can't expect sentences in other languages to be word-for-word translations of English sentences. So we study other languages to discover the range of constructions and features they contain—in order to find out about LINGUISTIC DIVERSITY.

The second reason for looking at examples from other languages is that linguists want to discover the common properties that languages share—their *homogeneity* or sameness. One of the most crucial discoveries of modern linguistics is that languages don't vary from each other at random, but are remarkably alike in many important ways. Certain features occur in all languages. For instance, every language distinguishes a word class of NOUNS (words like *tree*, *liquid*, *expression* and *enjoyment*) from a word class of VERBS (words like *liquefy*, *learn*, *enjoy* and *grow*), although some languages have no other major word classes. (Chapter 2 examines word classes.) To discover this kind of information, linguists need to examine a representative sample of languages from different language families and different geographical areas.

Most linguists want to uncover the central patterns common to all languages. Although specific constructions are not generally universal (= common to all languages), all languages use a subset of the same basic tools of grammar. Each language has a word-list or LEXICON which its speakers share, and that word-list always contains words from several different classes. All languages combine these words into phrases and sentences, and speakers can manipulate the order of the phrases for various purposes—perhaps to ask questions, or to emphasize different parts of a sentence, or to show who's doing what to whom. This is syntax, and it forms the subject matter of the chapters ahead.

1.2.2 How to read linguistic examples

1.2.2.1 *The layout of examples*

Your first task as a syntactician is to learn to make use of examples from other languages. This book contains examples from over 100 different languages. Of course, I don't speak most of these—the examples come from other linguists, or from native speakers of the language (and sometimes native-speaker linguists). But I can utilize these examples because linguists set them out in a specific way for students and researchers who don't speak the language.

Examples of this special layout occur in the two Spanish illustrations in (24) and (25). Each consists of three lines. The first line is from the source language under consideration. The third line is a translation from the source language into English. You need this line to know what the original example means, but it's not the most important part of the example, because it only tells you about English—it tells you nothing about the source language. The really important line is the second one, called the GLOSS. The gloss is a literal translation of the original language. Each meaningful part of the original is translated, whether it corresponds exactly to a word in English or not. Look back at (2): French *ne* is GLOSSED (translated) simply as NEGATIVE because there's no English word that directly corresponds to it.

To see why the gloss is so important, consider (26) and (27), from Japanese and from Welsh. I have left out the gloss line. Both examples mean the same thing in the sense that they can receive the same English translation:

(26) Sensei-ga gakusei ni tegami-o kaita.   (Japanese)
      'The teacher wrote a letter to the student.'

(27) Ysgrifennodd yr athro lythyr at y myfyriwr.   (Welsh)
      'The teacher wrote a letter to the student.'

Let's suppose the point I'm trying to make is that sentences in Japanese, Welsh and English all have different word orders. Unless you happen to know both Japanese and Welsh, you won't be able to work this out from (26) and (27). In (28) and (29) I give the full examples, with glosses:[2]

(28) Sensei-ga   gakusei   ni   tegami-o   kaita.   (Japanese)
      teacher   student   to   letter   wrote
      'The teacher wrote a letter to the student.'

(29) Ysgrifennodd   yr   athro   lythyr   at   y   myfyriwr.   (Welsh)
      wrote   the   teacher   letter   to   the   student
      'The teacher wrote a letter to the student.'

Now we can compare the word orders of the three languages. First, the word for 'wrote' (a verb) has a different position in all three languages: at the end of the sentence in Japanese, at the beginning in Welsh, and somewhere in the middle in English—to be precise, after the phrase *the teacher*. This tells us right away that not all languages have the same sentence structure as English. Second, in both Japanese and English, the phrase '(the) teacher' is initial in the sentence, so Japanese and English have an important feature in common. In fact, at least 80 per cent of all languages would start their version of our sentence with the 'teacher' phrase. Welsh is different: its sentences start with the verb meaning 'wrote', a pattern found in perhaps 12 per cent of the world's languages. Third, both Welsh and English have the same order in the phrase 'to the student', whilst the Japanese in (28) has the opposite word order: *gakusei ni*, literally 'student to' (note the absence of a word for 'the' in the Japanese).

这一部分对于我们解读语言实例以及在不同的语言之间进行比较很有帮助，需要仔细阅读。

Using the glosses we can work out quite a lot about the word order differences—and similarities—between the three languages. Other facts about Japanese and Welsh emerge from the glosses too: for example, Japanese has no equivalent to either 'the' or 'a', and Welsh has no word for 'a'.

You should now begin to see the importance of the gloss. On reaching a three-line example in the text, you should start at the bottom and work upwards, reading the translation first, then examining the gloss, then looking at the source language. Keep in mind that the English may bear little resemblance to the original source. In (28) and (29), the examples are pretty similar to the English, word-for-word (even if the word orders are different), but this certainly isn't always the case: (30) is from Rapa Nui, the Polynesian language of Easter Island.

(30) E   tagi   ā   te   poki.   (Rapa Nui)
     NONPAST   cry   PROGRESSIVE the   boy
     'The boy is crying.'

Apart from the word order differences (as in Welsh, the verb meaning 'cry' is (almost) at the beginning of the sentence), Rapa Nui has various other interesting features. In the English, *is* indicates that the crying is now, i.e. not in the past. The Rapa Nui example has no word for 'is', and instead a small word *e* indicates 'nonpast'. Second, in English the *-ing* ending on *cry* indicates an ongoing action, i.e. the boy hasn't finished crying. Rapa Nui has a separate little grammatical word to indicate this: the 'progressive' word (meaning an unfinished action). Neither of these features of Rapa Nui can be discovered from the English translation, of course. So you always need to read the gloss carefully, thinking about whatever point is being made in the surrounding text. It should be clear by now that if you only read the last line of an example, you won't find out about any language other than English!

1.2.2.2 *Lexical and grammatical information*

Glosses contain both LEXICAL information, printed in normal type, and GRAMMATICAL information, printed in small capitals. Lexical information means ordinary words which are translations (or paraphrases) of the original language. In (28) and (29) the glosses contain only lexical information. The Rapa Nui example in (30), though, has two items glossed as NONPAST and PROGRESSIVE (which indicates an ongoing action). This information concerns grammatical categories such as TENSE and ASPECT (more on these in Chapter 2, pages 43 and 44). The point is that there are no separate words in English—members of the English LEXICON or vocabulary—that can translate this grammatical information, so it is glossed using the technical terms that describe its function in the source language.

All languages contain grammatical information. In (31) we show this by suggesting a precise gloss of an example from English, treating it as if it were a foreign language, and representing the grammatical information, as usual, in small capitals.

(31) The   student-s   ask-ed   for   these   book-s.
     DEF.ART   student-PL   ask-PAST   for   DEM.PL   book-PL
     'The students asked for these books.'

Taking these glosses as illustration, we can now explain the usual linguistic conventions. There are some familiar lexical items, 'student', 'ask', 'for' and 'book', but I've glossed *the* by referring to the grammatical information it represents: it's a DEFINITE ARTICLE—a word meaning 'the', as opposed to an INDEFINITE ARTICLE—a word meaning 'a'. I also glossed *these* as DEM.PL: *these* is a DEMONSTRATIVE word, a 'pointing' word from the set *this, that, these, those*. It's also PLURAL, therefore used before a plural word like *books*. Throughout the book, though, I will normally try where possible to use glosses you can recognize as words.

Apart from the lexical and grammatical information, the gloss also contains pieces of information separated by a dash (-). A dash preceding or following a piece of grammatical information in the gloss means that the grammatical element is attached to the word, or to another grammatical element, and can't be a separate word. Crucially, though, such grammatical elements have their own meaning. So the glosses *book*-PL and *student*-PL indicate that *books* and *students* are plural nouns; -*s* is a plural ending. And -*ed* is a past tense ending. I've also used the dash in the first line in (31) to indicate the boundaries in the source language between the grammatical information and the lexical items, although not all examples in this book follow this convention.

Grammatical elements attached to the beginning or end of a word, or to other pieces of grammatical information, are called AFFIXES (meaning something attached). Generally, then, a dash in the gloss indicates an affix, such as the plural -*s*. Grammatical affixes come in two main varieties: suffixes and prefixes. English plural -*s*, progressive -*ing* and past tense -*ed* are SUFFIXES: they're attached to the end of words. PREFIXES are attached at the beginning of words; examples from English are *un*- as in *untidy* and *re*- as in *re-seal*.

Elements of meaning such as 'ask' and 'past tense', 'un-' and 'plural' are known as MORPHEMES. As you can see, some of these represent independent words, but not all. The study of word forms is known as MORPHOLOGY, and though this is generally outside the scope of this book, we will often meet examples that show the interface between morphology and syntax—morphosyntax. Glosses in an example essentially inform the reader about the morphosyntax of the words used, as well as just giving their literal meaning.

Sometimes, we recognize that a word contains more than one piece of information, that is, more than one morpheme, but these meaning elements have no discernible boundaries. For instance, if (31) had been *The students took these books home*, we would recognize that the verb *took* is past tense, just as *asked* is, but *took* is irregular, and doesn't have a past tense -*ed* suffix. We can't tell what part of *took* means 'past'. Linguists generally indicate this in the gloss using a colon (:) or a dot: thus, *took* would be glossed 'take:PAST' or 'take.PAST'. This convention means that a single source word contains more than one morpheme (such as 'take' and 'past tense') but there are no clear boundaries between these morphemes.

Morpheme, 词素，是最小的有意义的语法单位。

Morphology, 形态学，研究词的结构或形式。

We also use this convention if we just don't wish to show the boundaries in a particular example, usually for the sake of keeping things clear or simple for the reader. Illustrating again with *asked*, I could show it as in (31) as ask-ed, with the hyphen indicating a morpheme boundary in the source word, and gloss it as ask-PAST, again showing the morpheme boundary. Alternatively, I could show *asked* in the source line, and ask.PAST in the gloss. Typically, we use this convention when we don't need to emphasize the detailed morphosyntax of the example.

1.2.2.3 *The categories of person and number*

In this section I discuss the conventions used to represent the grammatical categories of PERSON and NUMBER, using examples from French and Kwamera (spoken in Vanuatu in the Pacific).

If you have learnt a foreign language, you will probably be used to meeting tables of verb forms like Table 1.1, from French.

Table 1.1

Present tense of French *parler* 'to speak'

	Singular	Plural
1st	je parle	nous parlons
2nd	tu parles	vous parlez
3rd	il/elle parle	ils/elles parlent

Such tables, known as PARADIGMS, display the set of related forms that a particular lexical word has in a given grammatical context. The paradigm in Table 1.1 shows the set of forms that make up the present tense of the verb *parler* 'to speak'. Reading down the column headed Singular, the forms mean 'I speak, you (singular) speak, he/she speaks'. In the column headed Plural, the forms mean 'we speak, you (plural) speak, they (masculine/feminine) speak'. (Note that unlike English, French has distinct masculine and feminine forms for 'they', *ils* versus *elles*.)

The labels 1st (FIRST), 2nd (SECOND) and 3rd (THIRD) in the first column designate the grammatical category called PERSON. First person indicates the speaker, or a group of people that includes the speaker: so both the 'I' and 'we' forms are first person. Second person indicates the addressee(s): the 'you' forms. Third person indicates some third party, an individual or group other than the speaker and addressee: the 'he/she/it' and 'they' forms.

The category of NUMBER refers to the distinction between SINGULAR (one person) and NON-SINGULAR (more than one person). In French, as in most European languages, number is either 'singular' or 'plural'. Note, though, that French distinguishes between *tu parles* 'you (singular) speak' and *vous parlez* 'you (plural) speak'. English once had this distinction too: *thou* meant 'you (singular)', equivalent to *tu*; and some varieties of modern English also have second person plural forms such as *you all* or *yous* (for instance, *yous* occurs in parts of both northeast and northwest England). Some languages divide non-singular into several categories, such as a category referring to two people (a DUAL), a category for three people (a TRIAL), and additionally a plural, used for referring to more than three people. For example, the Polynesian language Kwamera has just such a system.

Kwamera also has more PERSON distinctions than are familiar in European languages. First person in this language divides into INCLUSIVE and EXCLUSIVE forms. 'Inclusive' means 'we (as in me and you, speaker and addressee)', and 'exclusive' means 'we (speaker and other party, excluding you, the addressee)'. Imagine that a friend says 'We could go and see a film tonight'. You reply 'We? Do you mean you and me (*we inclusive*) or you and your boyfriend (*we exclusive*)?' English doesn't have different forms of 'we' to specify this information, but Kwamera does:

(32) a. **sa-ha-**akw (Kwamera)
    1INC-PLURAL-break.up
    'We all break up.' (inclusive 'we')
  b. **ia-ha-**vehe
    1EXC-PLURAL-come
    'We came.' (exclusive 'we')

Before going any further, it's vitally important that you understand how to read the information in examples like this. The English translations in (32) contain several words—four separate words in (32a), for instance. But the Kwamera source examples each contain just *one* word, though this incorporates several distinct pieces of lexical and grammatical information. I'll explain using (32a), where there is a verb STEM, *akw*, and two prefixes attached to it—prefixes are grammatical elements which precede a stem. The *ha-* form closest to the verb stem means 'plural', and the *sa-* form on the outside means 'first person inclusive'. Together, these prefixes buy the meaning 'inclusive we'. English and Kwamera differ in a crucial way here. English has a separate pronoun *we*—it's a distinct, independent word on its own, not part of the verb. This is known as a FREE PRONOUN. But in the Kwamera, there is no separate word for 'we' at all: instead, that meaning is expressed by using grammatical elements attached to the verb itself. The forms *sa-* and *ia-* can't be separated from the verb, and don't occur on their own, and so are known as BOUND PRONOMINALS (there is more discussion of this in Chapter 4, Section 4.3).

Note that in Kwamera, there are separate affixes representing the categories of PERSON and NUMBER, whereas in English the pronoun *we* represents both person (1st) and number (plural) simultaneously. So the pronominal prefix *ia-* in (32b) represents not 'I' or 'we', but just first person: it only becomes 'we' when the plural prefix *ha-* follows. This means that the same 'first person exclusive' form *ia-* also translates as 'I':

(33) **ia-**pkagkiari-mha (Kwamera)
    1EXC-talk-NEG
    'I didn't talk.'

In future examples, I gloss person and number as in Table 1.2, unless the language has some special inclusive and exclusive forms as in Kwamera. The first and second columns give the glosses and their meaning—this is grammatical information—and the third column lists the pronouns which in English are associated with this grammatical information, to help you remember.

Table 1.2

Glosses for person and number

Gloss	Meaning	English pronouns
1SG	first person singular	'I/me'
2SG	second person singular	'you [singular]'
3SG	third person singular	'he/him; she/her; it'
1PL	first person plural	'we/us'
2PL	second person plural	'you [plural]'
3PL	third person plural	'they/them'

> 请思考，我们是否也可以制出一个类似"Glosses for person and number in hinese"的表格？

If the gloss specifies just the person, '1', '2' or '3', but doesn't mention singular or plural, this means that the particular language being glossed does not have number distinctions in this instance.

1.2.2.4 Writing systems and glosses

> 请思考，世界上共有哪几种书写系统？另外，请根据规范的要求，使用英语撰写一个汉语的句子实例。

Not all languages use the Roman alphabet (the one you're reading now). For example, Russian uses the Cyrillic alphabet, and Chinese and Japanese both use writing systems based on characters rather than an alphabet. But there usually exist conventions for writing such languages in the Roman alphabet, and this enables linguists to make use of the examples. I mostly follow the published source that my data come from, although some labels for glosses are changed to bring them into line with my practice. Additionally, I standardize glosses that are more detailed or less detailed than we need. Occasionally I simplify by not glossing some item, especially if we haven't yet met the appropriate grammatical term. I will often omit the tones in examples from languages such as Chinese: these specify pronunciation and are not vital to our discussion of syntax. Finally, note that some languages don't have a writing system at all, since they've never been written down. In this case, linguists typically give a phonetic representation of the original language. For that reason, some of the examples don't start with capital letters; the phonetic alphabet doesn't follow the conventions of a writing system.

1.3 WHY DO LANGUAGES HAVE SYNTAX?

Speakers manipulate sentences in all sorts of ways because they're trying to convey different meanings. Syntax allows speakers to express all the meanings that they need to put across. In the simplest cases, this might mean altering the basic word order of a sentence, to emphasize or downplay a particular phrase, or to ask a question, or else grouping words together in different ways to modify the meaning. This section gives a preliminary idea of some of the typical syntactic constructions found in languages, and demonstrates that languages really do have syntactic structure.

这一部分并不是真正要解释语言具有句法的原因, 其目的在于介绍一些关于句法结构的基本概念。

1.3.1 Word order

In English, the WORD ORDER is pretty fixed. There are three main elements in the sentence in (34): *Kim*, the one drinking the tea; *drank*, the verb which expresses what Kim did; and *the tea*, expressing what is being drunk. We use the term 'word order' (more accurately, as we will see later on, 'CONSTITUENT order') to discuss the order in which these three main parts of a sentence occur in a language. In English, the three elements occur in the order shown in (34a). This is the normal word order, and all variants of it are impossible (therefore starred) except for (34f), which has a restricted special usage.

Constituent, 成分, 指句子结构中具有区分性的句法单位。

(34) a. Kim drank the tea.
 b. *Kim the tea drank.
 c. *Drank Kim the tea.
 d. *Drank the tea Kim.
 e. *The tea drank Kim.
 f. The tea Kim drank.

Most of the logically possible variations are impossible in English. However, each of the word orders in (34) is attested (= found) amongst the world's languages, though some are much more common than others (see Chapter 6). The three most common basic word orders in languages other than English are those of (34a), (34b) and (34c). We saw in Section 1.2.2.1 that Japanese has the basic word order of (34b), and Welsh the basic order of (34c). Malagasy, spoken in Madagascar, has the basic order in (34d). The two word orders in (34e) and (34f) are the rarest basic word orders in the languages of the world, although they are found in the Carib language family of the Amazon basin. For example, Hixkaryana has the word order in (34e).

汉语的基本词序属于哪一个?

It is generally possible to determine the basic, neutral word order in a language, but the flexibility or rigidity of the basic word order differs widely amongst the world's languages. English has a fixed basic word order, whilst Russian has a very flexible word order, and Japanese allows many different orders provided the verb comes at the end of the sentence, as in (28). In English, some of the starred (ungrammatical) word orders in (34) might just about be permissible in poetry, but not in the spoken language or in prose. Example (34f) may initially sound odd to you, but it can be used to FOCUS on what it was that Kim drank; the phrase *the tea* is FRONTED from its usual position as given in (34a), so becomes more prominent. Try adding a bit of context: Kim visits an eccentric aunt who makes tea and beer out of strange garden plants: *The tea, Kim drank ___, but the home-made nettle beer, she really hated ___*. The gaps are used to show the normal position of the fronted phrases *the tea* and *the home-made nettle beer*. In technical terms, this construction involves fronting what is known as the DIRECT OBJECT of the verbs *drank* and *hated*: the direct object (or just 'object') of *drank* is *the tea* (the 'thing drunk') and the object of *hated* is *the home-made nettle beer* (the 'thing hated'). Example (35) shows a published example of the same object-fronting construction; the context is that the writer is learning to fly a microlight aircraft:

(35) **The last exercise, a stall while climbing**, I didn't do ___ well.

(From *Travels with Pegasus*, Christina Dodwell. Sceptre, Hodder & Stoughton, 1989)

In (35) the fronted object is shown in bold, and again its more usual position is marked by a dash. Object-fronting is, in fact, quite rare in English. It's known as a MARKED (= unusual) construction, whilst the usual basic word order as in (34a) is termed UNMARKED.

> Marked（有标记的）和 unmarked（无标记的）是成对的概念，在此处，前者指比较少见的、特殊的结构，而后者则指比较常见的结构。

Often there are stylistic reasons for changing basic word order. The fronted phrase in (35) is rather long, and sounds clumsy in the usual object position: *I didn't do the last exercise, a stall while climbing, well*. In (36) we illustrate a different kind of word order change, which involves breaking up a rather long phrase by moving part of it to the right. The phrase in bold type moves rightwards from its basic position following the word *estimates*, shown by the gap:

(36) Estimates ___ vary greatly **about the number of fluent speakers** (i.e. *of Esperanto*).

(From *The Cambridge Encyclopedia of Language*, David Crystal. Cambridge University Press, 1987)

This avoids the clumsiness of a long initial phrase *estimates about the number of fluent speakers* before the short phrase *vary greatly*. (Compare the normal word order in *Estimates about this vary greatly*.) As (34) showed, English has a generally inflexible word order in the sentence, but optional modifying phrases can be reordered quite easily, as is the case for the *about* ... phrase which modifies (= expands on) the word *estimates*.

The examples in (37) and (38) again involve rightward movement of a phrase. In both cases the moved phrase is the object of a verb—as it was in (35)—but you don't need to be able to define what an object is in order to find the phrase that's moved. Try and work out the basic word order, find the phrase that's moved, and indicate where it has moved from by using a dash, as I did above. Then say why you think the writer chose this construction, rather than using the basic word order of English:

(37) It may harm your defence if you do not mention when questioned something which you later rely on in court.

(From *1994 Criminal Justice and Public Order Act*)

(38) Mrs Verwoerd struggled to read without her glasses a statement appealing to Nelson Mandela to give the Afrikaner a *volkstaat*.

(From the *Guardian*, 21.8.95)

I indicate the moved phrase by following the usual linguistic practice of enclosing it inside square brackets: [...]; the brackets signify the beginning and end of a phrase. Here are the answers to the exercise:

(39) It may harm your defence if you do not mention ___ when questioned [something which you later rely on in court].

(40) Mrs Verwoerd struggled to read ___ without her glasses [a statement appealing to Nelson Mandela to give the Afrikaner a *volkstaat*].

In (39), the basic word order would be *I mentioned something when questioned*, not **I mentioned when questioned something*. But because the bracketed object in (39) is a particularly long phrase ('heavy' is the technical term) it's allowed to shift from its normal position, and indeed sounds better that way. Similarly in (40), the basic word order has to be *She read a statement without her glasses* not **She read without her glasses a statement*. But again, the object is heavy: it's the whole phrase *a statement appealing to Nelson Mandela to give the Afrikaner a volkstaat*. So the preferred position of this heavy phrase is not its basic position, but a position to the right of the shorter phrase *without her glasses*.

If you previously had no idea how to determine the OBJECT of a verb, look at the position of the gaps in (39) and (40). Both gaps immediately follow verbs, namely *mention* and *read*. The objects are the 'thing mentioned' and the 'thing read' here: both these phrases in some sense complete the meaning of the verb, and so are often known as the COMPLEMENTS of the verb. The normal position for a direct object in English is immediately following the verb. I discuss these technical terms in more detail in Chapter 2, but these features will help you identify objects in the next section. Please review this section before moving on if you weren't previously familiar with the grammatical term 'object'. We return to word order in Chapter 6.

1.3.2 Promotion and demotion processes

The syntactic variations in Section 1.3.1 involved simply reordering the elements of a sentence. But syntactic changes can have much more radical results than this. Section 1.1, in the discussion of Indonesian, introduced the idea of promotion processes—making a word or phrase more prominent in the sentence. There are also demotion processes, which make part of the sentence less prominent. Here I give a preliminary introduction to another construction involving promotion and demotion—the PASSIVE—in English and Japanese (more in Chapter 7).

世界上的事物往往是成对出现的，有阴则有阳，有男则有女，语言的研究也是如此，有单数（singular）就有非单数（non-singular），有主动就有被动，有升格（promotion）就有降格（demotion）。

The passive is illustrated in bold type in (41) and (42), and is an extremely common construction in both spoken and written English.

(41) The women and boys with crates converged on the boats and **their catch was counted out by the market boss**.

(From *Travels in Mauritania*, Peter Hudson. Flamingo, 1990)

(42) His normal work was filing girls' teeth to points, although **pointed gnashers were considered a bit old-fashioned by the girls here**.

(From *Travels with Pegasus*, Christina Dodwell. Sceptre, Hodder & Stoughton, 1989)

Compare these passive constructions with the sentences in (43) and (44), which are their counterparts in meaning, but are both ACTIVE constructions:

(43) The market boss counted out **their catch**.

(44) The girls here considered **pointed gnashers** a bit old-fashioned.

Before reading further, please try to figure out what properties differentiate the active from the passive constructions. Use the correct technical terms where you know them. Start by deciding on the grammatical role of the phrases in bold type in (43) and (44), and see what role these same phrases have in the passive constructions. What purposes do the two different construction types seem to serve? Can you describe any additional grammatical features?

First, assume that active sentences are the more basic; they are, for instance, learnt much earlier by children than are passives. Two properties of the passive occur in any language which has the construction: (i) the passive involves PROMOTION of an object phrase to a new position in the sentence, known as the SUBJECT position, and (ii) the phrase that used to be in the subject position undergoes DEMOTION. Let's go through this technical passage carefully. The phrases in bold in the active constructions in (43) and (44) are in the OBJECT position: they each immediately follow the verb (*counted out*, *considered*) and they express what is being counted out, what is considered. In (41) and (42), the phrases *their catch* and *pointed gnashers* appear in a new, promoted position in the sentence. They have changed their grammatical function, and become the subjects of the passive sentences. How do we know that these phrases are now subjects? One major indication is that *their catch* and *pointed gnashers* appear immediately before the verb, in the normal sentence-initial position of English subjects. (We will see more tests for subjecthood in English in Chapter 2, page 50.) This advancement to subject position in (41) and (42) makes the promoted phrases more salient: it focusses attention on *their catch* and *pointed gnashers*. By contrast, the phrases that were the subjects of the active

在成对的两种结构中，它们之间的基本构成要素是相同的。一种结构往往是更为基本的（可以说是无标记的），而另一种结构（可以说是有标记的）则可以被认为是由基本结构转换而来的。

sentences in (43) and (44), namely *the market boss* and *the girls here*, are no longer subjects. In the passive sentences in (41) and (42) they have been demoted to a lower position. Demotion in this case means that they are consigned to a *by*-phrase, outside the core of the sentence: hence, these phrases have ceased to act as subject. Notice that this *by*-phrase is entirely optional: we could omit it, and just have, for instance, *Their catch was counted out*. Compare that optionality with what we find in the active sentence in (43): both the subject *the market boss* and the object *their catch* are core elements of the sentence, and neither can be omitted. (Try this.)

You should now be starting to have some feeling for the purpose and usual positions of different parts of the sentence. Before leaving the topic of the passive construction, note that in English (and in many other languages) it is signalled by changes in the form of the verb: compare (45a) and (45b), where the verbs are in bold type.

(45) a. Kim **broke** the vase. (active)
b. The vase **was broken** by Kim. (passive)

The examples in (46) show the corresponding properties in Japanese. Example (46a) is the active sentence, (46b) its passive counterpart:

(46) a. Sensei ga John o sikat-ta. (active) (Japanese)
teacher SUBJECT John OBJECT scold-PAST
'The teacher scolded John.'
b. John ga sensei ni sikar-**are**-ta. (passive)
John SUBJECT teacher by scold-PASSIVE-PAST
'John was scolded by the teacher.'

In (46a),³ the 'teacher' phrase *sensei ga* is the subject, and *John* is marked as the object of the 'scold' verb by the *o* marker. In (46b), *John* is promoted to subject position and the 'teacher' phrase is demoted. It appears in the equivalent of a *by*-phrase, *sensei ni* 'teacher by'—note that Japanese has a different word order from English here. The verb also has a special passive suffix, *-are*. Please make sure you understand the way these examples are structured before moving on.

Passives and other promotion and demotion constructions are discussed in detail in Chapter 7.

1.3.3 All languages have structure

All languages—whether living or dead—have syntactic structure, including, of course, sign languages (such as British Sign Language). This means that a language doesn't just consist of strings of words, but that the words group together to form phrases, and the phrases group together to form larger phrases and sentences. Linguists describe this phrases-within-phrases pattern as HIERARCHICAL STRUCTURE.

人类的语言多种多样，但是所有的语言都表达相同的思想和概念，都有句法结构。在所有的语言中，句子不是由一堆词语随意堆积到一起的，而是有其内在的层次结构，都是由词构成短语，短语跟短语组成更大的短语，直至组成句子。

Embedded sentence, 嵌入句, 指一个句子中嵌入另外一个句子或一个小句中嵌入另一个小句的结构。

Recursion, 递归, 各种语法结构的关系是有限的, 但是在语言单位的组合过程中, 可以反复无限地使用这些有限的规则, 从而使句法结构复杂化。递归性可以使得有限的规则产生无限的句子, 是人类语言的基本属性之一。

One kind of hierarchical structure is seen in EMBEDDED **sentences**. In this construction, a sentence occurs within another sentence, such as *Chris told Lee [Kim couldn't swim]*. This property is known as RECURSION. Here, the sentence in brackets—*Kim couldn't swim*—is the embedded sentence. It serves to tell you what it was that Chris told Lee. More examples of recursion from English are given in (47): the embedded sentences are again in square brackets.

(47) I wonder [if Lee will arrive late].
The claim [that she doesn't like Kim] is very surprising.
[That we've no coffee left] isn't my fault.
We asked [how to get to the station].

For the first three phrases in brackets in (47), you can check that they really are sentences by removing the words *if* and *that* which introduce them: you can then get perfectly good independent sentences such as *Lee will arrive late*. But this doesn't work for all embedded sentences, as is clear from *how to get to the station*; we will see much more on this in Chapter 3. Try to decide what properties this final example has that set it apart from the other embedded sentences in (47).

There are no limits to the number of embedded sentences that can be built up. So given a sentence like *Kim couldn't swim* we can turn it into *Lee thought that Kim couldn't swim*, then *I said that Lee thought that Kim couldn't swim*, and so on. This means it's never possible to construct a 'longest sentence', though of course a person's memory limitations will, in practice, constrain the number of embeddings.

I end this chapter with two short practical demonstrations that syntactic structure really exists, in other words that speakers of a language share the same mental representations of this structure. First, look at the examples in (48):

(48) a. I charged up the battery.
b. I charged up the street.

At first glance these sentences appear to be structurally identical. Of course, you might be aware when you read them that *charge* means something different in (48a) and (48b), but otherwise, the only difference seems to be that *street* replaces *battery*. And yet the syntactic behaviour of the two sentences is entirely different. As always, the asterisks indicate ungrammatical sentences:

(49) a. I charged the battery up.
b. *I charged the street up.

(50) a. *It was up the battery I charged (not the engine).
b. It was up the street I charged (not the corridor).

(51) a. *I charged up Lee's battery and (then) up Kim's too.
b. I charged up Lee's street and (then) up Kim's too.

Since native speakers of English agree about where the asterisks showing an ungrammatical sentence should be placed, we must all share an unconscious knowledge of the sentence structure of English. Even though pairs of sentences like those in (48) look the same, they in fact have different structures. Different sets of words group together to form phrases in each case, and linguists represent this using brackets:

(52) a.　I [charged up] the battery.
　　 b.　I charged [up the street].

In (52a) the brackets show that there's a phrase *charge up*. This makes sense if you think that the only thing you can do with a battery is charge it up; you can't charge it down, over, across, or anything else. So *up* belongs with *charge* in (52a). In (52b), it doesn't: instead, there's a syntactic unit *up the street*, which can be moved around the sentence for focus, as for example in (50b), It was **up the street** I charged. And in (52b), *up* can be replaced with a number of other words: I charged **down** the street/**over** the street/**across** the street and so on. The very fact that *up* forms a unit with *charge* in (52a) but with *the street* in (52b) is responsible for the patterns of (un) grammaticality in (49) to (51). We'll return in detail to questions of structure and the grouping of words to form phrases in Chapter 5.

对于本族语的人来说，他们会很自然地把（52a）中的 charge up 和（52b）中的 up the street 作为一个整体，这反映了人们心理之中句法结构的现实性。

As a second demonstration of syntactic structure, let's examine possessive -*'s* in English, as in *Lee's friend*. You might assume at first that this possessive ending simply attaches to a noun, a word such as *Lee* or *government*, as in *the government's dilemma*. But consider (53):

(53) a.　I saw the woman next door's children.
　　 b.　What was that guy who retired last month's name?
　　 c.　The student I lent the book to's room-mate said she'd left.

Each example in (53) shows that -*'s* actually attaches to the end of a whole phrase, not to the single noun at the end of the phrase: we know that the door doesn't have children, and that the answer to (53b) couldn't be *November*. And *to* in (53c) isn't even a noun (you may find this example a little odd, because it belongs in spoken rather than written English. Try saying it aloud a few times). Native speakers also know that you can't attach the -*'s* to the noun it logically seems to belong to: *What was that **guy's** who retired last month name?*. The fact that we agree where to attach the -*'s* shows once again that sentences do have structure, and that we have an intuitive knowledge of it. The phrases that -*'s* attaches to are shown in brackets:

(54) a.　[the woman next door]'s
　　 b.　[that guy who retired last month]'s
　　 c.　[the student I lent the book to]'s

Demonstrations of this nature could be given from any language, because the rules of the syntax of all languages are STRUCTURE DEPENDENT. This is why no language has rules that, for example, form questions from statements by reversing the order of the words in the sentence—such a rule wouldn't depend on the structure of the sentence at all, and so can't work. When, as linguists, we try to figure out the syntactic structures of a language, we rely on the judgements of native speakers to tell us whether our example sentences are possible or impossible (the latter being starred). These GRAMMATICALITY JUDGEMENTS, along with examples that are collected from a spoken or written corpus of the language, form the data of the science of linguistics. It doesn't matter that native speakers usually can't tell us why they feel that a particular sentence is good or bad; the very fact that they have these intuitions shows up the structural differences and similarities between sentences.

Checklist for Chapter 1

If you're not sure about the answers to any of the following, you are advised to look back and check on them before reading further.

- Do you understand how to read linguistic examples with glosses?
- Do you understand the distinction between lexical and grammatical information in a gloss?
- Do the categories of person and number make sense, including the distinctions that do not occur in English?
- Can you define the term BOUND PRONOMINAL?
- Do you have at least a preliminary feel for what promotion and demotion processes do?

FURTHER READING

An excellent general introduction to linguistics and to the views of linguists on language acquisition is Fromkin, Rodman and Hyams (2007). I can also strongly recommend Jackendoff (1993) and Pinker (1994). Baker (2001) is a recent introduction to the view of language learning most associated with the work of the linguist Noam Chomsky. Chomsky's idea that speakers possess a subconscious 'knowledge' of their native languages is explored accessibly in the early chapters of his (1986) book, *Knowledge of language*, and in the conversations set out in Chomsky (2012). On language change, see McMahon (1994) and Millar (2007). On person, see Siewierska (2004); on gender, see Corbett (1991); on number, see Corbett (2000); and on agreement, see Corbett (2006). Also on person, number and related issues see Whaley (1997: ch. 10) and Comrie (1989: ch. 9). The topics raised in Section 1.3 all appear again in later chapters: word order is in Chapter 6, promotion and demotion processes in Chapter 7, and syntactic structure in Chapters 4 and 5.

EXERCISES

1. In Chapter 1 I argued that dialectal forms of English cannot be criticized for lack of 'logic'. The tables below list both the standard English forms of the reflexive pronouns (the 'self' forms) and the forms found in a northern dialect of British English. Which dialect has the more regular pattern for the formation of its reflexive pronouns? Why? Be as specific as you can about how the reflexives are formed in each case, using the correct technical terms if you can.

Standard dialect	Northern dialect
myself	myself
yourself	yourself
himself	hisself
herself	herself
ourselves	theirself
yourselves	ourselves
themselves	yourselves
	theirselves

I've omitted *itself*, which is the same across all dialects, and doesn't shed any light on the question. Also, the form *myself* is generally pronounced more like *meself* in this northern dialect, but I take this to be a phonetic reduction which is not relevant to the question. The northern dialect has one more reflexive pronoun than standard English. What is it, and what do you think it's used for? (If you're not a native speaker of this dialect, you may find it helpful to look back at Section 1.1.) Some English speakers have a singular form *themself*: comment on how this fits into the set of forms in standard English, and say how it is used (if you're not a speaker who has this form, see if you can imagine how it's used).

Finally, do you think that 'more logical' equals 'better', as far as languages are concerned?

2. In Section 1.3.3 I referred to the -'s morpheme in English as the POSSESSIVE form. This term describes the function of the -'s suffix in noun phrases like *Kim's dog*, where it does indicate possession. But -'s doesn't always have a possessive meaning. For this reason, linguists often use the more general term GENITIVE, which indicates that there is a formal relationship between the elements in the noun phrase without specifying any meaning.

Task: Consider the following data, and try to classify the various different ways in which genitive -'s can be used to indicate semantic (meaning) relationships in the noun phrases. Feel free to add more data of your own. Generalize where possible, and be as precise as you can in your descriptions.

(1) Kim's denial/conclusion/problem
(2) the book's ending/the book's cover
(3) today's lecture/today's date
(4) the professor's book
(5) next door's kids
(6) the boy's inactivity
(7) that decision of the President's
(8) Lee's surprise (at the low price)
(9) the dog's death
(10) the newspaper's editor
(11) the woman's family
(12) the tree's growing habits

3. The data in this exercise are from Icelandic, a Germanic language which is related quite closely to English, and are taken from Sigurðsson (2006).

Task: All these examples illustrate a single, specific, grammatical difference between English and Icelandic. What is this? You should use the correct grammatical term, which is given earlier on in this chapter. If you find other syntactic differences between the two languages in any example, list these too. Finally, in what specific ways can you see that Icelandic is syntactically similar to English? Use the correct terminology wherever possible. **NB** The Icelandic alphabet includes some characters that are not used in English, but this has no bearing on the answer.

(1) Kona   sat   á   bekk.
    woman sat   on   bench
    'A woman sat on a bench.'

(2) Ég   keypti   skemmtilega   bók   í   morgun.
    I   bought   interesting   book in   morning
    'I bought an interesting book this morning.'

(3) Ólafur   er   prófessor.
    Ólafur   is   professor
    'Ólafur is a professor.'

(4) Það   er   maður   í   garðinum.
    there   is   man   in   garden.the
    'There is a man in the garden.'

(5) Sá   sem   er   að   tala   er   Íslendingur.
    the.one   who   is   to   talk   is   Icelander
    'The one who is talking is an Icelander.'

4. In (1) through (10) below are some more examples from Kwamera, and two closely related languages, Lenakel and Southwest Tanna, all languages of the Republic of Vanuatu in the southwest Pacific; data are from Lindstrom and Lynch (1994) and Lynch (1998). I give the original and the gloss, and your task is to suggest a translation. You will find it useful to look back at Section 1.2.2.3, where the Kwamera examples are discussed in the text.

Hint:
There is rarely just one correct way of translating each example; the important part here is to make sure you understand the role of the grammatical information in the glosses (in small capitals).

(1) t-r-uv-irapw (Kwamera)
    FUTURE-3SG-move-outwards

(2) t-r-am-apri (Kwamera)
    FUTURE-3SG-CONTINUOUS-sleep

Translate the 'continuous' prefix *am-* using an *-ing* form of the verb in English, as in *I was sleeping, I've been sleeping, I will be sleeping*. Both Kwamera *am-* and English *-ing* denote an ongoing action here.

(3) iak-imiki   kuri   u (Kwamera)
    1EXC-dislike dog   this

The prefix *iak-* is the form of the first person exclusive which occurs before vowels.

(4) k-rou-ánumwi (Kwamera)
    1INC-DUAL-drink

Note that the first person inclusive prefix, *k-*, does not have the same form as the first person inclusive *sa-* that we saw in (32a) in the text. The reason for this is that *sa-* is used in conjunction with a plural prefix, whilst *k-* co-occurs with a dual prefix.

(5) K-im-hal-vin-uas. (Lenakel)
    3PL-PAST-TRIAL-go.there-together

(6) R-im-avhi-in   mun (Lenakel)
    3SG-PAST-read-TRANS again

The suffix *-in* marks the verb as TRANSITIVE (more in Chapter 2): this means that it is understood to have an object (see Section 1.3.1), and this should affect your translation.

(7) Kimlu   i-imn-la-gin (Southwest Tanna)
    we.two.EXC   1PL-PAST-DUAL-afraid

(8) Kimlu   i-imn-la-hai   pukah (Southwest Tanna)
    we.two.EXC   1PL-PAST-DUAL-stab   pig

Recall from Section 1.2.2.2 that the dot '.' in a gloss indicates that the various pieces of grammatical information can't be separated from each other: the *whole* form *kimlu* in (7) and (8) therefore has the meaning (glossed as) 'we.two.EXC'.

(9) R-i-aamh nimwa vɨt ker (Lenakel)
he-PAST-see house good one

(10) Nimwa taha-n r-ɨ m-vɨt akɨn (Lenakel)
house POSS-his it-PAST-good very

There is an additional point of syntactic interest concerning the element glossed as 'good' in (9) and (10). Can you identify how these two examples differ?

5. The following data are all from Niger-Congo languages, a massive family of African languages covering almost a quarter of the total languages in the world.

Task: Examine each sentence and note as many grammatical differences in these examples as you can between English and each of the various source languages. Look for differences both in the syntax and morphosyntax, and describe these differences carefully, using the correct terminology where you can. The data are taken from Watters (2000) and J. Payne (1985a).

(1) è wúru tèe à bóa (Mende)
he cut stick with knife
'He cut the stick with a knife.'

(2) ba-tub-aka (Lobala)
3PL-sing-PAST
'They sang.'

(3) Halima a-na-pika ugali (Swahili)
Halima 3SG-PRES-cook porridge
'Halima is cooking porridge.'

(4) a. ɔ́ tẽ kɔ́ (Kru)
he buy rice
'He bought rice'
b. ɔ́ sé kɔ́ tẽ
he NEG rice buy
'He didn't buy rice.'

6. These data are from a Melanesian language called Tinrin, spoken in part of the islands of New Caledonia, in the southwest Pacific Ocean (Osumi 1995).

Task: (i) Figure out the function of the grammatical marker *nrâ* shown in each example in (1) through (6) in bold type, and not glossed. (ii) Decide why this marker does not occur in (7), (8) and (9).

Hints:
- Don't worry about the fact that Tinrin has another morpheme with the form nrâ, which occurs in (2), (4), (5), (6) and (9). This has a different meaning

altogether: it's a third person singular pronoun, and has no relevance to your answer.

- Tinrin has a grammatical category 'dual', like Kwamera, discussed in this chapter. But this is not relevant to your answer.

- It will help to compare the structure of (1) through (6), which have the nrâ marker in question, with that of (7) through (9), which do not. What syntactic factor distinguishes these two groups of data?

(1) rru   fi   pwere   ânrâmwâ   **nrâ**   truu   truu-truare
    3.DUAL   go   to   there   ???   the.DUAL   DUAL-brother
    'The two brothers went there.'

(2) nrâ   nyôrrô   **nrâ**   wa   mwîe   mwâ
    3SG   cook   ???   the   woman   that
    'That woman cooked (something).'

(3) u   truumwêrrê   mirrî   **nrâ**   nro
    1SG   always   hungry   ???   I
    'I am always hungry.'

(4) nrâ   tewùrrù   nranri   **nrâ**   toni
    3SG   tie.up   goat   ???   Tony
    'Tony tied up the goat.'

(5) nrâ   truu   tôbwerrî-nrî   **nrâ**   magasâ
    3SG   stay   close-PASSIVE   ???   shop
    'The shop is closed.'

(6) nrâ   tôbwerrî-nrî   **nrâ**   magasâ   rugi   midi
    3SG   close-PASSIVE   ???   shop   at   noon
    'The shop is/was closed at noon.'

(7) wa   mwâ   ha   hêê-rò
    the   house   this   belonging-me
    'This house is mine.'

(8) rri   truu   hubo   ei   nrü
    3PL   stay   near   to   2SG
    'They live near you.'

(9) toni   nrâ   tuo   nrî   padrêrrê-tave
    Tony   3SG   put   3SG   side-bed
    'Tony put it beside the bed.'

NOTES

1. Section 1.2.2 explains in detail how to read linguistic examples. You don't need to know any French to see the point that example (2) is making. The technique you should employ is to read the English translation, then carefully examine the second line of the example, which is the literal translation of the original language.
2. To simplify matters, I leave two small words in the Japanese unglossed: *ga* indicates that *sensei* '(the) teacher' is the subject (here, the one writing) and *o* indicates that *tegami* '(the) letter' is the object (here, the thing being written). These terms come up again later, and in Chapters 2 and 6, so don't worry if they are unfamiliar to you now.
3. The verb stem (the form before the affix is added) is *sikar*, but this changes to *sikat* before the past tense suffix *-ta*.

2

Words belong to different classes

章节导读

　　词是句法分析的基本单位，因此词类的识别具有重要的意义。对于中国学生来说，大家对词类的划分是非常熟悉的，我们都知道名词、动词、形容词等词类的区别，但是许多人的概念中词类划分的依据主要是词的意义，例如，名词是表示人或事物的名称，动词表示动作、行为，形容词表示性质、状态等。然而，依靠词义判断词类的划分往往是有困难的，原因之一在于词义本身不太典型，难以作为分类的依据；另外，不同的人对于"事物""动作""行为"等概念的理解也不尽一致，容易导致分类的差异。现在常用的分类方法是依据词汇的分布（即词在句子中所处的位置及其搭配）来分类，词汇在句子中具体的形态变化和功能也是词类判断的重要依据。

　　不同语言之下的词类的情况是不一样的，例如，英语中的介词数量较多，但是有些语言的介词数量很少，有的语言甚至没有介词。但是，几乎所有的语言都有动词和名词。词类可以被进一步分为开放类词和封闭类词。开放类词可以不断地有新词加入，而封闭类词则不行。对于不同的语言，其开放类词和封闭类词所包含的词类是不一样的。在英语中，形容词属于开放类词，但是在许多其他语言中它属于封闭类词。另外，我们还可以将词类区分为功能语类（functional categories）和词汇语类（lexical categories），前者是指那些只有语法功能、没有实际意义的词，而后者则只具有实际意义的词。在英语中，冠词、指示词、连词和代词都属于功能语类。

　　动词的主要功能在于表达述谓结构。世界上所有的语言都有动词，根据它所需的论元数量的不同，动词可以被分为不及物动词、及物动词和双宾语动词。与动词相关的语法范畴主要包括时态、体、情态和一致。时态和体都与时间有关，时态的区分可以以动词本身的形态变化为标记。在英语中有现在时和过去式的划分，而英语中的将来时则依靠如 will 之类的助动词来表达。虽然时态被认为是一种普遍的语法范畴，但是在某些语言中并没有时态。英语中有进行体和完成体两种，在其他语言中还有诸如惯常体之类的语法范畴。情态是表示讲话人判断一项陈述的真实程度的语法范畴，包括陈述语气、虚拟语气和祈使语气等。一致是两个成分之间的形式关系，如在众多的语言中，动词必须要与它的论元之间保持人称、性和数的一致。

名词的主要功能是用来做动词的论元，不同论元都承担着各自的题元角色，例如，施事者、承受者、体验者、受益者、工具等。从名词与动词的关系来看，名词可以充当主语和宾语。要确定一个名词是否为主语，我们可以从以下两个方面来判定：（1）英语中的主语控制主语与动词的一致；（2）通过代词的格标记。另外，名词还可以做谓语。与名词相关的语法范畴包括数、性、领属、格等。英语中有单复数之分，其他语言还有双数、三数等形式。对于许多语言来说，名词都有性的差别，有的是阴性与阳性的区分，还有的语言中名词有二十种以上的性的区别。领属是指名词所代表的物体与领有者之间的关系，包括可让渡领属关系与不可让渡领属关系两种。格也是一个与名词相关的重要语法范畴，用来表示句子中名词短语的语法功能。英语中与格相关的形态变化很少，但是某些语言则具有格的高度复杂的形态系统。有定性也与名词具有密切的关系，有些语言可以通过名词本身的形态变化来表示有定性，而英语则主要通过冠词、指示代词等的使用来表示有定性和无定性的区分。

形容词用来表示名词的属性，可以做定语和谓语。程度副词经常与形容词一起使用，对形容词的意义起到增强或减弱的作用。比较是与形容词有关的一个语法范畴，包括比较级、最高级和等同级三种。一致也与形容词具有一定的关系，因为在一些语言中，形容词必须要与他所修饰的名词在性和数上保持一致。在大多数语言中，形容词属于开放类词，但是在少数语言中它也属于封闭类词。

副词的主要功能是用来修饰形容词和动词。在许多语言中，副词往往与形容词具有形态上的关联性，因此许多副词是由形容词转化而来的，而在另一些语言中，副词和形容词之间并不存在形式的差异。

介词可以分为及物性介词和非及物性介词，及物性介词可以和名词一起构成介词短语，用来修饰动词。介词也被称为前置词，因为它一般位于名词之前，但是，在许多语言中，名词也可以放置在介词之前，因此被称为后置词。

Section 2.1 should be useful to readers who have little previous experience of word classes, or 'parts of speech'. This section concentrates on English. Then in Sections 2.2 to 2.5, we look at the major LEXICAL word classes occurring cross-linguistically, namely verbs (2.2), nouns (2.3), adjectives (2.4) and adverbs (2.5). Although all languages distinguish a class of verbs from a class of nouns, it is less clear whether or not all languages have a separate adjective word class, as we will see. Adverbs are widespread, but not universal. Section 2.6 discusses adpositions, also a widespread word class cross-linguistically. Each section discusses the distribution, function and MORPHOSYNTACTIC properties of the word class it describes. All the major word classes are associated with a typical set of grammatical categories. We concentrate here on the most common categories found cross-linguistically.

2.1   IDENTIFYING WORD CLASSES

2.1.1   How can we tell that words belong to different classes?

It is easy to demonstrate that words in a language fall into different classes. For example, only certain single words can fill the gap in (1) to complete the sentence:

(1)   Kim wanted to _____ .

The gap can be filled as in (2), but not as in (3):

(2)   Kim wanted to relax/depart/compete.

(3)   a.   *Kim wanted to relaxation/departure/competition.
        b.   *Kim wanted to underneath/overhead.
        c.   *Kim wanted to energetic/thoughtful/green/sad.

The words that can fill the gap are all VERBS. Verbs appear in a variety of other positions too, but if we have to find one word to complete (1), it must be a verb. So the words that are impossible in (3) are not verbs: they must belong to other word classes. Note that to try this test you don't need a definition of 'verb', because you're simply applying your knowledge of English: you know without being told that only certain words fit in (1). From now on, you can use this test as follows: any single word which can fill the gap in (1) to form a complete sentence must be a verb.

Before reading further, pick out which words from the list in (4) fit into the empty slots in (5):

(4)   squeamish, happiness, wolves, expect, below, suddenly, writes, Cornish

(5)   ___ became extinct in the eighteenth century.
      ___ seemed to be unpopular.
      I wonder whether ___ will ever return.
      ___ extinct! I don't believe it.
      That ___ could ever return seems unlikely.
      For ___ to be reintroduced to Britain might be a good idea.

> Gap test, 空位测试，是一种基于词汇分布的词汇分类方法。

Of course, only three words fit: *happiness*, *wolves* and *Cornish* (a language). As you probably expected, these words all belong to the same word class (they're all NOUNS) whilst words like *below* and *suddenly* and all the other words in (4) don't belong in this class. **Gap tests** work in all languages: there will always be positions in a sentence which can only be filled by a specific class of word. From now on, you can use the sentences in (5), adjusted as necessary in order to make sense, to test for the word class NOUN.

Very often, a word can belong to more than one word class. For example, the verb *escape* can fit into the gap in (1), but there's also a noun *escape* as in *The escape went badly*. There's a noun *official*, as in *Some officials are corrupt*, but there's also an adjective *official*, as in *our (un)official policy*. How do we determine the word class in these cases? Discovering the DISTRIBUTION of each word is one method: to do this, we find gaps that can only be filled by members of one particular word class.

> 这是词汇分类的形态方法。请思考，对于像汉语这样缺乏形态变化的语言来说，这种方法有效吗？

Another method involves looking at the form the word takes in different contexts; this is morphosyntax. For example, the verb *escape* can take the same *-(e)d* ending for the past tense which is found on other verbs such as *wandered*, *relaxed* and so on: *I escaped*. But the noun *escape* can't: **The escaped went badly*. And whilst nouns usually take the *-s* ending when they're plural, as in *some officials*, adjectives don't take this ending: **our officials policies*. In modern linguistics, word classes are distinguished largely by using evidence from distribution and form.

2.1.2 Starting to identify nouns, adjectives and verbs

In this section I demonstrate why we need formal tests to identify word classes, and I will show you how some of these tests work with simple examples from English. You may perhaps have learnt some informal semantic tests for identifying nouns, adjectives and verbs. A typical schoolroom definition of these three major word classes might be:

(6) a. A noun is the name of a person, place or thing.
     b. An adjective is a describing word which modifies a noun.
     c. A verb expresses an event, action, process or state.

Although such informal definitions based on meaning will identify many central members of a word class, linguists generally believe that they need to be supplemented by formal tests. One reason is that we may not all agree on, say, what counts as a 'thing' or an 'action'. Consider nouns like *sincerity*, *freedom* and *turbulence*: do these fit the definition in (6a)? Some nouns seem more like states than 'things'; others, like *tornado* or *tsunami*, are events, surely a verb-like property. So on a purely semantic basis, such words might seem to be verbs. But a formal distribution test shows clearly that these examples *are* nouns: they fit another typical noun slot such as: *A ___ can be dangerous.*

对于许多学生来说，他们对于词类划分的概念或者标准更多地来自于传统语法中的词义划分标准，要从事句法学的研究，还需要换一个角度。

Sometimes it won't be appropriate to use the article *a* in this test, for instance when the noun is plural: *Cheetahs can be dangerous.* Please try the test before reading further with some words that you think may be nouns, or with some words which have a word class that you're not sure of. What results do you get with *pomposity*, *impoliteness*, *incongruity*, *spinach*, *Batman*? Of course, for some nouns you'll need to adjust the test a bit so it makes sense (not everything is potentially dangerous!).

Let's take some more examples. How should we classify *kindness* in the sentence *Lee is kindness itself*? *Kindness* seems to describe a property that Lee has, and as *Lee is a noun*, we might assume *kindness* to be a 'describing' word: an adjective. But it's not: it fits a typical noun slot, as in *Kindness can be dangerous*, and (another formal test) it also takes the plural *-(e)s* ending of a typical noun—*kindnesses*—as in *Such kindnesses are rare*. Adjectives, such as *squeamish* and *expensive*, don't behave this way.

What word class do you think *engine* belongs to in *Kim is an engine driver*? It fits the informal definition of both noun and adjective: it's a thing, so must be a noun, but it also describes what Kim drives—it modifies the noun *driver*, so should be an adjective. Without additional evidence, it would be hard to decide categorically on the word class in this case. In fact, using formal tests we can confirm that *engine* is a noun and not an adjective. First, it doesn't have the same DISTRIBUTION as typical English adjectives, like *untidy* and *happy*, which fit into slots such as those in (7a). Example (7b) shows that *engine* doesn't fit these slots.

在下面的分析中，作者以分布的标准为主线，还谈到了词汇的形态和功能，它们也是判断词汇类别的重要依据。

(7) Some tests for adjective status in English:
     a. Kim looked really/too/very/quite ___ .
         Kim seems ___ .
         Kim's as ___ as Chris.

          Kim is so/less ___ .
    b.   *Kim looked really/too/very/quite engine.
          *Kim seems engine.
          *Kim's as engine as Chris.
          *Kim is so/less engine.

Second, *engine* can never take the typical adjective endings *-er*, *-est*, as in *untidier*, *happiest* (and nor can we say *more engine, *most engine). So *engine* never has the same set of word forms as an adjective either. But it does take the plural *-s* suffix of nouns, as in *Kim drives engines*.

Another way to use distributional evidence is to show that nouns and adjectives are MODIFIED by different word classes: they keep different company. So, like other nouns, *engine* can itself be modified by an adjective, such as *electric*. But it can't be modified by an ADVERB such as *electrically* (the meaning intended in (8) is that the engine is electric, not Kim):

(8)   Kim is an **electric engine** driver.
       *Kim is an **electrically engine** driver.

This is typical behaviour for a noun. But adjectives behave in a different way: they are not modified by other adjectives—such as *unbelievable* in (9)—but by adverbs, such as *unbelievably*. So the asterisks are the opposite way round in (8) and (9).

(9)   *Kim is an **unbelievable skilful** driver.
       Kim is an **unbelievably skilful** driver.

This distributional test distinguishes adjectives like *skilful* from nouns like *engine*. To account for all the examples seen here, we simply need to say that nouns such as *driver* can be modified either by adjectives (*skilful driver*), or by other nouns (*engine driver*).

Now consider verbs such as *vegetate* and *survive*: these don't seem to be events, actions, processes or states (or 'doing' words!), but the formal distribution test in (1) shows that they are indeed verbs (e.g. *Kim wanted to vegetate*). As before, you may have to adjust the test slightly in order to fit the meaning of the verb. Again, these verbs take the past tense *-ed* suffix (*vegetated*, *survived*). They also take two other endings that are found on verbs: *-s* and *-ing*. Only verbs in English take *all three* of these suffixes, *-ed*, *-s*, *-ing*. But unfortunately, it's hard to use these suffixes independently to identify verbs, since they each have other grammatical roles. For instance, *boring* has the *-ing* suffix and can be a verb: *Kim's boring me to death*. But it's an adjective in *Kim's very boring*, as we can tell by *very*, which only modifies adjectives: we don't get: **Kim's very boring me to death*.

The formal methods that linguists use to identify word classes concentrate both on MORPHOLOGICAL criteria and on SYNTACTIC criteria. Morphology is the study of word form. Recurring patterns in the form of words, particularly in the affixes that they take, indicate that a group of words belong to the same class. We've seen several examples already: for instance, the observation above that only verbs take all three endings *-ed*, *-s* and *-ing*. This kind of evidence is based on the MORPHOSYNTAX of verbs: the morphology that they take in specific syntactic contexts. We will see plenty more MORPHOSYNTACTIC CATEGORIES as we go along.

Syntactic criteria show that each word class has a unique pattern of distribution. First, there are certain slots in a sentence that can only be filled by members of one word class, as illustrated in (7) and elsewhere in this section. Second, each word class has its own specific set of modifying words—words that can or must accompany it, as in (8) and (9). And third, as we'll see in the following sections, each word class has a particular role in relation to other parts of the sentence: this is its function.

To summarize:

(10) **Linguistic criteria for identifying word classes**
    a.   What different forms can the word have in distinct syntactic contexts? (MORPHOSYNTAX)
    b.   Whereabouts in a phrase or sentence does the word occur, and what words can modify it? (DISTRIBUTION)
    c.   What work does the word perform in a phrase or sentence? (FUNCTION)

2.1.3 An illustration: How do speakers of a language identify word classes?

The methods that linguists use to distinguish between word classes are also used by ordinary speakers of a language, albeit subconsciously; linguists, however, apply them consciously to the language under investigation. Let's see how speakers of English identify word classes, using as an illustration two headlines from newspaper articles:

(11)   a.   Revived ferry sale fears dog islanders.
      b.   Treasury eyes wider prescription charges.
                                   (From the *Guardian*, 22.5.93, 20.5.93)

What do you think are the stories behind these headlines? If the writer was successful, you will have been led up the **garden path** for a moment, probably having to re-read the headlines to get their true meaning. Before reading further, decide exactly why the headlines catch us out, using the correct grammatical terms where you know them.

Garden path, 歧途，指一开始被认为正确后来又被确认错误的句子分析。歧途句（garden path sentence）在语言学研究中具有重要的作用。

The first story is about plans to privatize a Scottish ferry service, and the worries this has caused to the islanders. The second headline is about the possibility that prescription charges in the National Health Service will be extended by the Treasury. Both headlines exploit the fact that a single word form can often belong to more than one word class. Consider *fears*: in (11a) it's a NOUN, part of a larger NOUN PHRASE, *revived ferry sale fears*; these compressed constructions are common in headlines. On the other hand, in *Man fears dog*, the word *fears* is a verb.

Turning to *dog*, in *Man fears dog*, the word *dog* is a noun. But in (11a), *dog* is a VERB (meaning something like *worry*). The word *eyes* in (11b) gives us the same problem: *eyes* is more often a noun, but in (11b) it's in a position which can only be that of a verb. Of course, nouns aren't simply randomly interchangeable with verbs. We can tell that the words *dog* and *eyes* in (11) really are verbs by substituting more typical verbs:

(12) a. Revived ferry sale fears **disturb/jeopardize/irritate** islanders.
     b. Treasury **considers/postpones/denies** wider prescription charges.

How effective would the headlines be if we changed them as follows?

(13) a. Revived ferry sale fears **have dogged** islanders.
     b. Treasury **to eye** wider prescription charges.

These don't achieve the same effect at all because it's now (too!) obvious that *dogged* and *eye* are verbs. You don't have to know the meaning of 'verb' to pick up the various clues to word class that (13) contains—as a speaker of English, you use these clues subconsciously all the time.

In (11b) the form *eyes* was particularly clever, because out of context, it might be either a noun or a verb—both word classes happen to have an *-s* suffix in English, though it performs very different work in each case. So (11b) at first leads us astray by playing on the fact that the word *eyes* can be a noun or a verb. In (13b), though, the use of *to eye* makes it clear at once that *eye* is a verb. Nouns can't fit into that slot:

(14) *Treasury to **ear/denial/postponement** wider prescription charges.

Although evidence from morphology (word form) can often be used to distinguish word classes, it's not always available. Furthermore, some languages—such as Chinese or Vietnamese—have very few grammatical affixes. For example, nouns in Chinese are not marked for a singular/plural distinction, so for instance the word *xìn* translates as both 'letter' and 'letters'. In such languages there isn't much morphological variation, so word form won't usually help to identify word class.

Syntactic evidence to distinguish word classes typically is available, however. In (13a), the verb *dogged* is followed by *islanders*; and in (13b) the verb *eye* is followed by the noun phrase *wider prescription charges*. In fact, these phrases (or ones like them) have to be present, or else the sentences will be ungrammatical (check this for yourself). Here, then, is another distribution test for verbs: certain verbs must be accompanied by a noun phrase like *islanders* or *wider prescription charges*. In technical terms, as we saw in Chapter 1, this phrase is the OBJECT of the verb. Verbs that need an object (often termed a DIRECT OBJECT) are known as TRANSITIVE verbs.

For completeness, notice that there's also an adjective *dogged*—it has a different (two-syllable) pronunciation from the verb, and means something like 'determined'. The adjective occurs, for instance, in *these dogged islanders*, where it modifies the noun *islanders*. As you'll expect by now, it has a different distribution to that of a verb or a noun. For instance, using the tests in (7), we can get *Kim's as dogged as Chris* and *Kim is so dogged*, but a noun or verb won't work here: **Kim's as dog as Chris*.

The newspaper headlines in (11) make use of words from just three different word classes: *ferry*, *sale*, *fears*, *islanders*, *treasury*, *prescription* and *charges* are all nouns; *dog* and *eyes* are verbs, as is *revived* in this usage, and *wider* is an adjective. The majority of words in the headlines are nouns and verbs—these word classes are indispensable and, cross-linguistically, are always the most important word classes. All languages seem to have distinct classes of nouns and verbs, so these are true LANGUAGE UNIVERSALS (= a property found in all languages). Also, nouns and verbs in most languages are OPEN CLASS words: this means that we can add new words to these classes. For example, the nouns *byte*, *blog*, *software* and *laser* are all recent innovations in English, as are the verbs *breathalyse* and *decoke* (to remove carbon deposits from an engine).

请从汉语报纸上面找一个类似的新闻标题，看看能否做出类似的分析。

In English and other European languages, adjectives (and maybe adverbs) are also open class words, but not all languages have an open class of adjectives, that is, a class to which new adjectives can be added. For example, Igbo, a language of the Benue-Congo family spoken in Nigeria, has a CLOSED CLASS of adjectives with just eight words in it (see Section 2.4 and 2.5 for more discussion).

这是一个很有意思的知识，许多人可能认为开放类词和封闭类词的词类都是固定的，其实不然，在不同的语言之中，它们所包括的词类是不一样的。

Adding a couple of other typical headlines, we also find the word class PREPOSITION—shown in bold in (15)—but no other word classes. *Bird* is slang for a prison sentence—the headline is about a woman illegally feeding pigeons:

(15) MPs' report urges action **within** four years **on** design changes.
Pigeon woman is cured **by** spell **of** bird.
(From the *Guardian* 29.7.95)

Prepositions aren't open class words, and some languages have very few or possibly even no prepositions. English, however, has a large class of prepositions conveying many different meanings. From the newspaper headlines, you can see that in English the four classes N (nouns), V (verbs), A (adjectives) and P (prepositions) contain the words we need most when we're trying to write in 'telegraphese'. Cross-linguistically, we can expect the classes N, V and A to be the major LEXICAL word classes, containing most members, and expressing most of the important meanings.

Some prepositions don't really carry much meaning, and are used for purely grammatical purposes: *by* and *of* are like this in (15). Headlines can often dispense with words that mainly bear grammatical information. This is why headlines don't typically contain the grammatical 'little words' like ARTICLES (*the*, *a* in English) which don't have much semantic content; in other words, meaning. All languages have words that express grammatical information, such as definiteness (*the*) or indefiniteness (*a*), or the DEMONSTRATIVES (*this*, *that*, *these*, *those*), or negation (*not*);

a language may well not have counterparts to all these specific grammatical elements, but there will certainly be grammatical words of some kind. These purely grammatical words are known as FUNCTIONAL **categories**, and they contrast with LEXICAL categories, which are rich in meaning. Other functional categories include CONJUNCTIONS (such as *and*, *or*, *but*) and PRONOUNS (such as *she*, *her*, *they*, *them*). We will meet more as we go along.

> Functional categories, 功能语类，包括限定词、助动词、代词和连词，这些语类一般只有句法特征，没有词法或者形态特征。

We've now seen something of the way speakers of English 'decide' (subconsciously) the classes of the words they encounter. We've also begun to see how linguists discover the different word classes by running a set of diagnostic tests based on morphological and syntactic evidence.

To summarize, we've argued in this section that words fall into different classes. Evidence comes partly from morphosyntax: each word class has its own unique set of affixes. But morphological evidence of this kind is not always available, so syntactic evidence is vital too. Each word class fits into certain slots which are unique to it, and each class co-occurs with (keeps the company of) specific words from other classes. Furthermore, each word class has specific functions, performing certain tasks in a sentence.

> 总结：词类的判别依据包括形态、分布和功能三种。

We next turn to a wider examination of the major lexical word classes, looking at their typical behaviour cross-linguistically. Section 2.2 looks at verbs; Section 2.3, nouns; Section 2.4, adjectives; Section 2.5, adverbs; and Section 2.6, prepositions.

2.2 VERBS

2.2.1 An introduction to verb classes

> Predicate, 谓语，指传统的二分法中除了主语之外的其他必需成分的总和。谓语通常表达主语的动作、过程和状态。谓语包括动词、宾语、补语等成分。

The major function of verbs is to express what is known as 'predication'. A PREDICATE expresses an 'event' in the sentence, which may be quite literally an event (such as *collapse* or *explode*) but also includes actions, processes, situations, states and so on. Though the role of predicate is typically fulfilled by a verb, we will see later that this isn't always the case.

In all languages, verbs fall into various syntactic sub-classes, depending on the relationships they contract in a sentence. Three of the most important are discussed in this section, starting in (16) with the sub-class of intransitive verbs. The verbs are in bold:

(16) a. Lee **sneezed**.
The volcano **erupted**.
b. ótáù **síkáàna** (Mbalanhu)
night falls
'The night falls/is falling.'
c. **Bhéic** sé. (Irish)
yelled he
'He yelled.'

Each of these verbs requires a single participant, the entity involved in the event or action which the verbs express. The participants in these examples are *Lee, the volcano, ótáù, sé*. In linguistic terminology, we say that the participant is the ARGUMENT of the verb. ('Argument' is a technical term, and doesn't mean that the verb and the participant are quarrelling!) Verbs with only one participant or argument are called INTRANSITIVE verbs. Note that it may well be the case that this single argument is an entire phrase, maybe even referring to many people: **Lee and Kim** sneezed; **All the students in the class** sneezed. But nonetheless, the verb *sneeze* has just the one argument.

All the single words that can replace *sneezed* in (16) are also intransitive verbs: for example, *listened, died, overate, blushed* and *swore*. We see in (16) that the participant may be an animate being, and the verb may be an action, but this doesn't have to be so: we also find inanimate participants and verbs which are not actions: *The volcano erupted*; *Night falls*.

The next set of verbs are TRANSITIVE verbs, which means that each requires two arguments; the arguments are in bold in (17) and (18). For clarity, I use # to separate two arguments occurring in a row:

(17) a. **Ceri** rejected **my generous assistance**.
b. **Kim** avoided **the man who'd shouted at her**.
c. **Lee** broke **that priceless oriental vase**.

(18) Bhris sí # an chathaoir. (Irish)
break.PAST she the chair
'She broke the chair.'

So transitive verbs have two participants, such as the 'breaker' and 'thing broken' in (17c) and (18).

A third sub-class of verbs has three arguments; again, the arguments are in bold:

(19) a. **Lee** handed **the letter** # **to Kim**.
b. **Ceri** sent **some flowers** # **for Lee**.
c. **We** showed **the newspaper cuttings** # **to our friends**.

(20) **human** rassal-o **maktūb** # **le ʔabū-hum** (Chadian Arabic)
they send.PAST-3PL letter to father-their
'They sent a letter to their father.'

The verbs in (19) and (20) are DITRANSITIVE: their pattern is *X verb Y to/for Z*, as in *Kim gave a present to his grandmother*. Typically, the participants will be someone performing the action (for example, doing the handing over); an item being acted upon (for example, the item handed over); and a recipient (e.g. *ʔabū-hum* 'their father'). Many of these verbs can be either ditransitive or just transitive: for instance *buy* and *send*, as in *Ceri bought some flowers*. However, not all can: **Lee handed the letter*.

Argument, 主目,也被翻译成论元。句子的意义是由命题(proposition)来表示的,而命题中最重要的成分为谓词(通常为动词和形容词),谓词决定了句子的其他成分是否存在,那些由谓词决定的句子成分就是论元。根据谓词所需的论元数量,可以有一位谓词(one-place predicate)、二位谓词(two-place predicate)或三位谓词(three-place predicate)。这里提到的不及物动词就是一位谓词。一个命题表示一个事件,事件由一个谓词及其论元构成,而扮演谓词和论元这两个重要角色的,主要是动词和名词这两个类别。

Ditransitive verb, 指带双宾语的及物动词。

> **Linguistic convention**: The asterisk *inside* the parentheses (*...) means that the example is ungrammatical if we *include* the parenthetical phrase, but grammatical without it.

Before reading further, decide what class each verb in (21) falls into (the verbs are in bold).

(21) a. Lee and Kim both **capitulated** (*the issue).
 b. Ceri **gave** the children some flowers.
 c. *Lee **assassinated**.
 d. Sprouts, Kim **loves**, but cabbage, he **detests**.

You should have the following results. In (21a), *capitulated* is intransitive—it has only one argument, *Lee and Kim*: note that you can get this answer without actually knowing the meaning of the verb. *Gave* is ditransitive, although note that in (21b) the participants appear in a different order than that in (19): the recipient (*the children*) in this example comes before what is given. *Assassinated* is a transitive verb, which is why (21c) is impossible: its direct object is missing. Both verbs in (21d) are transitive: both *love* and *detest* have two arguments. You may have thought that these are intransitive verbs, because there is no argument immediately following the verb. But this is wrong, as we can tell because **Kim loves/detests* is ungrammatical. The direct object arguments, *sprouts* and *cabbage*, would normally be positioned immediately after the verb, but in (21d) each of them has been moved from its usual position, for emphasis. Even displaced in this way, *sprouts* and *cabbage* still fulfil the requirements of both verbs for an 'item loved/detested' participant. So even if an argument is displaced from its usual position, it still 'counts' as an argument of the verb that it's associated with.

In English, there are very many verbs that are 'ambitransitive': these can be either transitive or intransitive, such as *sing, cook, read, eat*. Fewer verbs can only be transitive (*devour, reject*) or only intransitive (*erupt, disappear*). This situation is not necessarily the same for all languages. For instance, in Jarawara, an Amazonian language (Dixon 2004b), about half the verbs are strictly intransitive, less than 20 per cent are strictly transitive, and maybe a third of the total are ambitransitive.

More verb classes are illustrated as we go along, in Chapters 3, 4 and 5. What we have seen in this section is that across all languages, verbs occur with specific 'core' arguments: these are the arguments required by the verb. The verb also selects the particular grammatical properties of its arguments, as we've seen. This relationship between a verb and its arguments is one kind of DEPENDENCY: a relationship contracted between elements in a sentence. We will see other kinds of dependencies throughout this book.

2.2.2 Verbs and their grammatical categories

Verbs have more cross-linguistic differences in the grammatical categories they express than any other word class. The major categories are illustrated here.

2.2.2.1 *Tense and aspect*

These are the most common morphosyntactic categories associated with verbs, and this discussion provides only a brief sketch of these extensive categories. Starting with English, you may be surprised to learn that morphologically speaking (in terms of form) English verbs have only two **tenses**, namely present and past:

(22) a. Kim **helps** Lee every day.
b. Kim **helped** Lee every day.

Tense, 时态，作为一种语法范畴，时态是动词表示的动作发生时间的语法标记。

The present tense of the verb in (22a) is marked by the *-s* inflection (ending), although this only occurs on the third person singular form: so in *I help(*s) Lee*, the verb has no actual suffix. This tense is sometimes referred to as 'non-past', a more accurate label, because most 'present' tense verbs don't refer to something that is happening right now. So (22a), for example, refers to a habitual event. The past tense in (22b) is marked with the *-ed* suffix, and this doesn't change for person and number. These *-s* and *-ed* endings are the only pieces of regular verbal morphology that represent tense in English, although *-s* actually has a dual role, as we'll see below.

What about the future tense? English certainly has ways of referring to future time: one is to use the present tense of an AUXILIARY element *will*: *She* **will** *help Lee tomorrow*. But the main verb, *help*, doesn't inflect here. There is no 'future' verbal morphology equivalent to the *-s* present tense or *-ed* past tense endings. The present tense of a verb can also refer to future time—as in *She leaves the country tomorrow*—or we can say *She is leaving the country tomorrow*, using another auxiliary, *is*. Note that the *-ing* suffix here isn't a tense marking: it can occur with any time reference, as in *She was leaving, She will be leaving*.

Tense is defined by Comrie (1985a: 9) as the 'grammaticalized expression of location in time'. The point is that different languages will 'choose' to grammaticalize (= represent grammatically) different contrasts in time—these are its tenses. This does not mean that a language can only refer to the points in time for which it has a morphological marker for tense, as we've already shown for 'future' in English. Other languages may have many more tense distinctions than English, or even fewer tenses, even none at all. Some Austronesian languages (e.g. Leti, Saliba) have no grammatical tense: there is no verbal morphology which represents tense in these languages, nor are there separate tense markers or auxiliaries. There are words that refer to time, however, such as Saliba *lahi* 'yesterday' and *malaitom* 'tomorrow'.

许多语言学家认为，汉语中也没有时态，但是对此句法学家还存在不同的意见。

Most languages have a basic two-way tense opposition: either between past and non-past tenses—like English—or else between future and non-future tenses. Within these major divides, some languages have much finer tense distinctions, particularly the African Bantu family, and native Australian and American languages. The Wishram-Wasco dialect of Chinook, a native American language spoken in the states of Oregon and Washington, has four past tenses represented by different inflections, or markings on the verb, shown in bold:

(23) a. **ga**-čiux   'He did it some time ago.'   (Chinook)
     b. **ni**-číux   'He did it long ago.'
     c. **na**-čiúxʷ-a 'He did it recently.'
     d. **i**-číux   'He just did it.'

Note that the tense inflections are prefixes in this language.

> Aspect, 体, 是另一个与时间相关的语法范畴，用来指示动词所表示的动作、事件或者状态是否正在进行还是已经完成。时态与体的区别在于，时态表示动作或事件所发生的时间，人们所关心的是事件发生在此前、此时还是此后；而体所关心的是事件发生的时间式样，是进行中的还是已经结束，还是刚刚开始，是瞬间完成的还是持续了一段时间，或者反复经历的。

A category closely related to tense is that of ASPECT. Aspect marks such properties as whether an action is ongoing or completed. For example, in *Kim was eating his dinner*, the verb *was* is past tense but we understand that the eating event wasn't over. This sentence has the PROGRESSIVE aspect, marked in English partly by the *-ing* suffix on the main verb, *eat*, but also by the addition of an auxiliary, a form of *be*. In *Kim has eaten her dinner* we have PERFECT aspect, referring to a completed action. Again, this is marked partly by changes in the verb form itself (*eaten*) and partly by adding another auxiliary, this time a form of *have*.

In other languages, aspectual distinctions are often captured entirely via the verbal morphology, without the use of auxiliaries. One such language with very rich systems of both tense and aspect is the Bantu language ChiBemba. These examples illustrate that it has an opposition between a progressive aspect (an event in progress) and a HABITUAL aspect (a repeated event):

> Habitual aspect, 反复体，惯常体，表示动作反复发生，又被认为是未完成体的一种。

(24) a. ba-**léé**-bomba   (ChiBemba)
        'They are working.' (progressive)
     b. ba-**là**-bomba
        'They repeatedly work.' (habitual)

And other languages have separate functional words that denote aspect, rather than marking it on the verb. Welsh and the other Celtic languages are good examples: the aspect markers are shown in bold in (25), and indicate an ongoing action (progressive) and a completed action (perfect):

(25) a. Mae Steffan **yn**   canu.   (Welsh)
        is Steffan PROGRESSIVE sing.INFIN
        'Steffan is singing.'
     b. Mae Steffan **wedi** canu.
        is Steffan PERFECT sing.INFIN
        'Steffan has sung.'

2.2.2.2 Mood

Mood is a grammatical category which marks properties such as possibility, probability and certainty. Languages tend to distinguish between actual events, as in (26a), and hypothetical events, as in (26b):

(26) a. Kim goes to Greece tomorrow.
b. Kim would go to Greece tomorrow if she were wealthy enough.

The MOOD used for actual events, as in (26a), is termed INDICATIVE. The mood in *Kim went to Greece yesterday* is also indicative: mood is an entirely separate property from tense. The hypothetical event in *Kim would go to Greece tomorrow* is expressed in English by a separate auxiliary element, *would*, rather than by a change in the form of the main verb *go* itself. Such auxiliaries (*would, could, should, might* and so on) are termed MODAL (i.e. 'mood') auxiliaries.

Indicative, 直陈式, 陈述语气。

Some languages have specific verbal morphology which is used for hypothetical events, termed the SUBJUNCTIVE mood. English has the remnants of such a system, although not all speakers use it. Please look at the verbs in bold type and work out what distinguishes these examples from ordinary indicative sentences:

a. ... if she **were** wealthy enough
b. I demand that this man **leave/be removed** at once!

When we use a past tense indicative form of the verb *be* we say *She **was** wealthy enough*, not (in standard English at least) *she **were***. But the past tense subjunctive form *were* is used for all persons and numbers, including first person singular: *If I were you* (speakers who don't use the English subjunctive have instead *If she **was** wealthy enough, If I **was** you*). The present tense subjunctive, in (b), uses just the bare uninflected form of the verb: *leave, be*. This contrasts with the third person singular of the indicative verb forms, *He leaves/is removed*: the subjunctive forms lack verbal agreement, such as the *-s* ending.

Other languages have a more extensive morphological subjunctive; (27) illustrates from German (I label the subjunctive SJTV in the gloss):

(27) Wenn du Zucker **hättest**, **könnten** wir jetzt Tee trinken. (German)
if you sugar have.2SG.SJTV can.1PL.SJTV we now tea drink
'If you had sugar, we could drink tea now.'

Both verbs in bold in (27) are marked for the subjunctive mood.

Cross-linguistically, it is common for verbs to be morphologically marked to show whether the event did or didn't happen, or might have happened but didn't in the end; or whether the speaker actually saw the event themselves, or merely heard it reported. European languages, however, are not rich in such categories, so you should beware of falling into the trap of thinking that 'familiar' languages are in any sense 'normal'.

在这一部分作者只是介绍了陈述和虚拟两种语气，除此之外，还有祈使语气（imperative mood）。

2.2.2.3 *Valency-changing processes*

Section 1.3.2 introduced the passive construction, which will be examined in detail in Chapter 7. The passive is the best known of what are termed VALENCY-CHANGING processes. These alter the 'argument structure' of the verb, changing its basic syntactic requirements for certain arguments. For instance, as we'll see in a moment, a transitive verb can become intransitive. If you've studied chemistry, you'll recognize the term 'valency', which linguistics has borrowed from the study of the properties of atoms.

In (28) we see a contrast between an ACTIVE and the corresponding PASSIVE construction, illustrated both from the Bantu language Chichewa, spoken in Malawi, and from the English translation. In both languages, (28a) is active and (28b) is passive (SU in the gloss is a 'subject marker'):

> (28) a. Kalulu a-na-b-a mkazi wa njovu. (Chichewa)
> hare SU-PAST-steal-ASPECT wife of elephant
> 'The hare stole the elephant's wife.'
> b. Mkazi wa njovu a-na-b-**edw**-a (ndi kalulu).
> wife of elephant SU-PAST-steal-PASSIVE-ASPECT by hare
> 'The elephant's wife was stolen (by the hare).'

In both Chichewa and English, the passive affects the arguments of the verb, and also the form of the verb itself. The noun phrase *mkazi wa njovu*, 'the elephant's wife', is the direct object in (28a), and becomes the subject in the passive (28b): in the terminology introduced in Chapter 1, it gets promoted to subject position. The subject of the active sentence, *kalulu*, 'the hare', is demoted in the passive: it becomes the object of a preposition *ndi/by*, or it can be omitted entirely. The valency of the 'steal' verb is altered in the passive: in (28a) it takes two core arguments, a subject and a direct object, while in (28b) it has only one core argument: *mkazi wa njovu*, 'the elephant's wife'. The phrase *ndi kalulu* 'by the hare' is not a core argument: it can be omitted entirely.

The passive in English is characterized by an auxiliary *be* or *get* (as in *It got stolen*) plus the PAST PARTICIPLE form of the main verb (*stolen, seen, killed*) but there's no specific passive affix. Chichewa, however, marks the passive directly on the verb, using the *-edw* suffix in (28b).

2.2.2.4 *Agreement*

Verbs in many languages 'agree with' one or more of their arguments (see Chapter 6). This means that various properties of the noun phrase arguments are also marked on the verb, the most common properties being person and number, and then gender or noun class. The situation most familiar to speakers of European languages is that of subject/verb agreement. English has very little verbal agreement—only the third person singular in the present tense is overtly marked (for example, *I play* versus *He play-**s***). This is the dual role of the *-s* suffix mentioned earlier: it represents both 3SG and present tense.

The Australian language Gunin also has subject/verb agreement, but in Gunin it is the gender of the subject that is cross-referenced (morphologically marked) on the verb, as shown in (29). Gunin has five genders, one denoting all humans (male or female) and four covering all non-human nouns (see Section 2.3.3.2 for more on gender).

(29) a. benyjin **bi-**yangga (Gunin)
man GENDER-goes
'The man is walking.'
b. leewa gadi **a-**yangga
dog run GENDER-goes
'The dog is running.'

Cross-linguistically, verbs often agree with their objects as well as their subjects. This example is from a Malayo-Polynesian language, Kambera:

(30) Nyuna na-tinu-nya na lau (Kambera)
she 3SG.SU-weave-3SG.OBJ the sarong
'She weaves the sarong.'

Here, the verb has markers representing both the subject and the object: the subject marker is the prefix *na-* and the object marker is the suffix *-nya*. Note that the verb here, *natinunya*, could actually form a perfectly good full sentence by itself. Literally, with its subject and object markers, it means 'she weaves it'; both the independent subject pronoun *nyuna* 'she' and the object *na lau* 'the sarong' could therefore be omitted quite happily. Far from being an unusual situation cross-linguistically, this is commonplace—though not in European languages. We say of such a verb that it has PRONOMINAL AFFIXES—morphological markers that can replace independent pronouns. Many more examples will occur throughout this text.

2.3 NOUNS

2.3.1 Semantic roles for noun phrases

Noun phrases (NPs) most typically function as the arguments of verbs. NP arguments can be classified both in terms of the semantic role that they fulfil and in terms of their syntactic function in a sentence (Section 2.3.2). First, we look at SEMANTIC ROLES, also known as thematic (or theta) roles. It is the verb that determines what semantic roles its arguments must take. Let's look at some examples.

(31) **Lee** handed the letter to Kim.
AGENT THEME RECIPIENT

Semantic role, 题元角色, 指体现论元与谓词的相互关系中所承担的语义角色。

语言中最主要的词类是动词和名词，即便是词类最少的语言中也会有名词和动词这两个基本的类别，因此名词和动词承担着句子主要语义内容的支撑。

(32) **Kim** detests sprouts.
    EXPERIENCER   STIMULUS

(33) **Spiders** frighten Lill
    STIMULUS   EXPERIENCER

(34) **The flowers** wilted.
    PATIENT

(35) **The ball** broke the window.
    INSTRUMENT   PATIENT

As you can see from these examples, there is no correlation between the number of arguments that a verb takes and the semantic role that these arguments fulfil. An AGENT is an animate being deliberately performing an action. Note that 'agent' and 'subject' are not equivalent at all: subjects are very often agents, but certainly not always. The subjects in (31) to (35) are shown in bold, and only in (31) is the subject an agent. None of the subjects in (32) to (35) are agents. Verbs like *love*, *fear* and *detest* have an EXPERIENCER subject—the animate being that experiences the feelings of love or hatred etc. In (33), the direct object *Lill* is also an EXPERIENCER. A STIMULUS prompts those feelings—clearly, not deliberately! A STIMULUS can be either an object, (32), or a subject, (33).

THEMES and PATIENTS are rather similar, and not all linguists distinguish between these roles. A THEME typically moves from one location or one person to another, like *the letter* in (31). A PATIENT (or undergoer), like *the window* in (35), is physically affected by the verb's action—so the window gets broken. A subject can also be a PATIENT, as with *the flowers* in (34): by wilting, the flowers undergo a physical change of state, but they certainly don't deliberately wilt, so that noun phrase is not the AGENT.

A RECIPIENT (or beneficiary) is a fairly self-evident term for *Kim* in (31): we expect a RECIPIENT to be an animate entity, though not necessarily human; in *Kim gave the toy to her dog, her dog* is a RECIPIENT. A rather similar semantic role is GOAL, as in *We sailed to the island*. Both GOALS and RECIPIENTS are introduced by *to* in English, but a GOAL clearly does not benefit from the verb's action.

Finally, an INSTRUMENT is used as the cause of the verb's action, as is the case for *the ball* in (35). Again this is clearly not a volitional act, so *the ball* is not an AGENT. An INSTRUMENT is often a prepositional object, as here: *We cut the wood with the new saw*.

There are certainly more semantic roles than are briefly mentioned here, but not so many more, and they are common to all languages.

2.3.2 Syntactic roles for noun phrases

We turn now to the syntactic functions of noun phrases. These are often known as **GRAMMATICAL RELATIONS**, because they define NPs in terms of their relationships with the verbs of which they are an argument. The two most important grammatical relations are SUBJECT and (DIRECT) OBJECT. The terms themselves have already been used several times; here I aim to give you a working idea of what subjects and objects are in English. Subjects typically have special properties that set them apart from the other grammatical relations, and Chapter 6 returns to the cross-linguistic properties of subjects and other grammatical relations.

In (36), the subject NPs are all in bold type. Before reading on, try to work out what features the subjects have in common, and what properties a subject has in English.

(36) a. **This woman** buys all the best apples.
 b. **All those people** are enjoying our apples.
 c. **Apples** were grown in that orchard.
 d. Apples, **she** really enjoys.

One hypothesis might have been that subjects all bear the same semantic role. But we already know from Section 2.3.1 that this is not the case: different verbs require their subjects to bear different roles. So in (36a) the subject is an AGENT, in (36b) and (d), an EXPERIENCER, and in (36c), a PATIENT (apples are the 'thing grown').

Looking at the distribution of the phrases in bold, we might conclude that subjects precede the verb in English. This is certainly true, and as noted in Chapter 1 it is indeed one of the ways we can tell subjects in English. It is definitely not true of all languages, though, as we saw for Irish in (16c), where the verb precedes the subject. Having observed that 'English subjects precede the verb', you may wonder if *every* NP that precedes the verb in English is a subject. We particularly need to know the answer to this in (36d), where two NPs precede the verb. Only *she* is marked in bold, though. How do we know that *she* is the subject and not *apples*? There are two ways of testing this, and these tests give us two further properties of subjects in English.

First, subjects in English control SUBJECT/VERB AGREEMENT: verbs and auxiliaries change in form to match or 'agree' with particular features of the subject, such as person and number. So in (36a) the verb *buys*, third person singular, agrees with the singular subject, *this woman*, whilst in (36b) and (36c) we get plural auxiliaries *are/were* to match plural subjects—*all those people* and *apples*. If you aren't quite satisfied that *apples* really is the subject in an example like (36c), perhaps because of its semantic role, note that the subject/verb agreement test proves that *apples* really is the subject: we get *Apples **were** grown* rather than **Apples **was** grown* (at least in standard English). This confirms that subjects are defined by their syntactic properties, not by their semantic roles. It also shows that we must distinguish between the semantic role and the grammatical relation of an NP: remember that subjects are often agents, but not always. Turning to (36d), the verb *enjoys* is a third person singular form: it agrees with *she* (3SG) and not with *apples*, which is plural. So *she* is the subject of the verb *enjoys*.

The second test for subjecthood in English involves CASE MARKING. Pronouns have a special form in English which is restricted to the subject position. This test is appropriate for the subject of a verb (or auxiliary) that is FINITE, such as *loves* (present tense) or *tasted* (past tense). We'll explore the verbal property of finiteness further in Chapter 3, but for now you can consider it to be equivalent to 'bearing tense'. The correct subject pronouns are in bold (examples are again from standard English):

(37) a. **She**/*her loves apples.
 b. **We**/*us don't grow that kind of apple.
 c. **They**/*them saw her/*she us/*we.
 d. Those apples tasted great to her/*she us/*we.

CASE means that the form of a noun phrase or a pronoun changes according to its grammatical relation (more details in Chapter 6). In the pronoun pairs *I*/*me*, *we*/*us*, *he*/*him*, *she*/*her*, *they*/*them*, the first member (underlined) is always a subject, so these forms *I*, *we*, *he*, *she*, *they*—known as NOMINATIVE case forms—can be used as a test for subjecthood in English. (The pronouns *you* and *it* are exceptional, and don't change in form no matter what their grammatical relation: *You like Lee/Lee likes you/Lee talked to you*.) Full NPs don't change in form in English either, so in (38) *my cousin* can be either the subject or the object of the verb, and the same is true of *his little girl*:

(38) My cousin kissed his little girl.
 His little girl kissed my cousin.

Summary of properties of subjects in English

- Normal position immediately before the verb.

- Control subject/verb agreement. Verbs and auxiliaries in the present tense agree with the subject in person and number (e.g. *She **sings*** vs. *They **sing***; *I **was** singing* vs. *They **were** singing*).

- Pronominal subjects (i.e. subjects that are pronouns) have a special subject form known as nominative case. These subject forms are: *I*, *we*, *he*, *she*, *they*. Note, though, that these forms only occur when the verb or auxiliary is finite.

If the example is such that you can't test one or other of these properties, as in (38), you can of course make the appropriate changes to allow you to use the tests (for instance, changing *his little girl* to *she*).

All of the empty slots in these examples from (5) above are subjects, and only an NP can fill every one of these:

(39) _____ became extinct in the eighteenth century.
_____ seemed to be unpopular.
I wondered whether _____ would ever return.
_____ extinct! I don't believe it.
That _____ could ever return seems unlikely.
For _____ to be reintroduced to Britain might be a good idea.

Before reading further, please try the tests for subjecthood on the examples in (39), filling in the gaps with words or phrases as you see fit, noting any problems you find and trying to think why these occur.

As we saw in Chapter 1, the object is the NP that in its usual position follows the verb in English. Objects of verbs fulfil the requirement of a transitive verb for a second argument, other than the subject. Some examples are shown in bold here: *Kim loves* **apples**; *Lee enjoys* **all the varieties of apples that we grow in the orchard**. Note that the whole of the phrase in bold type is the object in the second example.

A third grammatical relation is that of PREPOSITIONAL OBJECT, taken by the NPs in bold in *on* **the bus**, *by* **train**, *with* **three friends** and also by *her* in *to her*. The words *on*, *by*, *with* and *to* are prepositions (see Section 2.6). English subject pronouns have a special form that only subjects take, as we saw above, while the objects of both verbs and prepositions share the same form. For instance, words such as *her* and *us* can be the object of either a verb, like *saw*, or a preposition, like *to*.

Although the most typical function of NPs is as arguments of a verb, noun phrases can in fact also be predicates, expressing an event or a situation:

(40) a. Zainal **guru saya**. (Malay)
Zainal teacher my
'Zainal is my teacher.'
b. Marija **rebënok**. (Russian)
Mary child
'Mary is a child.'

The **NP predicates**, in bold, are *guru saya* 'my teacher' and *rebënok* 'a child'. The English translations also have NP predicates: *my teacher, a child*. However, in English the predicate NP is linked to the subject by *is*, a form of the verb *be*. Such linking verbs are known as COPULA verbs. In the examples in (40), though, there is no copula, which is actually a common situation cross-linguistically. In fact, even in English we can omit the copula to express disbelief: *Zainal a teacher? Who would*

NP predicate, 谓语性名词短语，指在有系动词的句子中出现在谓语位置上的名词短语。

ever have believed it?. This knowledge may also help you with the subject slot in '___ *extinct*' in (39), which also omits the copula.

Though noun phrases may be predicates, we have seen so far in this section that NPs most often function as participants or ARGUMENTS of verbs. These arguments can be classified in terms of their semantic functions (agent, theme and so on) or in terms of their syntactic functions, known as grammatical relations—for instance, subject, direct object, and prepositional object. We return to grammatical relations or GRAMMATICAL FUNCTIONS in Chapter 6.

2.3.3 Nouns and their grammatical categories

2.3.3.1 *Number*

Many languages mark nouns and noun phrases according to whether they are singular or plural. Typical examples are shown from an Austronesian language, Saliba, which like English has plural suffixes on nouns:

(41) a. natu-gu   b. natu-gu-**wao**   (Saliba)
         child-my   child-my-PLURAL
         'my child'   'my children'
     c. natu-m   d. natu-m-**wao**
         child-your   child-your-PLURAL
         'your child'   'your children'

Note though that only human nouns are marked for number in Saliba; number must be inferred from the context when discussing animals and inanimate objects.

Not all languages use plural nouns after numerals:

(42) a. ci/cŵn   b. pedwar ci   c. *pedwar cŵn   (Welsh)
         dog/dogs   four   dog   four   dogs
                           'four dogs'

In Welsh, the noun following a numeral must be singular, as in (42b), not plural, as in (42c).

Although the basic options for number are singular or plural, some languages also make finer distinctions, as we saw in Chapter 1, using DUAL forms for two items, and even TRIAL forms for three items. It's also common to find a distinction between COUNT nouns and MASS nouns, as in English (see Section 1.1.2). Count nouns, unsurprisingly, refer to items that can be counted (e.g. *dog, pen, bean*) unlike mass (or non-count) nouns (e.g. *furniture, air, oxygen, rice, wheat*). Normally, then, we don't expect non-count nouns to occur in the plural: *three rices. It is possible, though, to flout this convention in English; I'll leave you to think of some examples.

2.3.3.2 *Gender or noun class*

In many languages, nouns fall into different genders, also known as NOUN CLASSES. Typically, the classification is essentially grammatical, and may have only a loose correlation—or no correlation at all—with the semantic properties of the nouns. Gender may be marked on the noun itself. In Spanish and Italian, for instance, nouns ending in *-o* are usually masculine (Italian *il libro* 'the book') and nouns ending in *-a* are usually feminine (Italian *la casa* 'the house'); obviously, these classifications are purely grammatical. In some languages, such as German or French, nouns have gender but this is not typically marked on the noun itself; instead, the gender of a noun is marked on the articles, words for 'the' and 'a'. This is also true of the articles in the Italian examples above (*il* vs. *la*). In German, articles agree in gender with a singular noun, so the word for 'the' can be *der* (masculine nouns), *die* (feminine nouns) or *das* (neuter nouns). It is common for adjectives within the noun phrase to also agree with the noun in gender; see (64) below.

这里所说的性属于语法范畴，与名词本身的意义之间没有必然的联系，当某些涉及现实世界中实体的性别时，我们说的是它的自然性别。

If you have only met European languages up till now, you may consider it normal to have 'masculine' and 'feminine' genders. But numerous other languages have many more distinct genders, based very loosely on other semantic or biological categories, such as human and non-human. The Niger-Congo languages of Africa, probably the largest language phylum (= group of related languages) in the world, typically have extensive systems of noun classification. For instance, in the very large Bantu family, languages each have up to twenty genders, if the singular and plural for each noun class are included. The noun class is indicated in this family by a prefix on the noun itself. Our examples are from Northern Sotho, a Bantu language of South Africa:

(43) a. **mo**-tswadi b. **ba**-tswadi (Northern Sotho)
CLASS 1-parent   CLASS 2-parent
'parent'   'parents'

(44) a. **le**-oto   b. **ma**-oto
CLASS 5-foot   CLASS 6-foot
'foot'   'feet'

Here, class 1 indicates human beings, and class 2 is the plural of class 1. Class 5 (and its plural, class 6) indicates body parts, but is also used for nouns representing many other concepts, including natural phenomena, fruit and vegetables, various birds and animals, and nationalities, amongst other things. The meaning of a noun therefore does not correlate strictly with noun class.

2.3.3.3 *Possession*

Possessive constructions are often quite complex. For a start, a language may regard some types of noun as not referring to possessable things at all, including features of the natural world such as rocks or rivers. In terms of possessable nouns, it's very

> 如果领属物与领有者之间是临时的或非必然的依赖关系，那它就是"可让渡的"（alienable），如果它与领有者之间的关系是永久的或必然的，那它就是"不可让渡的"（inalienable）。

common to find a division between what is known as ALIENABLE and INALIENABLE POSSESSION. Typically, nouns for body parts or for a person's relatives are in the inalienably possessed class; these include terms for things that you can't put aside or dispose of. Alienable possession covers other types of noun, such as someone's belongings, animals or food. These examples are from Jarawara, a language of Southern Amazonia:

(45) a. Okomobi kaa taokana b. ami kaa jomee (Jarawara)
Okomobi POSS gun mother POSS dog
'Okomobi's gun' 'mother's dog'

(46) a. Okomobi teme b. ami tame
Okomobi foot.M mother foot.F
'Okomobi's foot' 'mother's foot'

Alienable possession is illustrated in (45), and inalienable possession in (46). You can see that alienable possession requires the use of an extra possessive morpheme, *kaa*, whereas inalienable possession merely involves placing two nouns side-by-side. Cross-linguistically, this is expected: alienable possession typically involves additional morphology, whilst inalienable possession just involves the juxtaposition of the nouns.

2.3.3.4 *Case*

> 汉语里的名词没有格的标记，其中的语法关系主要靠词序来表示，例如，"李四打了张三"和"张三打了李四"的意义就大不一样。

Case is a grammatical property that occurs in many languages, but by no means all, and indicates the grammatical relation (or grammatical function) of an NP in a phrase or sentence. Case marks, for example, whether a noun phrase is a subject or an object of a verb: it denotes the relationship the NP has to that verb. Not all languages have case marking: this means they don't mark the grammatical function of an NP on that NP in any way. English has very little case morphology: we saw earlier that only pronouns have a special form when they fulfil the grammatical relation 'subject' of a finite verb. Even then, the forms *you* and *it* have no distinctive case-marking. Some languages have even less case marking than English:

(47) a. Saya benci dia. (Malay)
I hate he/she
'I hate him/her.'
b. Dia benci saya.
he/she hate I
'She/he hates me.'

Note that the subject and object forms of each pronoun do not differ from each other in form, so that *saya* in Malay translates as both 'I' and 'me', and *dia* translates as *he/she* as well as *him/her* (the pronoun having no gender distinction either).

Conversely, some languages have rich case systems, such as Turkish, Finnish, Latin and the Slavonic languages (e.g. Russian and Polish). Examples from Latin are shown in (48). The 'nominative' case (NOM) indicates the grammatical relation of subject, and the 'accusative' case (ACC) indicates the grammatical relation of direct object:

(48) a. Nauta puellam amat. (Latin)
sailor.NOM girl.ACC loves
'The sailor loves the girl.'
b. Puellam nauta amat.
girl.ACC sailor.NOM loves
'The sailor loves the girl.'

Note how flexible the word order is in Latin: since the grammatical relation of the noun phrases is always marked on the NPs themselves, they don't have to occur in a fixed order, unlike in English. So (48a) and (48b) have the exact same meaning, no matter whether it's the subject *nauta*, 'the sailor', that's initial in the sentence, or the object *puellam*, 'the girl'.

2.3.4 Nouns, definiteness and determiners

Some languages, such as the Scandinavian languages Norwegian, Swedish and Danish, can mark **definiteness** morphologically—via a change in the form of the noun—as well as using a definite article, a word for 'the':

Definiteness, 有定性，指具体的、可识别的实体。

(49) a. mus-**en** (Swedish)
mouse-DEF
'the mouse'
b. den hungriga mus-**en**
the hungry mouse-DEF
'the hungry mouse'

多数语言在区分有定性和无定性时都像英语那样使用冠词表示，但是也有许多语言使用名词自身的形态变化来表示这一区分。

The suffix -*en* marks definiteness, and can co-occur with *den* 'the', as in (49b).

The noun itself doesn't have any 'definiteness' morphology in English. Many languages, including English, can distinguish definite from indefinite nouns by using a separate functional element—an article, such as the definite article *the* or the indefinite article *a/an*. Articles are members of a larger class of function words known as **DETERMINERS**. Some of the main sub-classes of English determiners are shown in (50), with the determiners themselves in bold:

Determiner, 限定词，与名词一起使用并以某种方式限定名词的意义。在英语中，限定词包括冠词the 和a，其次是 each/every、this/that、some/any 以及 both、all 等，这些词与冠词具有相同的句法分布，因此有理由把它们归为一类。

(50) a. Articles: **the** paper(s); **a** problem; **an** egg
b. Demonstratives: **this** paper; **these** papers; **that** egg; **those** eggs
c. *Wh*-determiners: **what** colour(s); **which** paper(s)
d. Quantifiers: **some** milk/eggs; **each** paper; **every** boy; **all** cases; **no** time; **most** eggs; **few** eggs; **much** time; **any** eggs

e. Possessive determiners: **my** child; **her/his** child; **our** child; **Lee's** child
f. Pronouns: **we/us** linguists; **you** boys

The reasoning behind classifying all these items as members of an overarching category 'determiner' is that we can only put one of them in the single slot before a noun in English: ____ N. For instance, we get *this child*, but not *this my child, or *these which eggs. However, the situation is actually not quite as simple as this, particularly with regards to the quantifiers (words like those in (50d), which specify quantity), because we do get phrases like *my every wish*, *some of the eggs* and so on, which have a more complex syntax.

Note also that in (50e), examples of possessive determiners include whole NPs such as *Lee's* in *Lee's child*, or *my cousin* in *my cousin's child*. These seem to fill the same position as single-word possessive determiners, and we can certainly choose only one of them in the pre-noun slot: we don't get **This is Lee's her child*. But if the 'determiner' position can be a whole phrase, it again suggests that the situation is quite complex syntactically.

Finally, it might seem strange to suggest that pronouns such as *we*, *us*, *you* should be placed in the class of determiners, along with words like *some* and *the*. But the fact that pronouns don't co-occur with determiners (*the she) suggests that pronouns aren't nouns. (Proper nouns—names—can't generally take determiners in English either, though they may in certain contexts: *The Kim Jones I know has black hair*; *I can hardly recognize the London I once loved*.) Interestingly, pronouns can often *replace* determiners, which suggests that they may indeed be in the same word class:

(51) **We/us linguists** aren't stupid. (*Compare*: These linguists …)
I'll give **you boys** three hours to finish the job! (*Compare*: those boys …)

One of the properties of such determiners (*we*, *us*, *you*) is that they can occur without a following noun:

(52) We ___ aren't stupid.
I'll give you ___ three hours to finish the job!

You might doubt that this is a general property of determiners, since *the* and *a* can't occur alone: ***The/a** *could be problematic*. However, plenty of other determiners can occur without a following noun and, as (53) shows, they have just the same distribution (= are found in the same places) as a full noun phrase:

(53) **These/those** ___ are good!
I'll give **some** ___ to Lee.
I'll give **that/this** ___ away.

For reasons like these, some linguists propose that noun phrases are really 'determiner phrases'; we return to this question in Section 4.1.8.

Determiners are paired only with nouns, and don't co-occur with other word classes. For example, we get *_Their expects are unrealistic_, where _expects_ is a verb— the noun _expectations_ would be fine. Knowing that determiners pair up with nouns, we can use them to test for word class. So if we're unsure whether or not, say, _singing_ can be a noun, we can try it with a determiner: _This singing is nice_; _Her singing is awful_. Since these are grammatical, we can conclude that _singing_ is a noun here.

Cross-linguistically, determiners are common. They typically occur either in initial position in the noun phrase, as in English and Japanese, or in final position, rather than in the middle of the phrase. This last point is clearly shown when the noun phrase also contains an adjective: (54) is from Akan, a Kwa language spoken in Ghana:

(54) mmea   nketewa   no   (Akan)
     women   PLURAL.small   the
     'the small women'

There are, though, many languages without the range of determiners that we find in English. For instance, many lack definite and/or indefinite articles (e.g. Russian, Finnish and Chinese). Some languages have one and not the other: for instance, Welsh has definite articles but not indefinite. But there are other ways of distinguishing definite and indefinite nouns, as illustrated by Chinese in (55) (the small functional element glossed as ASPECT serves here to indicate a completed event):

(55) a. Ta   mai   pingguo   le.   (Chinese)
        he   buy   apple   ASPECT
        'He bought an apple.'
     b. Ta   pingguo   mai   le.
        he   apple   buy   ASPECT
        'He bought the apple.'

你还能想出其他的汉语实例来吗？汉语中有哪些手段来区分有定性和无定性？

The word order in (55a) indicates an indefinite noun phrase (_an apple_), whilst in (55b) the word order shows the noun phrase to be definite (_the apple_).

2.4 ADJECTIVES

Adjectives indicate physical properties of nouns, including their size, shape, colour and so on. They also indicate qualities, such as 'good' or 'bad'. An interesting question is whether or not all languages have adjectives.

形容词可以被分为定语性和谓语性两种类型。对于定语性形容词来说，在英语等许多语言中，它们都出现在所修饰的名词前面，这与限定词有点类似，但是两者之间又存在明显的差异。首先限定词属于封闭类词，它的成员数量

2.4.1 Positions and functions of adjectives

There are two basic functions which ADJECTIVES and adjective phrases (APs) fulfil, known as the ATTRIBUTIVE and the PREDICATIVE functions. Attributive adjectives directly modify a noun, and normally have a fixed position. In some languages the adjective precedes the noun, as in English, Hungarian and Greek (the adjective is in bold):

(56) a **piros** autó (Hungarian)
    the red car

(57) i **omorfi** jineka (Greek)
    the beautiful woman

In other languages, such as French and Breton, attributive adjectives normally follow the noun they modify:

(58) un den **bras** (Breton)
    a man large
    'a large man'

We saw in Section 2.3.2 that NPs can have a predicative function; see (40) above. Adjective phrases can also be predicates, fitting into slots such as those in (59):

(59) a. He felt ___. She is/seemed ___.
    (very sad, quite hungry, amused, amusing)
    b. I find it ___ to think she's an acrobat.
    (fairly hard, impossible, most impressive)

As with predicate nominals, in some languages there is no copula linking the subject (here, *Ali*) to the predicate adjective phrase (here, *marah*):

(60) Ali marah. (Malay)
    Ali angry
    'Ali is angry.'

This construction can occur in certain contexts in English too, which is why we find examples like *Cornish extinct! I don't believe it.*

⟶

Before reading further, please look at the examples in (61). Most adjectives can occur in either the attributive or the predicative positions, but not all can. Using the appropriate terminology, describe the distribution of *awake*, *utter* and *mere*:

(61) The man was awake./*the awake man
    *The failure seems utter./an utter failure
    The mere fact of this amazed me./*The fact was mere.

⟵

Awake can only be used as a predicative adjective, not an attributive one. We can confidently classify it as an adjective, because like other adjectives it can be modified by words like *quite/more/most*, as in *quite/more/most awake*. *Utter* can only be an attributive adjective, and not a predicative one. Again, it takes at least some of the typical adjectival modifiers, as in *I felt the most utter fool*. Less obviously, *mere* is also an adjective, and can only have the attributive function; as adjectives go, *mere* is a rather atypical example. These examples show that like all the major word classes, adjectives fall into different sub-classes.

2.4.2 Adjectives and intensifiers

Just as nouns are paired with a class of functional elements—determiners—within the noun phrase, so adjectives also pair with a special set of function words, as we saw in the previous section; see also (7) above. Example (62) illustrates (in bold) some of these INTENSIFIERS (also known as DEGREE MODIFIERS) in German adjective phrases, and their English equivalents:

(62) **sehr** schwer   **zu** voll   **ganz** sicher   (German)
      very heavy   **too** full   **quite** certain

Other English examples of intensifiers include *rather*, *somewhat* and *enough*, though *enough*, unlike the other intensifiers, is placed after the adjective it modifies: *full enough*. Intensifiers specify the extent or degree to which something is, say, full or heavy. Intensifiers may precede the adjective they modify, as in English (generally) and German, or follow it, as in Breton *klañv kaer*, literally 'sick very', meaning 'very sick'.

Although the ability to occur with the intensifier *very* is probably the best test for adjective status in English, *very* can only modify adjectives which are GRADABLE, such as *heavy*, *cantankerous*, *supportive*—someone can be supportive, for instance, to a greater or lesser extent. So *very* is unlikely to occur with non-gradable adjectives such as *definitive*, *residual*, *syntactic*.

Gradable, 有级差的，指物体、人、思想等不同程度地具有某种特性。有级差形容词是表示某物能以程度描写的形容词。

2.4.3 Adjectives and their grammatical categories

It is common, though certainly not universal, for languages to have the morphosyntactic category known as COMPARISON. In English, we represent the comparison of adjectives in two different ways. The first is morphological, via changes in the form of the adjective itself: for instance, in *straight*, *straighter*, *straightest*, the base form of the adjective *straight* takes a COMPARATIVE suffix *-er* or a SUPERLATIVE suffix *-est*. The second method is via the addition of *more* or *most*, which are functional elements: *more honest*, *most honest*. Some languages have an extra degree of comparison that doesn't occur in English. For instance, the Celtic family has an EQUATIVE, used in the 'as <Adjective> as' construction. Where English simply uses the base form of the adjective, Welsh has an *-ed* equative suffix:

(63) Mae 'r cwpan cyn **llawn-ed** â 'r botel. (Welsh)
is the cup as full-EQUATIVE with the bottle
'The cup is as full as the bottle.'

The other morphosyntactic category for adjectives which is widespread is AGREEMENT. Adjectives are often marked to agree with the nouns they modify. This means that inherent features of the noun such as gender or number may also be shown (CROSS-REFERENCED is the technical term) on a modifying adjective; in some languages the case of a noun is also cross-referenced on the adjective. For instance, in French and many other European languages, adjectives agree in gender with the noun they modify, changing their form accordingly:

(64) a. le vin **blanc** b. la porte **blanche** (French)
the.M wine(M) white.M the.F door(F) white.F
'the white wine' 'the white door'

The noun *vin*, 'wine', is masculine, so the attributive adjective, *blanc*, appears in its masculine form too (as does the determiner *le*). The noun *porte*, 'door', is feminine, so we find the feminine form of the adjective, *blanche* (and also the feminine determiner *la*). It should be noted, though, that many French adjectives do not have distinct masculine and feminine forms. For instance, *noir* 'black(M)' is pronounced identically to *noire* 'black(F)'—it is purely a spelling rule which adds -*e* in the feminine, and does not reflect a genuinely different form.

2.4.4 Are adjectives essential?

We saw in Section 2.1.3 that not all languages have an open class of adjectives. For instance, Dixon (2004b) reports that the Jarawara language of Southern Amazonia has a closed class of fourteen adjectives, with meanings such as 'bad', 'another', 'big' and 'little', and 'young' and 'old'. Typically, if a language has only a few adjectives, their meanings are fairly predictable, covering properties such as size and quality. Foley (1991) reports that the Yimas language of New Guinea has only three clear examples of words that are unambiguously adjectives: *kpa* 'big', *yua* 'good' and *ma* 'other'; note the overlap in meanings with those mentioned from Jarawara.

How, then, do languages like these—and many others—manage without the huge, open class of adjectives familiar from European languages? What happens instead is that other major word classes, particularly nouns and verbs, take over the functions fulfilled in other languages by adjectives. We will look at two instances.

Our first examples are from Kwamera, an Austronesian language spoken in Vanuatu. Kwamera does have a class of attributive adjectives, as in *iakunóuihi óuihi nah*, literally 'child small that', i.e. 'that small child'. But in places where many other languages have a distinct class of predicative adjectives, Kwamera uses what appear to be verbs. The evidence that they are verbs comes from their morphology, or form. Let's start by examining the morphosyntax of some typical Kwamera verbs. In (65) the verb meaning 'dislike' has the first person singular *iak-* prefix. Note that there is no free pronoun for 'I' in this example. Instead, the 1SG pronominal prefix on the verb tells us the person and number of the subject: recall from Chapter 1 that this is known as a bound pronominal. The verb in (66) has two prefixes: *r-*, which is third person singular, agreeing with the subject *Iau* (a personal name); and *am-* meaning PROGRESSIVE (i.e. the talking is still in progress).

(65) **iak**-imiki   kuri   u   (Kwamera)
     1SG-dislike   dog   this
     'I don't like this dog.'

(66) Iau   **r-am**-agkiari   ihi
     Iau   3SG-PROGRESSIVE-talk   still
     'Iau is still talking.'

These same verbal affixes also occur on words which we translate into English as adjectives, such as 'big' and 'small', occurring in predicative positions:

(67) pukah   u   **r**-asori
     pig   this   3SG-big
     'This pig is big.'

(68) ianpin   **iak-am**-óuihi   ihi ...
     when   1SG-PROGRESSIVE-small   still
     'When I was still small ...'

As we discussed at the start of this chapter (Section 2.1.2), linguists use shared morphosyntax as one of the criteria for placing words within the same word class. Since, in predicative positions, the words for 'big' and 'small' take the same morphosyntactic prefixes as verbs, this is evidence that they actually are verbs in Kwamera.

Now we turn to Yimas, a Papuan language which, as noted, has a closed class containing three true adjectives. These form a tight unit with the noun they modify, and must occur immediately before the noun, not after it or separated from it. One of these adjectives is shown in (69):

(69) a.   kpa   nam   b.   *nam   kpa   (Yimas)
          big   house   house   big
          'a big house'

Other words denoting qualities in Yimas are either verbs or nouns. Starting with the 'adjectival' verbs, we find that these have very different properties from true adjectives. Consider (70):

(70) a.   *urkpwica   numpran   b.   urkpwica-k-n   numpran
          black   pig   black-TENSE-III.SG   pig.III.SG
                                         'a black pig'

Example (70a) is ungrammatical because *urkpwica* 'black' is not one of the three adjectives that can occur in this construction, right before the noun it modifies. Example (70b) shows the same stem, *urkpwica*, but—like a verb—this now has both a tense marker *-k* (which indicates that 'blackness' is a fixed property of the pig) and an agreement marker *-n*; this shows agreement with *numpran* 'pig' in noun class (Section 2.3.3.2), and this noun happens to be a singular noun from class III. Both of these suffixes are typical of verbs in Yimas. Moreover, unlike an adjective, the 'adjectival' verb doesn't have to occur immediately before the noun at all—it can occur after it, as in (71), or can even be separated from the noun completely:

(71) namarawrm   urkpwica-k-mampan
     person.I.DUAL black-TENSE-I.DUAL
     'two black persons'

Here we again see the 'adjectival' verb *urkpwica* 'black', again with the tense suffix *-k*, and again with an agreement suffix (*-mampan*), this time agreeing with a class I noun which is DUAL (referring to two people). Another way in which the stem *urkpwica* behaves like a verb is that it can, with an appropriate tense marker, show a change of state. This example shows a whole sentence, with the 'adjectival' verb agreeing with the noun class of the subject of the sentence, *narm*:

(72) narm   p-urkpwica-t
     skin.VII.SG VII.SG.SU-black-PERFECTIVE
     '(My) skin darkened.'

In English, we distinguish adjectives like *black* from change-of-state verbs, like *blacken* and *darken*. But in Yimas, the same verbal stem does all this work. In (72), *narm* 'skin' is a class VII noun, and the verb agrees with this, using the relevant subject agreement marker for this noun class (*p-*). The verb also has a 'perfective' marker, which in Yimas marks an event that was completed in the course of the day. The three true adjectives cannot behave in this way.

Yimas also has a class of 'adjectival' nouns (Foley 1991). For instance, to say something meaning 'I'm feeling happy', Yimas would use a construction like 'Happiness does/feels on me'. This example uses the 'adjectival' noun *wapun*, 'happy/happiness':

(73) wapun   kantk-n   amayak
     happy.V.SG   with-V.SG COPULA.1SG
     'I'm happy.'

This literally means something along the lines of 'Happiness is with me', and we can see that, like other nouns in Yimas, *wapun* belongs to a specific noun class (class V in this case), and triggers agreement (on *kantkn* 'with'), as do other nouns in the language.

In sum, it appears that many languages typically either use verbs in place of adjectives, or nouns, for example by saying something like 'Kim has kindness' rather than 'Kim is kind'. Are there, then, languages without a recognizable class of adjectives at all? This is a controversial issue, but in fact, two linguists from very different grammatical traditions have argued that all languages do have a formal class of adjectives: Baker (2003), from a Chomskyan generative grammar perspective, and Dixon (2004a), from the broadly functionalist/typological perspective. In some languages, we would have to conclude, this may be a very small class of adjectives, as in Yimas. Whether or not adjectives are an essential word class, they are certainly widespread cross-linguistically.

2.5 ADVERBS

2.5.1 Adverbs and adjectives

In English, central members of the traditional word class of adverbs are words like *suddenly*, *slowly* and *gradually*. These central adverbs are formed from the related adjectives by an affix *-ly*, which turns adjectives like *sudden* into *suddenly*, and so on. Similarly, in French, *-ment* turns *sage* 'wise' into *sagement* 'wisely', and so on. We can't, however, identify adverbs in English by their morphology. Numerous adjectives in English don't take the *-ly* affix at all: *big*, *small*, *ill*, *young* and many more. Some irregular English adverbs have the same form as the adjective: *She works fast/hard* but not **She works fastly/hardly*. Just to confuse matters, there's an entirely different adverb which does have the form *hardly*, as in *She hardly works*, but which has just the opposite meaning! Conversely, some *-ly* words are definitely adjectives, not adverbs: examples are *ungodly*, *kindly*, *ungainly*, *lonely*. We can tell that these are adjectives because they modify nouns but not verbs: *this ungodly hour*, but not **He speaks ungodly*. One of the chief functions of adverbs is to modify verbs, as in *Kim stopped suddenly*.

Traditionally, English adjectives are distinguished from adverbs because they don't generally occur in the same syntactic environment. Adjectives modify nouns, such as *song*, as in (74); and adverbs modify adjectives, such as *sad*, (75a), other adverbs, such as *lucidly*, (75b), and verbs, such as *spoke*, (75c). Here, we follow the linguistic practice of putting the phrase in square brackets and indicating its category (NP, AP etc.) at the left edge.

(74)   [NP a **strange** song]

(75)   a.   this [AP **strangely** sad] song
       b.   She spoke [AdvP **strangely** lucidly].
       c.   She [VP spoke **strangely**].

This set pattern of distribution is the only one possible in standard English: compare **a strangely song*, **She spoke strange lucidly*. In fact, in standard English adjectives and adverbs cannot occur in identical positions, but instead occur in what is called

> Complementary distribution, 互补分布, 这是来源于音系学的一个概念, 指两个语言要素不会同时出现。

COMPLEMENTARY DISTRIBUTION: where one occurs, the other doesn't, but together they cover all the available positions. So, adjectives modify nouns, but adverbs modify the other lexical word classes, namely adjectives, other adverbs and verbs. Together, adjectives and adverbs modify all the lexical word classes, and their environments don't overlap. We can predict which will occur in any given syntactic environment. Because adjectives and adverbs complement each other in this way, some linguists consider them to be sub-classes of the same word class. We could regard this to be the adjective class, since this is more basic in form.

To qualify as sub-classes of a single word class, there must also be grammatical properties common to both groups. Adverbs and adjectives fulfil this requirement too. First, they share modifiers: they take the same intensifiers, as in *very/quite/most unusual(ly)*. Second, they can both occur in the *as _____ as* comparative construction: *as miserable as Kim, as miserably as Kim*. Third, the comparative suffixes *-er, -est* occur on a few adverbs, such as *soon* (*sooner, soonest*) as well as on adjectives such as *red* (*redder, reddest*). There are some distinctions: (76) shows that, for example, the adjective *uncertain* can take a following *whether...* sentence, whereas the related adverb can't.

(76) He seems **uncertain** whether she's left or not.
*He spoke **uncertainly** whether she'd left or not.

But on balance, the evidence for treating the central class of *-ly* adverbs in English as a sub-class of adjectives seems convincing.

In many languages there is no formal distinction between adjectives and adverbs. German illustrates: in (77), *schlecht* 'bad' has the function of a predicative adjective, whilst in (78), it has the function typical of adverbs, modifying the verb.

(77) Er   ist   **schlecht**.   (German)
     he   is   bad
     'He is bad.'

(78) Er   singt   **schlecht**.
     he   sings   bad
     'He sings badly.'

Finally, let's consider words like *still* (as in *I'm still waiting*), *yet, always, already* and *sometimes*. These aren't related to any adjective, and can't take any of the typical adjective/adverb modifiers: **very already, *more sometimes*. However, since they modify verbs (*Kim always ate fruit, She still reads that newspaper*) we can indeed consider them to be a sub-class of adverbs.

2.5.2 The adjunct function

As a word class, 'adverb' has traditionally been rather problematic, since it's been used as a ragbag for any words that don't neatly fit into the categories of nouns, verbs or adjectives. For instance, in traditional grammar, words like *today*, *tomorrow*, *yesterday* and *tonight*, as well as phrases such as *this week*, *next week*, would be termed 'adverbs'. Here, we'll see that they are not adverbs, but are actually nouns or noun phrases (NP). They can occur in all the typical NP positions, with typical NP grammatical functions: as subjects, (79a); direct objects, (79b); and as the objects of prepositions, (79c):

(79) a. **Tomorrow/today/tonight/this week** seems fine.
b. I planned **tomorrow/yesterday** very carefully.
c. I'll finish it by **tonight/tomorrow/next week**.

And they can also take the *-'s* possessive ending, like other NPs: *today's bike ride*, *tomorrow's lectures*, *next week's wedding*. But unlike adverbs, they can't be modified by the intensifiers *very*, *quite* and so on: *very tonight, *quite tomorrow. So we can conclude that *today*, *tomorrow* etc. are not adverbs at all, and in this respect, the traditional view is incorrect.

Why, then, have these NPs traditionally been termed 'adverbs'? The reason is that—like adverbs—they often occur not as subjects, objects and so on, but rather as optional modifying phrases, for instance modifying a verb. Preposition phrases (PP) can also occur in this same context. Example (80) illustrates:

(80) We're leaving **next week/today/tomorrow** (NP).
We're leaving **in a week** (PP).
We're leaving **rather hurriedly** (AdvP).

What these elements (in bold) modifying *leaving* all have in common is not their word class, but rather, their syntactic function. All of them fulfil what is known as the ADJUNCT function in (80)—they are optional modifying phrases. Confusingly, this function is also referred to as the ADVERBIAL function, no doubt because it is often adverbs that fulfil this function. But as (80) shows, not all adjuncts are adverbs. As we will see in Chapter 3, adjuncts can also be entire modifying sentences.

Adjunct, 附接语, 指可有可无或者次要的成分, 附接语可以去掉而不影响其他部分的完整性。

2.6 PREPOSITIONS

2.6.1 Identifying prepositions in English

In English, though not in all languages, we find phrases like **under** *the floor*, **towards** *that conclusion*, **outside** *my house*, where a PREPOSITION (the word shown in bold) has combined with a noun phrase to form a preposition phrase (PP). Perhaps the most typical role of prepositions is to mark locative and temporal information in a language—that is, information concerning location and time. In English, prepositions such as *under, over, into, on* (*top of*), *beside, towards, in* (*front of*) mark location, whilst prepositions such as *before, during, after, while, until* and *since* mark temporal information: *before the meeting, during the war, until four o'clock*. Many prepositions express either kind of meaning: *after the game, after the traffic lights; over the bridge, over the summer*. Prepositions also express the manner in which an event is carried out: *with a knife, by means of poison, in a loud voice*, and so on. There are also metaphorical uses of prepositions: compare *against the kerb* (spatial) and *against my better judgement*.

In terms of function, many PPs are optional modifiers of verbs, as in *We left [before the meeting]*, *She sang [in a loud voice]*—the PPs are in brackets. In this grammatical function, a PP is an adjunct, as we saw in Section 2.5: an optional, modifying phrase.

Now let's start to identify the preposition class in English. Just like nouns, adjectives and adverbs in English, prepositions pair up with their own special set of modifiers: these are *straight, right, well* and *just*, and we can also add the more restricted modifier *bang*. All of these (underlined) immediately precede the prepositions (in bold) in (81):

(81) The weight is well/just **inside** the limit.
We were bang **on** target/**on** time.
She pushed the box well/right/straight/just **under** the bed.
Go straight/right **to** the top of the stairs!
The library is just/right **by/beside** the town hall.

Although the ability to take these modifiers is a good test for preposition status in English, it does need to be used with caution, because some of the modifiers can occur with word classes other than prepositions (e.g. *just fine*, where *fine* is an adjective). Also, not all prepositions work with all of these modifiers, most often because their meanings are not compatible. A final note of caution is that the purely grammatical preposition *of*, as in *the top of the stairs*, cannot take a modifier either. The modifiers do, however, enable us to identify various other words as prepositions when we might otherwise not have been sure of their word class.

First, let's consider words like *afterwards* and *nearby*. As we will see, these can be classified as intransitive prepositions: this means that they cannot take an object NP. So far, the prepositions we've seen were used transitively: they take an object NP. Examples are *inside the limit, on time, under the bed*, where the prepositional objects are underlined. Though most prepositions are transitive, a number can be used either transitively or intransitively, i.e. without an object: examples are *inside, over, before*, as in *That student was here before (the others)*, and *underneath*, as in *Put your case underneath (the bed)*. The prepositions *afterwards* and *nearby* differ only in that they are always intransitive:

(82) I'll see you right/straight/just **afterwards**.
She lives right/just **nearby**.

The co-occurrence with the modifiers *right, straight* and *just* identify *afterwards* and *nearby* as true prepositions.

Second, consider words like *upstairs*, *overhead* and *online*. Traditionally, these would be termed 'adverbs', but using the modifiers *just* and *right* as a test for preposition status, they are shown to be prepositions, and are again intransitive:

(83) She lives just/right **upstairs/downstairs**.
The plane flew just/right **overhead**.

Third, we can re-evaluate what are traditionally termed 'verbal particles'. The term refers to the small words that go together with verbs in 'phrasal verb' expressions like *run down*, *put back*, *take over* etc. Not only do they look identical to prepositions, these 'particles' are also classified as prepositions by the *right* test. The prepositions are again in bold:

(84) Lee ran his apartment right **down**.
Put those chocolates right **back**!

Prepositions are used widely in English, and though not all members of the word class behave in a standard way, they do share properties in common.

2.6.2 Postpositions

So far, we've considered words like *in*, *over*, *beside* in English, which are called 'prepositions'. When these prepositions are transitive, their object NP follows the P, as in *over the summer*. However, in some languages, the object NP always precedes the P, as in Japanese:

(85) a. tookyoo **kara**   (Japanese)
          Tokyo   from
          'from Tokyo'
      b. sono hito   **to**
          that person with
          'with that person'

In Japanese, these words in bold, *kara* 'from' and *to* 'with', are not prepositions, but POSTPOSITIONS: they follow the NP which is their object. The cover term for the whole word class is ADPOSITION, meaning both prepositions and postpositions.

In Chapter 4 we return to questions of word order of this kind.

2.6.3 Grammatical categories for adpositions

In most languages, there are no adpositional inflections: only the major lexical word classes noun, verb and adjective are typically associated with any morphosyntactic categories. In other words, we don't often expect to find 'endings' (or other kinds of affix) on prepositions and postpositions. However, a minority of languages do have inflected prepositions. Well-known examples are the Celtic and the Semitic families.

In the Celtic language Irish, for example, prepositions inflect to show person, number and gender:

(86) a. *le* b. *leis* c. *léithi* (Irish)
 'with' with.3SG.M with.3SG.F
  'with him' 'with her'

The preposition 'with' is *le* in its citation form (the one in the dictionary, for instance) but there is a distinct form of the preposition for each person and number, and distinct genders in the third person singular forms. In Irish, these inflected forms replace the free pronominal objects of prepositions that we find in most other languages (*with **him**, with **her*** etc.). So we can say that these prepositions have bound pronominal affixes; see 1.2.2.3 for a reminder of bound pronominals.

2.7 CONCLUSION

This chapter provides an overview of the distribution, function and morphosyntax of the major lexical word classes, verb, noun, adjective and adverb, as well as the adposition class. Word classes are distinguished by their morphosyntactic categories, their functions and by their patterns of distribution. 'Distribution' covers both the slots which words can appear in, and the modifying words that co-occur with them. We saw that specific functional elements (small, closed class words) often pair up with a particular lexical word class such as a noun or an adjective. To count as a distinct word class, a set of words must have some properties which distinguish them from other word classes in the language. If we don't find any such properties, then it would be unscientific to make artificial divisions in the data. It is important, then, not to expect all languages to look the same. For instance, we shouldn't think that just because, say, English and Italian have an open class of adjectives, then all languages must have one.

We have seen that grammatical information can be represented either morphologically (that is, via changes in the form of words from major classes) or, alternatively, by the use of separate 'functional' elements. Although both methods of representing grammatical information can occur within a single language, languages tend to lean towards one method or the other. Languages which have a lot of morphology represent grammatical information without needing many of the small, purely grammatical, function words. Good examples are the African Bantu languages, native American languages and, within Europe, Greek and the Slavonic family (Russian, Polish etc.), as well as non-Indo-European languages such as Finnish and Turkish. On the other hand, languages with little morphology, such as Chinese, Vietnamese, Cambodian and Malay/Indonesian, tend to need more of the small functional elements to represent grammatical information.

> **Checklist for Chapter 2**
>
> If you're not sure about the answers to any of the following, you are advised to look back and check on them before reading further.
>
> - Can you remember the three main criteria that linguists use to identify different word classes? (Section 2.1)
> - Can you remember how to apply these criteria to English to diagnose the word classes of noun, verb, adjective and preposition?
> - What are the major sub-classes of verb seen in this chapter? Give examples of each. (Section 2.2)
> - Do you recall the main properties of subjects in English? (Section 2.3)
> - Make sure you have at least a basic idea of the grammatical categories CASE and GENDER before reading further. What word class are these associated with? (Section 2.3)

FURTHER READING

Elementary reading on word classes in English can be found in Aarts (2013). A vastly more detailed treatment of word classes and most other aspects of English grammar can be found in Huddleston and Pullum (2002). A smaller, student's version is Huddleston and Pullum (2005). More advanced and technical readings on identifying word classes (also known as parts-of-speech) are Lyons (1966), Schachter (1985) and Emonds (1986), papers which tackle the problems from very different angles. A more advanced and technical discussion of the lexical categories verb, noun and adjective can be found in Baker (2003), a book which argues that these three word classes can be recognized universally, despite some claims to the contrary. Hurford (1994) is an indispensable guide for the beginning syntax student, providing definitions and examples of many of the concepts that I will be using throughout. See also Aarts (2013) for the concepts of 'subject' and 'object'. On grammatical categories, see particularly Anderson (1985) and Chung and Timberlake (1985). More detailed information can be found on aspect in Comrie (1976) and on tense in Comrie (1985a); see also Whaley (1997: ch. 12). General help with describing syntax and morphosyntax for the beginning student can be found in T. Payne (1997, 2006).

EXERCISES

1. This exercise is intended to help you consolidate the notion of 'subject' in English.

   Task: (i) Identify all the subjects in each of the following examples, using the tests established in Section 2.3.2. You can turn the noun phrases into pronouns where possible, in order to test for the nominative case forms, and you can change the tense of the verb or auxiliary, in order to test for subject/verb agreement. You can also try changing the person and number of the putative subjects, to see how this affects case and agreement. (ii) What categories of phrases form subjects in the data, apart from NPs? Give the examples and add any other examples you can think of. (iii) Flag up any problematic or interesting issues raised by these data, or other examples you've thought of. **NB** Some of these examples contain more than one clause (a concept discussed in Chapter 3); this means that there may be more than one subject in some examples.

(1) Despite the problems the military are having with the armed intervention, conditions on the ground for much of the population have improved markedly.

(2) Something wicked this way comes.

(3) Whether or not people believe in climate change depends on the current temperature.

(4) Given the circumstances they found themselves in during the winter, there's little expectation that the present government will survive.

(5) What was then the largest cathedral in the world was built by the Emperor Justinian in the sixth century.

(6) Just jealous of my vast wealth is what you are.

(7) Yesterday's stormy weather meant we couldn't even leave the house before midday.

(8) From Durham to Newcastle takes 15 minutes on the train.

(9) A stalemate in the negotiations led to the soldiers being forced to return to base.

(10) This week will be the only time you're working that early.

2. This exercise is intended to get you to think carefully about English word classes. In each of the following examples, decide on the word class of the items in bold. Consider the evidence given throughout this chapter and note any problems posed for it by the data here. Remember to include the evidence provided by the words which modify the items in bold, and try adding different modifiers to help with your diagnoses. Give as much evidence as possible for your answers, looking at the distribution, morphology (inflections) and function of the words. It will probably help to compile your own list of the relevant properties for nouns,

verbs, prepositions and adjectives. There are sixteen example sentences below; you should use at least ten of these in your answer.

Hints:
- Examples marked with % are restricted to certain dialects of English. Of course, you may not find them grammatical if you don't speak such a dialect, but the point is that they provide evidence for how words are used in certain varieties of the language.
- Some of the words pose quite a challenge; if you can see evidence pointing in more than one direction (for instance, some word might be an adjective or might be a preposition), note this too.
- Remember that words can fall into more than one class, in different contexts. Just because something is, say, an adjective in one context doesn't necessarily mean that it is an adjective in all other contexts.

(1) She lives just/right/really/%real **near** the shops.

(2) You can't get any **nearer** than the **nearest** supermarket.

(3) We're just **delighted** to hear your good news.

(4) We walked **lengthways** across the quad/**clockwise** round the gardens.

(5) She studies an **unwritten** language. *Compare*: *She unwrote the language.

(6) This film is **devoid** of meaning.

(7) It fell straight **apart** the moment I opened it.

(8) I'm still quite **undecided**.

(9) %We had a right **tasty** meal.

(10) **Afterwards**, we travelled **southwards towards** the mountains.

(11) I'm not **that bothered** about the exams.

(12) I'm not too **conversant** with **that software**.

(13) This proposal is well **worth considering**.

(14) The kids ran **aboard** (the ship) as **soon** as they could.

(15) The boat floated **downstream** and drifted **ashore**.

(16) Since the war, the journalist has lived **overseas**.

3. In (1) through (6) below are some examples from Malay.

   Task: (i) Go through them, noting as many grammatical differences between Malay and English as you can; there are around half a dozen things to spot. Use the correct grammatical terminology to describe your findings.

   (1) Saya sayang dia.
   I love he/she
   'I love him/her.'

   (2) Dia sayang saya.
   he/she love I
   'He/she loves me.'

   (3) Kawan saya doktor.
   friend I doctor
   'My friend is a doctor.'

   (4) Buku ini mahal.
   book this expensive
   'This book is expensive.'

   (5) Buku-buku itu murah.
   book-book those/the cheap
   'Those/the books are cheap.'

   (6) Maria membeli sepasang kasut untuk saya.
   Maria buy pair shoe for I
   'Maria bought a pair of shoes for me.'

   (ii) Can you say how Malay distinguishes the subject of the sentence from the object? Is this the same as English or different?

4. The following data are from the language Zina Kotoko, a Chadic language of Cameroon, and are courtesy of Anders Holmberg. First, examine each sentence and note as many grammatical differences as you can between English and Zina Kotoko; you should find up to six. Describe these differences using the correct grammatical terminology. Next, what grammatical similarities do you find between the two languages?

   (1) Mafu de majakwi
   tree.PL the tall.PL
   'The trees are tall.'

(2) Adam majakwa b'da.
    Adam tall.SG NEG
    'Adam is not tall.'

(3) Adam kwice asu de da ghika b'da.
    Adam cut meat the with knife NEG
    'Adam didn't cut the meat with a knife.'

5. Examine the data below, from Japanese, and try to figure out the function of the particle -*no*, which I have left unglossed. In (1) through (4), the particle is seen in its central usage. First, decide what this is.

   (1) Hanako-**no** musuko
       Hanako-NO son
       'Hanako's son'

   (2) boku-**no** haha
       I-NO mother
       'my mother'

   (3) Taroo-**no** hon
       Taro-NO book
       'Taro's book'

   (4) Yamada-**no** kaban
       Yamada-NO bag
       'Yamada's bag'

   In (5) through (9), the use of the particle is extended. In what way do these examples differ from the first four? How is the particle used? Finally, suggest a suitable gloss for -*no*.

   (5) kono e-**no** namae
       this painting-NO name
       'the name of this painting'

   (6) kaihatu-**no** keikaku
       development-NO plan
       'a plan for development'

   (7) sensoo-**no** hanasi
       war-NO story
       'a story about the war'

(8)   suugaku-**no**   sensee
        mathematics-NO   teacher
        'a mathematics teacher'

(9)   Tookyoo-**no**   tizu
        Tokyo-NO   map
        'a map of Tokyo'

The data in this exercise are taken from Tsujimura (1996) and Iwasaki (2002).

6. The data in this exercise are from three Melanesian languages, Nakanamanga (or Nguna), Fijian and Lenakel, and are taken from Lynch (1998). All data sets illustrate the fact that verbs in these languages have different morphosyntactic properties from verbs in many familiar European languages.

Task: A distinctive grammatical category is represented by a marker on some of the verbs in these three data sets. It is marked in bold but a gloss is not provided. The marker has the same function in all three data sets. (i) What function does the marker have? (ii) Under what circumstances does the marker occur, and under what circumstances does it not occur? (iii) Suggest a gloss for the marker. (iv) Discuss briefly any other interesting properties of the verbs in these examples. Throughout, the data you have are representative, so you have enough data to answer the questions. **NB** The marker in question takes distinct forms in the three languages, and also sometimes varies in form from verb to verb within a language; these facts do not affect your answers.

A.   Nakanamanga   (Nguna)

(1)   A   ga   munu.
        I   INTENTIONAL   drink
        'I'll drink.'

(2)   A   ga   munu-**gi**   noai   naga.
        I   INTENTIONAL   drink-???   water   that
        'I'll drink that water.'

(3)   A   ga   munu-**gi**-a.
        I   INTENTIONAL   drink-???-it
        'I'll drink it.'

B.   Fijian

(4)   E   bulu
        he   bury
        'He/she/it is buried.'

(5)   E   bulu-**t**-a   na   benu.
        he   bury-???-it   the   rubbish
        'He/she buried the rubbish.'

(6) E moce na gone.
he sleep the child
'The child slept/is sleeping.'

(7) E gunu yaqona o Seru.
he drink kava the Seru
'Seru is drinking kava.'

(8) E gunu-**va** na yaqona o Seru.
he drink-??? the kava the Seru
'Seru is drinking the kava.'

(9) E na lako mai o Jone.
he FUT go here the John
'John will come.'

(10) E rai-**ci** ira.
he see-??? them
'He saw them.'

(11) Eratou sā lako vata sara yani.
they.few ASPECT go together intensive there
'They (few) went off there together.'

(12) E loma-**ni** koya.
he love-??? her
'He loves her.'

C. Lenakel

(13) R-im-avhi-**in** mun.
3SG-PAST-read-??? again
'He read it again.'

(14) R-i-aamh nimwa vɨt ker.
he-PAST-see house good one
'He saw a good house.'

(15) R-im-eiua-**in** mun iik.
3SG-PAST-lie-??? again you
'He lied to you again.'

(16) R-im-ol nimwa vi.
3SG-PAST-make house new
'He built a new house.'

(17) K-im-hal-vin-uas.
3PL-PAST-TRIAL-go.there-together
'They three went off there together.'

3

Looking inside sentences

章节导读

我们从本章开始关注句子的内部结构。一个句子都有主语和谓语两部分组成，句子可以被分为简单句和复杂句。现代句法理论一般采用小句来指代简单句，所谓小句是只包含一个谓语的句子。有的小句不依附于其他小句，可以独立使用，因此被称为独立句或者独立小句。在英语以及许多其他语言中，一个独立小句必须要包含一个定式动词。定式是个比较复杂的概念，很难给出一个令人满意的定义，因为它与众多的语法范畴相关。英语中的定式动词需要表达时态，而在许多其他的语言中，定式往往与一致、数等语言范畴密切相关。在英语中，一个小句只能有一个要素是定式的，它要么是主动词，要么是助动词。英语中的 be、do、have 以及情态动词都属于助动词。助动词需和主动词一起使用，而且这个主动词往往是不定式动词。不定式动词是指句子中不标记时态、人称、性、数、一致等语法范畴的动词。英语中的不定式动词包括不定式和分词两种，定式动词总是出现在不定式动词之前。

复杂句是指包含两个或两个以上小句的句子，它往往以并列的方式把小句连接起来。从句法的角度来看，在一个复杂句中，通过并列方式连接起来的句子的地位是平等的，而通过嵌套方式构成的复杂句却不是如此，这类复杂句包含母句和从属小句。从属小句包括补语小句、附接小句和关系小句三种。补语小句的功能在于它充当母句中动词的论元，因此是必不可少的。附接小句在传统上也被称为状语从句，它并不充当动词的论元，因此属于非强制性的修饰成分。有些从属小句可以作为独立小句使用，但是在英语和许多其他语言中，所有的不定式小句都不能是独立小句。不论是补语小句还是附接小句，它们都有可能是定式的，也有可能是不定式的。某些语言对于从属小句的定式具有一定的限制，也有一些语言没有，但是，那些只包含不定式动词、而不包含定式成分的小句都属于从属小句。在复杂句中，在层级结构中居于最高位置的母句被称为根小句。根小句具有许多自身的特点，例如，根小句一定是定式的，另外它的词序也与嵌套小句有所不同。在英语中，只有根小句才有主语和助动词的倒置，才能构成附加疑问句。

世界上的绝大多数语言都有复杂句，但是它们的构成方式与大家熟悉的欧洲语言相比具有很大的不同。除了使用并列和套嵌之外，还有名词化和连动式两种构成复杂句的方法。连动式结构一般具有以下几个特点：（1）中间不允许插入其他的语言要素；（2）从意义的角度来看，几个并列的动词构成一个复杂的事件；（3）连动化的动词必须拥有同一个主语；（4）整个动词序列结构只有一个表示否定的标记词；（5）连动式动词不能单独标记时态、体、语气等语法范畴。

This chapter begins an examination of the internal structure of sentences which takes up the remainder of the book. Section 3.1 examines finite and non-finite verbs and auxiliaries, and distinguishes between simple sentences and complex sentences—sentences which contain other sentences. Subordination is the term used for a construction in which a sentence is embedded (or contained) within another sentence. Section 3.2 is an introduction to subordination in English and other languages. Although subordination is common cross-linguistically, not all languages seem to make much use of it. Section 3.3 examines some cross-linguistic variation in clause types, particularly in complex constructions.

3.1 FINITENESS AND AUXILIARIES

3.1.1 Independent clauses

Linguists often divide the sentence into two main parts: the SUBJECT and the PREDICATE. As we saw in Chapter 2, the central role (or 'head') in the predicate is normally filled by a verb, but we also find other types of predicate, such as adjectival predicates and nominal predicates. A verbal predicate consists of the head verb plus any phrases modifying the verb, or selected by the verb.

Let's examine the data in (1). In (1a), the subject is *Kim* and the predicate *waited*; in (1b) the subject is *these guys* and the predicate *like chips*; and in (1c), the subject is the whole phrase *The first-year students in our department* and the predicate is *bought a lot of books at this stage in the year*.

(1) a. Kim waited.
b. These guys like chips.
c. The first-year students in our department bought a lot of books at this stage in the year.

These examples each illustrate SIMPLE SENTENCES. 'Simple' here is a technical term, meaning 'consisting of just one clause'. To avoid conflict with the (non-linguistic) idea of a sentence as something that starts with a capital letter and ends with a full stop, here I introduce the more precise term CLAUSE. The term 'clause' has a specific meaning: it's a sentence that contains one predicate. As we will see in this chapter, some sentences contain only one clause, and others contain more than one clause. From the data in (1), you can see that it doesn't matter how long or 'complicated' a simple sentence is: (1c) is still a simple sentence because it contains just one predicate, therefore one clause.

The simple sentences in (1) stand alone: they aren't attached to any other clause, and are therefore known as INDEPENDENT SENTENCES or independent clauses. In English, and typically in other languages, an independent clause must contain a FINITE verb. We can identify finite verbs in English by the fact that they express tense information, which broadly speaking means information about the time of the event. The finite verbs in (1) are *waited*, *like* and *bought*. You can see easily that *waited* and *bought* are past tense, but what about *like* in (1b)?

Simple sentence, 简单句, 指没有从句和并列句而只有一个小句组成的句子, 其实简单句的结构有时并不简单。

Clause, 小句, 传统上用来指小于句子但是大于短语或词的结构单位, 但是现代句法学理论对此的定义有所不同: 只要是包含一个谓语的句子就被认为是一个小句。

Finite verb, 定式动词, 它在人称、数等方面与主语一致并标示时态, 与定式动词相对的是不定式动词。

How do we know that the verb *like* in (1b) is finite? Does it express tense? It has exactly the same word-form as *like* in *Kim wanted to like spinach*, where the verb definitely isn't finite. What evidence is there that *like* in (1b) is finite?

When you see a verb such as *like* in (1), you may wonder why we say that it's finite, since after all it has no inflections—no endings—and is in fact just the bare form of the verb. But although it may not be obvious from the form of *like* in (1), we know it really is finite because it has exactly the same DISTRIBUTION as other, clearly finite verbs. To test this, try changing the sentence so that you can see the tense (and agreement) suffixes: compare *This guy* **likes** *chips*, *These guys* **liked** *chips*, where there are obvious person/number or tense inflections. English makes things rather difficult for the beginning student, because the form of *like* in *These guys like chips* has no special morphology. This means that out of context, you can't tell whether a verb form with no inflections is finite or not—if I give you a verb form such as *enjoy*, it doesn't make any sense to ask whether it's finite unless I put it into a sentence. You can use the distribution test from now on to check whether any given verbal element in English is finite, changing the form of the verb as necessary so that you can see tense or agreement. In *I enjoy chips*, *enjoy* is indeed finite; but in *I don't enjoy*

chips, the verb *enjoy* is not finite—the finite part is the auxiliary *don't*. The next section explores the property of finiteness in more detail.

3.1.2 Finiteness

It is difficult to give a satisfactory definition of 'finiteness' that works cross-linguistically, because languages differ widely with respect to which of the morphosyntactic categories associated with verbs they express (Section 2.2). A verb that is finite is allowed to be the only verb in an independent clause (i.e. a clause that stands alone); therefore, if you find an independent clause with just one verb in it, it is likely to be finite. In English, as noted above, and indeed in many other languages, finite verbs are those expressing tense. But it's also common for languages not to express tense in the verbal morphology. Finiteness is often indicated by other grammatical categories associated with verbs, such as agreement for person and/or number. Strictly speaking, finiteness is a property of an entire clause, rather than just a verb, and for some languages, finiteness may well not be indicated via the verbal morphology at all. For instance, if a language has nominative case (see Chapter 6, pages 194 to 195), this typically occurs on the subjects of finite clauses, so this is another diagnostic. Finally, in some languages all clauses are finite, for instance Mohawk, Nahuatl, Nunggubuyu and Ainu.

Examples (2) through (4) illustrate independent clauses—and therefore simple sentences—in three very different languages, each of which expresses finiteness in distinct ways. The verbs and associated morphology are in bold:

(2) Dytyna **spyt'**. (Ukrainian)
child sleep.PRES.3SG
'The child is asleep.' (literally 'The child sleeps.')

(3) **Na-bànjal-ya** na ana-na lai nyungga. (Kambera)
3SG.SU-put-3SG.OBJ the child-3SG at me
'He left his child with me.' (literally 'He put his child at me.')

(4) Ape yu ati **o de**. (Ndyuka)
there your heart FUT be
'Your heart will be there.'

The Ukrainian verb is marked for tense and also the person/number of the subject; all this information is fused together, so that there are no separate morphological markers for 'present tense' or 'third person'. This is very common in the verbal morphology of European languages.

In the Kambera example, the finite verb has bound pronominals: person/number markers representing both the subject and the object. But there is no tense marker at all. The 3SG.SU prefix *na-* on the verb in (3) means a third person singular subject. This is translated as a pronoun *he* in English, but the Kambera has no independent pronoun here. The 3SG.OBJ suffix *-ya* marks a third person singular object, referring to the child. (You can refresh your memory for such glosses by re-reading Section 1.2.2.3.)

In Ndyuka, (4), the verb *de* 'be' itself has no morphology indicating tense (or any other morphosyntactic category), but there is an independent future tense marker, *o*. Therefore, the clause is finite.

Cross-linguistically, most independent clauses contain finite verbs, as in (2) through (4). Some languages, though, allow independent clauses consisting of a subject and a predicate that is non-verbal, as we first saw in Chapter 2. So in (5), the predicate (in bold) is just an adjective phrase *nadīf katīr* 'very clean', and this sentence contains no copula (i.e. no word for 'is'; Section 2.3.2):

(5) al-bēt dā **nadīf katir** (Chadian Arabic)
 DEF-house this.M.SG clean very
 'This house is very clean.'

3.1.3 Main verbs and verbal auxiliaries

In English only one element in any clause can be finite, but that element may be either a MAIN VERB or an AUXILIARY, sometimes called a 'helping' verb. A main verb typically has a much heftier semantic content (= meaning) than an auxiliary. For that reason, linguists also refer to main verbs as LEXICAL **verbs**. In (1) the finite verbs *waited*, *like* and *bought* are main verbs. In *We should leave*, the finite element *should* is an auxiliary. We demonstrated that (1b) has a finite main verb, *like*. If we change this to *These guys don't like chips*, the finite element is now the auxiliary *don't*, since it expresses the tense information. The distribution test from Section 3.1.1 shows that *like* is not finite here—it can't be replaced by *likes* or *liked* without an ungrammatical result: **These guys don't **liked** chips*, or **Kim doesn't **likes** chips*. You may recall the discussion of '*do*-support' in Section 1.1.2. Auxiliary *do* in examples such as *Kim doesn't like chips* is only there to negate the concept of 'liking', and it is *like* that carries the real weight.

If there's an auxiliary, it always co-occurs with a main verb, such as *leave* in *We should leave*. What about apparent counter-examples, such as *Kim hasn't read this book, but she **should**—*where no main verb follows auxiliary *should*? These can be regarded as a shortened form—the technical term is an ellipsis, meaning that some words have been omitted. Here, we have a shorter version of *she should read this book*, where the part containing the main verb is merely implied.

Lexical verb, 词汇动词，也称实义动词，是与助动词相对而言的，可以单独使用，而助动词则需要和实义动词一起使用来表达各种语法功能。

The finite auxiliaries in the simple sentences in (6) are shown in bold. These are the *only* finite elements here; in other words, any other verbs and verbal auxiliaries in these examples are non-finite. Your task is to work out the generalization (= a rule, a statement of the facts) about where a finite element occurs in the sequence of verbs and verbal auxiliaries in English. The finite auxiliaries include *'s*, the phonetically reduced form of *has*. Can you offer any evidence that the auxiliaries in bold really are finite?

(6) a. You **can** leave early again today.
 b. The people in the library **may** have been working late.
 c. Kim**'s** experienced a lot of problems lately.
 d. We really **do** feel sad about that.

The generalization is that the finite element always occurs first in the sequence of verbs/auxiliaries in English. In (6b) there are three auxiliaries, *may have been*, and one main verb, *working*, but it is only the first of these, *may*, which is finite. For (6c) and (d) you should be able to use the distribution test to show that the forms in bold are finite—you could replace these by past tense *had* (*Kim had experienced a lot of problems*) and present tense *does* (as in *She really does feel sad*). The auxiliaries *can* and *may* can be replaced by other finite auxiliary forms: *could*, *might*.

- **Modal auxiliaries**

MODAL AUXILIARIES are a group of independent words in English which express such concepts as permission, necessity or ability. In some languages similar kinds of meaning are expressed by verbal inflections. English MODALS are distinct from other auxiliaries, and also distinct from main verbs: first, the modals only occur in a finite form, and second, they don't take the third person singular *-s* inflection in the present tense. We don't get such forms as **She **mays** leave* or **Kim **wills** arrive soon*. They do, however, mostly have contrasting finite forms which are technically considered to be present and past tense, though their relationship to actual time reference is pretty complex in English. So in these pairs of modals, the first is present tense and the second, past tense: *can/could*; *shall/should*; *may/might*; *will/would*. *Must* is also a modal auxiliary, but it has no distinct past tense form. All these modals precede the bare uninflected form of the verb which is known as the INFINITIVE, such as *leave*, *arrive*. A few elements are generally regarded as modals (e.g. *ought*, *need*), and their meaning is consistent with other modal auxiliaries, but they have exceptional syntactic behaviour in various ways. For instance, they precede *to* + infinitive, as in *Lee **ought** to leave*, *I **need** to go*.

I've already noted that in English only one element per clause can be finite, and that this is the first in the sequence of auxiliary/verbal elements. You can be sure, then, that in sequences such as **may** *leave*, **will** *arrive*, **must** *sleep*, **can** *dream*, only the modal auxiliary (in bold) is finite, and therefore the main verbs (*leave*, *arrive*, *sleep*, *dream*) are all NON-FINITE here. This means that they carry no information about tense, person or number.

- ***Have*** **and** ***be*****: main verbs and aspectual auxiliaries**

The elements *have* and *be* in English have two distinct uses: they can be either main verbs or auxiliaries. Ellipsis aside, when they appear as the only verb in the clause, then by definition they must be the main verb. (7) illustrates MAIN VERB *have* and *be* (in bold):

(7) Kim **isn't** sure about that.
I **had** a cold last week.
Are you a friend of Kim's?

(8) illustrates *have* and *be* in their other function, as ASPECTUAL AUXILIARIES (in bold). Note that each example contains additional verbal elements, including the main verbs *leaving, written/played/sung, enjoying*:

(8) a. We**'re** just leaving.
b. Jo **has** often written/played/sung to me.
c. They **have been** enjoying better weather lately.

ASPECT is a grammatical category of verbs which expresses such information as whether the action of the verb is completed or unfinished (Section 2.2.2.1). Two kinds of aspect are illustrated in (8). Auxiliary *be*, along with the *-ing* form of the main verb, as in (8a), gives PROGRESSIVE aspect (an unfinished or ongoing action); *been enjoying* in (8c) is also progressive. In (8b), *has written/played/sung* illustrates PERFECT aspect, which in its basic meaning refers to a completed event, but one which still has relevance to the time of the utterance. In (8c), *have been* is another example of the perfect. Note from (8c) that progressive and perfect aspect can co-occur. Perfect aspect in English requires auxiliary *have* plus a special form of the main verb known as the PAST PARTICIPLE, which ends in *-ed* in regular verbs (*played*) and in *-en* in numerous irregular verbs (*written, stolen, forgotten*).

Main verbs *have* and *be* can also co-occur with auxiliary *have* and *be*: *She has **had** a cold recently*; *They have been **having** better weather*. The auxiliary forms are underlined, and the main verb forms are in bold type. These examples also show that in English, the main verb always comes after any sequence of auxiliaries. There can be three auxiliaries or more in one clause, as in (6b): *The people in the library may have been **working** late*.

To summarize our findings for English:

Finiteness and auxiliaries in English

- A normal simple sentence in English has *one* (and only one) finite element, which may be an auxiliary or a main verb.
- The finite element always occurs *first* in the sequence of auxiliaries/verbs.
- All other auxiliary and verbal elements in the clause are therefore NON-FINITE.
- The main verb always *follows* any sequence of auxiliaries.
- English *have* and *be* occur both as main verbs and as auxiliaries.

- Auxiliary *have* + past participle of verb gives the perfect aspect, e.g. *has written, has played*.

- Auxiliary *be* + *-ing* form of verb gives the progressive aspect, e.g. *is writing, is playing*.

3.1.4 Ways to express the grammatical categories for verbs

Many Indo-European languages (the family that English belongs to) also use the equivalents of 'have' and 'be' as auxiliaries, as does the entirely unrelated European language Basque. But cross-linguistically, there is a great deal of variation in whether auxiliaries are used at all, and if they are, what they are used for. In all languages, 'Auxiliaries are words that express the tense, aspect, mood, voice, or polarity [= negative or affirmative characteristics] of the verb with which they are associated: i.e. the same categorizations of the verb as may be expressed by means of affixes' (Schachter 1985: 41). This means that any of the morphosyntactic categories that are associated with verbs (see Section 2.2.2) can also be expressed by an auxiliary in some language or languages. We saw above that in English, morphosyntactic information about finiteness can be expressed on a main verb or on an auxiliary, but not both within a single clause. In some languages, a verb and an auxiliary in the same clause both carry the grammatical information, for example by both being marked for tense, as in the Australian language Warlpiri.

We can now see that there are three different ways of expressing all the grammatical categories for verbs: (a) via the verbal morphology itself, or (b) via an auxiliary, or (c) by using an independent word. Let's look at these three strategies now. We saw above, for instance, that English expresses progressive and perfect aspect using auxiliaries plus main verbs. The Brazilian language Bare doesn't use auxiliaries; instead, it expresses both progressive and perfect aspect just by inflections on the main verb (these affixes are shown in bold). This, then, is the verbal morphology strategy:

(9) yaharika   nu-tikuwá-**ni**   (Bare)
     now   1SG-lie-PROGRESSIVE
     'I am lying down now.'

(10) i-tíkua-**na**
     3SG-lie.down-PERFECT
     'He has lain down already.'

(Note that once again these examples do not contain actual independent pronouns for 'I' and 'he', just verbal inflections which perform the same work: first person singular in (9) and third person singular in (10). To remind you, these are known as pronominal affixes, or bound pronominals.)

Conversely, some languages have auxiliaries not found in English. Evenki, a Tungusic language of Siberia, has a negative auxiliary. In (11) the main verb *duku* 'write' is finite: it has tense and person/number inflections. But in (12) the finite negative auxiliary bears these inflections instead, and the main verb *duku* 'write' is non-finite (Section 3.1.5)—it no longer has the tense and agreement suffixes found in (11). The Evenki main verb and the auxiliary in (11) and (12) take the same basic affixes, although the PAST affix is pronounced rather differently in (12).

(11) Bi   dukuwūn-ma   duku-cā-w.   (Evenki)
     I   letter-ACC   write-PAST-1SG
     'I wrote a letter.'

(12) Bi   dukuwūn-ma   ə-ə̄-w   duku-ra
     I   letter-ACC   NEG.AUX-PAST-1SG   write-PARTICIPLE
     'I didn't write a letter.'

The English translation in (12) also uses an auxiliary, *didn't*, for the negation. But *do* is not inherently negative, whilst the Evenki auxiliary is. English expresses negation by using a separate morpheme, *not*, which can optionally be amalgamated with auxiliaries (*isn't, shan't, won't* etc.). So here we see the third method of expressing a grammatical category associated with verbs: by using an independent morpheme like *not*.

To summarize, this section has shown that the grammatical information associated with verbs is mainly represented in three different ways: with verbal morphology, with an auxiliary or by adding an independent word. These alternative means of expressing information (via separate words or via affixes) recur throughout grammars, not just in the verbal systems, and I will indicate other examples from time to time.

Major ways to express grammatical categories for verbs

- Via inflections on the main verb itself. See (2), (3), (9), (10), (11).
- Via a separate word or particle; an independent grammatical word. See (4);
- also English *not* as described above.
- Via an auxiliary. See (6), (8), (12).

3.1.5 Non-finite verbs

NON-FINITE VERBS in English are not marked for tense, person/number agreement or any of the other grammatical categories associated with finite verbs, such as aspect or mood. This is very often true of other languages as well, but not all, as we will see. I divide non-finite verbs into the two main types that occur cross-linguistically, INFINITIVES and PARTICIPLES. English has an infinitive plus two different participles.

- **Infinitives**

It is not easy to provide a satisfactory cross-linguistic definition of the term 'infinitive', and forms corresponding to the English infinitive are not particularly

不定式动词与定式动词相对比，在第一章的注释中我们已经提到，和其他学科一样，句法学包含了很多成对的概念，它们之间相互映衬，要理解一个就必须要理解另一个。

不同语言对于不定式的表现方式差异很大。

common in other languages. Some languages mark the infinitive with special inflections: for instance, French has the suffixes *-er* (as in *dessin-er* 'to draw'), *-ir* (as in *fin-ir* 'to finish') and *-re* (as in *vend-re* 'to sell'). In English, the infinitive is the bare verb stem, with no inflections: examples are *eat, relax, sing, identify, cogitate*. As we've already seen in this chapter, though, this property is not sufficient to identify an infinitive in English, since finite verbs in the present tense also have this same 'bare' form: *I sing, you sing* and so on, apart from the third person singular (*sings*).

We can identify English infinitives instead by their distribution. Modal auxiliaries in English require a following infinitive, as in *Kim must___ (that)*. An infinitive also occurs after *to* in environments such as *I had to ___ then; For you to ___ now would be good*. This *to* is an INFINITIVAL MARKER, not to be confused with the entirely different *to* which is a preposition (and, as a preposition, is followed not by a verb, but by a noun phrase).

A distributional test for English infinitives

- Following a modal auxiliary or form of auxiliary *do*, e.g. *must **leave**, could **eat** that cake, can't **relax**, does **love** chocolate*.

- Following the infinitival marker *to*: *To **err** is human, We ought to **be** leaving, I have to **arrive** on time, Kim wants Lee to **sing***.

Look at the examples in (13). Are the verb forms in bold type finite or are they infinitives? Can you provide evidence?

(13)   a.   Mel made the kids **leave** home early.
       b.   I saw him **blink**!
       c.   Let Kim **sing** in the choir? Never.

These are all infinitive forms. The easiest way to test this is to see if you can get a *-s* present tense affix in these contexts (the subject has to be third person singular, of course, to try this test). A finite verb allows this. But in (14), this affix can't occur, so the verbs are not finite:

(14)   a.   Mel made the boy **leave/*leaves** home early.
       b.   I saw him **blink/*blinks**!
       c.   Let Kim **sing/*sings** in the choir? Never.

The infinitive may be used in other languages where English has a finite verb. Compare the bracketed EMBEDDED clause in (15) with its English translation (Section

3.2 returns to embedding—a situation where a clause is inside another clause). In the Welsh, the clause in brackets has only an infinitival form of the verb *ennill*, 'win', (in bold). English, on the other hand, has a finite clause here: *Mair* **had** *won the prize*, where the finite element is auxiliary *had*.

(15) Meddyliodd Aled [i Mair **ennill** y wobr]. (Welsh)
think.PAST.3SG Aled to Mair win.INFINITIVE the prize
'Aled thought [that Mair had won the prize].'

Although infinitives are typically considered to be non-finite verb forms, some languages have infinitives which inflect for person and number—something we normally assume is a property of finite verbs only. Example (16) is from European Portuguese. The embedded clause (in brackets) contains the verb *aprovar* 'to approve', which has the *-r* infinitival ending. But like a finite verb, the infinitive has a third person plural suffix *-em*, agreeing with the 3PL subject *eles* 'they':

(16) Será difícil [eles **aprovar-em** a proposta]. (Portuguese)
be.FUTURE difficult they approve.INFIN-3PL the proposal
'It will be difficult for them to approve the proposal.'

Inflected infinitivals of this kind seem to stand mid-way between infinitives (non-finite verbs) and finite verbs. Their form is infinitival, but they behave rather like finite verbs: they have overt subjects, and they take person and number agreement markers.

- **Participles**

Participles are widespread cross-linguistically. In Indo-European languages, the term 'participle' is generally used to refer to the types of non-finite verbs which primarily co-occur with a finite auxiliary. Such an example is also given from Evenki in (12).

Cross-linguistically, participles are considered to be verb forms that can also be used in positions normally filled by adjectives or nouns. Two examples are given below from German. The words in bold are known as 'present participles'; though derived from verbs, they behave exactly like adjectives in modifying a noun, and in taking the same gender agreement suffixes that adjectives normally take. So in (17), *glaubend* takes the masculine ending *-er*, agreeing with a masculine noun, whilst in (18), *gehend* takes the feminine ending *-e*, agreeing with a feminine noun:

(17) ein **glaubend-er** Priester (German)
a.M believing-M priest.M
'a priest who believes' (literally, 'a believing priest')

(18) eine **gehend-e** Person
a.F walking-F person.F
'a person who's walking' (literally, 'a walking person')

It's quite common for languages to have a number of distinct participles (e.g. Basque, Armenian and Lezgian), though English only has two different participles. In languages other than English, verbal categories such as tense and aspect are often marked on participles, not just on finite verbs. Some languages, perhaps rather surprisingly from a European perspective, have only a CLOSED class of finite verbs, but an OPEN class of participles. For instance, in the Australian language Wakiman, the finite verb class has only around 35 members, whilst participles are a genuinely open class of verbs (Cook 1988).

We'll now consider in a little more detail the two distinct PARTICIPIAL forms in English—the *-ing* form and the *-ed/-en* form. Note that the morphology (each has its own suffix) distinguishes the participles from the English infinitive, which is the bare verb stem.

- **The *-ing* participle**

What traditional grammars term the 'present participle' is the *-ing* form of the verb which, together with auxiliary *be*, gives progressive aspect, as in (19a). But the *-ing* form doesn't only co-occur with an auxiliary: the verb form *laughing* also appears on its own in the other examples in (19).

(19) a. Kim was **laughing** loudly.
b. Kim kept on **laughing**.
c. **Laughing** loudly, Kim rushed into the room.
d. I found Kim **laughing** in the corner.

However, not all words with an *-ing* suffix are participles, or indeed verbs of any kind, as the usual distribution tests show. For instance, *boring* is clearly an adjective in *this very boring film*—it co-occurs with the adjectival modifier *very*. Compare this with *a (*very) sleeping child*, where *sleeping* is participial (i.e. a verb form), so can't be modified by *very*—remember that the asterisk inside the parentheses means that the example is ungrammatical if that word is included. Another English example is *a burning branch*, where again, the participial form *burning* does not behave like an adjective. Other *-ing* forms can be nouns; *singing* is a noun (a form traditional grammar refers to as a gerund) in such contexts as *Their singing was beautiful*.

- **The past participle**

The past participle of most English verbs has the *-ed/-(e)n* ending, as in *played, shown, seen, forgotten*. In English, this form of the verb, together with auxiliary *have*, gives the perfect aspect. Some examples (with the past participles in bold) are: *Have you **eaten** the cake?*; *Kim has **had** flu*. There are many irregularities in the form of English past participles. Though some verbs have distinct past participle forms (e.g. *eaten, known*), these are all irregular verbs. Regular verbs have past participles which are identical to their PAST TENSE, such as *worked, left, decided*: they both have an *-ed* ending. It is important that you understand the distinction between past participle (a non-finite form) and past tense (a finite verb). A simple distribution test can help you to tell which is which:

(20) **Distribution test to distinguish between English past participle and past tense**
   a.   Kim has ___ (that) already.
        PAST PARTICIPLE, e.g. *eaten, forgotten, written, left, decided, played*
   b.   Kim ___ (that) yesterday.
        PAST TENSE, e.g. *ate, forgot, wrote, left, decided, played*

In English, as well as a number of other European languages, such as French and German, past participles are also used in the PASSIVE construction (see Section 7.1) as in *This book was **written** last year*, or *It has been **made** into a film*.

English also often uses a past participle to modify a noun, as in *a boiled egg, a baked potato*. These are verbal rather than adjectival; for instance, they don't take any of the typical adjectival modifiers discussed in Section 2.4.

3.1.6   Co-ordination of clauses

So far in this chapter we have looked mostly at simple sentences: sentences containing only one clause. COMPLEX SENTENCES are sentences that consist of more than one clause. One way that complex sentences are formed is by CO-ORDINATION. In (21) we see three independent clauses. These simple clauses can be joined together, or CO-ORDINATED, to form a complex sentence, as in (22):

Co-ordination, 并列, 是语言中常见的一种句法关系, 由同类型的两个或者两个以上的范畴, 借用连词 and、but 和 or 组合而成。被组合的词、短语或者小句具有平等的句法地位, 每一个单独成分都可以在功能上代表原结构。

(21) Kim arrived early.
     Lee was half an hour late.
     Ceri didn't even show up.

(22) Kim arrived early **and** Lee was half an hour late, **but** Ceri didn't even show up.

The words in bold are CO-ORDINATING CONJUNCTIONS (another in English is *or*), used to CONJOIN (= join together) strings of simple sentences. In clausal co-ordination, each clause could stand alone as an independent clause, and there are no syntactic restrictions on the order of the clauses, though there may be pragmatic restrictions (the sentence may not make good sense if the clauses are re-ordered).

All the clauses in a co-ordination have equal syntactic status—no clause is dependent on any other. As we will see in Section 3.2, this is not the case in complex sentences involving SUBORDINATION.

3.1.7   Summary

Simple sentences consist of only one clause, and most contain a finite verb, although some languages allow sentences with no finite verb, or no verb at all. The finite element may be either a main verb or an auxiliary; a finite auxiliary always co-occurs with a main verb, which is usually non-finite. In English, the finite verb always appears before any non-finite verbs, and if there are any auxiliaries, the main verb always follows them. Cross-linguistically, non-finite verbs fall into two major categories: the infinitive, and participial forms of the verb, which often combine with aspectual auxiliaries to give various categories of verbal aspect. Simple sentences can be conjoined to give a type of complex sentence where all the clauses have an equal syntactic status: this is co-ordination. We turn next to an examination of subordination: a subordinate clause is one that is dependent on another clause in some way.

> ### Checklist for Section 3.1
>
> If you're not sure about any of these topics, please go back and revise before reading further.
>
> - What defines a simple sentence?
> - What are the typical properties of a finite verb? (Section 3.1.2)
> - What are the typical properties of auxiliaries? (Section 3.1.3)
> - What are the three different ways in which the grammatical categories for verbs may be expressed cross-linguistically? (Section 3.1.4)

3.2 INTRODUCTION TO SUBORDINATION

3.2.1 Complement clauses

Matrix clause, 母句, 又称主句 (main clause), 指一个小句套嵌其中的上位小句, 套嵌其中的句子被称为从属小句 (subordinate clause)。

In (23), the clauses do not all have an equal syntactic status. Each of these examples has two clauses: a MATRIX **clause**, which is the entire sentence, and a SUBORDINATE clause which is embedded within the matrix clause. The subordinate clauses are all in square brackets in (23), and the verbs in the matrix clause are in bold. The subordinate clause is dependent on the matrix clause, as we'll see in a moment:

(23) a. My friend **claimed** [(that) Ceri liked chips].
b. I **wondered** [whether/if Lee had gone].
c. They **want** [to leave before breakfast].

Each of the bracketed subordinate clauses is an obligatory ARGUMENT of the verb in the matrix clause. In other words, these verbs (*claim, wonder, want*) need a particular kind of syntactic phrase to complete their meaning. We can't have sentences like **My friend claimed* or **I wondered* or **They want*—these wouldn't be complete. In some of these cases, we could just have a direct object as the argument of the verb: for instance, *They want an egg*. Other verbs, though, like *wonder*, in fact require an argument which is an entire clause. The subordinate clauses specify what was claimed, wondered or wanted. Subordinate clauses that are selected by a verb in this way are known as COMPLEMENT **clauses**.

You can see from these examples that subordinate clauses have some distinctive properties. First, they are often introduced by a small functional element known as a COMPLEMENTIZER. In (23), *that*, *whether* and *if* are all complementizers. Complementizers can typically be omitted if they don't bear any real meaning, and this is true of English *that* in (23a). But *whether* and *if* couldn't be omitted. In fact, the matrix verb *wonder* selects a clause that starts with a complementizer of this kind, whereas *claim* selects a finite clause introduced (optionally) by *that*. We can't switch these around:

(24) a. *My friend claimed whether/if Ceri liked chips.
 b. *I wondered that Lee had gone.

Complement clause, 补语小句，也有人翻译成"标句词小句"。

Complementizer, 标句词，指用来标记一个补语性套嵌句的从属连词。

The verb in the matrix clause not only selects a subordinate clause, it selects a subordinate clause with specific properties, and often, a specific type of complementizer.

A second property of subordinate clauses concerns finiteness. Independent clauses in English must be finite, as we've seen. In complex sentences, the verb in the highest matrix clause, known as the ROOT clause, must be finite too. But many subordinate clauses contain only a non-finite verb form. This is the case in (23c), where *to leave before breakfast* is a non-finite clause. The verb *want*, then, selects a non-finite clausal complement. From the examples so far you should be able to see that these subordinate clauses are syntactically dependent on the matrix clause, or more specifically, on the verb in the matrix clause.

A third property of (some) subordinate clauses is also seen in (23c), *They want [to leave before breakfast]*. Here, the non-finite complement clause *to leave before breakfast* has no overt subject; it has only an understood subject, referring back to *they* in the matrix clause. This is a sure signal in English that we are dealing with a subordinate clause. An alternative option to (23c) is a non-finite subordinate clause with an overt subject: *They want [the girls to leave before breakfast]*. But then it is clearly understood that this subject, *the girls*, refers to a different entity from the matrix subject, *they*.

As we saw, a subordinate clause is part of the matrix clause, and so is said to be EMBEDDED (= contained) within it. We can indicate this embedding as in (25). The innermost square brackets show the subordinate clause, and the outermost brackets show the matrix clause; as you can see, the subordinate clause is entirely contained within the matrix clause.

Embedded, 套嵌的，与并列一样，套嵌也是构成复杂句的一种重要方式。

(25) [My friend claimed [that Ceri liked chips]].
 <------------------>
 subordinate clause
 <-------------------------------------->
 matrix clause

使用方括号[ ]来标记句子的构成成分是句法分析的一种通用做法。

In (26), we see another role that subordinate clauses (underlined) can fulfil:

(26) a. That Chris liked Lee so much really **surprises** me.
  b. For Mel to act so recklessly **shocked** everyone.

These subordinate clauses are known as CLAUSAL SUBJECTS (or SENTENTIAL SUBJECTS), because they are clauses, but also fulfil the requirement for the matrix verbs (in bold) to have a subject. You can see that each entire clause is in the subject position in both cases by replacing it with an ordinary noun phrase subject, the phrase in square brackets here:

(27) a. [This] really surprises me.
  b. [Mel's behaviour] shocked everyone.

Again, clausal subjects are embedded within the matrix clause, but this time, of course, they are in the subject position:

(28) [[That Chris liked Lee so much] really pleases me].
          ⟵———subordinate clause———⟶
     ⟵————————matrix clause————————⟶

Like the subordinate clauses in (23), these clausal subjects may be either finite (26a) or non-finite (26b). Both of them are also introduced by a complementizer: *that* introduces the finite clause, and *for* the non-finite clause. It's not too surprising that both of these complementizers are obligatory here, because they signal the start of a special kind of subject: an entire subordinate clause. For instance, having complementizer *that* at the start of the finite clausal subject prevents the hearer from assuming incorrectly that the noun phrase *Chris* is just the subject of the matrix clause: *Chris liked Lee so much really pleases me*.

Subordination is not generally restricted to a depth of just one embedded clause. In fact, in most languages (though perhaps not all), there is theoretically no limit to the number of subordinate clauses in complex sentences. For example, (23c) could be extended as *They want to know whether we'd expect to leave before breakfast* or *They want to know whether she thought we'd expect to leave before breakfast* (and so on). Such examples of RECURSION are typical, though recursion may be fairly restricted (or very uncommon) in some languages.

Looking further at complement clauses, we see that each complement clause in (29) to (31) is dependent on the matrix clause 'upstairs', and is contained, or embedded, within that clause. Each matrix verb selects the following dependent clause as its complement. This means that we have structures of the following kind, where each clause is nested inside the clause directly above it:

(29) They hope/want [to leave before breakfast].

(30) They hope [we'd expect [to leave before breakfast]].

(31) They want [to know [whether we'd expect [to leave before breakfast]]].

The brackets show the start and end of each clause. So in (30), for example, the matrix *expect* clause doesn't end after *expect*—it can't, because *expect* absolutely requires the presence of the dependent clause *to leave before breakfast*. Instead, the *expect* clause ends after *breakfast*, at which point it is complete. In (30) and (31), the *leave* clause is dependent on the *expect* clause—the verb *expect* selects the non-finite subordinate clause 'downstairs'. And the *expect* clause in turn is dependent on the clause above, and again, is selected by the verb in the clause above it (*hope*, *know*). So each of the highest clauses in (29) to (31) (the *hope/want* clause) in fact contains all the other clauses within it, as shown in (32):

(32) [They want [to know [whether we'd expect [to leave before breakfast]]]].

句末方括号数量的多少表示了句子层级的多少，数量越多，这个句子的层级就越多。

What we find, then, is not a linear sequence of clauses strung out one after the other, […] […], but rather, a HIERARCHICAL structure of clauses embedded within clauses: [… […]]. The *know*, *expect* and *leave* clauses here are all complement clauses, since they are required by the verb in the 'upstairs' clause. But the *want*, *know* and *expect* clauses are also—simultaneously—all matrix clauses as well, since they each select as a complement the clause 'downstairs'. So a clause can be at once both a matrix (from the Latin meaning 'mother') clause and a complement clause:

(33) [They want [to know [whether we'd expect [to leave before breakfast]]]].
                                                        complement to *expect*
                          complement to *know* **and** matrix clause for *to leave* …
             complement to *want* **and** matrix clause for *whether we'd expect* …
    matrix clause for *to know* … (and all below this)

At the moment, we are only talking about English, where complement clauses follow the verb that selects them. Later on we will see that in languages like Japanese, complement clauses precede the verb that selects them.

The subordinate clauses discussed so far are all complements because they are essential; they can't simply be omitted without loss of grammaticality. A complement is therefore an argument of the verb, just as, for instance, direct objects are an argument of a transitive verb. Clausal subjects, as in (26), are also arguments of the verb, just as much as the embedded clauses in examples like (23). For this reason, clausal subjects are traditionally termed 'subject complement clauses'.

However, not all subordinate clauses are complements—required arguments of a matrix verb. As we'll see next, some are optional.

3.2.2 Adjunct or adverbial clauses

Some embedded clauses are not selected by any verb, and instead are just optional modifiers rather than arguments:

(34) a. Mel will be there [when she's good and ready].
b. [If you're leaving early], please get up quietly.
c. [Kim having left early], we drank her beer.

The clauses shown in brackets are all ADJUNCTS, to use a term introduced in Chapter 2; this means that they are not obligatory. You can see this for yourself by removing them from (34); all the remaining sentences are fully grammatical. In traditional grammar, these optional subordinate clauses are known as ADVERBIAL CLAUSES. They add a very wide range of additional meanings, including information about time, location and manner, purpose, and reason or cause. The *if*-clause in (34b) is known as a CONDITIONAL clause. Here are some further English examples of **adjunct clauses**:

(35) a. Mel will come to work [after she gets paid].
b. [Because it was before dawn], we got up quietly.
c. We walked up the hill [(in order) to see the castle].
d. We walked up the hill [for Lee to see the castle].
e. We walked up the hill [so (that) Lee could see the castle].
f. [While shutting the window], I accidentally knocked over the flowers.

There are a number of points to note here. In English, and widely in other languages, adjunct clauses have just the same sorts of properties as **complement clauses**. They are often introduced by a complementizer. They may be finite or non-finite. Non-finite adjunct clauses sometimes have an overt subject (*for Lee to see the castle*) and sometimes only an understood subject (*in order to see the castle*; *while shutting the window*).

3.2.3 Identifying subordinate clauses

Beginning syntax students sometimes have difficulty identifying what is a clause and what is not. Finding the predicates is a good way to find the clauses, since each clause has just one. A complex sentence may contain a number of subordinate clauses—complements, adjuncts or both. To recognize all of them, again you need to look for the predicates.

Before reading on, examine the sentences in (36). The examples all contain subordinate clauses; sometimes just one, sometimes more than one. Each clause in (36) has a verbal predicate. (i) Pick out all the main verbs—some are finite and others are non-finite. Finding the main verbs should help you recognize where the clauses are: one main verb = one clause. Then (ii) try and decide which of the subordinate clauses are adjuncts and which are complements. In the case of the complement clauses, what verbs are they a complement to? I will leave this last task with you as an assignment for discussion.

(36)   a.   When Kim got on the train, someone said she'd left her rucksack in the middle of the platform on a trolley.
      b.   Unless we want to arrive late, we really need to be leaving now.
      c.   To get to class on time, set your alarm for about 6.15 every Wednesday.
      d.   To arrive on time feels brilliant.
      e.   I promise to cook the meal while you sort the groceries.

In (37) the main verbs are shown in bold:

(37)   a.   When Kim **got** on the train, someone **said** she'd **left** her rucksack in the middle of the platform on a trolley.
      b.   Unless we **want** to **arrive** late, we really **need** to be **leaving** now.
      c.   To **get** to class on time, **set** your alarm every Wednesday for about 6.15 in the morning.
      d.   To **arrive** on time **feels** brilliant.
      e.   I **promise** to **cook** the meal while you **sort** the groceries.

And all the complement clauses (including the clausal subject in (37d)) are underlined. Note that the whole of the complex sentence *unless we want to arrive late* is an adjunct to the *need* clause. However, that adjunct itself contains two clauses: a matrix clause with the main verb *want*, and its complement, the subordinate *arrive* clause. The adjuncts are:

(38)   when Kim got on the train
      unless we want to arrive late
      to get to class on time
      while you sort the groceries

At this stage, you will have noticed that I am beginning to use a great deal of the terminology which was introduced and defined in earlier sections and chapters. If you are finding it hard to keep things straight in your mind, you will need to do some revision before reading further, since I will be using the technical terms more often from now on without any reminder of their meaning. In any case, I recommend re-reading this section (3.2) up to this point before moving on.

3.2.4 Special properties of root clauses

In a complex sentence, the highest matrix clause in the hierarchical structure is the ROOT CLAUSE, also known as the MAIN CLAUSE: this is not embedded within any other clause. Stand-alone sentences—independent clauses—are of course never embedded within another clause, so are also main clauses. Independent clauses (*Kim likes tofu*) typically share syntactic properties with the highest matrix clause in a complex sentence, and so both clause types can be grouped together as root clauses. It is not uncommon, cross-linguistically, for root clauses of both kinds to display some special properties that are not shared by embedded clauses. For instance, embedded clauses in English may be finite or non-finite, but the main clause is *always* finite; in other words, it must contain a finite verb. And independent clauses in English must be finite too.

Another way in which root clauses often differ from subordinate clauses concerns word order. A root clause may have a word order that does not occur in embedded clauses, or vice versa. The Germanic languages are well known for this phenomenon, and below we will see some indications of it in English (which is a Germanic language). The illustration here, though, is from a Celtic language, Breton. Back in Chapter 1, we saw that Welsh, another Celtic language, has VERB-INITIAL word order: in other words, the finite verb comes first in the clause. We might expect that the closely related language Breton would be verb-initial too, but it appears from the ungrammaticality of (39) that this is not the case:

> Verb-initial, 动词开头, 指动词在小句的开始。一般语言的词序为 SVO（Subject + Verb + Object）, 但是也有的词序为 VSO。

(39) *Lenn ar wazed al levr.   (Breton)
     read.PRES the men the book
     ('The men read the book.')

Rather than (39), one grammatical version of this sentence would be (40), where the subject is initial in the clause:

(40) Ar wazed a lenn al levr.
     the men PRT read.PRES the book
     'The men read the book.' (*Literally*, '*It's the men that read the book.*')

It's also possible for the object of the verb to be initial in the clause:

(41) Al levr a lenn ar wazed.
     the book PRT read.PRES the men
     'The men read the book.' (*Literally*, '*It's the book that the men read.*')

However, if we make the verb-initial sentence in (39) into a subordinate clause (introduced by a small particle, *e*) then it's perfectly grammatical:

(42) Int a gav dezho [e lenn ar wazed al levr].
     they PRT think.PRES to.3PL PRT read.PRES the men the book
     'They think that the men read the book.'

So what is going on here? In fact, finite verbs are indeed initial in Breton—but generally, that order is not allowed in root clauses, only in embedded clauses. What happens in Breton (as in German) is that some element must precede the finite verb in a root clause; as we've seen, this could be the subject, the object, or indeed various other elements, such as an adjunct.

In some languages, of which English is generally said to be an example, root clauses do not have complementizers. This is definitely not a universal property. For instance, Swedish is a Germanic language quite closely related to English, and as (43) shows, it does have complementizers in root clauses. One of two complementizers can be chosen here (in bold):

(43) **Om/att** jag gillar blodpudding. (Swedish)
if/that I like black.pudding
'You bet I like black pudding!'

It's true that we don't get English sentences such as *That my friend likes chips* or *Whether/if it will rain today*. On the whole, then, we can agree that English typically lacks root clause complementizers. However, a common usage in some varieties of English has *so* in root clauses:

(44) Interviewer: Tell us about the new website, then.
Interviewee: **So** this site has been up and running for around a month.

This is clearly not the *so* of purpose adverbial clauses, as in *I'll stop talking so you can concentrate*—in fact, its only function seems to be to delineate the start of the clause. I consider, then, that *so* here is a root clause complementizer.

English root clauses have two other properties that will help you to distinguish them from subordinate clauses.

- **Only root clauses in English have subject/auxiliary inversion.**

The usual way of asking YES/NO or POLAR QUESTIONS in English (that is, questions expecting the answer *yes* or *no*) involves what is known as SUBJECT/AUXILIARY INVERSION. The subject of a root clause undergoes inversion (= switching of position) with a finite auxiliary. In a simple sentence, the word order in a statement is *Kim didn't like chips*, whilst the word order in a question is *Didn't Kim like chips?*. *Kim* is the subject, and *didn't* the finite auxiliary, which moves to the left of the subject. Some more instances of this are: *You can speak Italian fluently* (statement) and *Can you speak Italian fluently?* (question); *Lee has been sleeping badly* and *Has Lee been sleeping badly?*.

Now let's look at subject/auxiliary inversion in the root clause of some complex sentences:

Subject/auxiliary inversion, 主语/助动词倒置，此处指两者之间颠倒位置。

(45) a. If you're leaving early, **could you** make sure your alarm works?
b. **Can Mel** persuade Kim to cook us all a meal?

The inversion test will tell you whether a clause is a root clause or an embedded clause. Obviously, this test can only be used in finite clauses, since only *finite* auxiliaries can be inverted in this way. So we can't apply the inversion test in non-finite clauses: *****Having Kim** *left early, we drank her beer*. But we already know that all non-finite clauses are subordinate clauses anyway. Let's try the test in a complex sentence with a finite subordinate clause: *Your friend claimed that Ceri liked chips*. There are two finite clauses here: first, the *claimed* clause:

(46) **Did your friend** claim that Ceri liked chips?

This works (with *do*-support, as there's no other auxiliary), so we can be sure that *claim* is the verb of the root clause. But we can't do this in the embedded *like* clause:

(47) *Your friend claimed that **did Ceri** like chips?

This is ungrammatical, so confirming what we already knew: a clause introduced by complementizer *that* must be a subordinate clause.

Here we should add the proviso that inversion is in fact allowed in embedded clauses that are (or act like) a quotation of someone's words. So we find sentences such as *My friend said, '**Did Lee** think that Ceri liked chips?'* and *Ceri asked, **could they** be a little quieter?*.

- **Only root clauses in English can have tag questions.**

Tag questions are usually 'tagged onto' the end of the entire sentence, and they have a pronoun as their subject which matches the subject of the root clause. Since they also use subject/auxiliary inversion, tag questions too are only found in root clauses or when quoting speech. Example (48) illustrates, with the finite verb/auxiliary of the root clause and its associated tag in bold:

(48) a. We **persuaded** Kim to cook a nice meal, **didn't we**?
b. For you to act so hastily **was** unexpected, **wasn't it**?
c. If you're leaving early, you **should** ensure that your alarm works, **shouldn't you**?
d. Kim having left early, we **drank** her beer, **didn't we**?

As usual, if there's no finite auxiliary in the root clause, then *do*-support is required, as in (48a) and (d). Note that when the root clause is affirmative, the tag is negative, and vice versa: *She hasn't gone yet, has she?*.

Tag questions can't be formed from embedded clauses, even if they're finite, as (49) shows—these sound very odd:

(49) a. *I wondered whether Lee had gone, hadn't he?
b. *If you're leaving early, you should ensure that your alarm works, aren't you/doesn't it?

In (49b), there are two subordinate clauses: the *leaving* clause (an adjunct) and the *works* clause (a complement). Forming a tag associated with either of these is impossible. We can only form a grammatical tag question from the root clause, as (48c) above shows.

There are a few exceptions, so some caution is needed: if the root clause verb is a verb like *think* or *say*, we can, in fact, get embedded tag questions, such as *I think we're leaving soon, aren't we?*. Verbs of this kind (*believe* is another one) that allow root constructions in their complement clauses are often known as 'bridge' verbs.

3.2.5   Some cross-linguistic variation in subordination

So far, we have only seen examples of complement clauses that *follow* the main verb that selects them, as is the case in English and in European languages generally. The next two examples both have a complement clause which *precedes* the verb that selects it. We will be looking at word orders like this in more detail in Chapter 4. For now, you need to understand that in (50) and (51), the matrix verbs meaning 'know' and 'want' select an embedded clause, just as in English, but that this clause (bracketed) precedes the verb that selects it:

(50) ʔah   [ce   k'ew   ew   tum-tah]   hatiskhi?   (Wappo)
     1SG   that   man   fish buy-PAST   know
     'I know that man bought fish.'

(51) ʔah   [ce   k'ew   ew   tum-uhk]   hak'se?
     1SG   that   man   fish buy-INFIN   want
     'I want that man to buy fish.'

In (50), the subordinate clause is finite, as we can tell from the past tense marker on the verb, and in (51), the subordinate clause is infinitival.

In English, verbs such as *try* and *want* select subordinate INFINITIVAL clauses, as in *Kim tries/wants/hopes [to **leave** before breakfast]*, where the infinitival clause (containing the infinitive *leave*) is bracketed. Rather than having an overt (pronounced) subject, such clauses often have an *understood* subject, referring back to the subject of the matrix clause—we understand that the person leaving will be *Kim*. In English, many matrix verbs can select either an infinitival clause, or alternatively a finite clause, as their complement. So we can also have *Kim hoped [that she could leave before breakfast]*. But not all languages have infinitives. So what do the embedded clauses selected by the equivalent verbs look like in such languages? The examples in (52) and (53) are from Modern Greek, and the embedded clauses are in brackets. (SJTV is a subjunctive marker, used to mark some event that hasn't actually happened yet).

(52) o   Sokratis theli   [i   Afrodhiti na   ton   filisi]   (Greek)
      the Socrates want.3SG   the   Aphrodite SJTV him   kiss.3SG
      'Socrates wants Aphrodite to kiss him.'

(53) i   Maria   prospathise [na   diavasi   ena   vivlio]
      the Mary   tried.3SG   SJTV   read.3SG one   book
      'Mary tried to read a book.'

A literal translation of (52) would be something like 'Socrates wants that Aphrodite kisses him' and of (53), 'Mary tried that she reads a book'. In other words, the embedded clauses are both *finite* in Greek: as in the matrix clauses, both verbs in the embedded clauses have a third person singular inflection.

3.2.6 Summary: Properties of subordinate clauses and root clauses

- Complement clauses and adjunct (or adverbial) clauses are both types of subordinate clause. A third major type of subordinate clause has not been discussed in this section: the relative clause. This is the construction underlined here: *I never like the food* that they serve in the canteen. Relative clauses are optional, so are in fact a type of adjunct. We will explore them in detail in Chapter 8.

- Complement clauses serve as arguments of the verb (or other lexical 'head') in the matrix clause. For that reason, they are typically obligatory.

- Adjunct clauses are not arguments, but optional modifying elements. These are traditionally termed adverbial clauses.

- Not all subordinate clauses would be possible as independent clauses. All non-finite clauses are impossible as 'stand-alone' clauses, in English and in many (though not all) languages.

- Both complement and adjunct clauses in English can be finite or non-finite. Some languages have more restrictions on the finiteness of subordinate clauses, though many do not. Any clause that *only* has a non-finite verb, and no finite element at all, will generally be a subordinate clause of some kind.

- Both complement and adjunct clauses in English may begin with a complementizer. English root clauses typically do not, but root clause complementizers are common cross-linguistically.

- Root clauses often have special properties cross-linguistically. In English, they are identified by their ability to take subject/auxiliary inversion and tag questions. In some other languages, root clauses have a special word order that differs from the word order in subordinate clauses.

3.3 MAJOR CROSS-LINGUISTIC VARIATIONS

The majority of languages have complex sentences of some form, but not all languages share the type of complex sentences found in English. The kind of subordination used in familiar European languages is not universal, although it is also widespread outside Europe. But many languages have strategies which seem to avoid the type of complementation common to European languages. This section examines some of the main cross-linguistic variations in clause types.

3.3.1 The co-ordination strategy

The first alternative strategy is CO-ORDINATION. Compare the Kambera examples in (54) and (55) with their English translations. The gloss CONJ indicates a conjunction; see Section 3.1.6.

(54) Ku-ita-ya **ba** na-laku la Umalulu. (Kambera)
1SG.SU-see-3SG.OBJ CONJ 3SG.SU-go to Melolo
'I saw him going to Melolo.'

(55) Ku-rongu-kau **ba** u-ludu.
1SG.SU-hear-2SG.OBJ CONJ 2SG.SU-sing
'I heard you sing.'

Starting just for comparison with the English translations, the constructions *I saw him going*, *I heard you sing* are examples of COMPLEMENTATION: the verbs in each matrix clause (*see* and *hear*) select a non-finite subordinate clause which contains the verbs *going* and *sing*. As we have seen above, it's common in English to have a finite verb in the matrix clause which selects some kind of non-finite subordinate clause—one way to tell that we have a subordinate clause in the English translations in (54) and (55) is the very fact that they are non-finite. (If you are not sure that *sing* really is non-finite here, note that the verb cannot take the *-s* inflection for present tense third person singular: **I heard him sings*.)

Complementation, 补足，就是在谓语部分给动词补上它所必需的成分，即补语。

But the Kambera equivalents use co-ordination rather than subordination. Literally, the Kambera examples could be translated as 'I saw him and he went to Melolo' and 'I heard you and you sang'. These English translations are also grammatical, of course, but they aren't the normal way of expressing things. In each case in the Kambera, there are two clauses, linked with the conjunction *ba*, and both of these clauses are root clauses: neither one is dependent on the other, but instead, each clause has an equal status. All the verbs in the Kambera examples here are finite.

>─────>─────>

Before reading further, it is vital to study the glosses carefully in (54) and (55) and try to understand how these examples are constructed. What is the work done by each piece of grammatical morphology (glossed in small capitals) which is attached to the verb stems? Describe these markers: which are prefixes and which are suffixes? What are verbal affixes of this kind called, using the correct terminology?

←——————←——————←

Pronominal affixes, 代词性词缀，又称黏着性代词。

These examples from Kambera do not have independent pronouns. Instead, the verbs have what are often called PRONOMINAL AFFIXES, or bound pronominals. In (54), the verb meaning 'see' has a pronominal prefix which is a first person singular subject marker *ku-*—this gives the 'I' of the English translation—and a pronominal suffix *-ya*, a third person singular object marker, which gives the 'him' of the translation. The verb meaning 'go' is also finite in (54)—in the Kambera, of course, and not in the English translation. It has a third person singular subject pronominal prefix *na-*, indicating that 'he' is going to Melolo. So these pronominal affixes—subject and object markers on the verb—fulfil the function which in English is performed by independent pronouns. In (55), the verb meaning 'hear' again has pronominal affixes *ku-* and *-kau*, marking both subject and object, giving the 'I' and 'you' meanings, and *uludu*, 'sing', is again finite, marked *u-* for the second person singular subject (the 'you' form). The subject markers here are prefixes on the verb, the object markers suffixes.

3.3.2 Nominalization

Nominalization, 名词化，指由其他范畴（尤其是动词短语或句子）派生出名词短语的过程。经过名词化的小句需要依附于母句，不能成为独立小句。

A second syntactic strategy which regularly occurs instead of European-style subordination is known as NOMINALIZATION, a widespread strategy in South American languages and Austronesian languages, amongst others. Nominalization means 'making something into a noun'; specifically, we are talking here about the process of turning a verb into a noun. That noun, plus any modifiers it has, then occurs in typical noun phrase positions, such as the object or subject position in a sentence. English, in fact, has such a strategy, as (56) shows:

(56) a. Kim hated [Lee('s) **losing** his licence].
b. [Lee('s) **losing** his licence] surprised Kim.

The noun *losing* is a NOMINALIZED form of the verb *lose*. We can tell that *losing* is a noun here because of the (optional, and perhaps slightly formal) possessive *-'s* marker in *Lee's*, which only occurs in a noun phrase. In (56a), the bracketed phrase is the object of *hated*, and in (56b), the subject of *surprised*. These nominal *-ing* constructions are traditionally known as GERUNDS in English.

Now compare this Kambera example, where the nominalized clause is in brackets:

(57) Nda ku-mbuti-nya [na tàka-mu] (Kambera)
NEG 1SG.SU-expect-3SG.OBJ the arrive-2SG
'I did not expect you to arrive.'

Literally, this means '*I didn't expect it, your arrival*', which is definitely not very natural English; but the Kambera is perfectly natural. The verb meaning 'arrive' is clearly nominalized here because it occurs with a determiner, *na* 'the', which is a property of nouns.

Example (58) shows a similar example from a native American language, Comanche, with the nominalized clause again bracketed:

(58) [u-kima-na]   nɨɨ   supana'ʔi-ti   (Comanche)
     his-come-NOMINALIZER   I   know-ASPECT
     'I know that he's come.'

Here, instead of a finite subordinate clause, as in the English translation, we find a nominalization: the verb *kima* is turned into a noun form with a nominalizing suffix *-na*, and then it takes a possessive marker *u-* 'his', rather like the examples in (56) had the possessive marker *-'s*.

Nominalizations of this kind are still examples of subordination, because the nominalized clause is dependent on a matrix verb (*Lee('s) losing his licence* couldn't occur as an independent clause, for instance). The next section discusses a construction that doesn't involve subordination.

3.3.3 Serial verbs

As we have seen from English and other languages, the type of complementation familiar from European languages involves an embedded clause which is subordinate to a matrix clause. This strategy is widespread cross-linguistically, but not all languages make much use of subordination. A different but very common strategy, known as VERB SERIALIZATION, occurs widely in the world's languages, for instance in Chinese, in many African languages, and in many of the languages of New Guinea.

Example (59) illustrates a serial verb construction from Nupe (a language of Nigeria), showing two finite verbs simply following one after the other:

(59) Musa **bé**   **lá**   èbi.   (Nupe)
     Musa came   took   knife
     'Musa came to take the knife.'

Verb serialization, 连动式, 指不用任何的连接词就把两个或者两个以上的动词或者动词短语并列的现象, 由此而产生的结构被称为连动式结构(serial verb construction, SVC)。

English and other European languages only allow *one* finite verb in each clause—that is, a verb marked for such categories as tense and/or person and number (we don't get **Musa comes takes the knife*). In English, each clause contains just one main verb. In serial verb constructions, though, two main verbs occur within a single clause. Both are finite. Both belong to a single predicate. In the English translation of (59), there's a matrix clause with a finite verb, *Musa came*, and an embedded clause with an infinitival verb, *to take the knife*, but in the Nupe serial construction the two verbs form a single predicate: there is no subordinate clause.

Let's look at the typical properties of serial verb constructions. First, it's very common across languages with serialization that no elements at all are allowed to intervene between the two serial verbs, which is not too surprising if they are closely tied together in a single predicate. This is the case in (59), from Nupe, and it's also true of Bare, an extinct language formerly spoken in Brazil and Venezuela. In the Chinese example below, also, the direct object *men* 'door' does not intervene between the serial verbs *la-kai* 'pull open':

(60)   Ta **la-kai** le men.   (Chinese)
        he pull-open PERF door
        'He pulled the door open.'

In some languages, though, if the first of the two serial verbs is transitive, an object noun phrase can occur between them, as in (61). Here, the object of the transitive verb *mú* 'took' (*iwé* 'book') intervenes in this way between the serial verbs *mú* and *wá* 'came':

(61)   ó mú ìwé wá   (Yoruba)
        he took book came
        'He brought the book.'

The same happens in (62), where there's a transitive verb *kpá* 'take', with an object *kíyzèé* 'knife', and this immediately follows the verb:

(62)   ù kpá kíyzèé mòng ówl   (Vagala)
        he take knife cut meat
        'He cut the meat with a knife.'

A second property of serialization is that the meanings of the two serial verbs together often make up a single complex event. So in (61), the meaning could literally be seen as 'He took the book and came', which is more or less possible in English, but which instead we denote with *bring*—which means to get something and take it to your destination.

Third, the two finite verbs in a serialization must have the same subject. This is crucial to the claim that they are both part of a single clause. We see this in (59), with the subject *Musa*; it's also shown in the Yoruba example in (61), where there is only one subject, *ó* 'he', but it is shared by the two verbs; and it's shown again in the Vagala example in (62), where the subject *ù* 'he' is shared by the two verbs. Another way that this shared subject is sometimes expressed is shown in (63), from Bare: crucially, the two verbs must both have the same bound pronominal prefixes showing person/number, here *nu-*, giving the meaning 'I':

(63)   **nu**-takasã **nu**-dúmaka   (Bare)
        1SG-deceived 1SG-sleep
        'I pretended (that) I was asleep.'

Note that once again, the English translation uses a finite subordinate clause, (*that*) *I was asleep*, while the Bare has only one clause.

Contrast (63) with an example of SUBORDINATION in Bare, (64) (some of the following Bare examples are slightly adapted). This is not a serial construction, but instead is very like the English, with an adjunct clause (in brackets) before the matrix clause:

(64) [mientre-ke **nu**-nakúda-ka] **i**-mare-d'a kubati (Bare)
while-SEQUENTIAL 1SG-go-SEQUENTIAL 3SG.M-steal-ASPECT fish
'While I was coming in, he stole the fish.'

Despite the fact that the two verbs *nunakúdaka* and *imared'a* in (64) follow one after the other, we can tell that this isn't a serial construction because each verb has a different subject. Again, this is shown not by independent pronouns as in the English (*I, he*) but by the two different bound pronominal prefixes, *nu-, i-*, on the two verbs, indicating the person and number (and gender) of the two different subjects: the 'go' verb has the 1SG subject marker (meaning 'I') and the 'steal' verb, the 3SG masculine subject marker (meaning 'he'). The verbs are therefore in separate clauses.

A fourth property of serialization is that there is only one marker of negation for the whole serial verb construction. In (65), this is the negative marker *hena*:

(65) hena **nihiwawaka nu-tšereka** nu-yaka-u abi (Bare)
NEG 1SG.go 1SG-speak 1SG-parent-F with
'I am not going to talk to my mother.'

The two serial verbs, *nihiwawaka* and *nutšereka*, both share the negative marker *hena*.

Compare (65) with (66), which is not a serial verb construction, but instead has two separate finite clauses, each with their own negative marker, *hena*:

(66) **hena**-ka ini-hisa **hena** in-hiwawaka (Bare)
NEG-DECLARATIVE 2PL-want NEG 2PL-go
'If you do not want, do not go.'

Fifth, the serial verbs can't be marked independently for such grammatical categories as tense, aspect or mood, but must share the same tense etc. This is either marked on each verb, or else occurs just once but is shared by both verbs. A good example is the Chinese perfect aspect marker *le*, seen in (60) above; this only occurs once for the whole serial construction. Another such category is the Bare 'sequential' marker *-ka*; this occurs only on one verb in a serial construction:

(67) nuni hena nu-kiate-d'áwaka nu-yuwahada-**ka** (Bare)
I NEG 1SG-fear-ASPECT 1SG-walk-SEQUENTIAL
'I'm not afraid of walking.'

(Note that we again have the same bound pronominal subject markers *nu-* on each verb in the serial construction, and the single shared negative marker, *hena*.)

We can compare (67) to an example of subordination in Bare, where we find that each verb in the two subordinate clauses takes the sequential *-ka* marker. In (68) the 'roll' verb is in the root clause, and the two other verbs, meaning 'see' and 'sleep', are in two subordinate clauses; the English translation is just the same in this respect. *Both* the verbs in the embedded clauses take a *-ka* marker.

(68) nu-khuruna hnumiye ibeuku nu-yada-**ka** sepultura tibuku
1SG-roll 1SG.hammock when 1SG-see-SEQUENTIAL tomb over
nu-duma-**ka**
1SG-sleep-SEQUENTIAL
'I rolled up my hammock when I saw that I had slept over a tomb.'

Finally, if the serial verb construction seems exotic, note that something similar was common in sixteenth-century English (the time of Shakespeare). An example would be ***Come live*** with me and be my love; constructions of this type have also survived especially in American English, as in *Let's **go eat**!* for example.

3.3.4 Summary

Section 3.3 has shown that languages do not necessarily share the same syntactic strategies as the familiar European languages. Finite and non-finite subordination, where one clause is embedded inside another clause, is widely used in many language families, including non-European ones. But it's important to realize that it's not the only possible strategy. The two major alternative constructions are nominalization (a verb converted to a noun, so that the dependent clause takes on the properties of a noun phrase) and serialization, which does not involve any subordination, but instead has two finite verbs within the same predicate.

Checklist for Sections 3.2 and 3.3

If you're not sure about any of these topics, please go back and revise before reading further.
- Are you clear about how to recognize complement clauses? How do adjunct clauses differ from complements?
- How can you identify root clauses in English? (Section 3.2 covers all these points.)
- What are the three main strategies in use cross-linguistically, in addition to the kind of subordinate clauses familiar from European languages? Do you understand how these distinct strategies work? (Section 3.3)

FURTHER READING

Hurford (1994) is helpful for further illustrations concerning both simple and complex sentences, auxiliaries and main verbs, matrix clauses and embedded clauses. Huddleston and Pullum (2002, 2005) provide comprehensive information about English clauses. On what are termed 'complementation strategies', the topic of Section 3.3, Dixon (1995) is good but advanced reading, which should only be tackled after you've finished this book. Whaley (1997: ch. 15) covers all types of complex clauses. See also T. Payne (1997, 2006).

EXERCISES

1. This exercise concerns a set of words that are possible candidates for status as English modal auxiliaries: *dare, need, ought (to), used (to)* (the last two in their auxiliary uses are often represented by linguists as *oughta, useta*). All of these display both auxiliary and main verb syntactic properties. A set of properties is taken to be diagnostic of auxiliaries in English. Four central ones, some of which we've already met in Chapter 3, are the NICE properties:

   a. **Negation**—an auxiliary, but not a main verb, can be directly negated by *not*:
      (i) We *do/should/may* not talk about that./*We talk not about that.

   b. **Inversion**—an auxiliary, but not a main verb, can invert with the subject:
      (ii) *Can/might/did* Lill bake a cake for me?/*Baked Lill a cake for me?

   c. **Code**—an auxiliary, but not a main verb, can be used with an ellipsis (omission):
      (iii) Lill said she'd water the plants, and she *did/will/should* too.
         *Lill said she'd water the plants, and she watered too.
      (iv) Kim could run a marathon, and so *could* Lee.

   d. **Emphasis**—an auxiliary, but not a main verb, can bear contrastive stress for emphasis:
      (v) You say you might not go, but you **might**.
         You don't think he read it, but he **did**.
         *You don't think he read it, but he **read**.

   Some additional properties are shared by standard English modal auxiliaries. They don't take the third person singular present tense -s suffix (*She **mays** leave or *Kim **wills** arrive*), whilst main verbs do. And the auxiliaries in the standard set are also unlike main verbs in that they don't have an infinitive (*She wants to may*) and don't have an imperative (*May leave!* vs. *Leave!*).

   Task: Using the diagnostics presented above, work out (i) the ways in which *dare, need, ought(a)* and *useta* behave like modal auxiliaries, and (ii) the ways in which they behave like main verbs. There is no single 'right' answer, in part because different dialects of English have different usages of these words. Below

I suggest some data that should get you started, but you'll need to provide some additional data of your own. Make sure you list such data in your response. Organize the answer clearly. **NB** No grammaticality judgements are provided below, since mine may well differ from yours. Decide for yourself which are grammatical in your dialect and which are not.

(1) I daren't leave./I don't dare leave./He dares leave./He dare(s) not leave./He daresn't leave.

(2) Dare you (to) pick up that spider?/Do you dare pick up that spider?

(3) I might not dare to pick it up./Well, Lill dared to pick it up.

(4) Kim used not to/usen't to take any exercise./Kim didn't use to take any exercise.

(5) Used Kim to take any exercise?/Did Kim used to take any exercise?

(6) She ought to stop eating so much chocolate./She oughtn't to eat that./She didn't ought to eat any sweets at all.

(7) Ought/oughtn't she to stop eating chocolate?/Did she ought to stop eating chocolate?

(8) I needn't go./He need not/needn't go./He doesn't need to go.

(9) Do you need to leave?/Need you leave so soon?

(10) Kim needs a holiday.

2. Section 3.2 presented some tests for distinguishing root clauses in English from subordinate clauses. One construction discussed there shows up again in the data in (1) through (7).

Task: (i) What construction is it? (ii) What properties seem to trigger the appearance of this construction in these examples? Use the ungrammatical sentences as contrast to help work out your answers.

(1) Not for any money would Lill pick up a spider. Neither will I, actually.
*Sometimes will Lill pick up a spider.

(2) Rarely have we seen such snow before.
*Last winter have we seen such snow before.

(3) Never again must those students take the last train to Durham.

(4) Under no circumstances should you press the red button.
*Under certain circumstances should you press the red button.

(5) Seldom can you find a better bargain than at Den's Dealership.
*Any day of the week can you find a better bargain than at Den's Dealership.

(6) Not till after the weekend might those who are on strike return to their desks.

(7) Only after 22.00 will there be another train.

(iii) What issues are suggested by these additional examples?

(8) She said that under no circumstances could she learn Irish.

(9) I knew that not even on Sundays/only on Sundays could my daughter lie in bed till midday.

3. This exercise asks you to consider the possible positions and functions of complementizers cross-linguistically.

Task: Examine the data in (1) to (13) and work out: (i) what kinds of functions the complementizers (in bold) appear to have in these examples; and (ii) what appear to be the possible positions that complementizers can take in the clause, cross-linguistically? Discuss each data set separately where necessary.

Hints:
- Regarding question (i), the function of a complementizer is basically to signal a clause boundary; for instance, complementizer *that* in English introduces embedded declarative clauses, but not interrogative ones: *Kim wondered whether/*that they'd be late*. Some of the complementizers in the data indicate specific information about the type of clause they occur in. The complementizer glosses are deliberately vague, so you will need to study each example carefully.
- The markers NOM (nominative) and ACC (accusative) in the Japanese data set are used to case-mark the subject (NOM) and the object (ACC) of a clause, as outlined in Chapter 2.
- As was the practice in the text of Chapter 3, square brackets indicate the start and end of an embedded clause in these data.

A. **Yaqui** (Noonan 1985)
(1) Tuisi tu?i [**ke** hu hamut bwika-**kai**]
very good COMP the woman sing-COMP
'It's very good that the woman sings.'

(2) Tuisi tuʔi [**ke** hu hamut bwika]
    very good COMP the woman sing
    'It's very good that the woman sings.'

(3) Tuisi tuʔi [hu hamut bwika-**kai**]
    very good the woman sing-COMP
    'It's very good that the woman sings.'

(4) *Tuisi tuʔi [hu hamut bwika]
     very good the woman sing
     ('It's very good that the woman sings.')

B. Japanese (Tsujimura 1996; Kuno 1978)

(5) a. Hanako-ga susi-o tukurimasita
       Hanako-NOM sushi-ACC made
       'Hanako made sushi.'
    b. Hanako-ga susi-o tukurimasita **ka**
       Hanako-NOM sushi-ACC made COMP
       'Did Hanako make sushi?'

(6) Taroo-ga [Hanako-ga kuru **to**] itta
    Taroo-NOM Hanako-NOM come COMP said
    'Taroo said that Hanako was coming.'

(7) Taroo-ga [Hanako-ga oisii susi-o tukutta **to**] itta
    Taroo-NOM Hanako-NOM delicious sushi-ACC made COMP said
    'Taro said that Hanako made delicious sushi.'

C. Irish (McCloskey 1979; Ó Siadhail 1989)

(8) Deir sé [**go** dtuigeann sé an scéal].
    say.PRES he COMP understand.PRES he the story
    'He says he understands the story.'

(9) Deir sé [**nach** dtuigeann sé an scéal].
    say.PRES he COMP understand.PRES he the story
    'He says he doesn't understand the story.'

(10) Deir sé [**gur** thuig sé an scéal].
     say.PRES he COMP understand.PAST he the story
     'He says he understood the story.'

(11) Deir sé [**nár** thuig sé an scéal].
     say.PRES he COMP understand.PAST he the story
     'He says he didn't understand the story.'

(12) **Ní**   dheachaidh   mé   ann.
      COMP   go.PAST   I   there
      'I didn't go there.'

(13) Chuaigh   mé   ann.
      go.PAST   I   there
      'I went there.'

4. In Section 3.1.4 we looked at some ways of forming clausal negation cross-linguistically. The Evenki example in (12) has a special negative auxiliary, whilst English has an independent negative word, *not* (though this is often optionally attached to auxiliaries, giving forms like *can't* and *shouldn't*). This gives us two of the major three ways of expressing grammatical categories listed in Section 3.1.4. The third strategy is to express negation via an inflection on the verb itself, for instance a negative prefix or suffix. All three strategies are exemplified below in (1) to (9).

Task: Work out which strategy—negative auxiliary, negative particle or verbal inflection—is used for the negation in each example that is negative. (There are some positive examples for comparison.) Make sure you cite clear evidence for each answer. If any cases cannot be decided straightforwardly, or display more than one strategy, explain why. Finally, point out any *relevant* grammatical features or changes in the negative examples, especially where these don't occur in corresponding positive examples. You will need to study the source line and gloss of the examples carefully for this.

Hint:
A negative auxiliary can be distinguished from a negative particle like *not* because an auxiliary expresses some of the grammatical categories associated with verbs generally, such as tense, person and/or number. An independent negative particle is just invariable, so will not be marked for any of these morphosyntactic categories. You can see this by comparing (11) and (12) in Chapter 3, and re-reading the discussion of these examples.

(1) a. Si   ə-tci-si   bū-ra   (Orok)
         you   NEG-PAST-2SG   give-PARTICIPLE
         'You didn't give.'
     b. Si   ə-tcil   bū-rə-si
         you   NEG-PAST   give-PARTICIPLE-2SG
         'You didn't give.'

                                                                (J. Payne 1985a)

(2) a. Gwall   ampart   eo   va   breur.   (Breton)
         very   competent   be.PRES.3SG my   brother
         'My brother is very competent.'

    b.   Gwall   ampart   n'   eo   ket   va   breur.
        very   competent   NEG   be.PRES.3SG   NEG   my   brother
        'My brother isn't very competent.'

(Press 1986)

(3) a. ama-wa-t   b. ta-ka-wa-t   (Yimas)
      1SG(SU)-go-PERF   NEG-1SG(SU)-go-PERF
      'I went.'   'I didn't go.'

(4) a. na-wa-nan   b. ta-pu-wa-nan
      3SG(SU)-go-NEAR.PAST   NEG-3SG(SU)-go-NEAR.PAST
      'He went yesterday.'   'He didn't go yesterday.'

(Foley 1991)

(5) a. Anghofia / anghofiwch y caws!   (Welsh)
      forget.IMPER.SG / forget.IMPER.PL the cheese
      'Forget the cheese!'
   b. Paid / Peidiwch ag anghofio 'r caws.
      NEG.IMPER.SG / NEG.IMPER.PL with forget.INFIN the cheese
      'Don't forget the cheese.'

(6) a. xola-xa-si   b. xola:-si-si   (Nanai)
      read-PAST-2SG   read-NEG.PAST-2SG
      'You were reading.'   'You weren't reading.'

(T. Payne 1997)

(7) a. ʕomar muʕallim-un   (Standard Arabic)
      Omar teacher-NOM
      'Omar is a teacher.'
   b. laysa r-ražul-u muʕallim-an
      NEG.3M.SG the-man-NOM teacher.ACC
      'The man is not a teacher.'
   c. lays-at muʕallit-an
      NEG-3F.SG teacher.FEM-ACC
      'She is not a teacher.'

(8) a. T-Tullaab-u ya-drus-uu-n
      the-students-NOM 3-study-M.PL-INDIC
      'The students study.'
   b. T-Tullaab-u laa ya-drus-uu-n
      the-students-NOM NEG.PRES 3-study-M.PL-INDIC
      'The students do not study.'
   c. T-Tullaab-u lam ya-drus-uu
      the-students-NOM NEG.PAST 3-study-M.PL
      'The students did not study.'

(Aoun et al. 2010)

(9) a. Mae   Aled   yn   darllen   y   llyfr.   (Welsh)
       be.PRES.3SG Aled   PROG   read.INFIN the   book
       'Aled is reading the book.'
    b. Dydy   Aled   ddim   yn   darllen   y   llyfr.
       NEG.be.PRES.3SG   Aled   NEG   PROG   read.INFIN the   book
       'Aled isn't reading the book.'

5. Examine the English sentences in (1) to (8).

   Tasks: (i) Mark in bold type the main verb (i.e. the lexical verb) in each clause. This will help you find where the clauses are. (ii) Decide which is the root clause in each example, and underline its main verb. (iii) Give at least one piece of evidence for the root status of each of these root clauses you've picked out, using the tests established in Section 3.2. (iv) Underline each of the subordinate clauses. Give at least one piece of evidence that each clause you've chosen really is a subordinate clause, using the criteria established in Section 3.2. (v) List the adjunct clauses and (vi) the complement clauses, giving some evidence for your decision in each case. (vii) Say which matrix verb each of the complement clauses is a complement to.

   Hint:
   Here is an example that I've done for you: *Kim has sometimes wondered how to cope with unexpected visitors.*

   (i)   Kim has sometimes **wondered** how to **cope** with unexpected visitors.
   (ii)   Kim has sometimes <u>**wondered**</u> how to cope with unexpected visitors.
   (iii)   The *wondered* clause is the root clause here because (a) it can take a tag question: *Kim has sometimes wondered how to cope with unexpected visitors, hasn't he?* and (b) it can take subject/auxiliary inversion: *Has Kim sometimes wondered how to cope with unexpected visitors?* These tests are not relevant for the *how to cope …* clause as this is non-finite.
   (iv)   There is just one subordinate clause, <u>how to cope with unexpected visitors</u>. This can only be a subordinate clause in English, because it's non-finite.
   (v–vii) This is a complement clause; the complement to *wondered*. Wonder obligatorily selects an embedded interrogative clause (i.e. a clause introduced by a question word such as *how, why, whether* and so on).

(1) Lee knows it's illegal but she still photocopied the entire book.

(2) Kim can't accept that the earth was only formed 5,000 years ago.

(3) That student with the unbelievably bright red sweatshirt over in the corner often stays in the gym till around 11pm.

(4) Since you write so well, we intend to hire you to work on the student newspaper.

(5) That you could spend so much time with Kim frankly amazes Lee.

(6) Yesterday evening, both the manager of the bar and the receptionist at the desk were expecting to give that part-time job to the guy with the faded jeans.

(7) Before the sun rose, we'd already run about three miles.

(8) Meet me in my office for a brief chat after class has finished.

6. The examples in (1) to (6) are from a Melanesian language, Tinrin, first seen in Chapter 1, and are taken from Osumi (1995). They all show verb serialization, so you will need to re-read Section 3.3.3 before starting.

Task: (i) Work out what typical properties of verb serialization these examples show. Compare the grammatical and ungrammatical sentences where shown. Be as explicit as possible in your answer, and use the correct grammatical terminology. Then (ii) decide how and under what circumstances the serialization in (1) to (4) differs from the serialization in (5) and (6). The forms *ri, rri, nrî, u* and *nrâ* are all pronouns.

(1) a. u nrorri gadhu peci ei toni
1SG give waste letter to Tony
'I wasted a letter by giving it to Tony.'
b. *u nrorri peci ei toni gadhu
1SG give letter to Tony waste
('I wasted a letter by giving it to Tony.')

(2) a. ri ve fi toni
1PL.INC take go Tony
'We took Tony away.'
b. *ri ve toni fi
1PL.INC take Tony go
('We took Tony away.')

(3) a. rri ve mê arròò
3PL take come water
'They brought water.'
b. *rri ve arròò mê
3PL take water come
('They brought water.')

(4) a. nrâ   nyôrrô   mê   ò
         3SG   cook   come   pot
         'She cooked and brought the pot dish.'
     b. *nrâ   nyôrrô   ò   mê
         3SG   cook   pot   come
         ('She cooked and brought the pot dish.')

(5) ri   ve   nrî   fi
     1PL.INC   take   3SG   go
     'We take it/him away.'

(6) rri   ve   nrî   mê
     3PL   take   3SG   come
     'They bring it.'

4

Heads and their dependents

章节导读

在上一章我们学习了句子的类型及其主要的构成方式，本章我们将在此基础上进一步讨论短语的结构。短语一般由中心词和依附成分构成。中心词在整个短语中起着关键性的作用，它决定了短语的类型和意义，与整个短语具有相同的分布，而且决定着依附成分的性质。中心词要选择特定的词类作为它的依附成分，它要求依附成分要与自己的语法特性（例如，性、数等）相一致。另外，在许多语言中，某些中心词要求是名词短语的依附成分使用特定的格。

在一个短语之中，除了中心词之外，其他部分都属于依附成分。依附成分可以被分为附接成分和补语两种。我们可以进一步从强制性、数量两个方面来看两者之间的区别。附接成分总是非强制性的，它只是对所修饰的中心词做出一些附加的说明，因此与中心词之间的关系是松散的，而补语则一般是强制性的、必不可少的，它与中心词的关系密切，而且受到它的制约。当然，形容词和名词的补语一般不是强制性的。从数量来看，一个中心词可以有多个附接成分来修饰，而补语的数量则要受到中心词的制约。例如，不及物动词不需要补语，带双宾语的及物动词要求有两个短语作补语。介词短语以介词为其中心词，当它们做附接成分时，可以使用不同的介词，而当它们做补语时，需要使用特定的介词。我们无法根据某一短语的类别来判断它是附接成分还是补语，因为同一个短语在不同的语境中，既可以做补语，也可以做附接成分。

对于英语和许多其他的语言来说，一个短语的中心语一般都位于短语的开始位置，但是也有的语言并非如此。我们可以根据这一点把语言划分为中心词居首的语言和中心词居尾的语言。除英语外，其他像凯尔特语等都属于中心词居首的语言，而日语、土耳其语等都属于中心词居尾的语言。中心词和其依附成分之间具有不同的句法关系。例如，在介词短语中，依附成分是中心词的宾语；在动词短语中，依附成分是中心词的论元。在各种不同的语言中，这些句法关系可以标记在中心词上，也可以标记在依附成分上，我们也可以以此为基础把语言分为中心词标记语言和依附成分标记语言两种类型。许多北美土著语属于中心词标记语言，而包括英语在内的印欧语系的语言更多地属于依附成分标记语言。另外，对于一些缺少形态变化的语言来说，中心词和依附成分都不作标记，因此被称为零标记语言，汉语就是一种零标记语言。

Section 4.1 looks at head words and their dependents within a phrase. Section 4.2 looks at the positioning of heads within their phrase, examining a major typological division into head-initial and head-final languages. Section 4.3 examines the properties of head-marking and dependent-marking languages, another important typological distinction between languages.

4.1 HEADS AND THEIR DEPENDENTS

This section examines the concept of 'head of a phrase', and then moves on to discuss what types of phrases are selected by each class of head as obligatory COMPLEMENTS, and what types of phrases accompany each head as optional modifiers.

4.1.1 What is a head?

In any phrase, we distinguish between the word that is the overall HEAD of the phrase, and other words which are DEPENDENTS to that head. The heads of the phrases in (1)—in bold—are bracketed, and their word class indicated with a subscript: 'N' for noun, 'V' for verb, 'A' for adjective and 'P' for preposition. All the other words or phrases are dependents to those heads:

(1) a. very bright [$_N$ **sunflowers**]
    b. [$_V$ **overflowed**] quite quickly
    c. very [$_A$ **bright**]
    d. quite [$_{Adv}$ **quickly**]
    e. [$_P$ **inside**] the house

The head is the most important word in the phrase, first because it bears the crucial semantic information: it determines the meaning of the entire phrase. So the phrase *very bright sunflowers* is 'about' sunflowers; *overflowed quite quickly* is about

Head, 中心词，有时也称为 center 或者 nucleus，指短语的中心成分或者在句法上起主导作用的词。具有中心词的结构可以被称为向心结构（endocentric structure），该类结构的分布在功能上相当于它的中心词。与向心结构相对的是离心结构（exocentric structure），该类结构没有确定的中心或中心词。在现代句法学研究中，更多的学者认为所有的句法结构都是向心的。

Dependent, 依附成分，指一个短语中依附于中心词并受其制约的成分。

something overflowing; and so on. To take other examples, *a brass statue* means *a kind of* statue, not a kind of brass, so the head is *statue*; *vegetable stew* is *a kind of* stew, not a kind of vegetable, so the head is *stew*. The word class of the head therefore determines the word class of the entire phrase. Since *very bright sunflowers* in (1a) is headed by a noun, it is a noun phrase (NP); *overflowed quite quickly* in (1b) is headed by a verb, so is a verb phrase (VP); *very bright* in (1c) is an adjective phrase (AP); *quite quickly* in (1d) is an adverb phrase (AdvP); and in (1e), *inside the house* is a preposition phrase (PP) headed by the preposition *inside*.

Second, in all the examples in (1) the head is the only word that has the same DISTRIBUTION as the entire phrase. Wherever the whole phrase can occur, it's possible to substitute just the head. For instance, we could say either *Kim liked very bright sunflowers*, or just *Kim liked sunflowers*; we could say *Go inside the house* or just *Go inside*. We can say *The sunflowers were bright* but not **The sunflowers were very*—therefore, *bright* rather than *very* must be the head of the AP.

It follows that the head can't normally be omitted (setting aside contexts where a head has just been mentioned, and is then omitted, as in *Are you angry?* answered by *Very!*). So the third property of heads is that they are the one obligatory item in the phrase.

There are many contexts, however, in which the dependents to a head can't be omitted either. For instance, in the Verb Phrase *released the hostages*, there's an obligatory dependent noun phrase, *the hostages*: we can't just say **The soldiers released*. And the preposition phrase *beside the wood* has an obligatory NP too, *the wood*; we don't get *She lives beside. The reason these dependents can't be omitted is that the heads in each phrase require them to be there: we say that the heads select certain dependents as their COMPLEMENT. Two familiar instances are illustrated in this paragraph: a transitive verb like *release* or *enjoy* requires an object NP, and so does a transitive preposition like *beside* or *into*. The fourth property of heads, then, is that they may select an obligatory dependent, a phrase of a particular class (such as NP) and with specific semantic properties: we can say *She lives beside the wood*, but not **She lives beside the speculation*.

In order to have a 'phrase' of some kind, we minimally require the presence of a head; the phrase may additionally contain some (optional or obligatory) dependents. A verb phrase, for instance, must contain a verb and often contains other words too. Knowing this, we can capture certain GENERALIZATIONS (= the simplest and most accurate statement of the facts) about the structure of sentences. For example:

- The subject of a clause is a phrase of one word or more which is headed by a noun (so it's an NP).

- The PREDICATE of a clause (see Section 2.2.1 and Section 3.1.1) is normally a VP; this phrase may contain just a head verb such as *overflowed*, giving us sentences like *The bath overflowed*, or else the VP can contain dependents, as it does in the sentence *The bath overflowed quite quickly*.

Distribution, 分布, 此处指中心词的使用环境和范围。一个中心词的使用和功能与整个短语是相同的。

Generalization, 概括, 指对观察到的语言事实做出解释的规则或原则, 或对语言事实做出普遍性的陈述。概括是语言学研究的重要一环, 是透过现象看规律的工作所必不可少的。

4.1.2 The influence of heads on their dependents

Heads play a crucial role in determining certain properties of their dependents. This section examines three kinds of DEPENDENCIES involving a relationship between a head and its dependent(s).

First, in all languages, heads select dependents of a particular WORD CLASS: only dependents of a certain category can occur with each kind of head. For example, in English, a head noun can be modified by an adjective such as *bright* as in (1a), but a noun can't be modified by an adverb such as *brightly*: **very brightly sunflowers*. And a head verb is modified by an adverb rather than an adjective, so we get *spoke sincerely*, but not **spoke sincere*.

Another example comes from the Austronesian language Kambera: (2) shows that an adverb *lalu* 'too' can modify a verb, (2a), but not a noun, (2b).

(2) a. Lalu   mbana-na   na   lodu.   (Kambera)
       too   hot-3SG   the   sun
       'The sun is too hot.'
    b. *lalu   uma
       too   house

Before moving on, look carefully at (2a) and work out how the Kambera example differs from English in the way it expresses the concept 'hot'.

The English translation of (2a) uses an adjective, *hot*, but the Kambera has a *verb* meaning 'to be hot', and it's this that *lalu*, 'too', modifies. We can tell that *mbana* is a verb here by the fact that it takes a third person singular subject agreement marker, agreeing with *na lodu*, 'the sun'.

A second way in which heads may determine properties of their dependents is by requiring the dependents to AGREE with various grammatical features of the head (see Chapter 2 for discussion of the grammatical categories associated with different heads). One example is GENDER in NPs. Not all languages have grammatical gender, but in those that do, gender is an inherent property of nouns. The dependents to a head noun often display gender agreement with that head. Example (3) illustrates from French:

在许多语言中，性是名词固有的属性。

(3) a. un   livre   vert   b. une   pomme   verte   (French)
       a.MASC   book(M)   green.MASC   a.FEM   apple(F)   green.FEM
       'a green book'   'a green apple'

It might seem slightly odd here to say that the nouns have a specific gender, because we can't actually see that from examining the head nouns themselves here. We actually only get to see the gender from the agreement. In (3a), the head noun *livre*, 'book', is masculine, and so requires the masculine determiner *un*; the adjective occurs in its citation form (= the one speakers typically cite if asked to give the word) when it is masculine: *vert*. The noun *pomme* 'apple' in (3b) is feminine, and requires the feminine form of the determiner, *une*, and the distinctive feminine form of the adjective, *verte*. So the determiner and the adjective agree in gender with the head noun. Children learning French must also largely learn the gender of nouns from the agreement they trigger, since few nouns announce their gender by their own form.

Third, in many languages certain heads require their noun phrase dependents to occur in a particular grammatical CASE (see Section 6.3 for more details). Case is a property of NPs which indicates their grammatical function in a phrase or a clause (Section 2.3.3.4): in languages that have case, NPs are marked in different ways depending on what function they fulfil. Specifically, the NP dependents of verbs and prepositions are often required to occur in a special form (see Section 2.3.2 for discussion of English pronouns): the verb or preposition is said to GOVERN the case of its dependent. For instance, a transitive verb has two arguments, therefore two dependent NPs: the subject and the object. These two NPs fulfil a different function from each other, and in many languages, the subject and the object also differ in form from each other: they are marked with different cases. So in the Japanese example in (4), the subject and object are marked in distinct ways, showing their different functions: the case markers are affixes on the nouns in Japanese. The NP which is the subject of the verb is in the NOMINATIVE case, and the object NP is in the ACCUSATIVE case. Nominative can generally be considered 'the case that subjects have' and accusative, 'the case that objects have'.

> 在此处所说的格（case）是语法意义上的，不是像施事、受事之类的语义格。另外，中心语决定名词短语的格，这种情况在生成语法中被称为管辖（government）。

(4) Kodomo-**ga**   hon-**o**   yon-da.   (Japanese)
    child-NOM   book-ACC   read-PAST
    'The child read the book.'

In this section we have seen various kinds of DEPENDENCY: a relationship contracted between elements in a phrase or a sentence. These dependencies are (a) the selection of a specific type of argument by a head; (b) agreement: the copying of features from a head to its dependents; and (c) government by a head.

4.1.3 Summary: The properties of heads

To summarize, the main points made about heads so far in this section are:

- The head bears the central semantic information in the phrase.
- The word class of the head determines the word class of the entire phrase.
- Heads are normally obligatory, while other material in a phrase may be optional.

- Heads select dependent phrases of a particular word class; these phrases are sometimes obligatory, and are known as COMPLEMENTS.

- Heads often require their dependents to agree with some or all of the grammatical features of the head, such as gender or number.

- Heads may require their dependent NPs to occur in a particular grammatical case. This is one form of a relationship traditionally known as GOVERNMENT: a head is said to govern the case of its dependent.

4.1.4 More about dependents: Adjuncts and complements

The dependents are all the remaining words in a phrase other than the head. Traditionally, dependents are classified into two main types: ADJUNCTS and COMPLEMENTS. We've met these terms before in Chapter 3, so if you need to revise the relevant sections, this would be a good point. Adjuncts are always optional, whereas complements are frequently obligatory. The difference between them is that a complement is a phrase which is *selected* by the head, and therefore has an especially close relationship with the head; adjuncts, on the other hand, provide optional, extra information, and don't have a particularly close relationship with the head. Let's first consider some adjuncts. In (5), the heads are again bracketed, and the phrases which are the adjuncts are now in bold:

(5)   a.   **very bright** [$_N$ sunflowers]
       b.   [$_V$ overflowed] **quite quickly**
       c.   [$_V$ talks] **loudly**
       d.   [$_V$ sings] **in the bath**

As adjuncts, these phrases in (5) are optional. The adjuncts provide additional information about such things as appearance, location or the manner in which something was done. Adjective phrases such as *very bright* and adverb phrases such as *quite quickly* or *loudly* are typical adjuncts. Preposition phrases (such as *in the bath*) are often adjuncts too. Evidence that the PP *in the bath* in (5d) is an adjunct comes from the fact that it can be replaced by any number of different PPs, using virtually any head preposition: *before breakfast, at the bus-stop, on the way to work, in the waiting room* and so on. The verb *sing*, then, can have as an optional modifier any PP that makes sense: it doesn't place any syntactic or semantic restrictions on what that PP looks like. Such a PP is a typical adjunct: its form is not constrained by the head verb. Note that *overflow, sing* and *talk* in (5) are all intransitive verbs—the presence of an adjunct doesn't affect the transitivity of a verb.

Example (6) shows some heads and their complements, again in bold:

(6)   a.   [$_V$ admires] **famous linguists**
       b.   [$_V$ wondered] **whether to leave**
       c.   [$_V$ resorted] **to the instruction manual**
       d.   [$_A$ fond] **of chips**

e. [_p_ inside] **the house**

Recall that a verb or a preposition which is TRANSITIVE requires an object NP as its complement. *Admire* in (6a) is transitive: the direct object NP is the complement of a transitive verb. Some verbs are always transitive, such as *release* in *The soldiers released the hostages*: such verbs must have an NP as their complement. Other verbs may be either transitive or intransitive: so *sing*, for instance, can also be transitive, as in *Kim sings folk songs*. The preposition *inside* in (6e) is transitive: it has a complement NP. Like verbs, some prepositions are always transitive (*beside*, *into*) whilst others are sometimes transitive and sometimes not.

The head verbs in (6b) and (6c) aren't transitive, because they don't have objects, but they do nonetheless have complements: the clause selected by *wonder* is its complement, as is the PP selected by *resort*. Compare the PP that is an adjunct in (5d) with the complement PP *to the instruction manual* in (6c). The preposition in the adjunct PP could be almost any preposition (*in*, *on*, *over*, *above*, *beside* etc.), but in the complement PP we can only use *to*: you have to *resort **to*** something, and can't *resort about something or *resort at something, for instance. In fact, the verb *resort* selects a complement PP which must be headed by the preposition *to*. Similarly, the adjective *fond* selects as its complement a PP headed by *of*. When a verb or adjective specifically selects the exact head preposition within a dependent PP in this way, it indicates that the dependent PP is the complement to that verb or adjective.

补语一般在位置上要更加靠近中心词。

Complements therefore have a much more important relationship with the head that they modify than adjuncts do. In English, and frequently in other languages, a complement typically occurs closer to the head than any adjuncts. Illustrating with dependents to a head verb, we get *We met the new students yesterday* but not **We met yesterday the new students*, where *the new students* is the complement (the verb's direct object) and *yesterday* is the adjunct. We can often use this preferred ordering of dependent phrases as a test for their status as complement or adjunct.

This section ends with two exercises which examine further the distinctions between complements and adjuncts.

⟶ ⟶ ⟶

An intransitive verb such as *disappear* doesn't have any complement. We don't get sentences like **The magician disappeared the white rabbit*, since the verb can't have an object NP. So why is (7) perfectly grammatical, even though *disappear* is followed by a noun phrase?

(7)   The magician disappeared the following day.

⟵ ⟵ ⟵

The fact that *disappear* is intransitive doesn't mean that *no* other phrase can follow it; we clearly accept, for example, *The magician disappeared in a puff of smoke*. The PP *in a puff of smoke* is an ADJUNCT. So the answer to the exercise is that *the following day* is also an adjunct. Despite being an NP, it isn't the object of the verb; in fact, it's not a complement at all. A good test for direct object status is the PASSIVE construction (see Section 7.1): a transitive verb such as *admire* in *All our friends admired Mel* can be passivized to give *Mel was admired by all our friends*. For this construction to work, the verb must have an object. We don't get **The following day was disappeared by the magician* precisely because *disappear* is not transitive and *the following day* isn't its object.

> **Linguistic convention**: The asterisk *outside* the parentheses *(...) means that the example is ungrammatical *without* the parenthetical phrase, but grammatical if we *include* it.

This exercise requires you to figure out why the adverbs can be omitted in (8) but not in (9). By convention, we indicate that a word or phrase is optional by putting it in parentheses.

(8) I wrote the report (carefully).
     Kim practises (carefully).
     They walked (carefully) on the ice.

(9) You should treat sensitive people *(carefully).
     You have to tread *(carefully).
     You need to handle Ming vases *(carefully).

The answer is that in (8), the adverbs are adjuncts, whereas in (9) we have three verbs that take adverbs as COMPLEMENTS. *Treat* in (9) has two complements: the direct object NP *sensitive people* and the adverb; *handle* has the same two classes of complement, object NP plus adverb. And *tread* has just the adverb as its complement. Note that a very small set of verbs take adverbs as complements.

These exercises show that knowing the word class of a phrase does not tell us whether it's a complement or an adjunct. So, although NPs are often complements, an NP can be an adjunct within the VP, as in (7); and although AdvPs are typically adjuncts, they can in fact be complements to verbs, as (9) shows.

4.1.5 More about verb classes: Verbs and their complements

Verbs are the heads which select the most varied types of complement, and linguists classify verbs mainly according to what complements they select. This section is a reminder of the major sub-classes of verbs, and it also introduces some new sub-classes. The complements are contained within the verb phrase which the verb heads. In this section I show the whole VP in square brackets, and the complements to each verb in bold.

- INTRANSITIVE verbs such as *gurgle*, *elapse*, *capitulate* and *expire* take no complement at all. They may, however, have an adjunct within the VP, as in *Lee [capitulated **within three minutes/gracefully**]*.

- TRANSITIVE verbs take an NP complement (the direct object): examples are *assassinate*, *rewrite*, *imitate*, *release* and *cultivate*.

- Often, a verb can be ambitransitive; either transitive or intransitive: *Lee [left **Kim**]* or *Lee [left]*.

- A number of verbs have the particular kind of transitive/intransitive alternation shown in *The sun [melted **the ice**]* versus *The ice [melted]*. Note that the ice is the OBJECT of the transitive verb but the SUBJECT of the intransitive verb. Other verbs of this class are *burn*, *sink* and *grow*, as in *The forest fire burned **the trees**/The trees burned*; *The torpedo sank **the ship**/The ship sank*.

- DITRANSITIVE verbs have two complements, either an NP and a PP, or two NPs. The complements are separated by # in (10):

(10)   Kim [$_{VP}$ gave **the chips** # **to Lee**]/[$_{VP}$ gave **Lee** # **the chips**].

Give is one of a number of verbs in English that have both a direct object NP (*the chips*) and what is sometimes termed an INDIRECT OBJECT (*to Lee*): in English the indirect object really has no special properties, but is just a PP usually headed by *to* or *for*. As (10) shows, though, there's also an alternative construction with two NP complements. Other verbs that behave like *give* are *send*, *show*, *write* and *buy*. Often, such verbs have an alternative classification as transitive verbs, so we get both *I wrote **a letter** # **to Kim*** and *I wrote **a letter***.

- Some verbs also take an NP and a PP complement, but don't have an alternation with an NP—NP complement of the kind shown in (10):

(11)   Kim [$_{VP}$ put **the potatoes** # **into the pan**].
       Kim [$_{VP}$ exchanged **her car** # **for a new bike**].
       *Kim put the pan the potatoes.
       *Kim exchanged a new bike her car.

- PREPOSITIONAL verbs take a PP complement, shown in bold in (12):

(12)   a.   This cake [$_{VP}$ consists **of fruit and nuts**].
       b.   I [$_{VP}$ applied **for a new job**].

As noted above, the PP complement is headed by a specific preposition, the choice of which is determined by the verb: with a dependent PP, this is the main test for complement status. So you can only *apply for* a job, and not **over* or **against* a job. Some more prepositional verbs are seen in *resort to NP*, *rely on NP*, *glance at NP*, *look after NP* and *long for NP*. Adjunct PPs, on the other hand, generally aren't headed by any specific preposition, and crucially, they are optional.

- Some verbs select both a direct object NP and a clausal complement, as in (13). The clausal complement to *persuade* can be either FINITE, *that they should leave early* or INFINITIVAL, *to leave early*.

(13)   Kim [VP persuaded **his friends # that they should leave early/to leave early**].

Verbs like *convince, allow, encourage, force* and *permit* are also in this category, although some of these only select infinitival complement clauses.

- Often, a verb can appear in more than one sub-class. For example, *remember* may take no complement at all: it can be intransitive, as in *I can't remember*. But it can also be a transitive verb, as in (14a), or it can take one of three different kinds of clausal complement, either finite, as in (14b), or non-finite, as in (14c) and (14d). As usual, all the complements (in bold) are contained within the VP headed by *remember*:

(14)   a.   Chris couldn't [VP remember **that long shopping list**].
        b.   Chris [VP remembered **that they'd left it on the shelf**].
        c.   Chris [VP usually remembers **to pick up the list**].
        d.   Chris [VP remembered **leaving it on the shelf**].

The finite complement clause in (14b) has an overt subject *they* whilst the two different types of non-finite complement clauses in (14c) and (d) have only an 'understood' subject, referring to *Chris*. Because there is no overt subject in these cases, some linguists regard such complements as less than clause-sized phrases, rather than a full clause. Here, I will assume they are clauses.

The non-finite complement in (14c) is an INFINITIVAL **clause**, containing the infinitive form of the verb *pick up*. In (14d), English has the non-finite *-ing* form of the verb in *leaving it on the shelf*. This is a clause type which Huddleston and Pullum (2002; see ch. 14) refer to as a GERUND-PARTICIPIAL clause: they argue that, contrary to what is normally proposed in traditional grammar, English has no distinction between a 'gerund' category and a 'present participle' category.

This section does not give a comprehensive list of verb classes, but it illustrates some of the most common sub-classes of verb found not just in English, but cross-linguistically.

Infinitival clause, 不定式小句。

4.1.6 Other heads and their complements

在谈到中心词和它的依附成分时，研究者关注最多的是动词短语，其实其他类型的短语也有中心词和依附成分之分：介词短语以介词为中心词，形容词短语以形容词为中心词，名词短语以名词为中心词。

Heads other than verbs can also select different complement types. Prepositions, adjectives, adverbs, nouns and complementizers are discussed in this section. Again, their complements are shown in bold type.

- Prepositions have notable variety in their COMPLEMENT STRUCTURE, although less than verbs. We have already seen that some prepositions are always transitive, whilst others may be intransitive too. There are also prepositions that are only intransitive, such as *nearby*, as in *She lives just nearby*; we don't get **She lives nearby the bank*. We can tell that *nearby* is truly a preposition by the fact that it co-occurs with the modifiers *just* and *right* (see Section 2.6): *She lives right/just nearby*. A number of prepositions take clausal complements, as *before* does in *Kim left before **the bus arrived***, where *the bus arrived* is an entire clause. And prepositions sometimes take PP complements, as *from* does in *He emerged* [PP *from* **under the blankets**].

- Adjectives occasionally take an obligatory complement, but this is rare. For instance, *fond* and *devoid* both take an obligatory PP complement headed by the preposition *of*, as in *fond **of fruit*** and *devoid **of meaning***; hence the ungrammaticality of **This speech is totally devoid*. A much larger number of adjectives take an optional PP complement, again headed by a specific preposition; some examples are *bad/good **at spelling***, *sorry **for your friend*** and *free **from any doubts***. Some adjectives (such as *sorry, happy, angry, glad, delighted*) take an optional CLAUSAL complement, as in *Kim felt* [AP *sorry* **that their friends weren't around**]. And adverbs sometimes have an optional complement too:

[AdvP *unfortunately **for me***], [AdvP *independently **from her parents***].

We've seen so far, then, that verbs and prepositions often have an obligatory complement, and adjectives very occasionally do.

- The last major word class is that of nouns. Some complements to N are shown in bold in (15):

(15) a. J. S. Blogg is [NP a manufacturer **of tyres**].
 b. [NP Lee's belief **in extraterrestrials**] is misguided.
 c. [NP Her assertion **that Martians would land soon**] astounded me.
 d. They repeated [NP their demand **for the library to stay open later**].
 e. [NP Our decision **to leave**] came as no surprise.

Nouns often take optional complements, but not obligatory complements. One exception is the noun *denizen*: you have to be a denizen *of* somewhere, such as *denizens of the local bar*. Complements to N may be PPs, as in (15a), *of tyres*, or *of the local bar*, and (15b), *in extraterrestrials*. The specific preposition within these PP complements is *selected* by the head noun, and this shows that these truly are complements. Some nouns take optional clausal complements, as in (15c) and (15d). (15c) has a finite complement clause—*that Martians would land soon*, and (15d) and (15e) both have infinitival complement clauses—*for the library to stay open later* and *to leave*.

- The final word class in this section is that of COMPLEMENTIZER, a small, closed word class. A complementizer (abbreviated as C) is a function word such as *that*, *for*, *whether* which introduces a clause, as we saw in Chapter 3. The clause it introduces is the complement to the head C, and the whole phrase (complementizer plus clause) can be termed **CP**, a complementizer phrase:

  CP，标句成分短语，指以标句词为中心词的短语，CP 是一种重要的语法结构，在生成语法中具有特殊的地位。

  (16) a. Mel said [$_{CP}$ that **she was leaving**].
       b. [$_{CP}$ For **Kim to go too**] would be surprising.
       c. I don't know [$_{CP}$ whether **you should go**/whether **to go**].

  As the examples in (16) show, some complementizers—such as *that*, (16a)—select a finite clause as their complement. Others—such as the prepositional complementizer *for* in (16b)—select a non-finite clause. And some can take either a finite or a non-finite complement clause, such as *whether* in (16c).

4.1.7 Summary: The main properties of complements vs. adjuncts

Here I give a brief summary of a vast topic, in order to help you to keep straight the major distinctions between the two kinds of dependent phrases.

(i) Optional vs. obligatory phrases?
- Adjuncts are always optional phrases. They have a fairly loose relationship with the head that they modify.
- Complements are often obligatory phrases, particularly the complements to verbs and prepositions. They have a close relationship with the head that they modify, and are selected by that head. Complements to adjectives are generally not obligatory, however (*I'm cross* **with Lee**, *I'm tired* **of working**). Complements to nouns are essentially optional (*our hopes* **for reconciliation**, *the decision* **to leave early**).

(ii) Limited vs. unlimited number of dependent phrases?
- A given head may be modified by a potentially unlimited number of adjuncts.
- A given head selects a strictly limited number of complements. Most heads have just one complement (e.g. a transitive verb or transitive preposition each select one object), though two or three complements are also fairly common: (*She put* [**the book**] [**on the shelf**]).

(iii) Properties of PP dependents

- PPs that are adjuncts are typified by having a wide range of head prepositions (*Lee danced in the ballroom/on the carpet/under the chandelier/for an hour* etc.).
- PPs that are complements are typified by having a specific head preposition in each of their usages (*We glanced at the clock*, *She sticks to her diet*, *They came across a small hut*).

(iv) Word class of complements and adjuncts
- We can't tell whether a phrase is a complement or an adjunct from its word class. For instance, an NP is most often a complement (to a head verb or preposition), but NPs can also be adjuncts (*He left last week*). An adverb is most typically an adjunct (*Kim sings loudly*) but can be an obligatory complement, as in *Kim treats Lee badly*.

4.1.8 Is the noun phrase really a determiner phrase?

In Section 2.3.4, I introduced the closed class of words called DETERMINERS (words like *the*, *a*, *some*, *this*, *these*) which, I proposed, pair up with nouns to form a noun phrase. In this chapter we have followed the traditional view that the noun is the head of the phrase; under this view, the determiner is one of its dependents. Some linguists consider the determiner to be a particular type of dependent known as a SPECIFIER; we could consider this a kind of adjunct that has a fixed position within the phrase (in English, preceding the head noun). On this view, the other closed class words that pair up with adjectives, adverbs and prepositions respectively (see Chapter 2) are also specifiers: this covers words like *very* in the AP *very happy* and the AdvP *very happily*, and words like *right* and *just* in the PPs *right inside* and *just underneath*. More use will be made of the term 'specifier' in Section 5.3.4.

However, a different view holds that in fact, the determiner is the head of the 'noun phrase', so that this phrase should really be considered a **determiner phrase** (DP). Under this view, the phrase has a head D, with an NP as its complement, as shown in (17): the head is *this* and its complement NP is in bold.

Determiner phrase, 限定词短语, 即名词短语, 这一概念主要是从形式化的角度提出来的。在英语和许多其他的语言中, 动词短语的第一个词是动词, 形容词短语的第一个词是形容词, 介词短语的第一个词是介词, 只有名词短语的第一个词不是名词, 往往是一个限定词。因此, 为了形式的统一, 研究者提出了 DP 的概念。这与 CP 有许多相似之处。

(17) [$_{DP}$ this [$_{NP}$ **box of dates**]]

Although the determiner *this* is clearly not the semantic head—the most important element in the phrase in terms of meaning—determiners do fulfil a number of the other criteria for head status outlined in Section 4.1.1. For instance, (Section 2.3.4) many determiners can have the same distribution as the entire 'noun phrase', as in *I'll take this/that/these/those/either/some*. Here, the DP consisting just of a determiner fulfils the need for the verb to have a direct object. The same is not true of the complement NP *box of dates* in (17): **I'll take box of dates*, which cannot occur as the direct object. This suggests that, indeed, the determiner *this* is the syntactic head. It's also the one obligatory part of the phrase in (17), which is more evidence for its head status. Furthermore, most determiners specifically select either a singular or a plural NP—*this box of dates* but *these boxes of dates*. So we can say that the head D requires its NP complement to agree with certain properties of the head. It seems, then, that various D elements may indeed select an NP as their complement.

The issue of whether D or N heads the 'noun phrase' is not explored further here, and I will continue to refer to a phrase like *this box of dates* as a 'noun phrase' without taking a stance on the DP hypothesis. Note, though, that the idea of a function word, D, heading a DP has parallels to the less controversial proposal that a function word, C (complementizer), heads a clause, which we then term CP.

4.1.9 Phrases within phrases

The dependents of a head are themselves grouped into phrases, and each smaller phrase has its own head which in turn has dependents. For instance, in the phrase *very bright sunflowers* in (1a), *very bright* is a dependent—an ADJUNCT to the head *sunflowers*. But in (1c) we see that *bright* is the HEAD of its own phrase, the AP *very bright*. We can indicate this thus: [[*very* [*bright*]] *sunflowers*].

Linguists often indicate the way a phrase occurs within a larger phrase by enclosing the phrases within square brackets, or by drawing a tree diagram, as we see in Chapter 5. Consider the verb phrase [$_{VP}$ *sings in the bath*], which has the verb *sings* as its overall head. Within the VP there is an adjunct PP *in the bath*, headed by *in*. The brackets indicate the beginning and end of each phrase: [$_{VP}$ *sings* [$_{PP}$ *in the bath*]]. Within the PP there's a dependent NP, *the bath*, which we can also bracket: [$_{VP}$ *sings* [$_{PP}$ *in* [$_{NP}$ *the bath*]]]. In this way we get phrases nested within phrases which in turn are nested within phrases. As noted in Chapter 1, this nesting is termed '**hierarchical structure**', and is a property common to all languages. Each phrase has its own head and its own dependents. So although the PP *in the bath* is a dependent to the head of the whole VP, *sings*, this PP also has its own head and dependents. Within its own phrase a word can't simultaneously be both a head and a dependent. For instance, the preposition *in* is a DEPENDENT of the verb *sings* within the VP, but within its own phrase—within the PP *in the bath*—*in* is the HEAD.

Hierarchical structure, 层级结构。在句法分析中，句子的层级结构构可以用方括号来表示，另外树形图也可以很好地体现这一点。

> **Checklist for Section 4.1**
>
> Before reading further, you'll need to make sure that you understand what a COMPLEMENT is, and also that you're happy with the distinction between complement and ADJUNCT.

4.2 WHERE DOES THE HEAD OCCUR IN A PHRASE? HEAD-INITIAL AND HEAD-FINAL LANGUAGES

In this section I introduce a two-way system of classifying languages which looks at the position of the head in relation to its complements. There is a strong tendency, cross-linguistically, for the head to occur in a fixed position in relation to its complements, and for this order to be the same across all phrases within a language.

In HEAD-INITIAL languages the head *precedes* its complements, and in HEAD-FINAL languages the head *follows* its complements. The heads of each phrase are in bold type in this section.

4.2.1 Head-initial languages

English is a head-initial language. Example (18) shows that complements to V, P, A and N all follow the head (which is shown in bold):

(18) a. [$_{VP}$ **likes** chips]
b. [$_{PP}$ **into** the water]
c. [$_{AP}$ **fond** of chips]
d. [$_{NP}$ **admiration** for Kim]

In (18), both the head verb *likes* and the head preposition *into* precede their complement NPs, whilst both the head adjective *fond* and the head noun *admiration* precede their complement PPs.

The Celtic languages are all good examples of the head-initial type; I illustrate here with Welsh. As in English, the head P precedes its NP complement:

(19) [$_{PP}$ **dros** y ffordd] (Welsh)
   over the road

And the verb is also initial within the VP: in (20), *yfed* 'drink' precedes its complement, namely the direct object NP *paned o de* 'a cup of tea':

(20) Ddaru Ceri [$_{VP}$ **yfed** paned o de].
 PAST Ceri   drink.INFIN cupful of tea
 'Ceri drank a cup of tea.'

(21) [$_{VP}$ yfed [$_{NP}$ **paned** o de]]
   drink.INFIN   cupful of tea
 '(to) drink a cup of tea'

And in (21) we see that within the VP, there is an object NP which has the head noun preceding its PP complement. The object is *paned o de*, and the head noun *paned* 'cupful' is initial in that NP. You should also be able to see from (21) that the PP *o de* 'of tea' is again head-initial, with the preposition *o* preceding its NP complement.

My final examples of a head-initial language are from an Austronesian language, Tinrin. Example (22) shows that a head verb (in bold) precedes its complement clause within VP, and (23) shows that the head noun (in bold) precedes its complement PP:

(22) u [VP **tramwâ** mwâ ke maija wake] (Tinrin)
    I   know   that you much   work
    'I know that you work hard.'

(23) [NP **kò** rugi   beebòrrò   nrâ   mwîê]
         news   about drowning   POSSESSIVE   woman
     'the news of the woman's drowning'

4.2.2 Head-final languages

Examples of clearly HEAD-FINAL languages are Japanese, Turkish and Lezgian (a language spoken in Daghestan and Azerbaijan). Examples (24) through (27) illustrate from Japanese, with the head word again in bold in each phrase ('dative' is a special case that's often used for recipients, as here):

(24) Taroo-ga   [VP Hanako-ni   hana-o   **ageta**].   (Japanese)
     Taro-NOM   Hanako-DATIVE   flower-ACC   gave
     'Taro gave Hanako flowers.'

(25) Taroo-ga   [VP tana-ni   hon-o   **oita**].
     Taro-NOM   shelf-at   book-ACC   put
     'Taro put a book on the shelf.'

(26) [PP tomodati-**to**]
          friend-with
     'with a friend'

(27) [NP sono   tesuto   e   no   **zisin**]
          that   test   to   GENITIVE   confidence
     'confidence in that test'

Examples (24) and (25) show that in Japanese verb phrases, the verb is final: in each example the verb has two complements, and these both precede the verb. Example (26) shows that Japanese has a head P *to* 'with' which follows its complement *tomodati* 'friend'. So Japanese is POSTPOSITIONAL, not prepositional: see Section 2.6.2. Example (27) shows that the head noun *zisin* 'confidence' follows its complement *sono tesuto e no* 'in that test' (the genitive item *no* is a case marker, showing the relationship between the head noun *zisin* 'confidence' and its complement).

And from Turkish, I illustrate with an adjective phrase: the complement to the adjective (shown in bold) precedes that adjective, as expected in a head-final language. Note the very slightly different use of dative case here, too:

(28) koca-sın-a   **sadık**   (Turkish)
     husband-3SG-DATIVE   loyal
     'loyal to her husband'

汉语短语中中心词的位置并不一致，因此，关于汉语应属于中心词居首还是中心词居尾的语言，目前学者们尚未达成一致。

4.2.3 An exercise on head-initial and head-final constructions

This section asks you to work out the position of the head in a number of examples.

The examples in (29) through (32) comprise some head-initial and some head-final constructions. Using the glosses, first figure out what type of construction and what category of phrase each example illustrates (VP, PP etc.). Decide which word is the head in each phrase. Finally, determine whether each example illustrates a head-initial or a head-final construction.

(29) ʔawlād   ʔaxū-k   (Chadian Arabic)
     children brother-2.M.SG
     'your brother's children'

(30) nu-yaka-u   abi   (Bare)
     1SG-parent-F   with
     'with my mother'

In the sentences in (31) and (32), concentrate just on the phrases in brackets:

(31) Girki-v   [mindu omakta-va purta-va   buu-re-n].   (Evenki)
     friend-my   me   new-ACC   knife-ACC give-PAST-3SG
     'My friend gave me a new knife.'

(32) Da   so   wan sani   á   [bun fu   sama   nyan].   (Ndyuka)
     and   thus   a   thing NEG   good for person eat
     'Such a thing isn't good for people to eat.'

Examples (29) and (32) are head-initial, and (30) and (31) are head-final.

- In (29), from Chadian Arabic, we have a possessive NP with a head noun *ʔawlād* 'children'; this is a head-initial construction, in keeping with the strongly head-initial character of Arabic. Although the head isn't initial in the English translation, note that an alternative would be *(the) children of your brother*, in which the head *children* precedes its complement *of your brother*.
- The Bare example in (30) is a PP, in this language a postposition phrase: its head is the postposition *abi* 'with', which is preceded by its complement NP. So this is a head-final construction.
- Evenki is a Tungusic language spoken in Siberia. The construction in brackets in (31) is a VP with the verb *buuren* 'gave' in final position, preceded by its two

complements, *mindu* 'me' and *omaktava purtava* 'a new knife', so this is again a head-final construction.

- Ndyuka is a creole language of eastern Suriname. The example in (32) shows an AP (in brackets), *bun fu sama nyan*, with the head adjective *bun* 'good' preceding its complement, which is a whole clause *fu sama nyan* 'for people to eat'. Since the head precedes this complement, this is therefore a head-initial construction.

4.3 HEAD-MARKING AND DEPENDENT-MARKING LANGUAGES

Section 4.2 examined one major cross-linguistic typology, known as head-placement. In this section we look at another important typological distinction: that between HEAD-MARKING and DEPENDENT-MARKING languages. Section 4.3.1 defines the terms and illustrates the constructions under discussion. Remaining sections give examples from languages of each type, construction by construction, ending by examining the wider picture of typological distinctions between languages.

4.3.1 Definitions and illustrations: Syntactic relationships between heads and dependents

Table 4.1 illustrates four different syntactic relationships—dependencies—between a head and its dependent(s). For ease of exposition, Table 4.1 shows each head before its dependents, but this shouldn't be taken to imply that only head-initial languages are under discussion; this is not at all the case, as we'll see.

Table 4.1
Syntactic relationships between a head and dependent

	Head	Dependent
i.	postposition/preposition	object NP
ii.	verb	arguments of the verb (e.g. subject, object)
iii.	(possessed) noun	possessor NP
iv.	noun	adjective

First, I show these four construction types in English; the relevant heads are given in bold:

i. **in** [$_{NP}$ the shower]   (**P** + NP)
ii. Kim **loves** Lee   (Su + **V** + Obj)
iii. Kim's **house**   (possessor NP + **N**)
iv. red **book**   (attributive adjective + **N**)

In this section we'll see that languages often mark either the head word or its dependent(s) in some way to signal the syntactic relationship between them. In such languages, either the head or the dependent(s) (or sometimes both) will occur in some special form, perhaps taking an affix, or exhibiting some other change in word form. Let's start with a preliminary illustration. In the noun phrase *Kim's house*, the HEAD is the noun *house* (because *Kim's house* IS A house) and the DEPENDENT is the possessor NP *Kim*. In English, the dependent occurs in a special form here: it has the possessive *-'s* affix. The possessed head noun, *house*, however, has no special morphology: it is in its basic form. The *-'s* affix shows the possessor NP *Kim* to be a dependent (of a particular kind) to the head *house*. Since it's the dependent that receives the *-'s* marking, rather than the head, then *Kim's house* is an example of DEPENDENT-MARKING. In a HEAD-MARKING language, on the other hand, the head noun 'house' would occur in some special form. We'll see an example in the discussion of possessive NPs in Section 4.3.4.

The fact that the syntactic relationship between a head and dependent may be marked either on the head or the dependent gives us a broad TYPOLOGICAL distinction (= a division into language types) between HEAD-MARKING and DEPENDENT-MARKING languages. Here's what we expect to find. Typical head-marking languages are those with extensive agreement or CROSS-REFERENCING. This means that heads such as verbs and nouns are marked to agree with grammatical properties of their arguments—properties such as number, person and gender. A reminder of such a language, Kambera, can be found in Section 2.2.2.4. For instance, we would expect a head-marking language to have markers on the verb indicating both the subject and the object.

<small>Cross-referencing, 相互参照, 此处指中心词和依附成分之间的一致性。</small>

Typical dependent-marking languages, on the other hand, have well-developed case systems: this means that the dependents are marked to show their grammatical relation, say to a head verb or preposition. For instance, subjects and objects themselves appear in a special form which shows that they fulfil these particular grammatical functions. We've already seen an example of this from Japanese in (4) above. Subjects bear a specific case (nominative), whilst objects take a different case, known as accusative. English displays a small amount of dependent-marking here too, although it's restricted to the set of first and third person pronouns, which have case distinctions such as *I/me* and *she/her* (see Section 2.3.2). English full NPs don't differ in case depending on grammatical function, so we get both *My sister saw the girl* and *The girl saw my sister*.

I turn next to examples of the four constructions in Table 4.1 from languages of both types. Dependent-marking languages are more familiar to most readers of this book than are head-marking languages, and so are illustrated first in each section below.

4.3.2 Head adposition and its NP object

<small>Adposition, 置词, 是前置词和后置词的统称。</small>

Recall from Chapter 2 that ADPOSITION is a cover term for preposition and postposition. In this section we will see examples of both head-initial and head-final PPs.

English, of course, generally has no marking at all on either head or dependent in this construction: *in the shower*. If the dependent NP is pronominal, though, once again we see the remnants of an older case system on the pronouns: *for him, for me*. This is dependent-marking.

4.3.2.1 *Dependent-marking in the PP*

First we focus on DEPENDENT-MARKING on the object of prepositions within the PP in German. The basic form of the NP meaning 'my friend' is *mein Freund*. If this NP is used as the object of a preposition, then it's a dependent to the head preposition. German prepositions mark their dependent NPs by requiring them to appear in some particular CASE. Example (33) illustrates with two different head prepositions, each requiring a different case:

(33) a. für mein-en Freund   b. mit mein-em Freund   (German)
         for my-ACC friend   with my-DATIVE friend
         'for my friend'   'with my friend'

German *für* 'for' selects an NP in the ACCUSATIVE case, and *mit* 'with' selects an NP in the DATIVE case: these case requirements are simply a lexical (unpredictable) property of the two prepositions. Although the noun *Freund* itself doesn't change from its basic form in either (33a) or (33b), the different cases of the two dependent NPs do show up in the different forms of their determiners: *mein-en* in (33a) but *mein-em* in (33b). The prepositions are traditionally said to GOVERN the case of their dependent NPs. Put another way, the syntactic relationship between the head preposition and its dependent object NP is signalled by giving the NP a special form. Note that there are no implications here for the meaning of the two NPs; their distinct cases are purely a formal requirement of the two different head prepositions.

Dative case, 与格, 又称承受格, 是名词或者名词短语的一种形式, 指受动词的状态或动作影响的人或物。

In (34) we see another PP with dependent-marking, from Chechen. This construction happens to be head-final: the head P is a postposition and so follows the dependent NP. Again, though, the object of the P, namely *beera-na* 'the child', is CASE-MARKED, and this time the case is shown directly on the noun itself: it's in the dative form:

(34) beera-**na**   t'e   (Chechen)
     child-DATIVE   on
     'on the child'

In both (33) and (34), each head adposition appears in its basic UNMARKED form; it's not marked with any information about the dependent at all. So there's no head-marking. The dependent NPs, on the other hand, appear in some specific case which shows that they bear the relationship of object to a (particular) head P. As noted above, case-marking is a classic form of dependent-marking.

4.3.2.2 Head-marking in the PP

In a PP which is HEAD-MARKING, the head P itself has a special form, whilst its dependent object receives no marking. You should be familiar by now with the fact that in many languages, verbs inflect to agree with their NP arguments. In a similar way, in some languages prepositions also inflect, changing in form to agree with their prepositional object in terms of grammatical features such as person, number, gender etc.; see Section 2.6.3. So the preposition itself takes person, number and sometimes gender markers. Example (35) illustrates:

(35) **ruu**-majk   jar   aachi   (Tzutujil)
     3SG-because.of   the   man
     'by the man/because of the man'

The preposition here is *majk*, and it has a third person singular prefix *ruu-*, agreeing with the dependent NP *jar aachi* 'the man' in person and number. So the syntactic relationship between head P and dependent NP is still signalled, but this time on the head.

A second example of head-marking within PP comes from Welsh. Most prepositions in Welsh inflect to agree with their pronominal objects. The basic form of the preposition meaning 'on' is *ar*, and three members of its INFLECTIONAL PARADIGM (see Section 1.2.2.3) are shown in (36):

(36) arna   i   arno   fo   arni   hi   (Welsh)
     on.1SG   me   on.3.M.SG him   on.3.F.SG her
     'on me'   'on him'   'on her'

The dependent pronouns in (36) retain their usual, unmarked form (they have no case marking) whilst the head preposition *ar* inflects to agree with the pronoun: *arna, arno, arni*. In the third person singular, the inflection is for person, number and gender. Inflected prepositions are found throughout the Celtic family (of which Welsh is a member) and in a number of other unrelated families, including Semitic (e.g. Arabic, Hebrew).

4.3.3 The clause: A head verb and the arguments of the verb

As noted above, English has dependent-marking in the clause only for a subset of pronouns, and not for full NPs at all. English has a tiny amount of head-marking in the clause, as we'll find later. See if you can figure out what this is before our discussion gets there.

4.3.3.1 Dependent-marking in the clause

The main verb in a clause has NP arguments which are its dependents. If we take a simple example of a transitive verb from the DEPENDENT-MARKING language Japanese, we see that the two dependents—subject and object—are each marked with a specific case (by affixes, shown in bold):

(37) Taroo-**ga** tegami-**o** kaita. (Japanese)
Taroo-NOM letter-ACC write.PAST
'Taroo wrote a letter.'

The head here, the verb *kaita* 'wrote', simply appears in its past tense form, and bears no information about its dependents. Specifically, it has no person or number inflections—no affixes to show who's doing the writing or what is being written. So there's no head-marking. But the dependent NPs are case-marked to show their relationship to the head verb: as we saw earlier, the subject of a verb in Japanese bears nominative case, and the object bears accusative case. Again we see that case indicates a dependent-marking construction.

German subjects and objects are also dependent-marked with different cases, again nominative for the subject of a verb and accusative for the object:

(38) Der Hund sah den Vogel. (German)
the.NOM dog saw the.ACC bird
'The dog saw the bird.'

(39) Den Vogel sah der Hund.
the.ACC bird saw the.NOM dog
'The dog saw *the bird*.'

From an English-speaking perspective, the examples in (38) and (39) might seem quite striking. In what way? What is the major difference here between English and German, apart from the fact that full NPs in German receive case marking?

The point here is that despite the different word orders in (38) and (39), both these examples in German mean the same thing, in terms of who is seeing whom. Example (39) has more focus on 'the bird', as the translation indicates. It's case-marking in German, rather than word order, as in English, that shows which NP is the subject (the nominative NP *der Hund* 'the dog') and which is the object (the accusative NP *den Vogel* 'the bird'). The grammatical function of each NP doesn't change, whichever position it has in the clause, and it's the case marking that enables German speakers to understand who is seeing whom in such examples. So languages with a lot of case marking of this kind often have quite flexible word order in a clause; we'll see more about this in Chapter 6.

4.3.3.2 *Head-marking in the clause*

Next we look at how the relationship between a head verb and its subject and object is marked in a HEAD-MARKING language. In Kambera, the head verb always has bound pronominals: affixes which show the person, number and grammatical relation (subject, object etc.) of its dependents. Note that in (40), there are no free pronouns for 'I' and 'him'. Instead, these meanings are 'understood' from the markers on the head verb: prefix *ku-* (first person singular subject) and suffix *-ya* (third person singular object):

(40) Hi **ku**-palu-**ya** (Kambera)
so 1SG.SU-hit-3SG.OBJ
'So I hit him.'

The PRONOMINAL AFFIXES are shown in bold. Bound pronominals are a classic indication of a head-marking construction: the head itself bears inflections giving information about its dependents, but there are no independent 'free' pronouns present. Most languages of this kind only use free pronouns (i.e. separate pronouns like *I* and *him*) for emphasis, or when the sentence would otherwise be ambiguous. This is the situation in Kambera: the language does have free pronouns, but in most sentences they aren't needed. But how does the person you're talking to know who the 'him' refers to? Just as in English, in natural discourse, the full noun phrase—for instance, the boy's name—might be mentioned once at the start of the discourse, or else it may be obvious from the context. Full NPs don't need to be explicitly present in most sentences.

Technically, then, there is no grammatical 'agreement' in examples like (40)— the pronominal affixes alone represent the arguments of the verb, and there is no independent subject or object that the verb could 'agree' with here. For this reason, some linguists reserve the term 'agreement' for constructions or languages in which a verb or other head really does agree with another element in the clause, and instead use the term CROSS-REFERENCING for languages like Kambera where pronominal affixes represent the arguments on their own.

Even when the NP dependents of the verb *are* present in the sentence, the head verb is still marked to cross-reference (or agree with) them, as in (41):

(41) [I Ama]$_S$ **na**$_S$-kei-**ya**$_O$ [na rí muru]$_O$. (Kambera)
the father 3SG.SU-buy-3SG.OBJ the vegetable green
'Father buys the green vegetables.'
(*Literally*, 'Father he-buys-it the green vegetable')

In (41) I've indicated both the subject itself, *I Ama* 'father', and also the subject marker on the verb with a subscript $_S$ (for 'subject'), and I've shown both the object NP *na rí muru* 'the green vegetable' and the object marker on the verb with a subscript $_O$ (for 'object').

Please make sure you're happy with this kind of head-marking before going further, because it will be vital for understanding later chapters.

4.3.4 Head noun and dependent possessor NP

I turn next to the syntactic relationship between a possessed head noun and the possessor NP which is a dependent to that head. We've already seen one example of dependent-marking in this construction in English—recall the discussion of *Kim's house*. The special pronominal forms *my, your, his, her, our, their* which replace possessive *-'s* (we don't say **them's house*) are also examples of dependent-marking.

4.3.4.1 Dependent-marking in the possessive construction

Our next example comes from a Papuan language called Mangga Buang (POSS is the 'possessive' marker):

(42) a. sa-te voow b. yi-te bayêên (Mangga Buang)
1SG-POSS dog 3SG-POSS village/house
'my dog' 'his/her village (*or* house)'

Note that in these examples, there is a possessive marker separate from the person/number marker, whereas English uses special possessive determiners here, *my, your, his, her* etc., which encapsulate both person/number *and* possession in a single form.

4.3.4.2 Head-marking in the possessive construction

Now consider the construction in (43), from the HEAD-MARKING language Saliba, an Austronesian language from the island of Saliba, Papua New Guinea:

(43) sine natu-**na** (Saliba)
woman child-3SG
'the woman's child'

The word order of the (dependent) possessor and the possessed (head) N in (43) is just as in English, but the possessor *sine* 'woman' has no marking, whilst the head *natuna* 'child' bears a third person singular suffix *-na* which marks agreement with the possessor, *sine*, 'woman': literally, (43) means 'woman child-her'.

4.3.4.3 Double marking in the possessive construction

It is, in fact, rather common for a language to mark *both* the head and the dependent in the possessive construction: such double marking (i.e. both head- and dependent-marking within a single construction) is illustrated in (44) from a Quechuan language called Ayacucho:

(44) a. runa-pa   wasi-n   (Ayacucho)
       man-GENITIVE   house-3.POSSESSIVE
       'a person's house'
    b. qam-pa   wasi-ki
       you-GENITIVE   house-2.POSSESSIVE
       'your house'

GENITIVE is a case marker—like *-'s* in *Kim's house*—which shows possession; in other words, it shows the relationship between the possessor and the thing possessed (the head N meaning 'house'). Like all case marking, this is an instance of dependent-marking. The head, though, is also marked in this construction to agree with the possessor: it indicates the PERSON of the possessor, so third person for *runa* 'man/person', the possessor in (44a), and second person for *qam* 'you' in (44b).

4.3.5 Head noun and dependent AP

I turn finally to a head noun and a dependent adjective that modifies it. There are no examples from English, since neither noun nor adjective are marked in any way.

4.3.5.1 *Dependent-marking in the noun + modifying adjective construction*

Dependent-marking means here that the attributive adjective agrees with properties of the head noun, such as gender and number. This occurs in many European languages; (45) illustrates from Spanish:

(45) a. el   niño   pequeño   b. la   niña   pequeña   (Spanish)
       the.M boy   small.M   the.F girl   small.F
       'the small boy'   'the small girl'

The head noun *niño* 'boy' is masculine, and the dependent adjective appears in its masculine form (*pequeño*) to agree with this; the noun *niña* 'girl' is feminine, and the adjective is therefore in its feminine form, *pequeña*. The French example in (3) also illustrated dependent-marking on a modifying adjective within the noun phrase. Note also that the determiners in (45) reflect the different genders of the two head nouns.

4.3.5.2 *Head-marking in the noun + modifying adjective construction*

Turning to the HEAD-MARKING construction, examples of the head noun itself being marked when it has an attributive adjective are not very common cross-linguistically, but they are characteristic of Iranian languages, such as Persian. Example (46) is from a Kurdish language of Iran, Hawrami. The word for 'horse' is *æsp*, but here this head is marked with a suffix showing that it has a dependent adjective, whilst the adjective receives no marking:

4. Heads and their dependents

(46) æsp-i   zıl   (Hawrami)
     horse-SUFFIX big
     'big horse'

4.3.6 An exercise on head-marking and dependent-marking

This short section asks you to work out for yourself which constructions are head-marking, and which dependent-marking.

In each example in (47) through (50) you need to (i) decide what kind of construction we're dealing with, and which word is the head; then (ii) examine the glosses to determine whether it's the head or its dependent(s) that bears the markers showing the syntactic relationship between the two. This tells you whether the construction is head-marking or dependent-marking.

Hint: Note that a head-marking language often has constructions consisting of just the head with appropriate person and number markers occurring as pronominal affixes (or bound pronouns). In such constructions, there may be no separate noun phrase dependents. Look back at the discussion of the Kambera example in (40).

(47) anū-tSī   pustaka   (Marathi)
     Anu-POSSESSIVE.3PL   book.3PL
     'Anu's books'

(48) sagasaga   e-na   (Saliba)
     mouth.of.the.river at-3SG
     'at the mouth of the river'

(49) a. Wisi   seuan-in   bi-mu-ban.   (Southern Tiwa)
         two   man-PL   1SG.SU-see-PAST
         'I saw two men.'
     b. Bey-mu-ban.
         2SG.SU/1SG.OBJ-see-PAST
         'You saw me.'

(The notation 2SG.SU/1SG.OBJ in (49b) indicates a marker which is a fusion of two separate pieces of grammatical information; here, a second person singular subject and a first person singular object.)

(50) a. rajul tawīl   (Chadian Arabic)
         man   tall.MASC
         'a tall man'

b. mara tawīla
   woman tall.FEM
   'a tall woman'

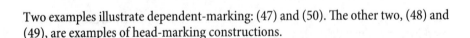

Two examples illustrate dependent-marking: (47) and (50). The other two, (48) and (49), are examples of head-marking constructions.

- In the Marathi possessor NP construction in (47), only the dependent (possessor) *Anu* is marked to show the relationship between possessor and possessed: it bears the possessive suffix (like English *-'s*) and it also agrees with the possessed head N, which is plural. The head noun, *pustaka* 'books', is simply marked as plural. So this example is dependent-marking.

- Example (48) is a postposition phrase from Saliba: the head P is at the end of the phrase. It's head-marking because the head P has the third person singular suffix *-na*, agreeing with the dependent NP *sagasaga* 'mouth of the river', which is the object of the postposition. This NP doesn't have any special markings to show it's a dependent. So (48) is parallel to the Tzutujil in (35) and the Welsh in (36), although both of those examples illustrate head-initial PPs, whereas in Saliba we have a head-final PP.

- The Southern Tiwa examples in (49) are full clauses, and are also head-marking: information about the verb's arguments are marked on the head verb as bound pronominals. The verb in (49a) is marked with a first person singular subject prefix *bi-*, but there is no independent subject pronoun for 'I'. The pronominal prefix *bey-* on the verb in (49b) fuses together two pieces of grammatical information: the subject is second person singular (standing for 'you') and the object is first person singular (standing for 'me'). Again, there is no separate subject or object pronoun in this example.

- The Chadian Arabic examples in (50) are dependent-marking. The adjective meaning 'tall' is a dependent of the head noun in each example, and agrees with that noun in gender.

4.3.7 Some typological distinctions between languages

Many languages fall fairly neatly into either the head-marking class or the dependent-marking class. Good examples of HEAD-MARKING languages are Abkhaz (a Northwest Caucasian language) and the native American language Navajo. In fact the indigenous language families of the Americas, and in particular North America, are nearly all head-marking: these families include Mayan (e.g. Jacaltec, Tzotzil), Athabaskan (e.g. Navajo), Iroquoian (e.g. Mohawk, Cherokee), Algonquian (e.g. Cree, Blackfoot), Siouan (e.g. Crow, Lakhota) and Salish (e.g. Squamish).

On the other hand, many languages from the Indo-European family (to which English belongs) are heavily DEPENDENT-MARKING, including German, Greek, Armenian and the Slavonic languages (e.g. Russian, Polish, Czech, Bulgarian etc.). But dependent-marking languages also predominate amongst the native Australian languages known as Pama-Nyungan (e.g. Dyirbal, Yidiny); the Northeast Caucasian languages (e.g. Chechen); and the Dravidian languages of southern India (e.g. Malayalam).

Another typological possibility is for the relationship between a head and its dependent not to be formally marked at all: this is known as ZERO-MARKING. Zero-marking—also known as neutral marking—typically occurs in languages which have very little morphology (= variation in the forms of words), such as Chinese, Vietnamese, and indeed English. In Chinese, for example, pronouns (and full noun phrases) have the same form whether they are subjects or objects:

(51) a. **Wo** changchang jian **ta**.   (Chinese)
         I   often   see   he
         'I often saw him.'
    b. **Ta** changchang jian **wo**.
        he   often   see   I
        'He often saw me.'

Example (51) shows that *wo* translates as either 'I' or 'me', and *ta* as either 'he' or 'him' (in fact, *ta* translates both 'he/him' and 'she/her'). So the dependent noun phrases aren't marked in any way in these Chinese examples. In other words, there is no CASE MARKING in Chinese: the dependents of a verb are not marked to show their relationship to that verb. And neither is there any head-marking, since the verb doesn't undergo agreement with either the object or the subject. Note that in such a language, the word order is crucial (as in English) to show who's doing what to whom. We can conclude that although many languages do have head-marking or dependent-marking, some languages have neither.

English has very little formal marking on either heads or dependents. Full NPs within a clause have no case marking. In PPs, such as *in the shower*, neither the head P *in* nor its dependent NP *the shower* is marked to show their syntactic relationship. The same is true of NPs with a modifying adjective, such as *red book*; English lacks the kind of dependent-marking seen in French, (3), Spanish, (45), and Chadian Arabic, (50), where attributive adjectives agree with the grammatical properties of the noun they modify. Nor do English nouns change in form when they have a dependent adjective, so there's no head-marking either. Largely, then, English is neutral marking.

However, English does have a small amount both of dependent-marking and head-marking. Taking DEPENDENT-MARKING first, we saw earlier that in possessive noun phrases like *Kim's house*, it's the dependent, *Kim*, which is marked (with the possessive -*'s*) rather than the head, *house*. We also saw that a subset of English pronouns display the vestiges of a CASE system, meaning a system whereby dependent NPs are marked to show their grammatical relationship to a head verb or preposition. Pronouns—but not full noun phrases such as *Kim* or *the cat*—have a different form according to whether they're a subject or an object:

(52) Kim saw the cat./The cat saw Kim.
She saw **him**./**He** saw **her**.
*Her saw he./*Him saw she.

So when the dependents of the verb are pronouns (first person or third person only), we find dependent-marking within the clause. And finally, a certain amount of dependent-marking occurs in the agreement within a noun phrase, as in *this book* versus *these books*: the determiner and the noun agree in number, though which is the dependent and which the head depends on whether or not we accept the DP hypothesis discussed in Section 4.1.8.

English could never be thought of as a HEAD-MARKING language. There is almost no head-marking on the verb: for example, the verb *see* is *saw* throughout the past tense, whatever its subject (or, indeed, object). However, limited head-marking does occur on English verbs in the form of SUBJECT/VERB AGREEMENT. The verb *be* displays some person and number distinctions, such as *I am* but *she is* and *we are*: this is head-marking because the verb changes in form to agree with its dependent subject pronouns. And in the present tense of regular verbs we find, for instance, *I like Kim* but *She likes Kim*, where the verb is head-marked (with an *-s* suffix) to agree with a third person singular subject. Note that of course, the *-s* suffix also indicates present tense, a property which has nothing to do with either head- or dependent-marking.

Languages which display a mixture of head- and dependent-marking properties are not at all unusual. One particularly common situation is that a language which is otherwise dependent-marking will have person and number affixes on the head verb marking agreement, particularly with the subject. This agreement is a head-marking pattern. German is a typical example, but many European languages (including non-Indo-European languages such as Basque) exhibit the same pattern:

(53) a. Ich **sehe** den Vogel. (German)
I.NOM see.PRES.1SG the.ACC bird
'I see the bird.'
b. Wir **sehen** den Vogel.
we.NOM see.PRES.1PL the.ACC bird
'We see the bird.'

For the most part, German is a typical dependent-marking language: dependent pronouns and full NPs are all case-marked, the subjects as NOMINATIVE and the objects as ACCUSATIVE. But (53) shows that German also has subject/verb agreement, which is head-marking, and this is much more extensive than in English. So in (53a) we have *sehe*, the first person singular form of the verb, when the subject is *ich* 'I', and in (53b) *sehen*, the first person plural form of the verb, when the subject is *wir* 'we'.

In fact, head-marking on verbs in the form of verbal agreement (particularly agreement with subjects) is highly prevalent cross-linguistically—even in languages which are otherwise systematically dependent-marking. We can regard this kind of head-marking as a property which is typical of both head- *and* dependent-marking languages, rather than seeing it just as belonging to the head-marking class of languages.

4.3.8 Summary

We have seen in this section that languages divide into various classes in terms of the head-marking versus dependent-marking typology. Some languages rarely mark the syntactic relationships between head and dependent at all; these are languages with very little morphology, such as Chinese, which can be considered a zero-marking language. Amongst languages that do mark the relationships, there are two major possibilities: the head may be marked or else the dependent may be marked. Some languages exhibit both head- and dependent-marking constructions. Finally, I noted that the occurrence of verbal agreement, a head-marking pattern, is particularly common, even in languages which are generally dependent-marking.

> **Checklist for Sections 4.2 and 4.3**
>
> If you're happy with the concepts discussed in these two sections, you're ready to read further. If you're not, I recommend revising before moving on.
>
> - Do you understand what we can call the HEAD-DIRECTIONALITY PARAMETER introduced in Section 4.2, which discusses whether a head precedes or follows its complements?
> - Does the typological distinction introduced in Section 4.3 between head-marking and dependent-marking languages make sense to you? Can you explain the four syntactic constructions used to illustrate this typology (outlined in Table 4.1)?

FURTHER READING

Information on the position of the head within a phrase (head-initial or head-final) can be obtained from Chapter 2 of Song (2001). One approach to heads and their dependents can be seen in Hudson (1984, 1990, 2007); in a different theoretical framework, see Radford (1988). Radford also provides extensive discussion of complements and adjuncts (though from a largely English perspective); see especially Chapters 1 through 5 (I recommend reading my Chapter 5 first). The question of whether or not the determiner heads the noun phrase has generated much interest over the years: two central papers are Zwicky (1985) and Hudson (1987). The seminal reading for Section 4.3 on head-marking and dependent-marking languages is Nichols (1986), though I don't recommend tackling this until you've finished this book.

EXERCISES

1. The examples in (1) through (5) all contain at least one noun phrase.

   Task: (i) Pick out all the NPs, and put them in square brackets. Make sure that you get the whole of each NP inside your brackets; i.e., the head noun and all its dependents. In some cases, an NP may have another NP embedded within it. Make sure you bracket these too. (ii) List all the subject NPs, all the direct object NPs, and all the NP predicates.

   (1) My idiot of a neighbour wastes stacks of water on his garden.

   (2) This is a planet that could engulf all the surrounding matter.

   (3) They encountered a bigger problem over the fees rise than they initially anticipated.

   (4) This is too long a story for me to tell you right now.

   (5) The only day currently available for your interview is March 12.

2. In Section 4.2 we saw that in many languages, heads have the same fixed position relative to their complements across all phrases. For instance, in many languages, a VP, PP and CP would all be consistently either head-initial or head-final: Welsh is a good example of the former, and Japanese the latter. However, not all languages display consistent ordering, either within phrases of the same category (for instance, within VPs) or across phrases of different categories (for instance, VPs might have a different order to PPs).

   Task: Study the three data sets in (1) to (3) and work out what the examples in each set show about head placement in the language illustrated. You will need to figure out for yourself the relevant phrase in each example: in most cases, it's only a phrase within the clause that is relevant to this exercise, rather than the whole clause. State what phrase type the salient phrase is in each example (e.g. VP, PP, AP, CP etc.) and say what it shows relative to the other data in the set.

   (1) Dutch
      a. Kleiner dan mij zijn niet veel mensen.
         smaller than me are not many people
         'Not many people are smaller than me.'
      b. Ik heb de toekomst gezien.
         I have the future seen
         'I have seen the future.'

(2) **Nupe** (Baker 2001; Baker and Kandybowicz 2003)
    a. Mi kpaye gànán Musa lá èbi.
       I think that Musa took knife
       'I think that Musa took the knife.'
    b. Èbi Musa lá o.
       knife Musa took COMPLEMENTIZER
       'It's a knife that Musa took.'
    c. Musa è lá èbi.
       Musa PRES take knife
       'Musa is taking the knife.'
    d. Musa á dukun si.
       Musa PERF pot buy
       'Musa has bought a pot.'
    e. Musa á etsu ya èwò.
       Musa PERF chief give garment
       'Musa has given the chief a shirt.'
    f. Musa má etsu èwò ya.
       Musa MODAL.AUX chief garment give
       'Musa knows how to give the chief a garment.'

(3) **German**
    a. Wir fahren den Fluss entlang.
       we travel.PRES.1PL the river along
       'We're driving along the river.'
    b. Wir fahren mit der Bahn.
       we travel.PRES.1PL with the train
       'We're going by train.'
    c. Er ist auf seine Arbeit stolz.
       he is on his work proud
       'He is proud of his work.'
    d. Er ist stolz auf seine Arbeit.
       he is proud on his work
       'He is proud of his work.'

3. This exercise illustrates the possessive construction in a range of different languages.

   Task: (i) Decide whether each example in (1) to (7) is HEAD-MARKING or DEPENDENT-MARKING, or displays both kinds of marking, or else is ZERO-MARKING (displaying no morphological indication of the relationship between the head and dependent), and give concise evidence for your conclusions. (ii) Work out why (4a) and (4b) might differ from each other.

Hint:
The Bantu language Makhuwa shown in (6) has extensive gender marking, with each noun belonging to a specific noun class; see Section 2.3.3.2 for a reminder. The noun class of each noun is shown in the gloss with a number on the noun itself; technically, Mawhuwa has up to 18 noun classes, though not all of these are distinct from each other in the modern language. If it helps, you can consider the two genders shown in (6) as parallel to the use of masculine and feminine gender in, say, French or Italian.

(1) beje   halgan-in   (Evenki)
    man   leg-3SG.POSS
    'the man's leg'

(2) jek   Petritesko   čavo   (Romani)
    a   Peter.GENITIVE   son
    'a son of Peter's'

(3) dee-n   aaxča   (Chechen)
    father-GENITIVE   money
    'father's money'

(4) a. xiri-con   Xijam   (Wari')
       house-3M.SG   (male name)
       'Xijam's house'
    b. pije'-nequem   Hatem
       child- POSS.3F.SG   (female name)
       'Hatem's child'

(5) a. le   rakles-k-i   dej   (Romani)
       the.M   boy-GEN-F   mother
       'the boy's mother'
    b. le   rakles-k-e   phrala
       the.M   boy-GEN-PL   brothers
       'the boy's brothers'

(6) a. ntsíná   n-áka   (Makhuwa)
       5.name   5-POSS.1SG
       'my name'
    b. ehópá   ts-áka
       10.fish   10-POSS.1SG
       'my fish'

(7) az   ember   ház-a   (Hungarian)
    the   man   house-3SG
    'the man's house'

The data in this exercise are from the following sources, example by example: Nedjalkov 1997; Matras 2002; Nichols 1986; Everett and Kern 1997; Matras 2002; van der Wal 2009; Nichols 1986.

4. The data in this exercise are from a Chadic language called Hdi, spoken in Cameroon, and are taken (slightly adapted) from Frajzyngier (2002). Examine all the data in (1) through (10).

   Task: (i) Work out the function of the morpheme *tá*, which I have left unglossed in these examples. Where exactly does it occur? (ii) Hdi and English display some interesting differences as regards the valency of verbs. What exactly are these differences, and which data items display them?

   (1) ngatsa-f-ngats-i   tá   lfid-a   lgut
       have-up-have-1SG   TÁ   new-GEN   cloth
       'I have new clothes.'

   (2) tsgha-da-f   xaxən   tá   sani
       put.up-away-up   they   TÁ   one
       'They sent up one (bag).'

   (3) ghwaghwa-ghwaghwa kri
       bark-bark   dog
       'A dog barked.'

   (4) si   midu-u
       PAST   inside-1DUAL
       'The two of us were inside.'

   (5) skwa-skw-i   tá   plis   nda   ma   na   hla
       buy-buy-1SG   TÁ   horse   and   female   DEM   cow
       'I bought a horse and a cow.'

   (6) nda   ngh-i   tá   pta
       STATIVE   see-1SG   TÁ   mat
       'I saw the mat.'

   (7) ta   skalu-lu   tá   skalu   girvidik
       IMPF   dance-SU   TÁ   dance(N)   night
       'They danced all night.'

   (8) nda   ngh-i   tà   pta
       STATIVE   see-1SG   on   mat
       'I saw (it) on the mat.'

(9) vra-k-vr-i   dzagha   ka   mbaz-i   tá   mbaza
    return-in-return-1SG home   then   wash-1SG TÁ   wash(N)
    'I returned home and washed.'

(10) ta   xanay   tsa   mndu   ya   tá   xani   dagala
     IMPF   sleep(V)   the   man   DEM   TÁ   sleep(N)   large
     'That man sleeps a lot.'

5. Before tackling this exercise, you should revise Section 3.3.3. In (1) through (4) you see some serial verbs in Yimas, a Papuan language of New Guinea. The data are all from Foley (1991), with some small adaptations.

Hints:
- The serial construction itself is a single grammatical word that comprises a number of distinct morphemes; in other words, no part of it can be split off and stand as an independent word. Each of the examples (1) to (3) is a single clause which contains only *one* grammatical word, which includes pronominal affixes and markers for tense and other categories. Make sure you understand this before moving on. In (4) there are also two independent words (for 'water' and 'canoe'), as well as the serial verb part. Again, this is a single clause.

- There are some elements in the glosses that need a few words of explanation. The gloss 'A' is for the 'agent' (here, the subject) of a transitive verb. We will see more about this term in Chapter 6. For instance, in (1) to (3) there is a verbal prefix *n-*, glossed as 3SG.A, meaning a third person singular agent; this gives us the subject 'he' in the translations. And in (4), there is a prefix *ka-*, glossed as 1SG.A, meaning a first person singular agent; this gives us the subject 'I' in the translations. Both of these markers are, of course, pronominal affixes. The gloss CONT (for continuous) gives an ongoing event, just like *walking* and *sitting* do in the English translations.

- Verb serialization can be formed in two different ways in Yimas, giving rise to two different interpretations. The two serial verbs in Yimas can be simply juxtaposed, i.e. placed next to each other, as is the case in (1), (2) and (3). This implies that the two events are simultaneous, or are very close (in time and space). Alternatively, the serial verbs can be connected by a morphological marker, most commonly *-mpi*, marked SEQ for 'sequential'; this construction is used for events that occur one after the other, so are sequential, but where one event did not cause the other. An example is (4). The serial verb construction always forms a single clause, despite having two verbs.

Tasks: (i) First, examine the serial verb constructions in (1) to (4) and decide which typical properties of verb serialization can be detected in these examples. Be as specific as possible in your answer.

(1) impa-n-yakal-kulanaŋ-kanta-k
3DUAL.OBJ-3SG.A-CONT-walk-follow-TENSE
'He was walking following those two.'

(2) pu-n-yakal-caŋ-tantaw-malak-ntut
3PL.OBJ-3SG.A-CONT-with-sit-talk-REMOTE.PAST
'He was sitting down conversing with them.'

(3) ura-n-irm-wampaki-pra-k
fire.OBJ-3SG.A-stand-throw-toward-TENSE
'He stood throwing fire toward (them).'

(4) arm-n   kay   i-ka-ak-mpi-wul
water-in canoe   SG.OBJ-1SG.A-push-SEQ-put.down
'I pushed the canoe down into the water.'

(ii) The serial verb examples in (5) and (6) are variants of (4), but both are ungrammatical; these are not possible constructions. Why not? Which principle of verb serialization do these violate? **NB** There is a certain freedom of word order in Yimas, meaning that independent words such as *kay*, 'canoe', can be found in various positions in the clause. But *in itself*, this is not at all relevant to your answer.

(5) *kay   i-ka-ak-mpi   arm-n   wul
canoe   SG.OBJ-1SG.A-push-SEQ water-in   put.down
('I pushed the canoe down into the water.')

(6) *i-ka-ak-mpi   kay   wul   arm-n
SG.OBJ-1SG.A-push-SEQ   canoe   put.down   water-in
('I pushed the canoe down into the water.')

The examples in (7) to (9), however, are *not* instances of verb serialization, but instead are examples of a 'dependent verb' construction. While the serial construction is a single clause, as noted in the *Hints*, the dependent verb construction comprises two *separate* clauses, as the English translations reflect. Instead of having a meaning that refers to a single complex event, pushing the canoe into the water, the dependent verb construction 'expresses two separate events, one followed in time by another' (Foley 1991: 326).

(7) kay   ak-mpi   i-ka-wul   arm-n
canoe   push-SEQ   SG.OBJ-1SG.A-put.down   water-in
'I pushed the canoe and put it into the water.'

(iii) The examples in (8) and (9) are variants of (7), again showing freedom of word order; both are fully grammatical. How, *specifically*, do these three examples differ from the serial verb constructions in (5) and (6)?

(8) kay   ak-mpi   arm-n   i-ka-wul
    canoe   push-SEQ   water-in SG.OBJ-1SG.A-put.down
    'I pushed the canoe and put it into the water.'

(9) ak-mpi   kay   i-ka-wul   arm-n
    push-SEQ canoe SG.OBJ-1SG.A-put.down   water-in
    'I pushed the canoe and put it into the water.'

(iv) In (10) we have another variant of the dependent verb construction. How does this differ from the three examples given so far? How does the fact that the dependent verb construction comprises two separate clauses predict this behaviour?

(10) kay   i-ka-ak-mpi   arm-n   i-ka-wul
     canoe   SG.OBJ-1SG.A-push-SEQ water-in SG.OBJ-1SG.A-put.down
     'I pushed the canoe and put it into the water.'

6. This exercise examines a construction known as 'quantifier float' in a variety of Irish English known as West Ulster English (data and discussion taken from McCloskey 2000). Standard English allows both of the constructions in (1), where (a) is said to have a floating quantifier (*all* or *both*), meaning that it's floating free of the phrase (*they*) that it modifies directly in (b):

(1) a. They have all/both gone to bed.
    b. They all/both have gone to bed.

Many varieties of English also allow questions of the kind in (2). (If you're not a speaker of such a variety, note that *what all*, *who all* etc. require that you answer with a list, and moreover, a full list; if you met Tom, Jack and Nicky in Derry, answering just *Tom* would not be what was required.)

(2) a. What all did you get for Christmas?
    b. Who all did you meet when you were in Derry?
    c. Where all did they go for their holidays?

What distinguishes West Ulster English is that it also allows questions of the kind in (3), which have quantifier float. The quantifier is said to be 'stranded' (left behind; not attached to the *wh*-word) in these examples:

(3) a. What did you get all for Christmas?
    b. Who did you meet all when you were in Derry?
    c. Where did they go all for their holidays?

Below are some further examples from the same dialect.

Task: (i) From (3), (4) and (5), formulate an initial hypothesis about where exactly (in syntactic terms) the floating quantifier is 'stranded' in this dialect;

note that (5b) and (5c) are ungrammatical, and this must be accounted for in your hypothesis too.

(4)   a.   What did you give all to the kids?
       b.   What did you put all in the drawer?
       c.   Who did you meet all up the town?

(5)   a.   What did she buy all in Derry at the weekend?
       b.   *What did she buy in Derry at the weekend all?
       c.   *What did she buy in Derry all at the weekend?

(ii) Next, consider the data in (6): are these examples consistent with your hypothesis? If so, well done; if not, please formulate a new hypothesis that correctly predicts the grammaticality of (6).

(6)   a.   Tell me what you got all for Christmas.
       b.   Tell me what you've been reading all.
       c.   I don't remember what I said all.

(iii) Next, consider the data in (7), which are ungrammatical; do these affect your hypothesis? If the answer is not at all, well done. If these data are not consistent with your hypothesis, can you formulate a new hypothesis that *is* consistent with all the data seen so far?

(7)   a.   *Who did you talk all to?
       b.   *What were you laughing all at?

(iv) Though the data in (7) are completely impossible, those in (8) are, according to McCloskey, only 'slightly degraded'; in other words, a linguistic analysis would have to account for them as possible data. In what way would these require your hypothesis to be amended?

(8)   a.   ?Who did you talk to all (at the party)?
       b.   ?Who was he laughing at all?

5

How do we identify constituents?

章节导读

任何句子都不是词汇的任意堆砌，而是具有一定的结构。一个句子由不同的成分构成，通过对成分的识别以及对成分结构的分析，我们可以深入地了解句子的结构，以及不同的句子结构对意义所产生的影响。我们有多种句法检验方法来确定一组单词是否是构成句子的成分。第一种方法是句子片段检验，如果一组单词能够用来回答一个简短的问题，那么它就是一个成分。句子片段检验还可以帮助我们认识成分的内部结构，帮助我们发现两个相似的成分实际上具有不同的结构。第二种方法是反问句检验，可以通过反问句而得到肯定的部分可以被认为是一个成分。第三种方法是分裂句检验，能够被用在分裂句的被强调位置的一组单词一定是句子的成分。第四种方法是移位检验，如果一组单词能够从它原来的位置移走，那么它就是句子的成分。

对于成分结构的分析，除了采用方括号之外，目前更为流行的做法是采用树形图的方式，它比较直观地表现出成分之间以及成分内部的层级结构。树形图一般由一系列加标记的节点构成，节点与节点之间由分叉相连。位于树形图上面位置的节点统制下面的节点，一个节点直接统制与其直接相连的下面的节点。两者之间构成母节点和子节点的关系，其中直接统制其他节点的节点为母节点，受其直接统制的节点为子节点。

在分析动词短语的结构或者绘制动词短语的树形图时，要注意区分短语动词和带介词的动词的区别，两者看起来非常相似，但是其内部结构差别很大。对于短语动词来说，动词本身和介词要视为一个整体，一般划分为 V+NP 的结构；而对于带介词的动词来说，动词和介词要分开，一般划分为 V+PP 的结构。

不同的语言所拥有的成分类型也是不一样的，例如，动词短语成分看起来在各种语言中是普遍存在的。但是有的语言学家发现巴斯克语和匈牙利语中就没有完整的动词短语这一成分。各种不同的语言成分具有不同的层级，有的是短语层次的，还有的是词的层次。另外，在两者之间还有一个中间层次，它比一个完整的短语要小，而且不能通过各种方法进行成分检验。现代句法学用阶标来表示这些不同的层次，词的层次不做任何标记，是零阶标，中间层次使用一个标记，是单阶标，短语层面使用两个标记，是双阶标。阶标这一概念的提出使得生成语法对于不同语言中成分结构的描述与分析具有了更强的普遍性。

This chapter returns to the theme of sentence structure, introduced in Chapter 1. We saw in Chapter 4 that phrases consist of a head word and its complements, plus any optional modifiers to that head. In this chapter we discover how to identify phrases, and how to distinguish a phrase from a random string of words. The phrases which make up sentences are known as the CONSTITUENTS of a sentence. We will see how constituents are represented in tree diagrams, and start to investigate how languages differ in terms of constituency.

5.1 DISCOVERING THE STRUCTURE OF SENTENCES

Section 5.1.1 demonstrates the existence of syntactic structure, in particular by looking at ambiguous phrases and sentences. Section 5.1.2 introduces three syntactic tests for constituent structure, and Section 5.1.3 examines the ways in which linguists formally represent constituent structure.

5.1.1 Evidence of structure in sentences

One way to show that syntactic structure actually exists is to examine sentences which are syntactically ambiguous; that is, sentences which have more than one meaning. Not all ambiguity is syntactic: some is lexical, as in *Lee went down to the bank*; does this mean 'the river bank' or 'the place where money is kept'? In other cases, though, ambiguity arises because we can't tell which words group together to form a phrase. This is syntactic ambiguity. For instance, a sentence like the following appeared in a British national newspaper, causing an unforeseen breakdown in communication.

(1) Black cab drivers went on strike yesterday.

Readers wrote in to say, what did it matter what colour the drivers were? But, of course, the newspaper actually intended *black* to modify *cab*, not to modify *cab drivers*. The two different meanings reflect the fact that the phrase *black cab drivers* has two different STRUCTURES. We can indicate this by using brackets to show which words group together; different bracketings indicate different phrase structures. Example (2) illustrates these different structures: the outraged readers had interpreted the sentence as in (2a), and the newspaper had intended (2b). (For readers unfamiliar with British culture, a 'black cab' is a particular kind of black taxi found in major cities.)

(2)   a.   [Black [**cab drivers**]] went on strike.
        b.   [[**Black cab**] drivers] went on strike.

In both (2a) and (2b), the whole phrase *black cab drivers* is a constituent of the sentence, hence is in brackets, but the differing internal brackets show that the words inside that phrase group together in different ways, depending on what *black cab drivers* actually means. In (2a), *cab drivers* forms a constituent, whereas in (2b), *black cab* forms a constituent. A **constituent** is a set of words that forms a phrase in a sentence. If you say aloud the distinct phrases in (2), you'll probably find that they each have a different intonation pattern; sometimes we show by our intonation which words group together to form constituents.

> Constituent,成分,指一个较大语言单位的构成成分。

Occasionally we can discover which words form constituents by looking at inflections, as in the case of English possessive *-'s* (see Section 1.3.3). The affix *-'s* attaches to the end of a phrasal constituent (an NP) giving *Lee's*, *the boy's* and so on, so we can use *-'s* to discover whether or not a string of words is an NP (and therefore a constituent). This gives some results that might initially seem surprising, as in (3):

(3)   I'll be back in [**an hour or so**]'s time.

Here, *an hour or so* must be a constituent, an NP, since *-'s* can attach to the whole phrase.

The *-'s* inflection can itself be the cause of syntactic ambiguity, because we can't always tell what constituent it's attached to:

(4)   The boy and the girl's uncle stayed to dinner.

This, of course, is ambiguous as to whether just one person stayed, or two, as the variants with tag questions make clear:

(5)   a.   The boy and the girl's uncle stayed to dinner, didn't he?
        b.   The boy and the girl's uncle stayed to dinner, didn't they?

> Constituent structure,成分结构,又称短语结构(phrase structure),指短语、小句或者句子中语言单位(即成分)的排列,用以说明它们之间的关系。

So in (4) there are two different meanings—or READINGS, to use the technical term—and, as we will see, each of these readings corresponds to a particular CONSTITUENT STRUCTURE, that is, a particular grouping of words.

The ambiguity in (4) lies in the phrase *the boy and the girl's uncle*. This whole string of words is a constituent of the sentence in both readings, but its internal structure is different in each case. We can't tell if *-'s* is suffixed to an NP *the boy and* *the girl*, in which case the uncle is related to both of them, or if *-'s* is just suffixed to an NP *the girl*, in which case the uncle is related to her, but not to the boy. Both options are possible, hence the ambiguity. The structures of the two alternatives are shown in (6), where the brackets mark out the two possible constituents that *-'s* can attach to:

(6) a.   [**The boy and the girl**]'s uncle stayed.   (one person)
     b.   The boy and [**the girl**]'s uncle stayed.   (two people)

Only in (6a) does the sequence *the boy and the girl* form a whole phrase, a constituent. This tells us that a sequence of words which forms a constituent in one environment need not necessarily do so in another environment. There is absolutely *no* rule of 'once a constituent, always a constituent'. To underline this point, compare the (a) and (b) sentences here:

(7) a.   The students wondered how cheap textbooks could be obtained.
     b.   The students wondered how cheap textbooks could be.
     a.'   The students wondered how [**cheap textbooks**] could be obtained.
     b.'   The students wondered [**how cheap**] textbooks could be.

In (7a), there's a constituent *cheap textbooks*, as we can tell by the fact that we can refer to this phrase by the single word *they*: *The students wondered how **they** could be obtained*. The relevant structure is shown in (7a'). But *cheap textbooks* isn't a constituent in (7b). Instead, *how cheap* forms a phrase in (7b), as you can see from (7b'). Here, *textbooks* is a separate constituent, which can again be replaced by *they*: *The students wondered how cheap **they** could be*. The examples in (7) show that we can't look at a string of words out of context and decide whether or not they form a constituent. We can only find this out when the string of words appears in a sentence, and when we can manipulate the sentence in various ways to discover its constituent structure. This requires a set of tests for constituency, like the pronoun test we used here: a pronoun such as *they* replaces a whole NP constituent.

5.1.2 Some syntactic tests for constituent structure

We have used the possessive *-'s* suffix—which only attaches to NP constituents—as a morphological test for constituency. But to discover all the constituents of a sentence (and not just NPs) we also need syntactic tests. One syntactic test is seen at the end of the previous section: a constituent can often be replaced by a pronoun, but a random string of words cannot. We now go on to examine more syntactic tests.

5.1.2.1 *The sentence fragment test*

The first test in this section utilizes shortened answers to questions. If I ask *Who went on strike?*, a reasonable answer is *Black cab drivers*. Answers like these which

Sentence fragment, 句子片段，指句子的某个组成部分。

are not full sentences are called SENTENCE FRAGMENTS, and they provide syntactic evidence about which words group together to form a constituent. A string of words that can be a sentence fragment must be a constituent. So here, *black cab drivers* is confirmed as a constituent of (1). Of course, it is still ambiguous, as its internal structure is not revealed. And if I ask *Who stayed to dinner?*, the answer is *The boy and the girl's uncle*, so this whole phrase is a constituent of (4), whichever internal structure it has. Both of these particular sentence fragments remain ambiguous, because there is additional constituent structure inside each phrase which differs, depending on the interpretation.

However, the sentence fragment test can often be used to discover more about internal structure. On hearing (4), someone might try to resolve the confusion by asking *But **whose uncle** stayed to dinner?*. A typical answer would be either (8a) or (8b), depending on which reading of the sentence you have in mind:

(8)   a.   The boy and the girl's.   (one person stays to dinner)
       b.   The girl's.   (two people stay to dinner)

In (8), the sentence fragment test confirms what we already discovered from (6): the whole sequence *the boy and the girl* is a constituent in the (a) reading, but in the (b) reading, *the girl* doesn't form a constituent with *the boy*. The fact that *-'s* can be attached to either possible sequence in (8) confirms that they are both able to be used as constituents.

We can also use the sentence fragment test for constituent structure to show that in (6b), the sequence *the girl's uncle* is a constituent.[1] Keep in mind the reading where two people stay to dinner. If you didn't hear the speaker too clearly, you might ask *The boy and **who** stayed to dinner?*. The answer is the sentence fragment *The girl's uncle*: this must therefore be a constituent. So we can bracket this phrase too, adding more information about the structure of (6b):

(9)   The boy and [[**the girl**]'s **uncle**] stayed.   (two people)

As (9) shows, constituents are in turn built up of smaller constituents. Thus we confirm what we already saw in Chapter 4, namely that phrases contain smaller phrases, with each phrase having its own head and dependent elements. In (9), *uncle* is the head of the phrase *the girl's uncle*, since this phrase is 'about' the uncle.

The sentence fragment test is one of the formal tests for constituent structure. Using such tests, we can discover whether two apparently similar sentences in fact have different structures. Consider the examples in (10) and (11): both contain words of exactly the same syntactic categories or word classes, and in just the same order, as (12) shows (to remind you, D is the category 'determiner').

(10)   Kim   wrote   that   book   with   the   blue   cover.

(11)   Kim   bought   that   book   with   her   first   wages.

(12)   N   V   D   N   P   D   A   N

We might assume, then, that these sentences share a syntactic structure. However, native speakers feel instinctively that (10) and (11) are different; the sentences tend, for instance, to have a different intonation pattern. In (10), *with the blue cover* is a phrase (a PP) modifying the head noun *book*—*a book with a blue cover* is a type of book. So this PP belongs with *that book*, forming a constituent with it in (10). But in (11), the PP *with her first wages* tells us how she bought the book, and not anything about the book itself. So that PP modifies *bought*—it is an adjunct to *bought*. Crucially, the PP in (11) doesn't modify the noun *book*, and so doesn't form a constituent with it.

The sentence fragment test for constituent structure supports these intuitive feelings. In each case, when we ask a question, we get different sentence fragment answers:

(13) What did she write? [**That book with the blue cover**]

(14) What did she buy?   a.   [**That book**]
      What did she buy?   b.   *That book with her first wages.

Example (13) shows that the entire sequence *that book with the blue cover* is a constituent of (10): it can be a sentence fragment. Example (14a) confirms that the sequence *that book* is a constituent of (11). And crucially, (14b) shows that the sequence *that book with her first wages* is not a constituent of (11): it can't be a sentence fragment (remember that the asterisk indicates an ungrammatical example). Contrasting grammatical and ungrammatical examples, as we have done here, is essential: you should use the ungrammatical examples to show that some sequence of words is *not* a constituent of the sentence you are working on.

- Please remember from now on that in the sentence fragment test, the question you ask should always be a *grammatical* one: the test is the answer itself.
- If a string of words from the original sentence can form a grammatical sentence fragment, it is likely that this sequence is a constituent of the original sentence.
- If the string of words is not grammatical as a sentence fragment, it most likely is not a constituent of the original sentence, though you need additional tests to confirm this.
- Square brackets are used to show where a constituent begins and ends. Please do not put brackets round a phrase *unless* it is a constituent. You may find it useful to use a wavy underline for a string of words which is *not* a constituent, as I have done in (14b).

此处概括了句子片段检验方法的几个核心要点，这对于句法分析非常重要。

5.1.2.2 *The echo question test*

ECHO QUESTIONS are our next test for constituent structure. These questions are used in English when the speaker doesn't hear part of the sentence, or else is rather incredulous: e.g. *You saw* **what**?. We use a *wh*-word (*what, which, who, when, why*

Echo question, 反问句，指要求对前面的话语的某一部分加以肯定

and so on, and including *how*) or a *wh*-phrase (*You saw **which film**?*) to replace just the part of the sentence that we want repeated, otherwise 'echoing' the speaker's words. The *wh*-word or phrase doesn't replace a random string of words, but can only stand for a constituent of the sentence:

(15) *Kim wrote **what** with the blue cover?

(16) Kim bought **what** with her first wages?

The grammatical echo question in (16) is fine because *what* replaces *that book*, which is a constituent of (11). But (15) is ungrammatical because *that book* is only part of a larger constituent *that book with the blue cover* in (10); crucially, *that book* itself is *not* a constituent in this case, and so can't be replaced by a *wh*-word. (We can, however, echo just a head noun on its own: for example, in (10) we can replace *book* with a *wh*-word, giving *Kim lost that **what** with the blue cover?*. The reason for this is that single words are also constituents.)

In fact, we've already used this test earlier: the echo question, *The boy and **who** stayed to dinner?*, only works when *who* replaces a constituent, such as *the girl's uncle*. So it's the question we'd ask if we were sure that two people stayed to dinner, and that one was the boy, but we weren't sure who the other person was. To summarize: in the echo question test, a *wh*-word or phrase can replace a constituent; if the resulting question is ungrammatical, though, the string of words which you've replaced is probably not a constituent.

5.1.2.3 *The cleft test*

A further test for constituent structure confirms our findings: the two sentences in (10) and (11) have different structures. In the CLEFT construction illustrated in (17), the string of words in the 'focus' position must be a constituent. So in (17), we can focus on the whole sequence *that book with the blue cover*, showing that this is a constituent:

(17) It was [**that book with the blue cover**] that Kim wrote.

But in (18), the sequence *that book with her first wages* is not a constituent, and so can't occur in the focus position of a cleft sentence. This confirms what we saw in (14b):

(18) *It was **that book with her first wages** that Kim bought.

Remember that we only bracket a string of words which is a constituent, so we bracket *that book with the blue cover* in (17), but not *that book with her first wages* in (18).

Our original sentence in (11) does, however, contain other word sequences which will fit into the focus position of a cleft sentence. For instance, we can focus on either *that book* or *with her first wages*, showing that both these phrases are separate constituents of (11):

(19) a. It was [**that book**] that Kim bought with her first wages.
b. It was [**with her first wages**] that Kim bought that book.

Putting the information from all three tests together, we can show what we've learnt so far about the constituent structure of (10) and (11) by using brackets, as follows:

(20) [Kim wrote [that book with the blue cover]].

(21) [Kim bought [that book] [with her first wages]].

The whole sentence is also in brackets in each case, since both examples occur as independent sentences, and are therefore constituents—if sentence fragments are constituents, then it's not surprising that whole sentences are also constituents. Although there are other constituents in each sentence, the brackets in (20) and (21) show as much information as we have up to now.

Of course, for our constituency tests to have real significance, we must be able to apply them to languages other than English, although not all tests apply equally well in all languages, because certain syntactic constructions may be absent. Cleft constructions occur widely. In the Irish examples below, (22a) shows the basic word order, and (22b) is a cleft construction with the noun phrase *an fear* 'the man' in the focus position:

(22) a. Bhí an fear ag péinteáil cathaoir. (Irish)
was the man PROG paint.INFIN chair
'The man was painting a chair.'
b. Is é [**an fear**] a bhí ag péinteáil cathaoir.
is it the man who was PROG paint.INFIN chair
'It's *the man* who was painting a chair.'

Similarly in the next examples, from Lekeitio Basque, (23a) has basic word order, whilst (23b) is a cleft construction, with focus on the fronted noun phrase *orreri mutillari* 'that boy' (the DATIVE case marking on this NP does the work of the preposition 'to' in English, showing the boy as the recipient):

(23) a. Premižúa orreri mutillari emon-dótze. (Basque)
prize that.DATIVE boy.DATIVE give-AUX
'They have given the prize to that boy.'
b. [**Orreri mutillari**] da premižúa emón dotzé-na.
that.DATIVE boy.DATIVE is prize give AUX-that
'It's to *that boy* that they have given the prize.'

From (23b), we can tell that *orreri mutillari* is a constituent of (23a).

5.1.2.4 *Displacement and dependency*

The constructions in Section 5.1.2 all illustrate an important property of human language: the ability to DISPLACE or MOVE a phrase from its basic position. The hallmark of such displacement is that a phrase is understood semantically as if it were in one position in the clause, but occurs physically (syntactically and audibly) in a different position in the clause. We can illustrate using the cleft examples seen earlier:

(24)　It was [$_{NP}$ that book] that Kim bought ___ with her first wages.

(25)　It was [$_{PP}$ with her first wages] that Kim bought that book ___ .

The gap in these examples shows the 'original' position of the displaced phrases. In other words, when you hear an example like (24), you understand it as if the displaced object NP *that book* were still in its normal linear position, following the verb *bought*. Importantly, the verb *bought* only has one direct object, and that syntactic fact does not change just because the object is displaced from its basic position in the usual constituent order. The same applies to (25): the displaced PP is understood as if it were in the typical adjunct position, following the direct object.

The displacement of a phrase sets up a DEPENDENCY between the displaced phrase and the 'empty' position associated with it: the displaced element provides the physical words we need, but its basic position specifies its syntactic role, for instance the role of 'direct object' in (24). The displaced element and the associated gap are of course one and the same entity—moving the object *that book* does not alter the argument structure of the verb *bought*.

It is likely that all languages have instances of displacement of one kind or another. We will see other examples as we go along.

5.1.2.5 *Summary*

Each of the tests for constituent structure in Section 5.1.2 works by harnessing the intuitions of native speakers of a language. The fact that speakers share GRAMMATICALITY JUDGEMENTS—intuitions about which sentences are possible and which aren't—shows that we have an unconscious knowledge of the word groupings in a sentence. The tests for constituent structure are just particular syntactic environments which can only be filled by constituents. Whenever we put a string of words that isn't a constituent into one of these environments, the result sounds impossible to native speakers. This UNGRAMMATICALITY (the technical term for such results) tells us that in such cases, the string of words isn't a constituent.

So far in Section 5.1, I have introduced these syntactic tests for constituent structure: (1) replacement by a pronoun; (2) sentence fragments; (3) echo questions; and (4) cleft sentences. The information about constituent structure which results from our tests can be represented by using square brackets to mark off the constituents, as I have done so far, or alternatively by using tree diagrams. We turn next to this topic.

Grammaticality judgement, 合乎语法性判断。合乎语法性是指一个句子与语法所定义的一系列规则相一致。在实际的操作中，要判断一个句子是否合乎语法可能会存在困难，因为对于同一个句子，操本族语的人有可能会做出不同的判断。

5.1.3 Introduction to constituent structure trees

In (26) and (27) I represent the structure of our two sentences in (10) and (11) by using **TREE DIAGRAMS**. As you can see, these are upside-down trees, with the root at the top, and branches descending from that root. The root of the tree is labelled 'S' for 'Sentence', and the clause is divided into two main branches, the subject and the predicate, as discussed in Section 3.1.1.

Tree diagram, 树形图, 是目前普遍采用的一种表示句子结构的方法。与自然界的树相比, 树形图一般是倒置的, 即根部在上面, 并由此生出一系列的分支。

(26)
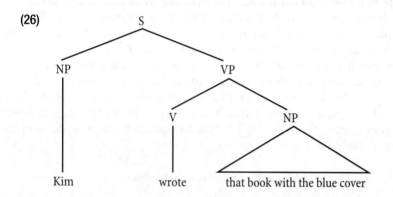

(27)
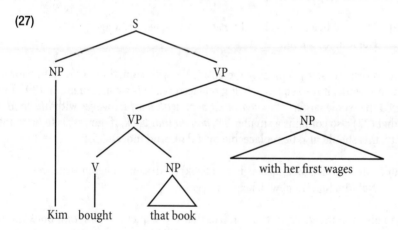

Let's now go through these tree structures. In each case there is a major split between the subject NP on the left branch and the predicate VP on the right branch. Both trees have a subject, *Kim*. The difference in structure in our two sentences lies within the VP, as we discovered from our tests on constituent structure, and this difference is reflected in the form of the two trees.

In (26), I have suggested that the verb and its object together form a verb phrase (VP). The VP has two branches, V (for verb) containing just the transitive verb *wrote*, and NP, the noun phrase which is the complement of *wrote*. This sequence, *that book with the blue cover*, is shown as a triangle, which indicates that the whole sequence forms a constituent. That doesn't mean that there is no more internal structure within that NP, just that so far, this is all we've discovered.

In (27), we again have a VP consisting of the transitive verb *bought* plus its complement, the object NP *that book*. However, we also have an ADJUNCT here, namely the PP *with her first wages*. Recall from Chapter 4 that an adjunct is a constituent which is syntactically optional, in other words not required in order to make the sentence grammatical: adjuncts are not arguments of the verb, and are therefore non-essential constituents. The structure which I've suggested for (27) reflects this by showing that if we add an adjunct to the VP, we don't get a different *kind* of phrase—it's still a verb phrase, but just one that contains more information. The structure is RECURSIVE, in that it has a VP within a larger VP.

In representing VPs in each tree, I have actually shown more structure than I gave in the brackets for each sentence in (20) and (21)—those examples did not include a set of brackets round the verb and its dependents. So we ought to check that the VP really is a constituent in each case. We can do this by using a different test for constituency: the *do so* test. A VP can be replaced by *do so* (or *did so* in the past tense) as follows:

(28) I thought that Mel [VP wrote that book with the blue cover].
No! Kim [VP *did so*].

(29) I thought that Mel [VP bought that book with her first wages]
No! Kim [VP *did so*].

Do so test, do so 检验。这种方法可以用于检验一个动词和它的依附成分是否是构成句子的成分。

The ***do so* test** works by replacing the entire VP with something that stands for it, and it only works if the sequence being replaced really is a constituent. In (29), I've replaced the whole larger VP *bought that book with her first wages* with *did so*. But note that (27) also contains a smaller VP, *bought that book*. If our test is to have any validity, this should also be replaceable by *did so*. And indeed it is:

(30) I thought that Mel [VP bought that book] (with some of her inheritance).
No! Kim [VP *did so*] with her first wages.

We can also use the *do so* test to confirm that the sequence *wrote that book* on its own does not form a VP constituent in (26). Once again, the contrast in grammaticality demonstrates the difference in structure between the two examples:

(31) I thought that Mel wrote that book with the blue cover.
No! *Kim **did so** with the blue cover.

The reason that *wrote that book* does not act like a VP here is because the sequence *that book* is itself not a constituent in this case, but rather is merely part of the larger NP *that book with the blue cover*, as we saw in Section 5.1.2. This whole NP is the object of *wrote*, so we can't take part of it and leave the rest behind. The underlining should help you see that *wrote that book* is not a constituent here:

(32)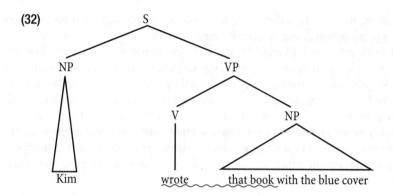

Let's look at two more examples which again contain words from exactly the same word classes and in the same order, but which again have different structures:

(33) My   brother   wrote   down   his   address.

(34) My   brother   applied   for   this   job.

(35) D   N   V   P   D   N

Tests for constituency show that (33) and (34) don't share the same syntactic structure, as you now have the chance to discover for yourself.

If we want to know whether, say, the sequences *down his address/for this job* form a constituent in each case, we can try putting each sequence into the focus position of a cleft construction. Please do this before reading further, and decide what the results show. Your cleft sentences will begin '*It was …*'. Bracket the constituent that you discover.

The cleft constructions should be:

(36) *It was **down his address** that my brother wrote.

(37) It was [**for this job**] that my brother applied.

Only (37) is grammatical: example (36) is impossible, which indicates that *down his address* is not a constituent in (33), and therefore it can't be placed in the focus position of a cleft sentence. In (34), *for this job* is a constituent, shown by the fact that it can be focussed in a cleft sentence. Once again, I remind you that we only bracket a string of words that is a constituent.

The tree diagrams in (38) and (39) show the structures of the two examples. The tree in (38) shows *wrote down* as a phrase, something I return to in Section 5.3.1. Note that in (38), *down* is not shown as part of the same phrase as *his address*, because we have proved by using the cleft construction that *down* doesn't form a constituent with *his address*. In (39), though, the preposition *for* forms a constituent with *this job*, as we have shown by the cleft test in (37). I should emphasize that a tree diagram simply illustrates the existence of constituents which we have already discovered by using our tests for constituent structure, and in turn, these harness our intuitions as native speakers of English.

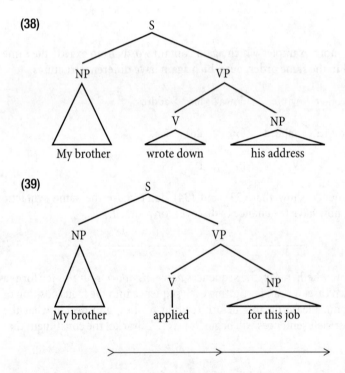

The tree in (38) also shows the sequence *his address* as a constituent, although we haven't yet seen any evidence for this claim. Basing your answer on the tests for constituency that we've used so far, what evidence is there that *his address* in (38) is indeed a constituent?

First, we can use the echo question test, where the *wh*-word *what* replaces the string *his address*, as in *He wrote down **what**?*. Second, the question *What did he write* *down?* can also be answered with *His address* as a sentence fragment, confirming that it's a constituent. And finally, we can use the cleft test:

(40)   It was [**his address**] that my brother wrote down (not his phone number).

I will leave you to apply the same tests to show that the sequence *my brother* is also a constituent of these sentences.

Tree diagrams can be drawn to show very detailed information about the syntactic structure of a phrase or sentence, or alternatively, some of the finer details can be omitted. Linguists choose to put more or less detail into their trees depending on what information they want to convey. So, for example, the tree in (39) indicates that *for this job* is a constituent, but it doesn't show whether there are any smaller phrases within this constituent. In fact, there are. The cleft test shows that the string of words *this job* is also a constituent in this example: *It was* [***this job***] *that my brother applied for*. Now that we know that *this job* is a constituent in this case, we can draw a more detailed tree to represent this: (41) gives more information about the structure than (39) does.

(41)

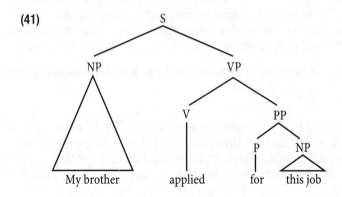

Tree (41) isn't a replacement for (39): it simply gives more information. Both trees would be used by linguists, depending on the level of detail we want to indicate. Tree (41) shows that *this job* is an NP constituent, nested inside a larger constituent *for this job*. If we are using brackets, one constituent is nested inside the other as follows: [*for* [*this job*]].

So, to summarize, exactly how much or how little structure we actually show within the tree diagram or the brackets depends on what we are trying to show. But if we are claiming that two sentences contrast in constituent structure, then the parts that differ must be shown in enough detail to make our claims clear.

和使用方括号一样，树形图也是一种工具，用来表示研究者对于句子结构的分析。在很多中国学生的心目中往往存在一种寻求标准答案的倾向，如果给出一个句子要求学生画出它的树形图，他们一定要知道标准的正确答案是什么。一个句子要画出什么样的树形图，细化到什么程度，这要依赖于我们研究的需要和对其句法结构的认识，树形图只是作为一个工具，只要按照给制的规范，能准确地表现出对句子结构的认识就可以了。

5.1.4 Summary

We have so far used the following syntactic tests for constituency: replacement by a pronoun, the echo question test, the sentence fragment test, the cleft test, and the *do so* test for VP status. We indicate which strings of words are constituents of a sentence in two ways: either by placing square brackets round the constituents, or by using tree diagrams. Most importantly, this section shows that we must use contrasting sets of grammatical and ungrammatical examples to argue for a particular constituent structure. Our analysis is valid only if we can show that it also rules out other logically possible analyses. So, as well as using the tests to show what the constituent structure of a phrase or sentence actually is, we also use them to rule out any alternative structures.

5.2 RELATIONSHIPS WITHIN THE TREE

This short section defines the technical terms used by linguists to discuss relationships between words and phrases in a tree diagram. It's common to use **LABELLED** BRACKETS or LABELLED TREE DIAGRAMS in which each relevant constituent has a label showing its category. Our trees include word class and phrase class labels such as V, VP, PP, P, NP, and so on, telling us that what's beneath that label is a PP, or a P, or an NP etc. This exact same information can be shown in labelled brackets. For example, the PP *for this job*, which we proved to be a constituent in (37), can be shown as follows:

> Labelled, 加标记的，所谓加标记就是给各种成分加上所属语法范畴的标签。

(42)   [PP [P for] [NP this job]]

These brackets are read like this: the whole constituent is a PP, since this is the label on the outermost brackets (by convention, only the left-hand bracket is labelled). The PP comprises two main constituents, a preposition *for* and an NP *this job*: as we saw, this noun phrase fits into the focus position of a cleft sentence, so must be a constituent. Each individual lexical item (word) is in fact also a constituent, so *for*, *this* and *job* here are constituents, though I haven't labelled or bracketed the last two items here. The words are the smallest constituents of a tree.

Let's now add more information into (41) to give a fully detailed tree diagram, showing *my* and *this* as D (determiners) and *brother* and *job* as Ns.

(43)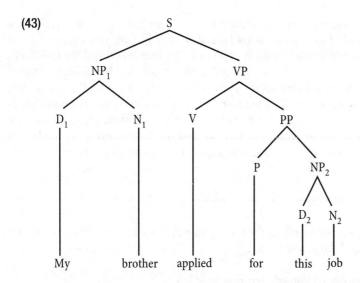

Using the tree in (43), I now introduce some of the technical terms used in syntax to describe tree structures. Recall that all the lines in the tree are known by the (reasonable!) technical term BRANCHES. Each point in the tree that has a category label or else an actual word attached to it is known as a NODE. In (43) we find PHRASAL nodes NP, VP and PP (nodes denoting the phrases in the tree), and also S. We also see in (43) the lexical nodes V, P, D and N (nodes indicating word-level elements), and the actual lexical items (words) *my*, *brother*, *applied*, *for*, *this* and *job*.

Despite the fact that I've used the label 'S', rather than calling the sentence a 'something phrase', the sentence is, of course, a phrase in its own right, and some linguists reflect this by terming the sentence 'TP', for **tense phrase** ('tense' in the sense of the tense of the verb). The idea is that a sentence is a phrase that denotes tense, though as we've mentioned earlier, it's not the case that *verbs* in all languages display the morphosyntactic category 'tense'. Here, I continue to use 'S', but you should be prepared for this not to be used in some frameworks if you go on to study theoretical syntax.

There are specific terms for the relationships between nodes in a tree. Each node IMMEDIATELY DOMINATES the next node below it, providing they are connected by a branch, and providing no other node intervenes. So for instance, within the PP, P immediately dominates *for*, D_2 immediately dominates *this*, and N_2 immediately dominates *job*. No other node intervenes between P and *for*, and so on. The node PP immediately dominates the two nodes P and NP_2, and NP_2 immediately dominates D_2 and N_2: again, no other nodes intervene.

A node which immediately dominates another node or set of nodes is their MOTHER: so, for example, PP is the mother of P and NP_2, and each NP is the mother of a D and an N. It won't surprise you that P and NP_2 are the DAUGHTERS of PP; and D_2 and N_2 are the daughters of NP_2, and so on. The lexical items *for*, *this* and *job* are the daughters of P, D_2 and N_2 respectively. In the same vein, the set of daughters

Tense phrase, 时态短语, 一个句子在大多数情况下被标记为S, 但是, 有时会根据研究者的不同看法而标记为不同的短语, 除了TP之外, 很多学者都把整个句子标记为CP（complementizer phrase）。

Daughter, 有的学者也把它翻译为"女（儿）节点", 但是从汉语的表达习惯来看, 可能翻译成"子节点"更为合适。

which share the same mother are known as SISTERS. So the nodes NP_1 and VP are sisters, and V and PP are sisters, as are D_2 and N_2, *this* and *job*, and so on.

However, the relationship between a set of nodes such as PP and the two nodes D_2 and N_2 is a different one: we say that PP DOMINATES D_2 and N_2 (though sadly we don't continue the analogy by using the term 'grandmother'). Note that PP doesn't IMMEDIATELY dominate D_2 and N_2 because the NP_2 node intervenes. But nonetheless an unbroken series of branches connects PP to D_2 and N_2: a branch first connects PP to NP_2, and then branches connect NP_2 to D_2 and N_2. When there's a path like this connecting the nodes in a tree, then the higher node is said to dominate the lower one.

Before reading further, work out the relationships between nodes in the tree in (43) by answering the following questions:

i. What nodes does S immediately dominate?

ii. What nodes does S dominate?

iii. Does NP_1 dominate P and NP_2?

iv. What nodes does VP dominate? Which are its daughters?

The answers are as follows:

i. S immediately dominates NP_1 and VP.

ii. S dominates NP_1 and VP, both Ds and Ns, V and PP, P and NP_2, and also *my*, *brother*, *applied*, *for*, *this* and *job*—in other words, all other nodes in the tree.

iii. No: NP_1 doesn't dominate P or NP_2 because there's no series of branches connecting the node NP_1 to these nodes (don't be misled by the fact that NP_1 is drawn higher up in the tree).

iv. VP dominates V, PP, P, NP_2, D and N, as well as *applied*, *for*, *this* and *job*. Only V and PP are its daughters, because VP immediately dominates only V and PP.

Note that if a node immediately dominates a set of nodes, it automatically also dominates them. So we said, for instance, that S both immediately dominates and also dominates NP_1 and VP.

Trees also show the groupings of words into constituents:

(44) Definition of a constituent in a tree diagram

A set of elements forms a constituent in a tree diagram **if and only if** there is a single node that dominates just these elements, and no other items.

> If and only if, 这是生成语法在下定义或者给出规则时经常用到的表达方法，有时缩写为 iff。

For instance in (43), the nodes *my* and *brother* form a constituent: they're both dominated by NP₁, and NP₁ doesn't dominate any other nodes.

Please look again at the tree in (43) and answer these questions:

i. Do *applied*, *for*, *this* and *job* form a constituent?

ii. Do *my*, *brother*, and *applied* form a constituent?

iii. Do *applied* and *for* form a constituent?

The answers are:

i. Yes: these nodes are all dominated by VP.

ii. No: there is no single node that dominates just the elements *my*, *brother* and *applied* and no others.

iii. No: although both are dominated by VP, VP also dominates *this* and *job*.

In this section I have introduced labelled tree diagrams and discussed the terminology for the relationships between the nodes in a tree. I will make use of these terms in the following section when I discuss more complex tree diagrams.

5.3 DEVELOPING DETAILED TREE DIAGRAMS AND TESTS FOR CONSTITUENT STRUCTURE

Section 5.3.1 uses the tests for constituent structure established in Section 5.1 to work out the structure of some phrases and sentences, and also introduces a new test: ellipsis. Section 5.3.2 introduces another diagnostic for constituency: co-ordination. And Section 5.3.3 considers whether all languages have the same constituents.

5.3.1 Verb classes and constituent structure tests

5.3.1.1 Phrasal verbs and prepositional verbs

Before turning to some detailed tree diagrams which represent sentences of English, I first discuss the differences between two verb classes: **phrasal verbs and prepositional verbs**. Let's examine two more sentences which may appear superficially similar, but in fact have different constituent structures:

短语动词（phrasal verb)和带介词的动词（prepositional verb）都是由动词加介词或者副词构成的动词结构，但是其内部结构差别很大。

(45) Those smugglers shook off their pursuers.

(46) Those smugglers relied on the weather forecast.

There is one clear indication that these two examples are syntactically distinct. In (45), we can take the preposition *off* and place it immediately after the direct object NP *their pursuers*, to give *Those smugglers shook their pursuers off*. The verb *shake off* is a transitive verb—it must have an NP complement, i.e. a direct object. In (46), we don't have a transitive verb, but instead we have a verb *rely* and its PP complement. The verb does not have a direct object at all, and if we attempt to put the preposition *on* after the NP, the result is ungrammatical:

(47) *Those smugglers relied the weather forecast on.

This test identifies very successfully one particular verb class: transitive PHRASAL VERBS such as *shake off* always allow the preposition to be placed after their object NP. These verbs are single lexical items comprising a V and a P: [$_V$ shake off]. We have, in fact, already met another example of a transitive phrasal verb in (33), namely *write down*, as we can confirm from the fact that we can get *My brother wrote his address down*. English has a vast number of phrasal verbs, both transitive and intransitive. Further examples of the transitive kind include *turn over, pull down, pick up, put out, switch on* and *break off*. As (48) shows, the preposition can follow the direct object (in bold) in each case. (For some of these, you may prefer to leave the preposition next to the verb. The point I am making is simply that it *may* follow the direct object.)

(48) a. We turned **the place** over.
b. They pulled **that old farm building with a thatched roof** down last week.
c. I'd pick **that snake** up carefully.
d. She broke **her last engagement** off very suddenly.

This test also allows you to identify the full extent of the direct object NP, because the preposition has to be placed immediately *after* that NP (and not in the middle of it). So for instance, in (48b) the test shows that the whole of the sequence *that old farm building with a thatched roof* comprises the direct object. The preposition *down* can be placed at the end of the direct object, but not elsewhere:

(49) *They pulled that old farm building **down** with a thatched roof last week.

As noted, English also has phrasal verbs which are—or can be—intransitive, such as *wake up, sit down, sleep in, turn out* (as in *Not many people turned out*) and *break down* (as in *The car broke down*).

Some English grammarians use the term 'particle' to refer to the *over, down, up, off, out* (etc.) part of the phrasal verb, but we can tell that they are truly prepositions by using the modifier *right*, which we saw in Section 2.6.1 to be a good test for preposition status. So for example, we get *Pull the handle **right** down, Break the plastic safety catch **right** off, There was a loud bang and I woke **right** up* and so on.

Now let's compare (46). There, we don't have a phrasal verb at all. Instead, the verb *rely* takes a PP complement, and this PP must be headed by the preposition *on*: we can only *rely **on*** something, not *rely for, *rely off, *rely over or *rely out. Verbs which select PP complements are known as PREPOSITIONAL VERBS. Their defining properties are that the PP is obligatory, and is headed by one specific preposition. Further examples of prepositional verbs include *believe in NP, hear from NP, see to NP, glance at NP, hope for NP, depend on NP* and *look after NP*, among many others. Quite often, the preposition has such a close relationship with the prepositional verb that not even one of the prepositional modifiers, such as *right, just* or *straight*, can intervene. These examples give you an idea of the variation that is found; of course, you may not agree with my judgements in each case:

(50) We rely just/*right on our good fortune.
 The politicians skated right/*just over these damaging issues.
 The grandparents looked *just/*right after the children.

Prepositional verbs, then, are a rather special set. On the other hand, if a verb merely has a PP adjunct—in other words, it is modified by an optional PP—the properties are entirely different. The head preposition can be readily changed: *I jumped **on** the wall/**off** the wall/**over** the wall/**behind** the wall* (and so on), and the PP can be omitted entirely, as it is not a complement. The choice of a modifier in the PP is also much freer:

(51) I jumped just/straight/right over the wall.
 We ran just/straight/right to the end of the beach.
 The vase fell straight/right off the shelf.

The verbs illustrated in (51) are not prepositional, since the PP is an adjunct rather than a complement. We reserve the term 'prepositional verb' for a verb with an obligatory PP complement.

5.3.1.2 *Tree structures for phrasal and prepositional verbs*

We already know that (45) and (46) must have different structures, because of the differing behaviour we uncovered in Section 5.3.1.1. Using constituent structure tests, we can discover which words group together. The tree diagrams in (52) and (53) give the end product of a set of tests, and I'll work back from these trees to demonstrate to you that the two distinct structures proposed here are correct. Bear in mind that a tree diagram is nothing more than a reflection of native speaker judgements about the structure of a phrase or sentence, gained mostly from applying tests for constituency.

Before reading further, I suggest you draw both trees for yourself on a sheet of paper, exactly as shown below. This will give you practice with tree-drawing, and also save you having to look back at my trees as I develop the arguments for their different constituent structures.

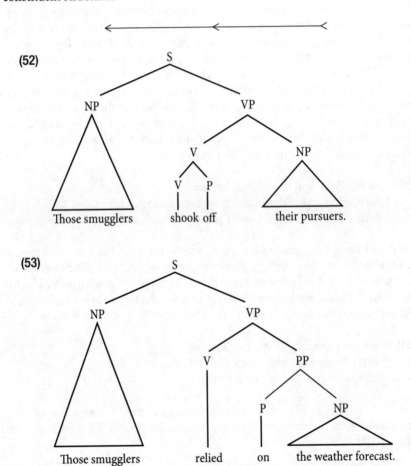

Every time we draw a tree diagram we are making a set of claims about constituent structure—about which words group together to form the phrases of a sentence. A tree is built up from our evidence of what these phrases are, which comes from tests for constituent structure. So let's start with evidence for the two main constituents in each tree: the subject and the VP predicate.

Our tests show that *those smugglers*, the subject in each sentence, is indeed a constituent. Both subjects can be sentence fragments:

(54) a. Who shook off their pursuers? [NP Those smugglers]
     b. Who relied on the weather forecast? [NP Those smugglers]

Second, both subject NPs can also appear in the focus position of a cleft sentence:

(55) a. It's [NP those smugglers] who shook off their pursuers.
      b. It's [NP those smugglers] who relied on the weather forecast.

And third, we can also replace both subject NPs with *they*, using a test for NP status introduced in Section 5.1.1. The word *they* is rather badly termed a 'pronoun'. Since it replaces a whole NP it's really a pro-NP: 'pro' means '(stands) for'. The cover term used for all pro-phrases is PROFORM: a proform takes the place of a sequence of words which form a constituent, and so any string of words that can be replaced by an appropriate proform must be a constituent.

A proform test can also prove the existence of the VP constituent, as we saw in Section 5.1.3. We use *do so* (or *did so* in the past tense) to stand for VP, therefore as a 'pro-VP':

(56) a. Those smugglers [VP shook off their pursuers], and the moonshine merchants [VP **did so**] too.
      b. Those smugglers [VP relied on the weather forecast], and these fishermen [VP **did so**] too.

Rather than repeating the whole VP, we can replace it with the proform. The *do so* test is a specific test for a VP constituent.

One of the other tests for constituent structure which was given earlier is the cleft construction. However, most dialects of English can't form a cleft using a VP constituent:

(57) *It's **shake off their pursuers** that those smugglers did.
      *It's **rely on the weather forecast** that those smugglers did.

This does not mean the cleft test is unreliable; it just means that VPs can't be focussed like this in English. In some languages, though, such as Irish, it's perfectly OK to focus VPs in the cleft construction. Given a sentence like (58), we can focus the VP to get (59), which is fully grammatical in Irish:

(58) Bhí   an   fear   ag   péinteáil   cathaoir.   (Irish)
      was   the   man   PROG paint.INFIN   chair
      'The man was painting a chair.'

(59) Is   [VP **ag**   **péinteáil**   **cathaoir**]   a   bhí   an   fear.
      is   PROG   paint.INFIN   chair   that   was   the   man
      '*It's painting a chair that the man was.'

This shows that the string *ag péinteáil cathaoir* is a constituent of (58). The lesson here is that sometimes a test won't work in a given language, but this may be due to some language-specific quirk. VP clefts are fine in Irish but not in English. We must make sure that our results are valid by using more than one test for constituency each time.

To confirm the existence of VPs in English I introduce another test for constituency: ELLIPSIS. Ellipsis means missing out part of the sentence, but the portion we miss out must always be a constituent:

Ellipsis, 省略, 这也是成分检验的一个重要方法, 如果一组单词可以被省略, 那么它们就是句子的一个成分。

(60) a. Those smugglers might [VP shake off their pursuers], and the moonshine merchants might [VP ___] too.
b. Those smugglers didn't [VP rely on the weather forecast], but these fishermen did [VP ___] for sure.

It's perfectly possible to repeat the VP from the first half of the sentence, but by omitting it as shown here, we prove that it really is a constituent.

You might have noticed, though, that some of the sequences which are constituents according to my trees in (52) and (53) cannot undergo ellipsis. First, in both trees there are sequences which are shown as NP constituents: *their pursuers* and *the weather forecast*. But if we omit these constituents from my sentences, the result is ungrammatical:

(61) a. *Those smugglers must shake off [NP their pursuers], and these moonshine merchants should shake off [NP ___] too.
b. *Those smugglers didn't rely on [NP the weather forecast], but these fishermen did rely on [NP ___] for sure.

Before we examine why the examples in (61) are ungrammatical, note that I haven't yet proved that there really is an NP constituent *their pursuers/the weather forecast* in both sentences. So first, find at least two tests for each phrase to confirm that they really are constituents.

For these NPs, you could use tests as shown in (62) through (65):

(62) **Echo questions**
a. The smugglers shook off [NP **who**]?
b. The smugglers relied on [NP **what**]?

(63) **Sentence fragments**
a. Who did the smugglers shake off? [NP **Their pursuers**]
b. What did the smugglers rely on? [NP **The weather forecast**]

(64) **Clefts**
   a.   It was [NP **their pursuers**] that the smugglers shook off.
   b.   It was [NP **the weather forecast**] which the smugglers relied on.

(65) **Proforms**
   a.   The smugglers shook [NP **them**] off.
   b.   The smugglers relied on [NP **it**].

Note also that the pronoun *precedes* the preposition when we have a transitive phrasal verb, as in (65a), but *follows* the preposition when we have a prepositional verb, as in (65b). This is the way each verb class always works in English, and it is a very reliable test. For instance, we can't have *The smugglers shook off them* for a transitive phrasal verb.

So if the NPs which we've tested from (52) and (53) really are constituents, as we've shown, why can't they be omitted in (61)? The reason is that both examples contain a head word which requires these NPs to be present—the NPs are complements, and the sentences are incomplete without these complements. So the transitive phrasal verb *shake off* requires a direct object NP in (61a), and in (61b) the transitive preposition *on* also requires an NP object. Constituents which form the complement to some head, particularly a head verb or preposition, are quite generally unable to be omitted. This means that the ellipsis test can't be used to diagnose the constituent status of such phrases.

Now let's examine the sequence *on the weather forecast*, which is shown as a PP in (53). First we need to confirm the constituent status of this string of words:

(66) **Sentence fragment**
   What exactly did the smugglers rely on? Oh, [PP **on the weather forecast**] of course!

(67) **Cleft**
   It was [PP **on the weather forecast**] that the smugglers usually relied.

(Some speakers may not be entirely happy with (67), but the test in (66) confirms that there really is a PP.)

Again, we might expect that if it's a constituent, then the PP could be omitted, but it actually can't be:

(68) *Those smugglers actually didn't rely [PP on the weather forecast], but these fishermen really did rely [PP ___], for sure.

Just as with (61), the reason for the ungrammaticality of (68) is that the PP we've omitted is a complement: prepositional verbs like *rely on NP* require the PP complement to be present, so again, we can't use the ellipsis test for constituent structure in a case like this.

For completeness, we should use the same tests to confirm a claim made by our tree in (52): the structure proposed there says that the sequence *off their pursuers* is *not* a constituent in *Those smugglers shook off their pursuers*. Recall that to prove that two sentences such as (52) and (53) have a different structure, we must give contrasting sets of grammatical and ungrammatical examples as evidence. Please formulate the relevant sentence fragment and cleft sentence in order to demonstrate that *off their pursuers* is not a constituent in this case. Remember that in the sentence fragment test, the question you ask must be grammatical: the test is whether the answer is grammatical or not.

The results are:

(69) **Sentence fragment**
Who did the smugglers shake off? *Off their pursuers.

(70) **Cleft**
*It was off their pursuers that the smugglers shook.

(Remember that we don't put non-constituents in brackets.) Even if you were not entirely happy with (67), I expect you'll agree that (70) is far worse. These ungrammatical examples confirm that there is indeed no PP *off their pursuers* in (52).

In this section we have justified the different structures proposed for phrasal verbs and prepositional verbs, using the tests for constituency introduced in Section 5.1. We have also introduced a new test: ellipsis, or omission. If we can omit some sequence of words, then there's a good chance that it's a constituent. We also showed that if a constituent is the complement of a verb or a preposition, then we generally won't be able to omit it, because it's required by the head V or P to be present.

5.3.2 The co-ordination test for constituency

Our final test for constituency is CO-ORDINATION. Sequences of words which are constituents can be CO-ORDINATED or CONJOINED with one another, provided that they are of the same syntactic category: so we can have NP + NP, or VP + VP, for instance. For example, the sequence *their pursuers* is an NP constituent in (52) and *the weather forecast* is an NP constituent in (53), and so each can be joined together with another NP:

(71) The smugglers shook off (both) [NP their pursuers] and [NP the revenue men].

(72) The smugglers relied on (both) [NP the weather forecast] and [NP their years of experience].

The two NPs in brackets in these examples have been conjoined using *and*, known as a CO-ORDINATING CONJUNCTION. Other such conjunctions in English include *but*, *nor* and *or*.

You may be wondering if the transitive phrasal verb *shook off* in (71) and the preposition *on* in (72) now have two object NPs. No, they do not: when two constituents of the same category are conjoined, they simply make one larger constituent of the same category, as in (73). So there is still only one object for the transitive verb in (71) and the preposition *on* in (72), but this NP may itself contain NPs embedded within it. The node label CONJ means 'conjunction'.

(73)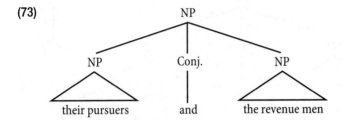

The co-ordination test can be used to confirm that a phrasal verb and a prepositional verb do have different structures, as we have proposed—look at your tree diagrams for (52) and (53). A prepositional verb contains a PP constituent, according to the tests we've seen so far. And indeed, the PP can be conjoined with another PP:

(74) The smugglers relied [$_{PP}$ on the weather forecast] and (also) [$_{PP}$ on their years of experience].

In (75), on the other hand, we can't conjoin *off their pursuers* with *off the revenue men*, because these two strings of words are not constituents of any kind:

(75) *The smugglers shook **off their pursuers** and **off the revenue men**.

The preposition of a phrasal verb like *shake off* isn't attached to the following NP, as we can see from the structure for phrasal verbs in (52): there is no node that dominates just the preposition and *their pursuers*, so this sequence doesn't form a constituent. Please look at your tree diagram for (52) to confirm this for yourself.

Finally, we can use the co-ordination test to discover more about the structure of one of the ambiguous sentences in Section 5.1: *The boy and the girl's uncle stayed to dinner*. You'll see that there's a conjunction *and* in this sentence. We can now show that there are two possible ways of co-ordinating constituents within the NP *the boy and the girl's uncle*, which accounts for the ambiguity. First, we can conjoin an NP *the boy* with an NP *the girl's uncle*, as in (76). This gives the reading in which two people stay to dinner:

(76)   [$_{NP}$ [$_{NP}$ the boy] and [$_{NP}$ the girl's uncle]]

In (76) the outermost brackets are labelled 'NP': this tells you the category of the whole phrase. Within this large NP, two smaller NPs are embedded, co-ordinated using *and*. The equivalent tree is in fact just the same as that in (73).

In the alternative reading of the phrase, where only one person stays to dinner, we conjoin an NP *the boy* with an NP *the girl*, as in (77): here, it's the uncle to both children who stays to dinner.

(77)

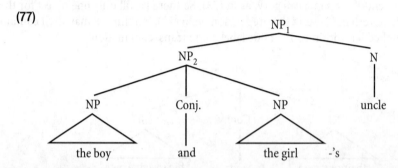

The tree in (77) says that the whole phrase is an NP (NP$_1$) which has two branches. On the left branch is NP$_2$, which immediately dominates the two conjoined NPs. Note that this whole phrase in NP$_2$ effectively replaces a single-word determiner such as *their*. On the right branch is the N *uncle*, the head noun of the *entire* phrase, NP$_1$. Again, numbering the phrases as I've done here is simply a useful way to make it clear which phrase we're referring to, when there are several phrases of the same category.

We've seen in this section that two strings of words can be conjoined if they're constituents, and (normally) of the same syntactic category. Conversely, if a sequence of words which does *not* form a constituent is conjoined with other material, then the result is always ungrammatical, just as in (75). Co-ordination can therefore be added to our set of tests for constituent structure.

5.3.3 Do all languages have the same constituents?

The answer to this question is no, they apparently don't. I illustrate this with VP. Most languages have a clear VP constituent, as can be shown, for example, using VP co-ordination. Examples (78) and (79) show conjoined VPs in Persian and in Malagasy (note that in Malagasy the subject—*Rabe*, a name—is at the end of the clause, rather than at the start):

(78) Jân   [$_{VP}$ xandid]   va   [$_{VP}$ dast   tekân   dâd].   (Persian)
     John   smiled   and   hand   sign   gave
     'John smiled and waved.'

(79) [$_{VP}$ Misotro   taoka]   sy   [$_{VP}$ mihinam-bary]   Rabe.   (Malagasy)
         drink   alcohol   and   eat-rice   Rabe
     'Rabe is drinking alcohol and eating rice.'

From this co-ordination we can conclude that there are likely to be VP constituents in both languages.

However, linguists have also used the standard tests for constituent structure to argue that some languages, such as Basque and Hungarian, have no VP constituent. In (57), we saw that VPs can't be clefted in English; nonetheless, other tests demonstrate that English clearly does have VPs:

(80) Kim says that he hasn't [VP drunk all the water]
    a. but he has [VP __].
    b. and he hasn't [VP __].
    c. but he has [VP **(done) so**].

In (80a) and (80b), we see that the VP can undergo ellipsis (it can be omitted); (80c) shows that one proform for VP in English is *so* (or *done so*). Now compare the same constructions in Basque (the argument and the data here are taken from Rebuschi 1989). The putative VP (i.e. the verb and its object, the sequence being tested) is shown in bold:

(81) Peio-k dio **ur guzia edan** du-ela. (Basque)
    Peio-CASE says water all drunk AUX-that
    'Peio says that he has drunk all the water.'
    a. *eta [VP __] du
       and AUX
       ('and he has')
    b. *baina ez du [VP __]
       but NEG AUX
       ('but he hasn't')
    c. *eta hala du
       and thus AUX
       ('and so he has')

(81a), (81b) and (81c) are all ungrammatical in Basque: there can be no ellipsis of a VP, as shown in (81a) and (81b), and nor does *hala*, 'thus', act as a VP proform. Nor, indeed, do any other standard tests indicate that Basque might have a VP constituent. So on these grounds, we can say that Basque appears to lack a VP altogether.

5.3.4 An introduction to the bar notation

This final section takes the reader somewhat beyond the simple tree structures seen so far in the chapter, and looks at a more advanced issue, though it uses exactly the same kind of argumentation. I use the co-ordination test for constituency to argue for the existence of another phrasal category which we haven't yet come across. This is a type of nominal phrase (= noun-type phrase) which is smaller than a full NP, but larger than just a head noun. I'm going to argue that a head noun together with its complement forms a constituent, which is termed N′ (pronounced **N-bar**).

N-bar 这一概念的提出代表着生成语法的一个重要发展阶段，与此相关的理论被称为 X-bar 理论。

The issue here is internal structure of the direct object NP in (82):

(82) I admired [$_{NP}$ the director's treatment of the issues].

First, you should satisfy yourself that the whole string labelled 'NP' really is a constituent: try the cleft test *It was ...*, and the sentence fragment test, using *What did you admire?*, in order to prove my claim. I will assume that your conclusions support me. As usual, this NP can be conjoined with another full NP, as in (83):

(83) I admired [$_{NP}$ the director's treatment of the issues] and [$_{NP}$ her sensitivity to the problems].

Each of the conjuncts (= sequences conjoined) in (83) is a full NP, as we can see from the fact that either of them could be the subject or object of a verb. Together, the two conjuncts form one large NP—the direct object of *admired*—although I haven't shown this in brackets in (83).

In (84), *admired* has a slightly different direct object. Here, I bracket the *entire* object NP, but without specifying its internal structure:

(84) I admired [$_{NP}$ the director's treatment of the issues and sensitivity to the problems].

Inside the full NP, two smaller strings of words are conjoined. Unlike in (83), however, the conjoined strings in (84) are not full NPs.

Before reading any further, decide what strings of words are actually co-ordinated in (84). Don't attempt to give their category, but just say what the conjoined sequences of words are.

The conjuncts are *treatment of the issues* and *sensitivity to the problems*. If you didn't get this, think about what (84) means; the specifier (Section 4.1.8) *the director's* applies to both conjuncts: it's both the director's treatment of the issues and her sensitivity that you admire. So within the direct object NP we have two conjoined strings as shown in bold in (85):

(85) I admired [$_{NP}$ the director's [$_{??}$ **treatment of the issues**] and [$_{??}$ **sensitivity to the problems**]].

If co-ordination is a reliable test for constituency, we must conclude that both of these sequences in bold are constituents. However, they're not members of any category we've seen before, which is why I indicate the category with subscript question marks instead of the real category labels.

So, we need to work out the internal structure of an NP such as *the director's treatment of the issues*. Perhaps your first thought is that the sequence *the director's treatment* might itself be an NP in our example. But in fact this string of words is not a constituent of any kind here, as we can prove by using the proform test. The appropriate proform in English for an NP which includes a possessive form is one of the set *mine, yours, his, hers, ours, theirs*, as, for example, in (86):

(86) I can't stand **his uncle**. Do you like **hers**?

Here, *hers* replaces an entire NP (such as *her uncle*). But it can't be used to replace the sequence *the director's treatment* in (87):

(87) *I admired **hers** of the issues.

This means that *the director's treatment* isn't a constituent here. To make matters clear, note that I am not claiming that *the director's treatment* can never be a constituent, just that it isn't one in (82).

We do know, though, from (85), that the sequence *treatment of the issues* is a constituent in our example, because of its ability to undergo co-ordination. So far, we have had no label for the type of constituents that are co-ordinated in (85). These mystery constituents consist of a head noun *treatment* or *sensitivity*, plus a PP complement to that head: *of the issues, to the problems*. So a head + complement is co-ordinated with another similar sequence, and the two conjuncts share a single specifier, *the director's*: both the treatment and the sensitivity are that of the director.

The structure we propose for *the director's treatment of the issues* is shown in (88). In (88) you can see that there is a constituent, *treatment of the issues*, which is labelled N'—this, then, is the category of the mystery constituent which was co-ordinated in (85).

(88)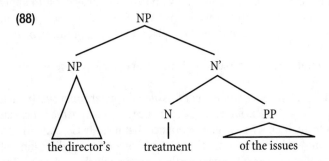

(89) I admired the director's [$_{N'}$ treatment of the issues] and [$_{N'}$ sensitivity to the problems].

You can see that N′ is not a full NP—the whole tree is an NP, with the specifier *the director's*—but rather, N′ is a smaller nominal phrase, an intermediate category smaller than an NP but larger than an N. This N′ consists of a head noun (*treatment*) plus a PP complement to that noun.

The minimal type of nominal element is a head noun: this is sometimes referred to as N^0 ('N zero'): the bare noun. Any nominal phrase which has a determiner or a full phrase in its specifier position must be an example of the *maximal* type of nominal phrase, which is NP. One instance of such an NP is *his uncle* in (86). And *hers* in (86) is also a full NP: we can tell because it's a PROFORM for the NP *her uncle*, and therefore must itself be an NP. The intermediate category N′, on the other hand, consists of the head plus its complement, but it has no determiner or other specifier. The N′ is still a phrasal category, but not a full NP.

So the general structure of noun phrases is as shown in (90). This structure shows that an NP immediately dominates a specifier and an N′. In turn, the N′ immediately dominates the head N (the notation N^0 is often used) and its complement.

(90)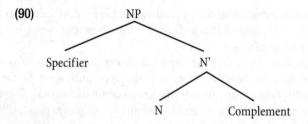

Before moving on, though, you should note that not all NPs have either a specifier or a complement—*hers* didn't in (86). This means that it is possible for an NP to consist of just its head noun, such as *cats* or *Kim*. Evidence that NPs containing only the head N are indeed full phrasal categories comes from the fact that they can co-ordinate with other NPs, as in [NP *Kim*] *and* [NP *her uncle*] *came to dinner*.

Returning to our intermediate category, we have seen one piece of evidence for the existence of an N′, from co-ordination. As I've noted, it's always best to apply more than one test for any putative constituent. And indeed, another piece of evidence for N′ comes from the fact that we can replace an N′ by a proform, *one*:

(91)   [NP This [N′ **treatment of the issues**]] is better than [NP that [N′ **one**]].

In (91), *one* stands for just the N′ *treatment of the issues*: the determiner *this* (which makes a phrase into a full NP) is excluded. If the sequence *treatment of the issues* can be replaced by a proform, then we have good evidence that it really is a constituent.

This section has presented evidence for the existence of an intermediate kind of nominal category, smaller than an NP but larger than a noun, which is called N′. The evidence was, first, that a sequence consisting of a head noun plus its complement could be co-ordinated with another similar sequence, so showing these sequences to be constituents; and second, that the sequence could be replaced by a proform *one*, again showing it to be a constituent.

5.4 SUMMARY

In Section 5.1 of this chapter, we presented evidence that sentences and phrases actually have syntactic structure. Using tests for constituent structure, we argued that various sentences which superficially appeared to be similar in fact have different structures. We represented syntactic structure using brackets or tree diagrams, which show the ways words group together to form phrases. Section 5.2 presented the standard terminology for describing the relationships between the nodes in a tree. In Section 5.3, we used the tests for constituency to work out the structure of a number of phrases and sentences, and produced labelled brackets and labelled tree diagrams to illustrate the constituent structure that we discovered. The syntactic tests for constituency used in this chapter are as follows: the sentence fragment test; echo questions; cleft sentences; proform tests; ellipsis; and co-ordination.

> **Checklist for Chapter 5**
>
> Although the remainder of this book does not engage further with the topic of constituent structure, you will definitely need to understand if it you're going on to further study of syntax.
>
> - Can you outline at least four different tests for constituency, and say how they're used?
> - Why do we use contrasting grammatical and ungrammatical examples in our tests?
> - What kinds of constituents cannot normally be omitted under ellipsis?
> - What is the difference between phrasal and prepositional verbs in English? Give some examples of each category and indicate how we can tell the difference.

FURTHER READING

Two introductory texts which concentrate on the grammar and structure of English, and which go significantly beyond what I have done in Chapters 2 through 5, are Börjars and Burridge (2010) and Lobeck (2000). Radford (1988) provides detailed (and relatively introductory) reading on constituent structure, tree diagrams and tests for constituency. At this stage you may not want to go beyond his Chapter 5. See also Aarts (2013) and Burton-Roberts (2010). For a more detailed account of how to treat the English possessive -'s, including proposed tree diagrams, I recommend consulting Burton-Roberts (2010). Moving on to more theoretically oriented treatments of syntax, Poole (2011) forms a good follow-up to the material discussed here.

EXERCISES

1. In the text of Chapter 5 I proposed that *one* is a proform for an N′ constituent. The examples below suggest that *one* can also be a proform for a different kind of constituent. What is this?

    (1)   Kim knows stacks of sea shanties, and Mel knows one too.

    (2)   I've seen a mockingbird, but Chris has never seen one.

    (3)   I've met several university presidents, but Lee has had dinner with one.

2. *Time flies like an arrow; fruit flies like a banana.* Explain clearly in syntactic terms how this pair of clauses work together as a nice example of a pun. Use the correct grammatical terminology plus relevant tests for constituent structure, contrasting the two clauses.

3. The two sentences in (1) and (2) below contain words from the same word classes, and in the same order, but they each have different syntactic structures.

    Task: (i) Using standard tests for constituency, work out what the constituents of each sentence must be. You should use at least two tests for each putative constituent. Your answers should include contrasting grammatical and ungrammatical examples which reveal the syntactic differences between (1) and (2). Use square brackets to indicate the constituents you find in each example, and remember to bracket constituents only, and not random strings of words. (ii) Next, draw labelled tree diagrams for (1) and (2), taking care that the trees correctly represent the constituent structures you discovered above.

    (1)   Kim glanced at the actor with a wig.

    (2)   Kim glanced at the actor through her binoculars.

4. The two sentences in (1) and (2) below again contain words from the same word classes, and in the same order, but again they each have different syntactic structures.

    Task: (i) Using at least three standard tests for constituency, work out what the constituents of each sentence must be. Your answers should include contrasting grammatical and ungrammatical examples which reveal the syntactic differences between (1) and (2). Can you provide any further evidence that (1) and (2) differ in structure? What sub-classes of verb does each example contain? (Don't worry if you prefer *stank* in (1); both past tense forms are acceptable!). (ii) Now draw labelled tree diagrams for (1) and (2), ensuring that the trees correctly represent the constituent structures you discovered above.

(1) The skunk stunk out my garden.

(2) The skunk slunk out my garden.

5. The data below are from Fijian, and are taken from Lynch (1998).

   Task: Examine the data and explain what they show about the grammar of possession in Fijian. Next, describe carefully how the possessive construction is formed. Your answer should account for all the data.

   Hint:
   The prefix glossed as POSS is a possessive marker. It has three distinct forms, depending on the semantic category of the item possessed. Your answer should note all three forms. However, you are not required to specify what factors determine the appearance of any particular form.

   (1) na   tina-qu
        the mother-my
        'my mother'

   (2) na   me-na   niu
        the POSS-his coconut
        'his coconut'

   (3) na   ke-mu   itaba
        the POSS-your photo
        'your photo'
        (i.e. a photo taken of you)

   (4) na   no-mu   itaba
        the POSS-your photo
        'your photo'
        (i.e. a photo you took or have)

   (5) na   yaca-qu
        the name-my
        'my name'

   (6) na   ke-mu   madrai
        the POSS-your bread
        'your bread'

   (7) na   me-qu   bia
        the POSS-my beer
        'my beer'

   (8) na   ulu-qu
        the head-my
        'my head'

   (9) na   no-qu   yaca
        the POSS-my name
        'my namesake'

   (10) na   tama-qu
        the father-my
        'my father'

6. Welsh is a VERB-INITIAL language: the finite verb or finite auxiliary appears first in the clause in unmarked (= normal) constituent order, as in (1), which has a finite auxiliary (meaning 'was') in initial position. This example also has a non-finite main verb *dweud* 'tell', lower down in the clause; this construction, then, is rather parallel to English *was telling*, which also has an auxiliary plus a non-finite main verb.

   (1) Oedd fy ffrind yn dweud ei hanes wrth yr athro y bore 'ma.
       was my friend PROG tell.INFIN her story to the teacher the morning here
       'My friend was telling her story to the teacher this morning.'

Changes in this basic order are used to focus other constituents. Examine the data in (2) through (6) (based loosely on Jones and Thomas 1977: 289).

Task: (i) State how constituents are focussed in Welsh (being as precise as you can), and (ii) state precisely what constituent is focussed in each example, giving its category and grammatical function. (iii) A translation for (2) is already provided; suggest appropriate translations into English for the remaining examples. (iv) In both (3) and (5) there are additional grammatical changes; can you say what these are?

Hint:
In some cases your translation into English may not sound very natural. The reason for this is that languages display differences in what constituents may be focussed or otherwise manipulated, as we have seen throughout this chapter. Provide the best translations you can, whilst trying to capture the meaning of the source language.

(2) Fy ffrind oedd yn dweud ei hanes wrth yr athro y bore 'ma.
my friend was PROG tell.INFIN her story to the teacher the morning here
'It was *my friend* who was telling her story to the teacher this morning.'

(3) Ei hanes oedd fy ffrind yn ddweud wrth yr athro y bore 'ma.
her story was my friend PROG it.tell.INFIN to the teacher the morning here

(4) Wrth yr athro oedd fy ffrind yn dweud ei hanes y bore 'ma.
to the teacher was my friend PROG tell.INFIN her story the morning here

(5) Dweud ei hanes wrth yr athro oedd fy ffrind y bore 'ma.
tell.INFIN her story to the teacher was my friend the morning here

(6) Y bore 'ma oedd fy ffrind yn dweud ei hanes wrth yr athro.
the morning here was my friend PROG tell.INFIN her story to the teacher

7. Examine the data in (1) through (6) from Malayalam, a Dravidian language spoken in India. These data (taken from Asher and Kumari 1997) all illustrate one particular construction which manipulates constituents in a certain way which was discussed in Chapter 5. However, I have left one crucial morpheme (part of a word) in the source language both unidentified and unglossed.

Task: (i) Identify what construction is illustrated in the data; (ii) work out *exactly* how this construction is formed in Malayalam; and (iii) work out what syntactic category of constituent (e.g. PP, NP etc.) is being manipulated in each separate Malayalam example. (To remind you, ACC is accusative case, indicating a direct object.)

(1) avan   bhaaryayooṭum   makkaḷooṭum   kuuṭe   taamasikkunnu
    he   wife.with   children.with together.with   stay.PRES
    'He stays with his wife and children.'

(2) ɲaan   raamaneyum   avanṟe   muunnaamatte   makaneyum   kaṇṭu
    I   Raman.ACC   his   third   son.ACC   see.PAST
    'I saw Raman and his third son.'

(3) avaḷ   viiṭṭilum   hoosṭṭalilum   taamasikkilla
    she   house.in   hostel.in   stay.FUT.NEG
    'She will not stay in the house or the hostel.'

(4) avan   eẓuttu   vrttiyaayum   vyaktamaayum   eẓuti
    he   letter   neatly   legibly   write.PAST
    'He wrote the letter neatly and legibly.'

(5) avan   kaappi   kuṭikkukayum   piṉṉe   vaṭa   tiṉṉukayum   ceytu
    he   coffee   drink.INFINITIVE   and.then   vada   eat.INFINITIVE do.PAST
    'He drank coffee and then ate vada.'

(6) uṇṇiyum   baabuvum   vannu
    Unni   Babu   come.PAST
    'Unni and Babu came.'

8. The data in (1) and (2) (from Clamons et al. 1999) are from a Cushitic language, Oromo, spoken in Ethiopia, Kenya and Tanzania. In the examples in (1), the subject of the sentence also has a special pragmatic property: it is a TOPIC, which Clamons et al. define as 'what the sentence or discourse is about'. The topic property is marked on subjects which are topics using a topic marker -*n*. The subjects in (2) are *not* topics. Subjects in general are marked with a 'subject case' marker (SU).

Task: Discover what grammatical change occurs in the sentence when its subject is also a topic. Articulate it as clearly as you can, using the correct grammatical terminology, and generalizing so that you cover all the data with a single statement. You are looking for a property which is common to all the grammatical data in (1) versus all the grammatical data in (2), but this property is manifested slightly differently from example to example.

Hints:
- The subject of the sentence can, of course, consist of one noun phrase conjoined with another noun phrase: for instance, in (1b) the 'girl' noun phrase and the 'boy' noun phrase are co-ordinated in this way to form a subject meaning 'the girl and the boy'. The subject will then have the grammatical properties of the two conjoined phrases together.

- English does not have a special topic construction, but topics are typically associated with a particular emphatic intonation. I've indicated this by using italics in the translations in (1).

- The background information above the examples is there purely to help you see where topics are used in Oromo. You can see from (1) that topics are normally a phrase which has just been mentioned in the discourse; this contrasts with the 'out-of-the-blue' sentence that you might find at the start of a story, as in (2a), or a sentence in which the participants clearly haven't been mentioned before, as in (2b, c). Note also that the translations in (1) and (2) differ subtly, reflecting the fact that the subjects are topics in (1) but not in (2).

- It will help you to compare (1a) with (2a), (1b) with (2b), and (1c) with (2c). The additional data are there simply to give you more clues.

(1) a. (i) (In answer to: What did the girl and the boy do?)
Intal-t-ií-n   hoolaa   bit-t-e.
girl-FEM-SU-TOPIC   sheep   buy-FEM-PAST
'*The girl* bought a sheep.'

    a. (ii) *Intal-t-ií-n   hoolaa   bit-e.
girl-FEM-SU-TOPIC   sheep   buy-PAST
('*The girl* bought a sheep.')

    b. (In answer to: What did the girl and the boy do?)
Intal-t-ií-n   -ifi   gurbaá-n   wal   lol-an
girl-FEM-SU-TOPIC   and   boy.SU-TOPIC   each.other   fight-3PL.PAST
'*The girl and the boy* were fighting.'

    c. (In answer to: Where was I when the boy came?)
Ati   -ifi   Salma-á-n   nyataa   godhu   tur-tan
you.SG   and   Salma-SU-TOPIC   food   make   were-2PL.PAST
'*You and Salma* were cooking.'

(2) a. (Passage at the start of a story, i.e. with no previous context)
Intala   takka-á   hoolaa   bit-e
girl   one.FEM-SU   sheep   buy-PAST
'A girl bought a sheep.'

    b. (In answer to: Who was fighting?)
Intala   -afi   gurbaa   tokko-ó   wal   lol-e
girl   -and   boy   one.MASC-SU   each.other   fight-PAST
'Some girl and boy were fighting.'

    c. (In answer to: Who was cooking?)
Ati   -ifi   Salma-á   nyataa   godhu   tur-e
you.SG   and   Salma-SU   food   make   were-PAST
'You and Salma were cooking.'

    d. (i) Intala-á   dhuf-e.
girl-SU   come-PAST
'The girl came.'

d. (ii) *Intala-á dhuf-t-e.
girl-SU come-FEM-PAST
('The girl came.')

NOTE

1 As you can probably tell intuitively, though, the sequence *the girl's uncle* is not a constituent in (6a), where the uncle belongs to both the boy and the girl.

6

Relationships within the clause

章节导读

一个小句主要包括名词短语和动词短语两部分，两者之间的关系可以由三种方式来表示：第一是成分顺序，核心名词短语在小句中一般都有固定的位置；第二是格的标记，主格名词短语是主语，而受格名词短语则是宾语；第三是动词和名词短语之间的一致。上述三种方法不是相互排斥的，许多语言都使用几种方法来表示名词和动词短语之间的句法关系。

世界上的语言有 SVO、SOV、VSO、VOS、OVS、OSV 等六种成分顺序。对于一种语言来说，往往其中有一种是基本的，被称为基本词序，而其他的则被称为有标记的词序。但是对于某些语言来说，我们很难判断哪一种词序是基本的，有时一个语言中的两种甚至更多的成分顺序都是常用的，都属于无标记的，有时一个语言中的母句和从属小句中的成分顺序有所不同，还有的时候，一个语言的句子一般没有独立的主语和宾语，因此，我们也难以判断基本的成分顺序。上述六种成分顺序在世界语言中的使用情况也是不一样，其中 SVO 和 SOV 两种是最为常见的。关于不同语言中的成分顺序，我们可以概括为以下两点：第一，绝大多数的语言都是以主语开头的；第二，绝大多数的语言都把动词放置于宾语之前。

从名词短语和动词之间的句法关系来看，名词短语可以作不及物动词的主语、及物动词的主语和及物动词的宾语三种情况，它们被视为动词的核心论元。总体上讲，世界上的语言存在受格和作格两种格的系统。在受格系统中，不及物动词的主语和及物动词的主语都使用主格形式，及物动词的宾语则使用受格形式。在作格系统中，及物动词的主语使用作格形式，不及物动词的主语和及物动词的宾语都使用通格形式。但是，上述区分并不绝对。在某些语言中，要采用哪一种格系统，要由具体的环境而定，在某些情况下需要使用作格形式，而在其他情况下则需要使用受格形式。名词短语的特性（例如，是否有生命等）、不及物动词的意义以及动词的时态和体等都有可能会影响到格的标记。

一致是指动词要与充当其论元的名词短语的人称、性、数等语法特性保持一致。汉语、日语、瑞典语等语言中不存在这种现象，动词不需要和任何名词短语保持一致。在印欧语系的语言中，动词只要与其主语保持一致，而在其他一些语言中，动词则要求与两个或者更多的名词短语保持一致。

主语和宾语是两个核心的语法关系，它们在各种语言中是普遍存在的。主语具有以下特性：（1）主语一般用来表示动作的施事者；（2）在无标记的成分顺序中，主语一般处于小句的开始；（3）在祈使结构中，主语一般会被省略；（4）主语控制反身代词和互相代词；（5）主语经常控制另一个小句中名词短语的指称特性；（6）其他位置的词经常会被升格到主语的位置。宾语是另一个重要的语法关系，它在受格系统中做二位谓词（即双论元动词）的补语。对于三位谓词来说，宾语往往有直接宾语和间接宾语之分。

After introducing the ways in which languages can indicate grammatical relations within the clause (Section 6.1), this chapter outlines in detail the major systems: constituent order (6.2); case systems (6.3); and agreement and cross-referencing (6.4). Section 6.5 looks at grammatical relations cross-linguistically, and asks whether there are universals. Section 6.6 is a case study of languages with 'free' word order, based on Warlpiri.

6.1 INDICATING GRAMMATICAL RELATIONS IN THE CLAUSE

In this chapter we investigate the relationships between verbs and their noun phrase (NP) arguments within the clause. All languages have intransitive clauses—clauses with a verb and just one NP participant, such as *The dog growled*—and transitive clauses—clauses with a verb and two NP participants, such as *The dog licked my friend*. The NP participants that occur in these basic clause types are known as CORE ARGUMENTS, and this chapter examines the ways in which the world's languages distinguish between core arguments.

There are three main ways in which a language may indicate the relationship between core NPs and the verbal predicate. First, each core NP may have a fixed position in the clause: such a system uses CONSTITUENT ORDER to indicate the relationship between NP participants and verb. In English, both subjects and objects have a fixed position, which is how we determine who killed who in a pair of sentences like *The snake killed the bird* and *The bird killed the snake*.

But core NPs don't have a fixed position in all languages. Core NPs in Latin can appear quite easily in different positions; both sentences in (1) have the same meaning, although the order of the NPs is different in (1a) and (1b):

(1) a. Puer-um   puella   audi-t.   (Latin)
             boy-ACC   girl.NOM   hear-PRES.3SG
             'The girl hears the boy.'
       b. Puella   puer-um   audi-t.
             girl.NOM   boy-ACC   hear-PRES.3SG
             'The girl hears the boy.'

This variation in constituent order is possible because in Latin, the form of the NPs themselves indicates what relationship they have with the verb: this is CASE MARKING. The NOMINATIVE NP (glossed NOM) signifies the subject and the ACCUSATIVE NP (glossed ACC) signifies the object of the verb. Nominative and accusative are grammatical terms for distinct cases. Latin, then, utilizes the second main way of distinguishing core NPs: by case marking. Subjects in Latin are not distinguished from objects by their position, but by being specifically marked as subjects or objects.

The third way in which a language can indicate the relationship between NP participants and the predicate is by verb AGREEMENT or CROSS-REFERENCING. Latin and English have a limited amount of agreement: the *-t* suffix on *audit* and the *-s* suffix on *hears* both indicate a third person singular subject (in English, this occurs only in the present tense). But many languages have far more extensive systems to indicate the participants via marking on the verb itself, typically in the form of pronominal affixes. Look back at Section 4.3.3.2: the head-marking language Kambera is a typical CROSS-REFERENCING language, where free pronouns are only used for emphasis or disambiguation. So in (2), there are no independent free pronouns meaning 'I' and 'you', and it's only the subject and object markers on the verb that determine who's doing the asking.

margin note: Nominative, 主格，指名词或名词短语充当动词主语时的形式；accusative, 受格，指名词或名词短语充当动词宾语时的形式。

(2) Jàka   **ku**-karai-**kai**   tiang …   (Kambera)
         if   1SG.SU-ask-2PL.OBJ   later
         'If I ask you (*plural*) later …'

In (2), the bound pronominal affixes on the verb (shown in bold) are clearly crucial, whilst in Latin and English, verbal agreement markers don't have much of a function in distinguishing subject and object.

These three systems—order, case and agreement—are not mutually exclusive: most languages use some combination of systems, although it is common for one to predominate. Sections 6.2 through 6.4 examine each system in turn. Section 6.5 then looks at noun phrases in terms of their GRAMMATICAL RELATIONS, or GRAMMATICAL FUNCTIONS.

6.2 ORDER OF PHRASES WITHIN THE CLAUSE

6.2.1 Basic and marked orders

As we saw in Chapter 1, linguists often talk about the 'word order' of a particular language. In fact, this term refers not to single words but to the order of PHRASES, so a better term is CONSTITUENT ORDER. Here, I concentrate on the order of the three major constituents in a transitive clause: subject, object and verb. In many languages, including English, subjects are distinguished from objects by having a fixed position for each NP, in the ordinary, basic constituent order. Given the three constituents S, O and V, there are six logically possible variations, and indeed all six orders do occur as a basic constituent order amongst the languages of the world:

(3) Mpša   e-lomile   ngwana.   (Northern Sotho)
     S   V   O
     dog   SU-bit   child
     'The dog bit a/the child.'

(4) Müdür   mektub-u   imzala-dı.   (Turkish)
     S   O   V
     director.NOM   letter-ACC sign-PAST
     'The director signed the letter.'

(5) Tuigeann   Bríd   Gaeilge.   (Irish)
     V   S   O
     understands   Bridget   Irish
     'Bridget understands Irish.'

(6) E   kamatea   te   naeta   te   moa. (Gilbertese)
             V   O   S
     3SG   kill.3SG   the   snake   the   chicken
     'The chicken killed the snake.'

(7) kaikuxi   etapa-vâ   toto,   papa   tomo   (Apalai)
     O   V   S
     jaguar   kill-PAST   3PL   father   3PL
     'They killed a jaguar, father's group.'

(8) anana   nota   apa   (Apurinã)
     O   S   V
     pineapple   I   fetch
     'I fetch pineapple.'

In the examples above, the constituent orders shown are all reasonably uncontroversial: they represent the basic order, or one of the basic orders, found in each of the languages. So, for instance, we can say Northern Sotho is an SVO language, and Turkish is an SOV language. However, saying a language has a certain basic constituent order doesn't mean that it never has any other orders. For instance, English has a basic SVO order, as in *They adore syntax*, but we can also use an object-initial order, as in *Syntax, they adore*, to give particular emphasis to the direct object, in this case *syntax*. An order which is used like this to focus on a constituent is known as a MARKED (= non-basic) order.

In some languages, it is not easy to decide on a basic constituent order. First, two (or more) orders may be UNMARKED—equally neutral. For instance, some verb-initial languages such as Fijian, Tongan and Samoan (all Austronesian languages) are not clearly definable as either VSO or VOS: both orders are frequent. Languages which allow all of the six possible constituent orders are common; which order is actually chosen depends on pragmatic factors such as focus, and which constituent is the topic of the sentence. Some languages with free constituent order do have one order which is clearly basic. So for example, the Slavonic languages Polish and Russian are SVO. The native American language Mohawk, on the other hand, has no single basic or dominant order; this is also a common pattern cross-linguistically. Some languages also have free or very unrestricted WORD ORDER in the most literal sense; we examine such languages in Section 6.6.

Second, some languages have a different order in root clauses and in subordinate clauses. For instance, a number of Germanic languages, including German and Dutch, have SOV order in embedded clauses but have unmarked SVO order in root clauses; see Section 3.2.4 for discussion of this phenomenon.

Third, it may not be possible to tell whether there's an unmarked word order because sentences don't typically contain independent subject and object NPs. This is typically the case in languages which are strongly HEAD-MARKING (see Section 4.3). The verb itself in such languages always has subject and object markers, as in (2), but in natural discourse there are very few clauses containing both a lexical subject and a lexical object NP (like *The bird killed the snake*), so we can't easily say what the order of S, O and V might be.

In instances like all these, the constituent order which is designated 'basic' often depends more on the theoretical allegiances of the linguist than on any properties of the language. The criteria linguists use to determine a basic constituent order include frequency, which means seeing how often each order occurs in a text, and neutrality, which means looking at sentences with no particular focus or emphasis. Native speakers also have strong intuitions about which order(s) are the most neutral, if any, and indeed whether or not word order changes make any difference to the meaning of a sentence.

6.2.2 Statistical patterns

The six basic constituent orders presented in Section 6.2.1 don't all have equal frequency. Statistically, we would expect to find the world's languages split evenly amongst the six possible orders. But in fact the basic orders SVO and SOV are by far the most frequent, between them covering around 80 per cent of the world's languages (roughly equally split). VSO is the only other major group, covering perhaps 9–12 per cent of languages, including Celtic (for example, Welsh and Irish), Semitic (for example, Biblical Hebrew and Classical Arabic) and Polynesian languages (such as Maori). Languages with the basic order VOS are much rarer, covering around 3 per cent of the world's total. As noted in Section 6.2.1, though, many verb-initial languages have both VSO and VOS as basic patterns. Both OSV and OVS were once thought not to exist as basic orders, and in particular the OSV order is extremely rare. But both are attested in the languages of the Amazon basin, as shown in (7) and (8). A certain amount of estimation is unavoidable in any figures given, not least because reliable information on basic constituent order is not always available.

Two major generalizations about constituent order in the world's languages emerge from the statistics. First, the vast majority of languages have subject-initial order (SOV, SVO), and even if subjects are not absolutely clause-initial, they generally precede objects (SOV, SVO, VSO). In one large language sample (Tomlin 1986), 96 per cent of the languages have subjects before objects. Why might this be? Subjects appear to be more salient than objects, which may account for their initial position: subjects typically initiate the action expressed by the verbal predicate, are often agents of that action or at least in control of it, and are often the topic of the clause. On the other hand, objects are prototypically the theme or patient, the entity which is acted upon, and are less likely as topics.

Second, the majority of languages place V next to O (in either order): again, over 90 per cent of a typical sample of languages do this. Only two constituent orders lack the VO/OV grouping—the extremely rare OSV order and the much more frequent VSO order. In VSO languages, though, there are often alternative orders available which do place O and V together. For example, many VSO languages have an SVO alternative order (e.g. Arabic and Berber). And the Celtic languages, though generally considered to be VSO (like the Irish example in (5)), also have a very frequent auxiliary-SVO word order, as in (9). In this order, the subject precedes the other main elements in the clause and a transitive verb and its object are also grouped together into a VP. Note that the finite element in this clause is the initial auxiliary, and the lexical verb *péinteáil* 'paint' appears in its infinitival form lower down in the clause:

(9) Bhí an fear [VP ag péinteáil cathaoir inné]. (Irish)
Aux S V O
was the man PROG paint.INFIN chair yesterday
'The man was painting a chair yesterday.'

This grouping of O and V which predominates cross-linguistically gives support to the traditional two-way division of the clause into a subject and a predicate, which in turn contains the verb and its object (see 5.1.3).

Examination of large statistical samples of languages also reveals that the word order *within* constituents correlates with the order of the major constituents themselves (see, for example, Dryer 1991). In Chapter 4, I introduced the idea that languages fall into two basic groups, HEAD-INITIAL and HEAD-FINAL.

Head-initial order

- The verb *precedes* its objects and complement clauses.
- Adpositions are prepositions, giving [P NP] order in PPs.
- Complementizers (such as *that, if, whether*) precede the clause they select as complement.

Head-final order

- The verb *follows* its objects and complement clauses.
- Adpositions are postpositions, giving [NP P] order in PPs.
- Complementizers follow the clause they select as complement.

It turns out that OV languages (the largest group is SOV) are very generally head-final, whilst VO languages (SVO plus all verb-initial languages) are characteristically head-initial. For example, OV languages are far more likely to have postpositions than prepositions: in a typical sample (for instance, Dryer 1991) around 96 per cent of verb-final languages are postpositional. On the other hand, VO languages are typically prepositional: only around 14 per cent of SVO languages have postpositions, and only 9 per cent of verb-initial languages. Similarly, in VO languages, complementizers such as *if* and *that* virtually always precede their subordinate clause, as in English. Conversely, in around 70 per cent of OV languages, the complementizers follow the subordinate clause; see for example the Japanese examples in exercise 3 in Chapter 3.

To summarize Section 6.2, for some languages constituent order is the major way to distinguish the grammatical relations (subject, object etc.) in a sentence. We expect such languages to have a fairly rigid constituent order, as is true of English, for example. Other languages have much more freedom of constituent order. These are typically languages which have case marking and/or a well-developed system of verb agreement: both these features allow subjects to be distinguished from objects even if the NPs don't have a fixed position in the sentence. The following two sections look in detail at case marking and agreement, starting with an examination of case systems.

6.3 CASE SYSTEMS

6.3.1 Ways of dividing core arguments

In Chapter 4, I introduced the concept of a head and its dependents. We saw that the relationship between these elements need not be marked morphologically at all (for instance, it's not indicated in Chinese): such languages have neutral marking. But if it *is* indicated, this can be either by marking on the head (head-marking) or on the dependents (dependent-marking). In languages with CASE systems, the noun phrase dependents are marked to show their relationship with the head element in the phrase or clause. This section concentrates on the relationships between a head verb and its NP arguments; case marking shows, for example, which NP is the subject and which the object.

We've often used the terms 'subject' and 'object'. But do these terms apply equally well to all languages? In this section, we'll see that it is helpful to distinguish between different types of subjects, in order to describe case systems that occur outside the familiar European language families. I will divide the CORE ARGUMENTS of a verb as shown in Table 6.1, and use the abbreviations S, A and O to designate their grammatical relations (Dixon 1972, 1979, 1994).

Table 6.1

The core arguments

Subject of an intransitive verb	S
Subject of a transitive verb	A
Object of a transitive verb	O

For example:

(10) The snake(S) hissed.

(11) The chicken(A) bit the snake(O).

Though the label 'S' is associated with 'subject', it specifically refers just to the 'single' argument of an intransitive verb, as in (10): I recommend using 'single' as a mnemonic for S. The label 'O' is clearly 'object'. And 'A' is for 'agent', which is the prototypical semantic role taken by the subjects of transitive verbs such as 'bite', 'examine' or 'regurgitate'. All languages must have some way of distinguishing the transitive subject, A, from the object, O, so that we can tell who gets bitten in an example such as (11). In languages like English, fixed constituent order does this work. What, though, if the constituent order is free? One solution is to ensure that A has a different *form* from O: this is the role of case marking.

A logically possible way of distinguishing the three core arguments would, of course, be to have a different marking for each of them. Such a language would distinguish three different cases, one for S, one for A, one for O; an example is given as (26) below. However, this is actually an extremely unusual system, cross-linguistically. The reason for this is undoubtedly because a much more economical system is attainable, using just two case distinctions. Only A and O need to be marked differently. There are no clauses with both an S and an A: they can't co-occur, because within any given clause the verb is either transitive or intransitive. Similarly, there are no clauses with both an S and an O: if the verb is intransitive, it just has an S, and not an O. So to achieve the most economical case system possible, there are two equally logical alternatives, both of which require just two case distinctions.

The first system marks S and A in the same way, and O differently. In other words, all subjects receive one case marking, and objects receive a different case. This is known as the NOMINATIVE/ACCUSATIVE pattern, and it occurs in most European languages (a notable exception is Basque). In Modern English, full noun phrases have no case marking, but we can see the relics of a previous nominative/accusative case system in the forms of the first and third person pronouns:

(12) We(S) left.
       We(A) like her(O).

(13) She(S) left.
       She(A) likes us(O).

We and *she* are NOMINATIVE forms, used for both S and A: in other words, all subjects have the same form. *Her* and *us* are ACCUSATIVE forms, used for O.

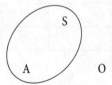

Figure 6.1
The nominative/accusative grouping

Because this grouping of S and A is so familiar from European languages, you may consider it entirely natural to case-mark all subjects in the same way. But remember that this is only one of the two equally economical ways of dividing the core arguments. The second system marks S and O in the same way, but marks A differently; this is known as the ERGATIVE/ABSOLUTIVE pattern:

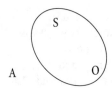

Figure 6.2
The ergative/absolutive grouping

ERGATIVE is the case of A—the subject of transitive verbs. ABSOLUTIVE is the case of both S and O, the subject of intransitive verbs and the object of transitive verbs.

A summary of the two systems is shown in Table 6.2. You can see that both case systems only require two distinctions. One system groups S with A (since they never co-occur and so won't be confused with each other); this is typically known simply as the accusative pattern. The other system groups S with O (they, too, never co-occur, so also can't be confused with each other); this is typically known simply as the ergative pattern.

Ergative case, 作格。在某些语言中及物动词的宾语和不及物动词的主语被赋予同样的格,为了描述这一类的句法结构,语言学家把及物动词的主语称为作格,而把及物动词的宾语和不及物动词的主语一起称作通格（absolutive case）。

Table 6.2
The major case systems

Accusative system	
A S	O
Nominative	Accusative

Ergative system	
A	S O
Ergative	Absolutive

In the following two sections I move on to an illustration of each of the main case systems in turn.

6.3.2 Nominative/accusative systems

I start with the most familiar system, NOMINATIVE/ACCUSATIVE (or just ACCUSATIVE). This system has an AS/O pattern: A and S are marked the same, O differently. Good examples are Latin, German, Japanese and Turkish, amongst many other languages. Subjects of both transitive and intransitive verbs are marked in the same way, with NOMINATIVE case. Objects of transitive verbs are marked with ACCUSATIVE case. This 'alignment' of NPs is sometimes indicated by using the notation S = A ≠ O.

(14) Puella   veni-t.   (Latin)
      girl.NOM   come-PRES.3SG
      'The girl(S) comes.'

(15) a. Puer-um puella audi-t.
    boy-ACC girl.NOM hear-PRES.3SG
    'The girl(A) hears the boy(O).'
 b. Puella puer-um audi-t.
    girl.NOM boy-ACC hear-PRES.3SG
    'The girl(A) hears the boy(O).'

Since the A and O arguments of the verb *audit*, 'hears', are in different cases, there is no problem determining which is which, despite the free constituent order illustrated in (15a) and (15b).

格是整个名词短语的属性，在某些语言中，格被标记在中心词上，而在另一些语言中，名词短语的格则通过限定词或者修饰中心词的形容词来体现。

Case is generally considered to be a property of an entire *noun phrase*, rather than just the head noun itself. In some languages, case is indeed marked on the head noun via changes in its morphology (= changes in its form), as in the Latin examples. But elsewhere, for instance in German, case is typically not marked on the head noun, but is marked instead on the determiners and any adjectives in the noun phrase:

(16) [Der gross-e Hund] knurrte. (German)
    the.NOM big-NOM dog growled
    'The big dog growled.'

(17) [Der gross-e Hund] biss [den klein-en Mann].
    the.NOM big-NOM dog bit the.ACC small-ACC man
    'The big dog bit the small man.'

The (masculine) head nouns *Mann* 'man' and *Hund* 'dog' in (16) and (17) don't undergo any morphological changes: they're in their basic form. But we can tell who gets bitten in (17) from the case marking shown on other elements in the NPs, namely the determiners and the adjectives. For instance, *der* is the nominative form of the definite article ('the') for masculine nouns, whilst *den* is its accusative form. The NP *den kleinen Mann* is thus shown as accusative, so it's the object, whilst *der grosse Hund* is nominative, so it's the subject.

6.3.3 Ergative/absolutive systems

The ERGATIVE/ABSOLUTIVE system (or just ERGATIVE) has an SO/A pattern: S and O are marked the same, and A is marked differently. Lezgian (a Daghestanian language spoken in the Caucasus) is a standard ergative language. The subject (A) of a transitive verb has ergative case, whilst the object (O) of a transitive verb and the subject (S) of an intransitive verb both have absolutive case. This ALIGNMENT of NPs is sometimes indicated by using the notation S = O ≠ A. Compare in particular the forms of the first person singular pronouns ('I/me' in the English translations) in (18) through (20).

(18) Za   zi   balk'an   c'ud   xipe-qʰ   ga-na.   (Lezgian)
    I.ERG   my   horse.ABS ten   sheep-for give-PAST
    'I(A) gave away my horse(O) in exchange for ten sheep.'

(19) Zun   ata-na.
    I.ABS   come-PAST
    'I(S) came.'

(20) Aburu   zun   ajib-da.
    they.ERG   I.ABS   shame-FUT
    'They(A) will shame me(O).'

In the English translations, the first person singular pronouns have the same form, *I*, both as an A and an S, whilst the O has a different form, *me*; this is the standard accusative case pattern. By contrast, in Lezgian the A form (*za*) *differs* from the S, and instead the S and O forms are identical (*zun*): this is the standard ergative case pattern. When the first person singular pronoun is an A—the subject of a transitive verb, as in (18)—it takes the ergative case, giving the form *za*. But when it's either an S (the subject of an intransitive verb) as in (19), or an O (an object) as in (20), it takes the absolutive case, giving *zun*.

Our second example comes from an ergative language spoken in Europe, namely Basque, which is a language isolate (= a language with no known relatives). Examples from the Lekeitio dialect are given in (21) through (23): compare the case marking of the word for 'man' in each example.

(21) Gixona-k   liburua   erosi   dau.   (Basque)
    man-ERG   book.ABS   buy   AUX.3SG
    'The man(A) has bought the book(O).'

(22) Gixona   etorri   da.
    man.ABS   come   AUX.3SG
    'The man(S) has come.'

(23) Gixona   ikusi   dot.
    man.ABS   see   AUX.1SG
    'I(A) have seen the man(O).'

The NP meaning 'man' has the ergative case suffix -*k* in (21), where it's an A, i.e. the subject of a transitive verb. When this NP is an S or an O, as in (22) and (23), it takes the absolutive case, which has no actual suffix here but is instead the basic form of the noun.

If you understand the data, but are having difficulty remembering which NPs group together in the ergative/absolutive system, I recommend the mnemonic 'Abso', for 'A-*but*-SO' grouping. I hope this helps!

Ergativity is not found in the European language families (Romance, Germanic, Celtic, Greek, Albanian and so on—to which Basque is unrelated), and is also very rare in Africa. However, it is common in Australian languages, and also occurs widely in Tibeto-Burman languages, Mayan languages (Central America), and a number of Papuan languages (New Guinea), amongst others. In other words, ergative systems are not purely localized, but are spread around the world. Dixon (1994: 10) estimates that perhaps one quarter of the world's languages can be described as ergative languages; clearly, then, the accusative system is far more common.

6.3.4 Split systems I

An important feature of all ergative languages is that they are never ergative in all aspects of their syntax and morphology, but instead have a combination of ergative and accusative properties. Often, a language doesn't use just one case marking system consistently for all instances of A, S and O, but instead has ergative case marking for some constructions and accusative case marking for other constructions. The term in widespread use for such a system is SPLIT ERGATIVE. What this means is that the S argument may align with either A or O, depending on the grammatical context. In some circumstances, then, the alignment pattern is S = A ≠ O (an accusative alignment) and in other circumstances it is S = O ≠ A (an ergative alignment).

> Split ergative, 分裂作格，在某些语言中，作格系统只用于一部分情形，其他情形仍采用受格系统。

As an illustration of a split system, consider an Australian language, Dyirbal, which treats full noun phrases differently from pronouns in terms of case marking. Noun phrases are marked according to the ergative/absolutive system, as in (24). In Dyirbal, and very typically in other ergative languages, there is no actual inflection for the absolutive form; we saw this in the Basque data above. Here, the simple noun root is used for absolutive case, whilst the ergative is marked with a suffix, *-nggu*:

(24) a. nguma   banaganʸu   (Dyirbal)
         father.ABS   returned
         'Father(S) returned.'
    b. yabu   banaganʸu
        mother.ABS   returned
        'Mother(S) returned.'
    c. nguma   yabu-nggu   buran
        father.ABS   mother-ERG   saw
        'Mother(A) saw father(O).'

The word for 'father' has the same case, absolutive, when it's an S (24a) and when it's an O (24c). The word for 'mother' is an S in (24b), and so again has absolutive case, but it's an A (transitive subject) in (24c), so here it has the ergative case. However, pronouns in Dyirbal employ a different system, as you now have the opportunity to work out for yourself.

Before reading further, please examine the sentences in (25) and work out how the case-marking system for pronouns differs from that of full noun phrases.

(25) a. ngana banaganʸu (Dyirbal)
we.NOM returned
'We(S) returned.'
b. nʸurra banaganʸu
you.NOM returned
'You(S) returned.'
c. nʸurra ngana-na buran
you.NOM we-ACC saw
'You(A) saw us(O).'

⸻

First and second person pronouns in Dyirbal have an accusative case marking system. So the S and the A pattern together: both are nominative, as in familiar European languages. The nominative form has no inflection, but just uses the bare root of the pronoun. The accusative form, the O, has an accusative suffix -*na*: compare the words for 'we' in (25a) and (25c).

Three major factors have been identified as responsible for triggering splits in the argument-marking system in ergative languages. First, properties of the NPs in the sentence (such as whether or not they are animate) can trigger a split. In the Dyirbal system, full NPs and third person pronouns employ the ergative system, (24), whilst other pronominals employ the accusative system, (25). An alternative found in some languages is that independent NPs exhibit an ergative alignment, whilst pronominal affixes employ the accusative system; see Section 6.4.4 on Warlpiri. Note that 'If pronouns and nouns have different systems of case inflection, then the pronoun system will be accusative, and the noun system ergative, never the other way round' (Dixon 1994: 84).

Second, in some languages (e.g. Dakota) the meaning of an intransitive verb may trigger the split, according to how much control its S argument exerts over the verb's action. With volitional verbs like 'run' or 'swim', 'retire' or 'resign', the subject is semantically an agent, or at least has control over the verb's action or performs it voluntarily. This type of S argument will be marked in the same way as the A argument of a transitive verb, which is not surprising as both S and A are agent-like in such instances. But with non-volitional intransitive verbs like 'blush' or 'fall' or 'die', the S argument is not at all in control of the verb's actions; we blush or fall involuntarily, not deliberately. So this type of S argument will be marked in the same way as the O argument of a transitive verb, which is again not surprising as S is semantically much closer to a typical object in such instances: it *undergoes* the verb's action (blushing or falling etc.) rather than initiating it.

Third, the tense or aspect of the verb can trigger a split: ergative marking typically occurs with completed events, so is expected with past tense verbs or those with perfective aspect, whilst accusative marking occurs with present tense verbs and those with imperfective aspect. Hindi and various other Indo-Iranian languages illustrate this situation.

Dixon (1994) also reports that a fourth, much rarer, factor which may trigger splits in argument-marking is the status of the clause as either a main or an embedded clause. Only a few ergative languages are known to exhibit this type of split.

Finally, I noted in Section 6.3.1 that languages which use a different case for each of the core arguments, S, A and O, are very rare. Such a TRIPARTITE system does occur in another split-ergative Australian language, Pitta-Pitta, where the split is triggered (the technical term is 'conditioned') by the tense of the verb. In non-future tenses (but not in the future tense), NPs each have a different case, depending on whether they are S, A or O. In (26), look especially at the first person singular pronouns, the words for 'I' (in bold):

(26) a. **nga-tu**   kat^{y}u-na   wat^{y}ama-ka   (Pitta-Pitta)
         I-ERG   clothes-ACC   wash-PAST
         'I(A) washed the clothes(O).'
    b.   nangka-ya   **ngan^{y}t^{y}a**   kunti-ina.
         sit-PRES   I.NOM   house-in
         'I(S) am sitting in the house.'
    c.   tupu-lu   **ngan^{y}a**   pat^{y}a-pat^{y}a-ya
         caterpillar-ERG   I.ACC   bite-bite-PRES
         'A caterpillar(A) is biting me(O).'

The pronoun for 'I' has ergative case in (26a), where it's an A; it has nominative case in (26b), where it's an S; and it has accusative case in (26c), where it's an O. These examples show that in Pitta-Pitta, the two main case marking systems—the ergative system and the accusative system—partially intersect.

Another kind of split ergative system is illustrated in Section 6.4.4 below.

6.3.5 Marked and unmarked forms

At this point we can discover why linguists often just use the terms 'ergative' or 'accusative' to describe the two systems: it is common for *just this one* member of each system to be the only NP that is overtly case marked, whilst the other member of each system is unmarked, i.e. has no special inflection for case at all. Instead we find the ordinary root of the noun or pronoun (the form with no inflections).

In an ergative system, if one form lacks overt marking it will be the absolutive NP, whilst the ergative NP has a special inflection. This is true of all the ergative systems illustrated so far, Lezgian, Basque and Dyirbal. Please confirm this by looking at the Dyirbal examples in (24): the absolutive forms are not inflected; the ergative form is.

In an accusative system, if one form lacks overt marking it will be the nominative NP, whilst the accusative NP has a special inflection. This is confirmed by (25): the nominative pronouns are not inflected, whilst the accusative one is.

In fact, we can make a generalization which works for both case systems: whichever case is used for the S argument (either absolutive or nominative), that will generally (with a few exceptions) be the NP that *lacks* any overt marking (Dixon 1994: 56f). Not only is the case used for S generally formally UNMARKED (= lacking special marking), as in the Dyirbal examples in (24) and (25), it's also functionally UNMARKED. This means it's more widespread in occurrence and more basic in terms of usage. For instance, the absolutive or nominative form is typically used as the citation form of a noun, generally the form given in a dictionary.

6.4 AGREEMENT AND CROSS-REFERENCING

6.4.1 What does verb agreement involve?

Case marking and verb agreement (also termed concord) are in fact two alternative (and sometimes overlapping) ways to represent the same information. Recall that the relationship between a head verb and its dependent NPs can be morphologically indicated either by DEPENDENT-MARKING (case) or HEAD-MARKING (agreement). As we saw in Chapter 4, it's very common for a language to have both verbal agreement with a subject and also case marking on the core NPs: see example (1) from Latin. This is an instance of case and agreement overlapping.

In this section we'll see that 'an accusative system' doesn't necessarily imply that the language has nominative/accusative *case*; the same applies to 'an ergative system'. The relationships between verb and core NPs may instead be shown by verb agreement, either following the accusative pattern or the ergative pattern. In other words, the verb agrees with certain of its dependents and not others.

Agreement, or cross-referencing, means that a head verb is formally marked to reflect various grammatical properties of its NP arguments; if you need to refresh your memory, look back at Sections 2.2.2.4 and 4.3.3.2. To take a simple example, a verb might be marked for third person singular when its subject is a singular NP, and third person plural when its subject is a plural NP. (English has a verb agreement marker for third person singular subjects, *-s*, but only in the present tense: *S/he sings*). Cross-linguistically, the most common categories involved in agreement are PERSON, NUMBER, GENDER (= noun class) and CASE. We will see that verb agreement can follow an accusative or an ergative pattern even when there's no actual case marking on the NPs themselves.

Logically, the options are for a verb to agree (i) with none of its arguments, (ii) with some but not others or (iii) with all its arguments, and in fact all of these possibilities occur, as we will see below. There are, then, languages with no verb agreement whatever, for example Swedish, Japanese, Chinese, Maori and Malagasy. Example (27) illustrates this for Chinese:

(27) a. Wo xihuan ta (Chinese)
I like he
'I like him.'
b. Ta xihuan wo
he like I
'He likes me.'

The verb has the same form, *xihuan*, no matter what the person and number of the subject pronoun. In fact, constituent order is the sole way of distinguishing the subject and object in these examples, since there's no case marking on the NPs either: the third person singular pronoun, for instance, is *ta* whether it's a subject or an object. Chinese illustrates a neutral alignment system.

We next turn to languages that do have verb agreement.

6.4.2 Nominative/accusative agreement systems

Within the Indo-European family, it is common for the verb to agree only with the subject, as for example in Italian, French, Spanish, German, Dutch and English. Subject-only agreement also occurs in Turkish and other Altaic languages, in Tamil and other Dravidian languages, and in Finnish and other Uralic languages. Examples (28) and (29) illustrate from French:

(28) Nous avons vu ce film. (French)
we have.1PL seen this film
'We(A) have seen this film(O).'

(29) a. Nous avons décidé.
we have.1PL decided
'We(S) have decided.'
b. Ils ont décidé.
they have.3PL decided
'They(S) have decided.'

法语采用受格系统，动词只需要与主语保持一致。

These three examples show that there is subject/verb agreement in French, expressed on the auxiliary here rather than the lexical verb. So auxiliary *avons* has a first person plural inflection to agree with the 1PL subject pronoun *nous*, and a third person plural inflection *ont* to agree with the 3PL subject pronoun *ils* (29b). The subjects of transitive verbs (A) and the subjects of intransitive verbs (S) are both marked on the verb in the same way, whilst the verb does not agree with the object, *ce film*, in any way in (28). We can therefore say that French has an ACCUSATIVE agreement pattern, or alignment: A and S pattern together, as opposed to O. Again, this alignment can be indicated as S = A ≠ O. French does not have case marking on NPs, however: as in English, only pronouns display the relics of an earlier case system.

The other possibility, also common cross-linguistically, is that the verb cross-references more than one of its arguments. So in Kambera, which also has an accusative alignment, the verb cross-references both the subject *and* the object: these markers are shown in bold type in (30). To help you see what refers to what, I've indicated both the independent subject NP and the bound subject marker on the verb with a subscript $_{SU}$. I also indicate both the independent object NP and the bound object marker on the verb with a subscript $_{OBJ}$:

(30) [I Ama]$_{SU}$ **na**$_{SU}$-kei-**ya**$_{OBJ}$ [na rí muru]$_{OBJ}$. (Kambera)
the father 3SG.SU-buy-3SG.OBJ the vegetable green
'Father buys the green vegetables.'

In Kambera, the subject marker is a prefix (i.e. it precedes the verb stem), and the object marker is a suffix (i.e. it follows the verb stem). Example (30) has an overt subject and object, but if these are omitted the sentence is still perfectly grammatical, because the bound pronominals alone serve to indicate both a subject and an object. Such a sentence then simply has the (less specific) meaning 'He/she buys it'. Look back at example (2) above to see an instance of this kind. As we saw there, and in Chapter 4, head-marking languages (such as Kambera) often have whole sentences consisting of just the verb with its inflections. Free pronouns are generally not required, since the pronominal person and number affixes on the verb provide all the information about the verb's arguments: again, see (2).

在该语言中，动词的前缀用来表示与主语的一致，后缀用来表示与宾语的一致。

In some languages, constituent order affects which agreement markers occur. So for example, in Northern Sotho, a Bantu language, the unmarked (= basic, usual) constituent order is SVO, as in (31) and (32):

(31) Mpša **e**-lomilê ngwana. (Northern Sotho)
dog SU-bit child
'The dog bit a/the child.'

(32) Di-mpša **di**-lomilê ngwana.
PL-dog SU-bit child
'The dogs bit a/the child.'

In (31) and (32) there is only a subject marker, a verbal prefix (shown in bold). This prefix agrees with the noun class and number of *mpša*, 'dog': this is a language with extensive gender marking, as we first saw in Chapter 2. (To be precise, the prefix *e-* is used for subject agreement with nouns from Class 9 (mostly animals), whilst the verbal prefix *di-* in (32) is a Class 10 agreement marker, which is the plural of Class 9. A *di-* prefix also occurs on the subject in (32), showing the noun as plural.)

In (33) and (34) we have two variations on (31). These examples both have a marked constituent order, namely OSV in (33) and SOV in (34). And in these marked orders, we find both the subject marker *and* an object marker, the prefix *mo-*. (This prefix agrees with the noun class of *ngwana*, 'child', which is Class 1, for human beings.)

(33) Ngwana mpša **e-mo**-lomilê. (Northern Sotho)
O S V
child dog SU-OBJ-bit
'As for the child, the dog bit him/her.'

(34) Mpša   ngwana   **e-mo**-lomilê.
    S   O   V
    dog   child   SU-OBJ-bit
    'As for the dog, it bit the child.'

Before reading further, try to figure out why an object agreement marker is required in (33) and (34) but not in (31) or (32). Don't worry about the specifics of the noun classes or genders; this is not relevant to your answer.

First, consider (31) and (32): only one NP precedes the verb, so a Sotho speaker can assume that the order is the normal SVO order. The speaker can therefore tell that the first NP in the clause is the subject. Variations in this normal constituent order are used in Sotho to make a constituent the TOPIC of the sentence, with the TOPICALIZED NP appearing in initial position. The translations of (33) and (34) give the effect of this topicalization with the formula *As for the X*. In these examples, there are *two* NPs before the verb, either one of which might potentially be the subject. But since there's a subject marker *e-* which agrees with 'dog' and an object marker *mo-* which agrees with 'child', a Sotho speaker can sort out who's biting who. In this instance, the subject and the object are in different noun classes, so the sentence is completely unambiguous. Note that these subject and object agreement markers on the verb occur in a fixed order (in all languages, the order of elements *within* words is generally fixed), although either ordering of the independent object and subject NPs in (33) and (34) is grammatical.

Topic, 话题, 句子的话题就是对其做出说明的那个实体。

If a language has object agreement, we can (with one or two exceptions) be sure that it will also have subject agreement: in other words, object agreement presupposes subject agreement. What about verbs which take more than two arguments, such as ditransitive verbs (see Chapter 4) like 'give' or 'buy'? In some languages, a verb agrees with or cross-references more than two arguments, although this is not particularly common. In (35), from an Australian language called Biri, the verb cross-references three arguments, all of which are expressed as suffixes on the verb stem, and are shown in bold:

(35) nhula   manhdha   yaba-nha-**la-ŋga-ŋgu**   (Biri)
     he   food   give-FUT-3SG.SU-3SG.OBJ-1.DU.DATIVE
     'He will give food to us two.'

The verb stem in (35) is *yaba*, and this has a future tense marker, followed by three pronominal affixes, or person/number markers: *-la* marks the third person singular subject (and there's also an independent third person subject pronoun *nhula*, 'he', here); *-ŋga* marks the third person singular object, agreeing with *manhdha* 'food'; and *-ŋgu* is a marker for first person dual ('us two'), and is also dative. Dative is a case often used to mark a recipient, which gives rise to the meaning of something being handed over to someone here.

In this section we have seen accusative systems of agreement: the verbs agreed with their subjects, or both with their subjects and objects.

6.4.3 Ergative/absolutive agreement systems

We turn now to systems with ergative alignment. When verb agreement follows the ergative pattern, it marks S (intransitive subjects) and O (all objects) in the same way and A (transitive subjects) differently. So we can say that S = O ≠ A. ERGATIVE AGREEMENT MARKING occurs in a number of Caucasian languages, and also in Mayan languages (Mexico and Central America). Our examples are from the North-West Caucasian language Abaza. In (36) we have an intransitive verb, and in (37) a transitive verb. In all these examples, the data consist simply of a verb with bound pronominal affixes showing the person and number of the participant(s): I have indicated in bold the function of each morpheme:

(36) a. d-thád. (Abaza)
S-V
3SG-go
'He/she's gone.'

b. h-thád.
S-V
1PL-go
'We've gone.'

(37) a. h-l-bád.
O-A-V
1PL-3SG.F-see
'She saw us.'

b. h-y-bád.
O-A-V
1PL-3SG.M-see
'He saw us.'

c. d-h-bád.
O-A-V
3SG-1PL-see
'We saw him/her.'

All the person/number markers are prefixes on the verb in Abaza: note that they have a fixed order, S-V and O-A-V, so it is always clear who's doing what. The prefixes show the SO versus A pattern characteristic of ergativity. Throughout, any S and O markers which refer to the same person/number have the same form. First, let's look at third person singular prefixes. In (36a) we have a 3SG S prefix *d-*, giving a meaning equivalent either to 'he' or 'she', and the same prefix occurs as the 3SG O prefix in (37c), giving rise to the 'him/her' meaning: thus, SO group together. Note that *d-* is only an SO form, and is of course not used to mark a third person singular A, since we're dealing with a grouping of SO vs. A here. Instead, the 3SG A prefixes in (37a) and (37b) occur in an entirely different form, and moreover they're differentiated according to gender (*l-* for the 3SG feminine, and *y-* for the 3SG masculine), which the SO form isn't.

Next, let's look at first person plural prefixes. In (36b) we have a 1PL S prefix *h-*, giving the 'we' meaning, and the same prefix occurs as the 1PL O prefix in (37a) and (37b), giving the 'us' meaning. The data contain an additional complication which you may have noticed: *h-* also means first person plural ('we') in (37c), where it's an A, rather than S or O. How then do native speakers of Abaza know what's going on? The answer is that because the order of prefixes is fixed, the data indicate clearly to an Abaza speaker that *h-* really is the A argument in (37c), the subject of the transitive verb, since it follows the O prefix. It is rather common for languages to 're-use' pieces of morphology in this way: as long as they are clear in their context, duplications of this kind don't appear to cause confusion.

6.4.4 Split systems II

A language with an ergative agreement system may have ergative case marking too (for instance, the North-East Caucasian language Avar) but it is also possible to have ergative agreement on the verb but no case marking on independent NPs—in fact, Abaza (illustrated above) falls into this category. There are also languages which have ergative case marking on NPs, but a nominative/accusative system of cross-referencing on the verb. The Australian language Warlpiri illustrates this system. Full noun phrases and independent (i.e. freestanding) pronouns are all marked with ergative/absolutive case. The agreement markers (in bold) are affixed to the auxiliary, the element in second position in (38) and (39):

(38) Ngaju   ka-**rna**   wangka-mi.   (Warlpiri)
     I.ABS   AUX.PRES-1SG.SU   speak-NONPAST
     'I(S) am speaking.'

(39) Ngajulu-rlu ka-**rna-ngku**   nyuntu   nya-nyi.
     I-ERG   AUX.PRES-1SG.SU-2.OBJ   you.ABS   see-NONPAST
     'I(A) see you(O).'

Look first at the independent pronouns in (38) and (39), which are marked according to the ergative/absolutive system. The S argument *ngaju* ('I') in (38) is absolutive, as is the O argument *nyuntu* ('you') in (39). Conversely, the A argument *ngajulu-rlu* ('I') in (39) is ergative. SO thus group together in opposition to A, as we anticipate in this system. We clearly see that the pronoun for 'I' has a different case according to whether it's the subject of an intransitive verb (S), as in (38), or a transitive verb (A), as in (39).

Now look in contrast at the verb agreement. This marks *both* instances of first person singular in the same way, with the suffix -*rna* designating any first person singular subject. So the affixes reflect a grouping of all subjects (AS) as opposed to all objects (O), namely a nominative/accusative system. The Warlpiri system is not at all unusual, whereas there are no known languages with accusative case systems but ergative agreement systems. This is, then, another way in which the accusative system predominates cross-linguistically.

6.5 GRAMMATICAL RELATIONS

6.5.1 Investigating core grammatical relations

In this section we examine the cross-linguistic properties of two major core grammatical relations, SUBJECT and OBJECT. To show that these concepts are valid, we need to demonstrate that certain linguistic phenomena are best described in terms of 'subject' or 'object'. For languages in the nominative/accusative class, it's clear that 'subject' and 'object' are valid categories: in the last few sections we've seen a number of illustrations of both case and verb agreement operating in terms of subject vs. object alignment. The examples seen so far show that certain languages are *morphologically* nominative/accusative. This means that the characteristic AS/O alignment is indicated by changes in the morphology (form) of the NPs, via case marking, or in the morphology of the head verb, via agreement, or indeed by marking on both NPs and verbs. However, the AS/O pattern is also pervasive in syntax itself. This means that many languages—including those with no case marking or even with ergative case marking—are *syntactically* nominative/accusative. In such languages there are a number of syntactic processes which revolve around the subject and object relations—in fact, particularly the subject, since this grammatical relation is by far the most important. We'll examine some of these processes in this section, and return to this topic in Chapter 7.

The subject relation is crucial cross-linguistically: subjects tend to control the syntax in a number of ways, as we'll see. However, it's hard to give a satisfactory definition of 'subject', because no single property is shared by all subjects in all languages. Instead, there's a set of properties typical of subjects, and each language is likely to exhibit a subset of these properties. We begin by looking at some of the main cross-linguistic properties of subjects (Section 6.5.2), and then turn to the question of subjecthood in specific languages (Section 6.5.3).

6.5.2 Subjects: Typical cross-linguistic properties

i. Subjects are normally used to express the AGENT of the action, if there is an agent.

ii. Subjects tend to appear first in the clause in unmarked (basic) constituent order. Recall that maybe 80 per cent of languages are either SOV or SVO, therefore subject-initial. But since that leaves many languages that are not subject-initial, we can't use this as a defining property.

iii. Subjects are understood as the missing argument in IMPERATIVE constructions. An imperative is a command such as *Sit!* or *Eat up your greens!*. Both intransitive and transitive verbs have an understood (or in some languages, overt) second person subject pronoun ('you') in the imperative.

Reflexive，反身的，小句中的主语和宾语指同一实体。反身代词和互相代词是生成语法中一个受到重点关注的问题。

iv. Subjects control REFLEXIVE NPs, that is, '-self' forms such as the English *herself*, *themselves*, and also RECIPROCAL NPs such as *each other*. So we get *My sister really admires herself*, where the NP *herself* (feminine singular) refers back to the feminine singular subject, *my sister*, but we don't get **Herself really admires my sister*. Note that we can't simply say that the reflexive must refer to a *preceding* NP. We see this in the Madagascan language Malagasy, which has VOS order, so the subject does not precede the '-self' form. Nonetheless, the subject determines the reference of the '-self' NP; that is, the subject determines which NP the '-self' form refers to.

(40) a. Manaja tena Rabe. (Malagasy)
respect self Rabe
'Rabe respects himself.'
b. *Manaja an-dRabe tena.
respect ACC-Rabe self
'*Himself respects Rabe.'

In (40b), *Rabe* is the object, as we can tell from its accusative case marker; only when *Rabe* is the subject is the reflexive sentence grammatical, as in (40a).

v. Subjects often control the referential properties of an NP in another clause. For instance, when two clauses are conjoined, as in (41), the subject of the second clause can be omitted because it is CO-REFERENTIAL with the subject of the first clause, *Chris*: I show the omitted NP with Ø. But it's only the subject that can be omitted, (41a), not the object, (41b). Moreover, the NP that's omitted has to refer back to the subject of the first clause, *Chris*, and not the object, *Lee*. The subscripts $_i$ and $_j$ here have no meaning of their own, but are simply labels to show which NPs co-refer (= designate the same entity).

(41) a. [Chris$_i$ phoned Lee$_j$] and [Ø$_i$ met him$_j$ later].
b. *[Chris$_i$ phoned Lee$_j$] and [he$_i$ met Ø$_j$ later].

Second, in many languages verbs like 'begin' and 'want' take an infinitival complement clause, as in *Kim began [to grate the carrots]*. The 'understood' subject of the 'grate' clause is co-referential with the main clause subject: we understand that it's Kim who is grating the carrots. But only the subject in the infinitival clause—and not the object—can be the 'understood' NP:

(42) a. Chris$_i$ wants [Ø$_i$ to meet this famous film star].
b. *Chris$_i$ wants [this famous film star to meet Ø$_i$].

Promotion，升格，指一个名词短语被从层级关系较低的位置移位到较高位置的过程。

vi. Subjects are the most usual target for **promotion** from other positions. For instance the PASSIVE construction promotes an NP from direct object position to subject position (see Chapter 7), turning *The students applauded her* into *She was applauded (by the students)*: the pronoun has the form *her* as an object, but *she* as a subject. Although not all languages have promotion processes, if a language has any promotion processes, then it will have ones that move some constituent into subject position.

6.5.3 An examination of subjects in specific languages

We turn now to an examination of subjects in particular languages. We look first at Icelandic (Section 6.5.3.1), which has nominative/accusative morphology and syntax, and so has a clear SUBJECT relation. Section 6.5.3.2 then turns to a morphologically ergative language, Lezgian, for which the notion of subject is more controversial. Section 6.5.3.3 examines Tagalog, which represents a language type different to both accusative and ergative. Section 6.5.3.4 asks whether there are universal grammatical relations.

6.5.3.1 *Icelandic*

Icelandic is a standard accusative language—subjects are usually in the NOMINATIVE case and objects in the ACCUSATIVE case:

(43) Ég sá stúlkuna.
 I.NOM saw.1SG the.girl.ACC
 'I saw the girl.'

Verbs in Icelandic agree in person and number with the nominative subject:

(44) a. Við dönsuðum.
  we.NOM danced.1PL
  'We danced.'
 b. Þeir dóu.
  they.NOM died.3PL
  'They died.'

However, some verbs are exceptional: their subjects take a case other than nominative. In (45), we have a dative subject, and in (46), an accusative subject, *hana* 'her' (the object is also accusative in (46)):

(45) **Henni** leiddist.
 her.DATIVE bored
 'She was bored.'

(46) **Hana** vantar peninga.
 her.ACC lacks money.ACC
 'She lacks money.'

These subjects with 'quirky' case don't trigger subject/verb agreement. In (47), the subject is a *plural* pronoun *þá*, 'them' (accusative), but we find the same form of the verb *vantar*, 'lacks', as in (46) where the subject is *singular*. Compare (44b), where the nominative *þeir* 'they' triggers agreement, giving a plural form of the verb:

(47) Þá   vantar   peninga.
     them.ACC   lacks   money.ACC
     'They lack money.'

So if these 'quirky' subjects don't trigger verb agreement, on what grounds can we say they're subjects? There are, in fact, a number of diagnostics for subjects in Icelandic, and the NPs with quirky case pass all of these tests. First, subjects can undergo subject/verb inversion (see Section 3.2.4 on inversion in English). Example (48) shows that an ordinary nominative subject inverts with the finite verb to form a yes/no question, and in (49), we see that a dative subject also inverts. The subjects are in bold type:

(48) Hafði   **Sigga**   aldrei   hjálpað   Haraldi?
     had   Sigga.NOM   never   helped   Harold.DATIVE
     'Had Sigga never helped Harold?'

(49) Hefur   **henni**   alltaf   þótt   Ólafur   leiðinlegur?
     has   her.DATIVE   always   thought   Olaf.NOM   boring
     'Has she always thought Olaf boring?'

Even though there's also a nominative NP *Ólafur* in (49), this couldn't be inverted with the verb *hefur* 'has'.

Second, when two clauses are conjoined, the subject of the second clause can be omitted when it's co-referential with the subject of the first clause, just as in English: see (v) in Section 6.5.2 above. Example (50) illustrates with ordinary nominative subjects:

(50) Þeir   fluttu   líkið   og   (þeir)   grófu   það.
     they.NOM   moved   the.corpse   and   they.NOM   buried   it
     'They moved the corpse and (they) buried it.'

Turning next to a quirky subject, we see in (51) that the verb meaning 'like' takes a dative subject:

(51) **Mér**   líkar   vel   við   hana.
     me.DATIVE   likes   well   with   her
     'I like her.'

And it turns out that this dative subject can undergo this SUBJECT ELLIPSIS (= omission) too: the dative subject pronoun *mér* can be omitted in the second clause in (52):

(52) Ég   sá   stúlkuna   og   (mér)   líkaði   vel   við   hana.
     I.NOM   saw   the.girl.ACC and   me.DATIVE   liked   well with   her
     'I saw the girl and (I) liked her.'

In fact not only can a quirky subject *undergo* ellipsis, as in (52), it can also be the NP which *permits* ellipsis of another subject. This, then, is the third test for subjecthood. Example (53) has a dative subject in the first clause, and the nominative subject *þeir* can undergo ellipsis in the second clause:

(53) Þeim   líkar   maturinn   og   (þeir)   borða   mikið.
     them.DATIVE   likes   the.food.NOM   and   they.NOM   eats   much
     'They like the food and (they) eat a lot.'

Note that even though there is a nominative NP in the first clause, this is not the subject, and a missing subject can't refer back to it: the sentence couldn't mean, even jokingly, that the food eats a lot.

In sum, then, these (and other) tests for subjecthood in Icelandic show that subject NPs with quirky case really *are* subjects, despite the fact that they fail to trigger subject/verb agreement.

6.5.3.2 *Lezgian*

We saw earlier that morphologically ERGATIVE languages (i.e. those with ergative case and/or agreement) may be syntactically ACCUSATIVE. This means that syntactic constructions such as subject ellipsis utilize a grouping of the S and A arguments, as opposed to the O argument (S = A ≠ O). In fact, it is quite usual for languages which have morphologically ergative alignment to be accusative in terms of their *syntax*, and much rarer for them to have ergative syntax. We will see more on this in Chapter 7.

As we saw in Section 6.3.3, Lezgian is morphologically ergative: the case marking on NPs contrasts absolutive (on S and O noun phrases) with ergative (on A noun phrases, the subjects of transitive verbs): S = O ≠ A. It will help to review the discussion of (18) through (20) before reading further.

Evidence of syntactic accusativity in Lezgian comes from the fact that it has a SUBJECT grammatical relation (Haspelmath 1993). Let's look first at some basic data. The 'subject' consists of three NP types. The first two types are the A and S arguments: these are the two NPs that would constitute the 'subject' relation in an accusative language. To illustrate these two, we have the ergative-marked argument (A) of a transitive verb, as in (54), and the absolutive-marked argument (S) of an intransitive verb, as in (55). The NPs in bold type in (54) to (56) are the putative subjects.

(54) **Ruš-a**   gadadi-z   cük   ga-na.
     girl-ERG   boy-DATIVE   flower.ABS   give-PAST
     'The girl gave a flower to the boy.'

(55) **Ruš**   elq̓wena   q'uluqʰdi   kilig-na.
     girl.ABS   turn   backward   look-PAST
     'The girl turned around and looked back.'

The third potential 'subject' is the experiencer argument of verbs with meanings such as 'want', 'see' and 'be afraid', which in Lezgian take the DATIVE case, as in (56); cross-linguistically, this use of dative case for the semantic role of experiencer is quite common.

(56) **Ruša-z**   ada-qʰaj   kič'e   x̂a-na-č.
     girl-DATIVE   he-of   afraid   be-PAST-NEG
     'The girl wasn't afraid of him.'

Note that all three putative subject NPs have different cases, so we certainly can't identify 'subjects' by their morphological case in Lezgian. Furthermore, although the NP in bold in (55) is absolutive, not all absolutive NPs are subjects, of course: the O noun phrase *cük* 'flower' in (54) isn't. Similarly, not all dative NPs are subjects: *gadadiz* 'boy' in (54) isn't the subject—dative case here identifies the indirect object (see Section 6.5.4). If there is a 'subject' grammatical relation in Lezgian, then, it cuts across the morphological case marking.

So why would anyone think that Lezgian has a 'subject' relation? Constituent order provides some indication that all three NP types in bold in (54) through (56) pattern together: all have the same clause-initial position, which, as we know from Section 6.2, is the most common position for subjects cross-linguistically. But position alone won't uniquely identify subjects in Lezgian, because the constituent order is actually very free, so other NP types can be initial in the clause.

However, we can test for subjects using a construction parallel to that in (42) in Section 6.5.2—please look back to check on this—in which an embedded infinitival clause has an understood subject that refers back to the main clause subject. Look first at the English translations in (57) through (59) to get the idea of the construction, which is very similar in the two languages: the infinitival clause is the complement of a finite verb 'wants' in the matrix clause. The main difference is that in Lezgian, the infinitival clause (shown in square brackets) precedes the finite verb *k'anzawa* 'wants', whilst in English the embedded clause follows *wants*. Crucially, the *understood* subject in Lezgian (marked with Ø) can only be one of the three NP types tentatively identified above as forming a 'subject' category: either an ergative subject (an A), an absolutive subject (an S) or a dative subject.

(57) Nabisata-z_i [[$_{\text{NP Erg}}$ Ø$_i$]   ktab   k'el-iz]   k'an-zawa.
     Nabisat-DATIVE   (Subject)   book   read-INFIN   want-IMPF
     'Nabisat wants to read a book.'

(58) Nabisata-z_i [[$_{\text{NP Abs}}$ Ø$_i$]   qʰüre-z]   k'an-zawa.
     Nabisat-DATIVE   (Subject)   laugh-INFIN   want-IMPF
     'Nabisat wants to laugh.'

(59) Nabisata-z$_i$ [[$_{\text{NP Dative}}$ Ø$_i$] xwa akwa-z] k'an-zawa.
Nabisat-DATIVE (Subject) son see-INFIN want-IMPF
'Nabisat wants to see her son.'

We know what case the understood subject would have in each example by looking at what happens in ordinary finite clauses with overt (= pronounced) subjects: the verb for 'read' takes an ergative subject, the verb for 'laugh' an absolutive subject, and the verb for 'see' a dative subject. Compare (60): here, the understood NP is again absolutive, but (60) is ungrammatical because this absolutive NP is an O, an absolutive *object* (Musa is the one being sent) rather than an S, an absolutive *subject* as in (58).

(60) *Musa-z$_i$ [didedi [$_{\text{NPAbs}}$ Ø$_i$] šeherdi-z raqur-iz] k'an-zawa.
Musa-DATIVE mother.ERG (Abs.Object) town-DATIVE send-INFIN want-IMPF
('Musa wants to be sent to town by his mother.')

In sum, the Lezgian data show that even a morphologically ergative language may display syntactic accusativity, and indeed there does seem to be evidence for a subject relation in Lezgian.

6.5.3.3 *Tagalog*

In this section we will examine a language which resists clear classification into either the accusative or the ergative type, and seems in fact to have a totally different marking system for NPs. In Tagalog and other languages of the Philippines, NPs are not case-marked, but they are each preceded by a marker (which we can consider a preposition) that indicates their SEMANTIC ROLE (see Section 2.3.1). The preposition *ng* marks both agent and theme; *sa* (or *mula sa*) marks locative—i.e. indicating location, and glossed as 'from' in (61); and *para sa* marks beneficiary, glossed as 'for' in (61). However, in every sentence *one* of the NP participants must be chosen to be the TOPIC of the clause, and it is marked as such by a special preposition, *ang*, which replaces the marker the NP would have otherwise. The topic is shown in bold in each example. (Note that the topic is always understood to be definite, whilst the other NPs can be understood as definite or indefinite.)

Also, the verb itself has an affix that marks the semantic role of the NP chosen as topic: I've indicated this role beneath the gloss for the verb in each example. This marking is clearly a kind of verb agreement, but it is different from either the accusative system or the ergative system in that it does not operate in terms of the grammatical function of the NP arguments. In examples like (61), any one of the NP participants can be marked as the topic—and whichever semantic role the topic has will be indicated on the verb, resulting in a verb marked to agree with one of the properties 'agent', 'theme', 'locative' or 'beneficiary'; this is shown in the different morphology that the verb has in each example in (61). To see this, you'll need to study the Tagalog data itself, as the gloss doesn't reflect the morphological distinctions.

(61) a. Kukuha **ang babae** ng bigas sa sako para sa bata.
FUT.take.out TOPIC woman THEME rice from sack for child
AGENT.TOPIC
'The woman will take some rice out of a sack for a/the child.'

b. Kukunin ng babae **ang bigas** sa sako para sa bata.
FUT.take.out AGENT woman TOPIC rice from sack for child
THEME.TOPIC
'A/the woman will take **the rice** out of a sack for a/the child.'

c. **Ang sako** ay kukunan ng bigas ng babae para sa bata.
TOPIC sack be FUT.take.out THEME rice AGENT woman for child
LOCATIVE.TOPIC
'The sack will have rice taken out of it by the woman for the child.'

d. **Ang bata** ay ikukuha ng bigas ng babae mula sa sako.
TOPIC child be FUT.take.out THEME rice AGENT woman from sack
BENEFICIARY.TOPIC
'The child will have rice taken out of the sack for him/her by the woman.'

It's clear, then, that Tagalog isn't morphologically marked in accordance with either the accusative system or the ergative system, either by case marking or by verbal agreement.

However, as we have already noted, a language may nonetheless be *syntactically* accusative despite not being morphologically accusative. Does Tagalog fit this pattern? Looking at the syntactic behaviour of NPs, it turns out that some processes operate in terms of topics, irrespective of their semantic and syntactic role. But there are also other processes that operate in terms of a grouping of the A and S noun phrases, whether or not they are topics: this is a syntactically accusative pattern, and suggests that there may after all be a 'subject' in Tagalog.

Let's look first at a process that targets topics: the 'all' construction. In (62) we see that *lahat*, 'all', is understood as modifying whichever NP is the topic. In (62a) the topic is the agent, so *lahat* must modify the A noun phrase, meaning 'the children'. But in (62b) we have a theme topic, referring to the 'thing written', so *lahat* must modify the O noun phrase, meaning 'the letters'. Note that *lahat* is not even adjacent to this latter phrase, *ang mga liham*, in (62b):

(62) a. Susulat lahat **ang mga bata** ng mga liham.
FUT.write all TOPIC PL child THEME PL letter
AGENT.TOPIC
'All the children will write letters.'

b. Susulatin lahat ng mga bata **ang mga liham**.
FUT.write all AGENT PL child TOPIC PL letter
THEME.TOPIC
'The/some children will write all the letters.'
not 'All the children will write letters.'

Since linguists don't normally consider a grouping of A and O to form any grammatical relation, the 'all' construction favours a view of Tagalog as not having subjects.

Now consider a syntactic process in Tagalog that targets S and A noun phrases—the classic 'subject' pairing—and not topics. Our examples are complement clauses with an understood subject. You will find it helpful to look again at the discussion of similar examples given earlier on before reading further: see (42) from English and (57) through (59) from Lezgian. In the Tagalog construction, the 'missing' subject is always an S or an A, whether or not it's a topic. In the examples in (63), the topic of each matrix clause (the 'hesitate' clause) is the agent, *siya*, meaning 'he' (the suffix *-ng*, which I have left unglossed, indicates that an embedded clause follows). In the embedded clause, however, the topic is different in each example:

(63) a. Nagatubili   siya-ng   [humiram   ng   pera   sa   banko].
         hesitate   he.TOPIC-NG   borrow   THEME   money   from bank
         AGENT.TOPIC   AGENT.TOPIC
         'He hesitated to borrow money from a/the bank.'

    b. Nagatubili   siya-ng   [hiramin   **ang**   **pera** sa   banko].
         hesitate   he.TOPIC-NG   borrow   TOPIC   money   from bank
         AGENT.TOPIC   THEME.TOPIC
         'He hesitated to borrow **the money** from the bank.'

Remember that these 'borrow' clauses are embedded clauses with an understood subject. In both embedded clauses in (63a) and (63b), this understood subject is the agent (referring back to 'he' in the matrix clause), an A noun phrase. In (63a), the missing agent NP in the 'borrow' clause happens also to be the NP chosen as the topic, as we can tell from the form of the verb, which, as you'll recall, is marked for the semantic role of the topic. In (63a), then, there isn't an overt *ang*-NP—an overt topic—because this topic is the 'understood' NP. But in (63b), the topic of the embedded clause is the theme (thing borrowed), namely *ang pera* 'the money', yet the understood subject of that clause is still the A noun phrase (referring back to 'he'). So topics are clearly *not* the targets for the ellipsis (the omitted part) in this construction. In fact, this process of NP ellipsis suggests that Tagalog is syntactically accusative, at least in this one construction. In other words, the understood subject can be either an S or an A argument (i.e. any type of 'subject'), but not an O argument. Any process that treats S and A noun phrases together—and O arguments differently—suggests that the language operates at least part of its syntax in terms of a nominative/accusative alignment. Tagalog may indeed, then, have a SUBJECT grammatical relation consisting of S and A.

6.5.3.4 *Language universals?*

We are left with the indication that the 'subject' relation is very important cross-linguistically, even occurring in some languages which are not otherwise nominative/accusative in their morphology and elsewhere in their syntax. Should it be considered a language universal? Some linguists argue that it should not. For instance, Dryer (1997) argues that there are no universal grammatical relations, discussing data from Dyirbal, Cree, Cebuano and Acehnese which are particularly problematic for a view that 'subject' is a universal category. This view is supported by Croft (2001); see also Haspelmath (2007). We will leave this an open question. However, it is clear that recurring properties in grammatical relations *are* found cross-linguistically, among languages of very different syntactic types and from totally unrelated language stocks. It seems, then, that these properties may reflect some universal features, even if these are not fully understood at present.

Finally, we saw in Section 6.5 that languages which have ergative (or no) case marking may nonetheless exhibit nominative/accusative syntax. Is the opposite situation ever seen—in other words, can a language be syntactically ergative even if it doesn't have ergative/absolutive case morphology? Linguists used to think not, but more recently it has been shown that this situation does exist (Donohue and Brown 1999). Certainly, though, it is very rare.

6.5.4 Objects

The other major grammatical relation is that of OBJECT, in accusative systems the complement of a two-argument verb. There is plenty of morphological evidence for the existence of an object relation in languages with nominative/accusative morphology, since the O argument is designated by a special case (accusative) and/or verb agreement. This chapter contains examples of a case-marked O from languages as genetically diverse as Latin (1), Turkish (4) and Dyirbal (25). (Recall from Section 6.3.4 that Dyirbal is largely ergative, but its first/second person pronouns have an accusative case system.) Verb agreement with the O argument is shown in several examples: see (30) from Kambera and (39) from Warlpiri.

Syntactic evidence for the O relation is more limited than for subjects, but in many languages only an O can be passivized (see 1.1.1, 1.3.2 and also Chapter 7 for a demonstration of this). Recall that in Icelandic, we find certain constructions in which a noun phrase doesn't receive the expected case marking, but instead gets a 'quirky' case: examples of *subject* NPs with quirky case were given in Section 6.5.3.1. Icelandic also has certain *object* NPs with quirky case, so we can see how these act in terms of typical object behaviour. It turns out that not only do ordinary accusative O arguments undergo passivization, so too do O arguments with quirky case. An example of a quirky object is the NP *mér* in (64): this is not accusative, as objects typically are in Icelandic, but rather it is dative:

(64) Þeir   hjálpuðu   **mér**.   (Icelandic)
      they.NOM   helped   me.DATIVE
      'They helped me.'

Like other objects, however, this O can be promoted to subject position, giving (65). Note, though, that the dative case remains on this NP—it doesn't become nominative—though its position is the standard clause-initial position of the subject in Icelandic:

(65) **Mér**   var   hjálpað.   (Icelandic)
me.DATIVE was   helped
'I was helped.'

Verbs such as 'give', 'send' and 'show', which take three arguments (**X** gave **Y** to **Z**), can in some languages be said to distinguish a DIRECT OBJECT from an INDIRECT OBJECT. In accusative languages with extensive case systems, the direct object bears accusative case, whilst what is traditionally termed the indirect object bears **DATIVE case**, as in Turkish, German, Greek and Latin. The indirect object is typically the 'recipient' or 'goal' NP, such as *mir* in (66):

(66) Mein   Freund   gab   **mir**   sein   Fahrrad.   (German)
my.NOM   friend   gave   me.DATIVE   his.ACC bicycle
'My friend gave me his bicycle.'

> Dative case, 与格, 在使用词的形式变化表示语法关系的语言中, 与格是名词短语所取的一种形式, 一般表示间接宾语关系或与英语中 to 或 for 表示的意义相类似的意义, 但是, 不同的语言与格的使用方式有很大的差异。

The dative is also used for this same purpose in many ergative languages: see (54) from Lezgian. Cross-linguistically, then, the central use of the dative case is to designate the NP that's the recipient or the beneficiary or the goal of a three-argument verb.

But this type of NP does not always get a special case. For instance, although in Ancient Greek most three-argument verbs have an accusative direct object and a dative indirect object, the verb for 'teach' is exceptional in that both of its complements (the NPs meaning 'the boy' and 'the music') have accusative case:

(67) Edidaxan   [ton   paida]   [tēn   mousikēn].   (Ancient Greek)
taught.3PL   the.ACC   boy.ACC   the.ACC   music.ACC
'They taught the boy music.'

In fact, in English and many other languages there is little justification for distinguishing an 'indirect object' from any other object. Very often, the recipient NP looks just like a direct object—in what is known as the **DOUBLE OBJECT construction**, the recipient immediately follows the verb and has the same case marking as any object, as in *Kim lent **me** the book*. Alternatively, the recipient appears in an ordinary PP headed by 'to' or 'for', as in *Kim made a cake **for me***. In other words, there's neither a special case nor any special syntactic behaviour associated with the NP that traditional grammar calls the indirect object.

In Section 6.4 we saw that a ditransitive verb such as 'give' may agree with all three of its argument NPs—see (35) from Biri. However, a more common situation is that only two arguments of a three-argument verb are actually marked on the verb. One is always the subject, but languages differ in terms of which other NP the verb agrees with: it can be either the NP with the semantic role of theme (such as 'thing given'), or else the recipient. Commonly, the verb agrees with the *recipient*

> Double object construction, 双宾语结构。在英语中, 包含直接宾语和间接宾语（与格）的句子可以有两种形式: 一种是介词性与格结构（prepositional dative construction）, 为 V + NP + to/for + NP; 另一种是双宾语结构, 为 V + NP + NP, 这种现象被称为与格交替（dative alternation）。

NP, rather than the 'thing given'. Example (68) illustrates from Warlpiri, which, as we saw in (38) and (39) above, has ergative case marking but accusative verb agreement:

(68) Ngaju-ku ka-**npa-ju** karli yi-nyi nyuntulu-rlu.
me-DATIVE PRES-2SG.SU-1SG.OBJ boomerang give-NONPAST you-ERG
'You are giving me a boomerang.'

There are two agreement suffixes in (68). The first, -*npa*, marks the subject ('you'). There is no agreement marker for *karli*, 'boomerang', on the verb at all, but the second suffix is a 1SG marker which cross-references the recipient, the dative NP *ngajuku*, meaning 'me'. What's more, the 1SG agreement suffix -*ju* is the same suffix that is used to mark the first person singular O argument of an ordinary transitive verb (as in 'You saw me'). It appears, then, that in some languages the recipient functions as a kind of object. Perhaps it's not too surprising that the verb marks the recipient here: recipients are typically human, or at least animate, and thus arguably more important than an inanimate theme NP such as *karli*, 'boomerang'.

6.6 FREE WORD ORDER: A CASE STUDY

Having examined case, agreement and grammatical relations, we are now in a position to return to the topic of word order. We have already seen that languages with extensive case marking on noun phrases typically allow much variation in constituent order (see, for example, the German data in Section 4.3.3.1, and also the discussion of Japanese in Section 8.3). The same is true of languages with extensive head-marking on the verb, such as Kambera. The current section shows that some languages also allow extremely free *word* order, in the most literal sense. One such language is Latin; another is Navajo. Our illustrations, though, are from Australian languages, and in particular, Warlpiri. To remind you, Warlpiri exhibits a split ergative system: it has ergative/absolutive case for independent noun phrases and pronouns, but an accusative system for the pronominal affixes marked on the auxiliary (Section 6.4.4 above).

First, we illustrate the fact that Warlpiri has free *constituent* order: the only restriction is that the auxiliary, expressing tense and person/number marking, must be in second position in the clause.

(69) a. Ngarrka-ngku ka wawirri panti-rni. (Warlpiri)
man-ERG AUX.PRES kangaroo.ABS spear-NONPAST
'The man is spearing the kangaroo.'
b. Wawirri ka panti-rni ngarrka-ngku.
kangaroo.ABS AUX.PRES spear-NONPAST man-ERG
'The man is spearing the kangaroo.'
c. Panti-rni ka ngarrka-ngku wawirri.

spear-NONPAST　　AUX.PRES　　man-ERG　　　kangaroo.ABS
'The man is spearing the kangaroo.'

These three as well as the other three orders of S, O and V are all possible, with no single basic order. Two further Warlpiri examples are shown in (70):

(70)　a.　Jarntu-jarra-rlu　lpa-pala-jana　　　　　　　ngaya　　nya-ngu.
　　　　　 dog-DUAL-ERG　 AUX.IMPF-3.DUAL.SU-3PL.OBJ　cat.ABS　see-PAST
　　　　　'The two dogs were looking at the cats.'
　　　b.　Ngaya　lpa-pala-jana　　　　　　　 jarntu-jarra-rlu　nya-ngu.
　　　　　 cat.ABS　AUX.IMPF-3.DUAL.SU-3PL.OBJ　dog-DUAL-ERG　　see-PAST
　　　　　'The two dogs were looking at the cats.'

These two sentences mean the same thing, and indeed would be considered the same sentence by a Warlpiri speaker (Shopen 2001: 191). Hale (1983: 5) reports that 'different linear arrangements count as repetitions of each other' in Warlpiri. However, Shopen notes that moving an element to clause-initial position in Warlpiri signals its pragmatic importance, making the initial element the focus or topic of the sentence.

Next we see that constituents can also be split up in Warlpiri, so that the word order is literally free: the auxiliary must still be *either* the second constituent (71a), *or* second word (71b), but this remains the only restriction. (Actually, the auxiliary attaches to the end of the first constituent or first word in the clause, though the notation here doesn't show that.) So a noun phrase such as *wawirri yalumpu*, 'that kangaroo', can appear either as in (71a) or as in (71b):

(71)　a.　**Wawirri**　　　**yalumpu**　kapi-rna　　　　panti-rni.　(Warlpiri)
　　　　　 kangaroo.ABS　that.ABS　　AUX.FUT-1SG.SU　spear-NONPAST
　　　　　'I will spear that kangaroo.'
　　　b.　**Wawirri**　　　kapi-rna　　　　panti-rni　　　　**yalumpu**.
　　　　　 kangaroo.ABS　AUX.FUT-1SG.SU　spear-NONPAST　that.ABS
　　　　　'I will spear that kangaroo.'

In (71b) we have a DISCONTINUOUS CONSTITUENT; the elements of the absolutive O noun phrase in bold type are not contiguous. It's possible for the O argument to be freely split up in this way because the case marking identifies its components as belonging to the same, absolutive NP (though, quite typically for absolutive case, there is no overt case suffix here).

Let's now turn to some more complex examples. In (72a), there's a continuous A constituent, *maliki wiringki* 'big dog'. But in (72b) and (c), the individual elements of this constituent are not contiguous, but instead are split up in two different ways:

(72)　a.　**Maliki**　**wiri-ngki**　Ø-ji　　　　　yarlku-rnu.　(Warlpiri)
　　　　　 dog　　　big-ERG　　AUX.PAST-1SG.OBJ　bite-PAST
　　　　　'The/a big dog bit me.'
　　　b.　**Maliki-rli**　Ø-ji　　　　　yarlku-rnu　**wiri-ngki**.

Discontinuous constituent, 非连续成分, 指属于同一构成成分但是被其他成分隔开的句子的几个部分, 例如, 在 The player picked the ball up. 这一句子中, 短语动词 pick up 就是一个非连续成分。

dog-ERG AUX.PAST-1SG.OBJ bite-PAST big-ERG
'The/a big dog bit me.'
c. **Wiri-ngki** Ø-ji yarlku-rnu **maliki-rli**.
big-ERG AUX.PAST-1SG.OBJ bite-PAST dog-ERG
'The/a big dog bit me.'

Before reading further, please examine the examples in (72) and indicate what the difference is between the (a) sentence on the one hand and the (b) and (c) sentences on the other. Use the correct terminology to describe this. Why might this difference occur, do you think?

In (72a), there is only one ergative case marker, the suffix *-ngki*, and it's attached to the end of the whole the A argument, which here is a continuous NP. But in both (72b) and (72c), each element of the discontinuous NP has an ergative suffix. It wouldn't be ungrammatical to use an ergative suffix on *maliki* in (72a) too; but crucially, that suffix can't be omitted in (72b) and (72c), where the NP is discontinuous. Again, the case marking identifies each subpart of the discontinuous A argument.

In (71) and (72), only one NP is discontinuous. However, in free word order languages it's also perfectly possible to have, say, both of the arguments of a transitive verb as split NPs. This example is from another Australian language, Kalkatungu, which 'exhibits a marked tendency to represent noun phrases discontinuously' (Blake 2001b: 419). Here, the two discontinuous NPs are interleaved:

(73) **Tjipa-yi** tjaa **kunka-ngku** pukutjurrka lhayi **nguyi-nyin-tu**. (Kalkatungu)
this-ERG this branch-ERG mouse kill fall-PARTICIPLE-ERG
'The falling branch killed the mouse.'

The elements in bold type are the subparts of the ergative A argument which means 'the falling branch', and each has an overt case suffix which identifies them as ergative. The underlined elements *tjaa pukutjurrka* form the O argument, and these receive no overt case marking; this is, of course, superfluous, since the A argument is already marked. Thus, having affixes just on the subparts of one NP is enough to ensure that there's no ambiguity. Once again, I stress that discontinuous phrases in these languages are by no means exceptional—quite the opposite, in fact.

We might wonder whether, in free word order languages, we should use the term 'constituent'; after all, if noun phrases can be split up so readily, is it appropriate to describe the syntax of these languages in terms of 'constituency' at all? It has sometimes been claimed not (e.g. Evans and Levinson 2009). Instead, it may be more appropriate to describe the syntax solely in terms of DEPENDENCIES, so that in examples like (71) to (73), what really counts is the word-to-word relationships, as indicated, for instance, by the case markings on each related element.

Nonetheless, it seems that constituent structure does play a role in free word order languages. In Warlpiri examples like (72), sentences with continuous NP arguments don't have just the same range of meanings as those with discontinuous constituents (Hale 1983; Austin and Bresnan 1996). The discontinuous constituents in (72b) and (72c) give rise to an additional meaning, which is 'The/a dog bit me and it was big.' But the continuous NP in (72a) has the 'merged' meaning: it can *only* mean 'The/a big dog bit me'. This distinction clearly suggests that NP constituents really do exist in the language. In addition, we saw that Warlpiri requires the auxiliary to be in second position in the clause: what precedes it can be an NP (71a), or a single word of some kind, including a noun (71b), a verb (69c), and a particle. Crucially, a random sequence of words which don't form a constituent *cannot* precede the auxiliary; this, then, is one test for constituent structure in Warlpiri. If constituents have a different syntactic status to random strings of words, this again suggests that constituents are real in such languages. Finally, examples like (72) showed that in Warlpiri, only the final element in a continuous NP constituent needs to be case marked—(72a) vs. (72b/c). This indicates that there truly is an NP in (72a): it acts as a unit, so each of its subparts doesn't need a case affix. It seems clear, then, that constituent structure does play a vital role even in free word order languages.

Interestingly, there is apparently no correlation amongst Australian languages between the existence of discontinuous NPs and the appearance of free constituent order; for instance, Austin and Bresnan (1996) report that Diyari has discontinuous NPs but prefers a fixed SOV constituent order. Moreover, though Warlpiri has an extensive system of bound pronominal marking in the auxiliary (Section 6.4.4), it also appears that, cross-linguistically, this is not a necessary condition for the appearance of split NPs: case marking on independent NPs and pronouns is enough to allow for discontinuous constituents. So for instance, the Australian languages Jiwarli, Dyirbal and Yidiny all have discontinuous NPs but lack the pronominal cross-referencing affixes that characterize the Warlpiri auxiliary.

I hope to have shown definitively in this final section that if we only looked at English and its close relatives, we'd be missing out on a great deal of knowledge about the potential of the human language faculty. I also hope that by this point, you're feeling more comfortable about analysing examples from 'exotic' languages. More are to come in Chapter 7!

6.7 SUMMARY

This chapter has examined three different ways in which languages represent the relationships between core NPs and the verbal predicate on which they are dependent: constituent order, case marking and verb agreement. All languages use at least one of these methods, and often more than one. Constituent order may be very free or very fixed. In languages with free constituent order (or word order), it is more likely that there will be some system of either dependent-marking (case) or head-marking (agreement) in order to identify the grammatical relation of each core NP participant. The two main case systems are the accusative and the ergative systems. Some languages, such as Chinese, have neither case nor agreement. But even in languages without morphological case, the need to recognize grammatical relations is evident in the syntax. Syntactic constructions generally follow either an ergative or an accusative pattern, the accusative being by far the most common.

> ### Checklist for Chapter 6
>
> If you are uncertain about any of these points, I recommend revising before moving on.
>
> - What are the three major ways in which languages can indicate grammatical relations within the clause?
> - What single-letter terms are used to indicate the three main NP functions, and what grammatical relation does each of these represent? Give an example of each.
> - What are the two major alignment systems, which group the three main NP functions in two distinct ways?
> - What are some of the typical properties of subjects, cross-linguistically?
> - What does it mean for a language to have discontinuous constituents?

FURTHER READING

Good places to start on the topics of constituent order, case and agreement would be T. Payne (2006) and Whaley (1997), moving on to Comrie (1989: ch. 4 and ch. 6). The seminal work on constituent order and word order is Greenberg (1966). More recent proposals can be found in Hawkins (1983) and in Tomlin (1986); see also the large body of work by Matthew Dryer, for instance Dryer (1991). On case, see Blake (2001a). On grammatical relations, see Palmer (1994) and the collection of papers in Aikhenvald et al. (2001). On agreement, see Corbett (2006). All of these are textbook treatments and are much recommended. On ergativity, Dixon (1994) is a more advanced read, but absolutely central and very worthwhile. The properties of subjects in Section 6.5.2 are largely taken from Keenan (1976); see also Comrie (1989: ch. 5). The Warlpiri data are largely taken from the work of Ken Hale, a brilliant linguist who undertook extensive fieldwork on endangered languages.

EXERCISES

1. Examine the data in (1) through (3) below (all taken from Stucky 1983). These are simple sentences from the Bantu language Makhuwa, spoken in Tanzania and Mozambique, and they show that the order of phrases is very free in this language. Makhuwa marks both subject and object with cross-referencing agreement prefixes on the verb. The APPLIC suffix on the verb is an 'applicative' marker; it's this that gives the sense of preparing porridge for someone, rather than an actual preposition meaning 'for', which marks the recipient in the English. This construction is discussed further in Chapter 7.

   (1) Araarima   aho-n-ruw-el-a   mwaana   isima.
        Araarima   SU-OBJ-prepare-APPLIC-PAST   child   porridge
        'Araarima prepared porridge for a child.'

   (2) Isima   Araarima   aho-n-ruw-el-a   mwaana.
        porridge   Araarima   SU-OBJ-prepare-APPLIC-PAST child
        'Araarima prepared porridge for a child.'

   (3) Aho-n-ruw-el-a   Araarima   mwaana   isima.
        SU-OBJ-prepare-APPLIC-PAST   Araarima   child   porridge
        'Araarima prepared porridge for a child.'

   Each sentence contains four phrases—a subject, a verb, a direct object and an indirect object—but they appear in a different order. In fact, any of the 24 (!) possible orders of the four phrases can be used, given the right context.

   Now consider complex sentences: given a subject, a verb and an embedded clause, there are six logically possible orders of these three phrases. However, only three out of the potential six orders are grammatical. The orders actually found in Makhuwa are:

   - Subject-verb-embedded clause (4),

   - Verb-embedded clause-subject (5),

   - and in addition, verb-subject-embedded clause (I haven't illustrated this, but you should be able to reconstruct it).

   (4) Araarima   aheeew-a   [wiira   nt'u   aho-thek-a   iluwani].
        Araarima   SU.hear-PAST   that   someone   SU.build-PAST   fence
        'Araarima has heard that someone built a fence.'

   (5) Aheeew-a   [wiira   nt'u   aho-thek-a   iluwani]   Araarima.
        SU.hear-PAST   that   someone   SU.build-PAST   fence   Araarima
        'Araarima has heard that someone built a fence.'

Task: Work out what the three unattested (= non-occurring) phrase orders are and state the generalization about possible phrase orders in Makhuwa. In order to do this, you'll need to look at what the three attested orders and then the three unattested orders have in common. Why might a language have such a restriction, do you think?

2. Examine the data below (slightly adapted from Van Valin 1985) from Lakhota (a native American language, specifically a Siouan language of South Dakota, Montana and Manitoba) and answer questions (i) through (iv).

(i) Which argument(s) of the verb, if any, does the verb agree with?
(ii) How is agreement (or cross-referencing) indicated in Lakhota? Give the details.
(iii) Using the data in (1) through (3) as comparison, try to figure out why (4) and (5) are grammatical, but (6) is ungrammatical. The notation '≠' indicates that the Lakhota form is not a possible way of translating the English sentence given.
(iv) In light of your answer to (iii), why do you think (7) is ungrammatical? What generalization can be made about the grammatical vs. ungrammatical examples?

(1) wičháša ki mathó wą Ø-Ø-kté
man the bear a 3SG.OBJ-3SG.SU-kill
'The man killed a bear.'

(2) mathó wą wičháša ki Ø-Ø-kté
bear a man the 3SG.OBJ-3SG.SU-kill
'A bear killed the man.'

(3) wičháša ki mathó óta wičhá-Ø-kté
man the bear many 3PL.OBJ-3SG.SU-kill
'The man killed many bears.'

(4) wičháša ki ixʔé óta Ø-yąke
man the rock many 3SG.SU-see
'The man saw many rocks.'

(5) wičháša ki mathó óta wíčhá-Ø-yąke
man the bear many 3PL.OBJ-3SG.SU-see
'The man saw many bears.'

(6) *wičháša ki ixʔé óta wíčhá-Ø-yąke
man the rock many 3PL.OBJ-3SG.SU-see
(≠'The man saw many rocks.')

(7) *ixʔé   ki   hená   hokšíla   wą   Ø-pi-phá
    rock   the   those   boy   a   3SG.OBJ-3PL.SU-hit
    (≠'Those rocks hit a boy.')

3. In Welsh, the verb agrees with one of its argument NPs, but the conditions on this agreement are somewhat different than in more familiar European languages such as English, French or German. Study the following data, and answer these questions.

   (i)   Which NP argument does the verb agree with in Welsh? (Name its GRAMMATICAL RELATION.)
   (ii)   What MORPHOSYNTACTIC CATEGORIES of the NP does the verb agree with?
   (iii) What are the restrictions on this agreement?
   (iv)   Why are (3), (4) and (8) ungrammatical? Why is the starred alternative in (9) ungrammatical?
   (v)   How could you change (4) to make it grammatical, while retaining the meaning?

   Hints:
   - All data given here are entirely regular, and no data are missing. You have enough information to answer the questions without having to make guesses.
   - Welsh has VSO (verb-subject-object) word order, but this is not relevant to your answer.

   (1) Gwelodd   y   bachgen   ddreigiau.
       see.PAST.3SG   the   boy   dragons
       'The boy saw dragons.'

   (2) Gwelodd   y   bechgyn   ddreigiau.
       see.PAST.3SG   the   boys   dragons
       'The boys saw dragons.'

   (3) *Gwelson   y   bechgyn   ddreigiau.
       see.PAST.3PL   the   boys   dragons
       (≠ 'The boys saw dragons.')

   (4) *Gwelson   ein   ffrindiau ddreigiau.
       see.PAST.3PL   our   friends   dragons
       (≠ 'Our friends saw dragons.')

   (5) Gwelais   i   ddreigiau.
       see.PAST.1SG   I   dragons
       'I saw dragons.'

(6) Gwelodd hi/o ddreigiau.
　　see.PAST.3SG she/he dragons
　　'She/he saw dragons.'

(7) Gwelson nhw ddreigiau.
　　see.PAST.3PL they dragons
　　'They saw dragons.'

(8) *Gwelodd nhw ddreigiau.
　　see.PAST.3SG they dragons
　　(≠ 'They saw dragons.')

(9) Aeth/*Aethon y bechgyn allan.
　　go.PAST.3SG/go.PAST.3PL the boys out
　　'The boys went out.'

(10) Aethon nhw allan.
　　go.PAST.3PL they out
　　'They went out.'

4. Examine the following data in (1) through (3) (from Blake 1977) and determine what case system is found in the Australian language Yalarnnga: either nominative/accusative alignment (S = A ≠ O) or ergative/absolutive alignment (S = O ≠ A). Make clear what the evidence is for your conclusion. I have indicated the different case markers on the NPs in the gloss by marking one case with **X** and the other with **Y**.

(1) ngia wakamu
　　I.**X** fell
　　'I fell.'

(2) kupi-ngku ngia tacamu
　　fish-**Y** I.**X** bit
　　'A fish bit me.'

(3) nga-tu kupi-∅ walamu
　　I-**Y** fish-**X** killed
　　'I killed a fish.'

5. Examine the data from Swahili in (1) through (4) below (from Dixon 1994).

Task: (i) Determine first whether verbal cross-referencing agreement in this language represents a nominative/accusative system or an ergative/absolutive system. Make clear what the evidence is for your conclusion.

Hint:
Remember that the same form may sometimes be used for marking a particular person/number combination in more than one case, as in the Abaza data in (36) and (37) in the text of Chapter 6.

(1) tu-li-anguka
1PL-PAST-fall
'We fell down.'

(2) m-li-anguka
2PL-PAST-fall
'You all fell down.'

(3) m-li-tu-ona
2PL-PAST-1PL-see
'You all saw us.'

(4) tu-li-wa-ona
1PL-PAST-2PL-see
'We saw you all.'

(ii) Now describe the position of the agreement affixes in Swahili as concisely and accurately as you can, using the correct terminology.

6. Examine the data in (1) through (6) below (from Anderson 1976 and Otsuka 2005) and determine what case system is found in Tongan, either nominative/accusative alignment (S = A ≠ O) or ergative/absolutive alignment (S = O ≠ A). Make clear exactly what the evidence is for your conclusion. Finally, describe precisely how case is represented in Tongan. In this exercise, I've simply indicated all the case markers with the *same* gloss, CASE. Of course, they are not all the same, and different markers have different roles in the clause. You will need to work out for yourself which is which, by figuring out the role of each marker! (The character that looks like a quotation mark is a letter of the alphabet in Tongan, and represents a specific consonant, a glottal stop. It has no relevance to the answer here.)

(1) na'e lea 'a e talavou
PAST speak CASE the young.man
'The young man spoke.'

(2) na'e ma'u 'e sione 'a e ika
PAST get CASE Sione CASE the fish
'Sione got the fish.'

(3) na'e alu 'a tevita ki fisi
    PAST go CASE David to Fiji
    'David went to Fiji.'

(4) na'e tamate'i 'a kolaiate 'e tevita
    PAST kill CASE Goliath CASE David
    'David killed Goliath.'

(5) na'e ma'u 'e siale 'a e me'a'ofa
    PAST get CASE Charlie CASE the gift
    'Charlie received the gift.'

(6) na'e kai 'a e ika 'e sione
    PAST eat CASE the fish CASE Sione
    'Sione ate the fish.'

7. This exercise asks you to investigate patterns of verb agreement in Standard Arabic (Aoun et al. 2010).

   Task: Work out the system of subject-verb agreement in the data shown in (1) to (15) below. Account for the grammaticality patterns in all the data given: your answer must cover the ungrammatical as well as the grammatical data. Generalize where possible, so that you produce the most concise account of the agreement facts that is consistent with the data.

   Hints:
   - Arabic typically allows two distinct constituent orders within the clause: SVO and VSO, though some other word orders occur too.
   - Patterns of verbal agreement and pronominals in Arabic reflect distinctions between masculine and feminine gender, but this is not inherently relevant for your account.
   - Arabic is a pro-drop or NULL SUBJECT language (Section 1.2), which is why the subject pronouns are shown in parentheses in some of the examples. This means that they are optional in the positions shown.
   - The verbs in (1) to (12) are perfective (translated as past tense); the verbs in (13) to (15) are imperfective (translated as present tense). Again, this is not inherently relevant for your account.

   (1) ʔakal-at l-muʕallimaat-u
       ate-3F.SG the-teacher.F.PL-NOM
       'The (female) teachers ate.'

   (2) l-muʕallimaat-u ʔakal-na
       the-teacher.F.PL-NOM ate-3F.PL
       'The (female) teachers ate.'

(3) ʔakala   l-muʕallim-uun
    ate.3M.SG   the-teacher.M.PL-NOM
    'The (male) teachers ate.'

(4) *ʔakal-uu   l-muʕallim-uun
    ate-3M.PL   the-teacher.M.PL-NOM
    ('The (male) teachers ate.')

(5) l-muʕallim-uun   ʔakal-uu
    the-teacher.M.PL-NOM   ate-3M.PL
    'The (male) teachers ate.'

(6) * l-muʕallim-uun   ʔakala
    the-teacher.M.PL-NOM   ate-3M.SG
    ('The (male) teachers ate.')

(7) kataba   r-risaalat-a   l-ʔawlaad-u
    wrote.3M.SG the-letter-ACC   the-children-NOM
    'The children wrote the letter.'

(8) (hum)   katab-uu   l-kitaab-a   ʔams
    they.M   wrote-3M.PL   the-book-ACC   yesterday
    'They (male) wrote the book yesterday.'

(9) (hum)   qaraʔ-uu   d-dars-a
    they.M   read-3M.PL   the-lesson-ACC
    'They (male) read the lesson.'

(10) qaraʔ-u   (humu)   d-dars-a
     read-3M.PL they.M   the-lesson-ACC
     'They (male) read the lesson.'

(11) *qaraʔa   (humu)   d-dars-a
     read.3M.SG they.M   the-lesson-ACC
     ('They (male) read the lesson.')

(12) *hum   qaraʔa   d-dars-a
     they.M   read.3M.SG   the-lesson-ACC
     ('They (male) read the lesson.')

(13) ta-drusu   T-Taalibaat-u
     3F.SG-study   the-students.F.PL-NOM
     'The (female) students study.'

(14) T-Taalibaat-u   ya-drus-na
    the-students.F.PL-NOM 3-study-F.PL
    'The (female) students study.'

(15) ya-drus-na   (hun)
    3-study-F.PL   they.F
    'They (female) study.'

8. For this exercise it will help you to revise Sections 6.5.2 and 6.5.3, on subjects. Recall from this section that in Icelandic, the subjects of some verbs take what is known as 'quirky' case. Now examine the Icelandic data in (1) through (3) (the data and arguments on which this exercise is based are from Sigurðsson 1991). You will see that the QUANTIFIER in bold type meaning 'all' (which 'quantifies' the number of boys) agrees in case with the subject of the clause, as well as in number (plural, here) and gender (masculine, here):

(1) Strákarnir   komust   **allir**   í   skóla.
    the.boys.NOM   got   all.NOM.PL.M   to   school
    'The boys all managed to get to school.'

(2) Strákana   vantaði **alla**.
    the.boys.ACC   lacked   all.ACC.PL.M
    'The boys were all absent.'

(3) Strákunum   leiddist **öllum**.
    the.boys.DATIVE bored   all.DATIVE.PL.M
    'The boys were all bored.'

Next, examine the data in (4) through (6). These examples are parallel to the construction from Lezgian discussed in Section 6.5.3, and it will help you to revise this particular section.

Task: (i) How can we account for the case marking (as well as the number and gender marking) found on the quantifier meaning 'all' in each of the examples in (4) through (6)? (ii) What does the quantifier agree with?

(4) Strákarnir   vonast til [að komast   **allir**   í   skóla.]
    the.boys.NOM hope   for to get   all.NOM.PL.M   to   school
    'The boys hope to all get to school.'

(5) Strákarnir   vonast til [að vanta ekki **alla**   í   skólann.]
    the.boys.NOM hope   for to lack not   all.ACC.PL.M   to   the.school
    'The boys hope to not all be absent from school.'

(6) Strákarnir   vonast til [að leiðast ekki **öllum**   í   skóla.]
    the.boys.NOM hope   for to bore   not   all.DATIVE.PL.M to   school
    'The boys hope to not all be bored in school.'

7

Processes that change grammatical relations

章节导读

在上一章，我们学习了主格/受格和作格/通格两种区分语法关系的系统，并讨论了世界上各种语言中表示各种语法关系的方式，包括成分顺序、格的标记以及动词和名词短语之间的一致等。其实，动词和它的论元之间的关系并不是静止不变的，在大多数语言中，我们都可以通过名词短语的升格和降格的过程来改变动词的配价。

被动结构存在于世界上的大多数语言中，它一般被认为是由主动结构转换而来的。它有两个主要特点：第一，主动结构中及物动词的主语和宾语这两个核心论元都在语法功能上发生了改变。主动句的宾语被升格为被动句的主语，而主动句的主语则被降格或被省略。第二，动词本身的配价也发生了改变，在主动结构中，动词有两个核心论元，而在被动结构中只有一个核心论元。无人称结构是指某些语言中动词处于不变的第三人称形式的一种结构。这一结构也有可能存在于被动结构之中，但是与被动结构所不同的是，无人称结构并不产生新的主语。另外，被动结构的动词都是及物动词，而无人称结构也可以用于不及物动词。无人称结构的主要功能是通过把原来主动句的施事者降格或者删除以达到转变句子焦点的效果。

反被动结构在含有作格/通格系统的语言中比较常见。与被动结构一样，反被动过程也适用于及物动词，并且通过名词短语的升格和降格使之成为不及物动词。在反被动过程中，一种情况是原来主动句中作宾语的名词短语被降格，不再是动词的核心论元，或者干脆被省略。另一种情况是原来主动句中通格的名词短语被升格而成为主语。另外，动词的形态也有可能会发生变化以表示反被动的过程。

在英语中，句子 My brother sold Sue his bike. 被认为是句子 My brother

sold his bike to Sue. 中与格移位的结果。在某些语言中同样存在类似的语法关系的转换，词类转换的结果就是应用语态结构。这一结构的特点包括：（1）旁格名词短语或者间接宾语被升格到宾语的位置；（2）原来的宾语被降格而成为第二个宾语或者旁格；（3）动词的形态也有可能发生变化以标记应用语态结构。在很多语言中，应用语态结构产生的新的直接宾语还可以进一步升格到主语的位置，从而构成被动结构。

被动结构、反被动结构和应用语态结构都可以通过升格或降格来改变动词论元的位置，但是不会增加动词论元的数量。与上述三种结构所不同的是，使役结构则可以使原来句子的主语降格，并产生使役施事者这一论元作为新的主语，而且还经常产生一个新的使役谓词。

Valency, 配价，在本章中，动词的配价就是它的论元结构或者它所要求的论元数量。

Chapter 6 examined the two major systems used in languages to distinguish grammatical relations, the nominative/accusative system and the ergative/absolutive system. It also examined the ways in which the grammatical relations may be represented cross-linguistically: constituent order, case marking and verb agreement. This chapter shows that grammatical relations between a verb and its arguments are not static: most languages have ways of changing the **valency** of a verb via processes of promotion and demotion of NPs. Section 7.1 examines the best-known of these valency-changing processes—the passive construction. Section 7.2 looks at a process often found in ergative systems, known as the antipassive. Sections 7.3 and 7.4 introduce another two valency-changing processes, the applicative and the causative constructions.

7.1 PASSIVES AND IMPERSONALS

7.1.1 The passive construction and transitive verbs

Consider the pairs of sentences in (1) through (3):

(1) a. Kim took some great photos with that old camera.
    b. Some great photos were taken (by Kim) with that old camera.

(2) a. We broke that Ming vase yesterday.
    b. That Ming vase was broken (by us) yesterday.

(3) a. Three cups of tea have revived the nurse.
    b. The nurse has been revived (by three cups of tea).

In each example, the (a) sentences are said to be ACTIVE and the (b) sentences PASSIVE (in traditional grammars, this is sometimes known as 'passive voice', as opposed to 'active voice', but we will not be using these terms here).

Before reading further, examine each pair of sentences in (1) to (3), and list as many syntactic and morphosyntactic differences as you can between the active sentences and the passive sentences. Use the correct grammatical terminology to the best of your ability.

The active (a) sentences all have a transitive verb—a verb that has a subject and a direct object. By contrast, the passive (b) sentences all have only a subject, and no object: they have become intransitive. The NP that was the original subject in the active sentences (*Kim, we, three cups of tea*) has been DEMOTED in the passive: it is no longer a subject, but instead appears inside an optional PP headed with *by*. This means that it's no longer a core NP: it is no longer an argument of the verb. Thus, the original subject of the active sentence doesn't necessarily appear in the passive sentence at all: we can also say simply *Some great photos were taken with that old camera*, *That Ming vase was broken yesterday* and *The nurse has been revived*. The NP that was the original direct object in the active (a) sentences has been PROMOTED in each (b) sentence, becoming the subject of the passive sentence. Finally, the verbs in the passive sentences differ in form from the verbs in the active sentences. The passives all contain the PAST PARTICIPLE form of the verb: *taken, broken, revived*; and they all contain a form of *be* as an auxiliary (in bold): **were** *taken*, **was** *broken*, *has* **been** *revived*.

Demote, 降格, 指从高一等级的语法关系向低一等级的语法关系的转化, 是与升格相反的一个句法转换过程。在被动句中, 原来主动句中的主语被降格为宾语或者被省略。

The passive in English can therefore be recognized by the following signs:

- Subject of the active sentence > demoted to a by-phrase or deleted; removed from the core.
- Object of the active sentence > promoted to subject of the passive.
- Passive contains auxiliary be + past participle of the main verb.

How do we know for sure that the NPs *some great photos*, *that Ming vase* and *the nurse* really are the subjects of the passive sentences? After all, each of these NPs has the semantic role of THEME (or PATIENT)—what has been taken, what has been broken, the person being revived—and this is the role more usually associated with objects. We can tell that these NPs in the (b) sentences nonetheless are subjects because they trigger SUBJECT/VERB AGREEMENT, which, as we saw in Section 2.3.2, is one of the diagnostic properties for subjects in English. In (1b) the subject *some great photos* is plural, so we get **were** *taken*, whilst in (2b) the subject *that Ming vase* is singular, so we get **was** *broken*. The other test for subjecthood in English discussed in Chapter 2 was pronominal case: first and third person pronouns have a special form (nominative case) when they are subjects: *I, we, he, she, they*. The subject of the active sentence in (2a) is *we*, but in the passive, (2b), *us* does not have nominative case, so is no longer a subject. And the subject of (3b), *the nurse*, could be replaced by the nominative pronoun *he* or *she*, so confirming that this is a subject position.

Although not all languages have a passive construction, it is extremely common in a wide variety of languages. Basic passive constructions in all languages are formed from transitive verbs. There are two hallmarks of the passive. First, the CORE arguments of a transitive verb—its subject and object—both undergo changes in their grammatical functions. Specifically, the object of the active sentence is promoted to be the subject of the passive sentence, whilst the subject of the active sentence is either removed altogether in the passive (as in *Some great photos were taken with that old camera*) or else is simply demoted. 'Demotion' here means that the NP is still present, but is no longer one of the core arguments of a transitive verb (subject/object). Instead, the former subject becomes an OBLIQUE argument—for instance, it appears inside a PP, such as the *by*-phrase in English; oblique arguments are never subjects or objects, but instead occur in less prominent positions of the clause. Second, the verb has changed its valency: the number of core arguments that it takes (see Section 2.2.2.3). So the transitive verb in the active clause has two core arguments, a subject and an object, whilst the intransitive verb in the passive clause has only one, a subject. Verbs signal this alteration in valency by changing their own form in some way. For instance, in English we find *took* becoming *were taken* in the example (1). To summarize, the prototypical passive construction has the following properties cross-linguistically.

Obligue, 旁格, 有时也被翻译成"间接格""斜格", 是主格以外其他格的统称, 在英语中体现为介词的宾语或所有格形式。

The passive construction

- Applies to a transitive clause (the active clause) and forms an intransitive clause.
- Object promoted > subject.
- Former subject demoted > oblique argument, or is deleted; removed from the core.
- Changes occur in the morphology of the verb to signal passivization.

In English, as in numerous other European languages, there is no specifically passive form of the verb: the two distinguishing features of the passive construction, namely auxiliary *be* and the past participle verb form (*seen, stolen, played* etc.) both occur separately in different constructions: for instance, *I was singing; We've stolen them*. So neither auxiliary *be* nor the past participle alone indicate a passive construction in English: only when they occur together do we have a passive.

Examples (4) and (5) illustrate languages which, like English, have an auxiliary-plus-main-verb kind of passive. The (a) sentences are active, the (b) ones passive, and the auxiliary verbs are in bold.

(4) a. Der   Frost   verdarb   den   Apfel.   (German)
       the.NOM frost   spoil.PAST   the.ACC   apple.
       'The frost spoilt the apple.'
    b. Der   Apfel **wurde**   vom   Frost verdorben.
       the.NOM apple become.PAST   by.the.DATIVE frost spoil. PAST PARTICIPLE
       'The apple was spoilt by the frost.'

(5) a. Eglurodd   y   darlithydd   y   sefyllfa.   (Welsh)
       explain.PAST the lecturer   the situation
       'The lecturer explained the situation.'
    b. **Cafodd**   y   sefyllfa   ei   egluro   (gan y   darlithydd).
       get.PAST   the situation its explain.INFIN by   the lecturer
       'The situation was explained (by the lecturer).'
       (Literally, 'The situation got its explaining by the lecturer.')

As (4b) shows, some other languages also use the past participle form of the verb in the passive construction, as English does, but this is by no means universal. Welsh, for instance, doesn't have a past participle, and the main verb just has one non-finite which is not specific to passives such as (5b). According to Keenan (1985a), the most common auxiliaries occurring in passive constructions cross-linguistically are verbs like 'be', 'become', 'get' and 'receive', as illustrated in (4) and (5). In fact, English also has a commonly used *get* passive, as in *My bike got stolen*.

在英语中，被动结构要使用动词的过去分词形式，但是这种做法在世界上的其他语言中并不普遍。

In the German examples, we can tell that the former object of the active clause becomes the subject of the passive clause by the change in its case-marking: *den Apfel* in (4a) is accusative, the case of direct objects in German, whilst *der Apfel* in (4b) is nominative, the case of subjects.

Instead of the auxiliary-plus-verb kind of passive, many languages have a specifically passive form of the main verb: this is known as a **MORPHOLOGICAL PASSIVE**. Each language illustrated in (6) through (8) has a special passive marker on the verb, shown in bold in each (b) example. This affix is the only change in the verb form that indicates the passive. As before, all the (a) sentences are active, and the (b) sentences passive.[1]

Morphological passive, 形态被动式，指通过动词本身形态的变化而不像英语那样需要助动词来构成被动结构。

(6) a. Si   Juan ha   dulalak   si   Jose.   (Chamorro)
       PN   Juan 3SG.SU follow   PN   Jose
       'Juan followed Jose.'
    b. D-**in**-ilalak   si   Jose   as   Juan.
       -PASSIVE-follow   PN   Jose   by   Juan
       'Jose was followed by Juan.'

(7) a. Neko-ga   sakana-o   tabeta.   (Japanese)
       cat-NOM   fish-ACC   eat.PAST
       'The cat ate the fish.'
    b. Sakana-ga   neko-ni   tabe-**rare**-ta.
       fish-NOM   cat-DATIVE   eat-PASSIVE-PAST
       'The fish was eaten by the cat.'

(8) a. E   kamate-a   te   naeta   te   moa.   (Gilbertese)
       it   kill-it   the   snake   the chicken
       'The chicken killed the snake.'
    b. E   kamate-**aki** te   naeta   (iroun te   moa).
       it   kill-PASSIVE   the   snake   by   the   chicken
       'The snake was killed (by the chicken).'

Note also here that in Japanese, a language with nominative/accusative case-marking, we again see the changes in case that result from the promotion of the object to the subject position, and the demotion of the erstwhile subject. In the passive in (7b), the 'fish' NP *sakana* has become nominative, the case of subjects in Japanese, and the 'cat' NP *neko* has been demoted from subject position to an oblique (i.e. non-core) position, marked by dative case.

In fact, passive constructions occur most typically in languages which, like German or Japanese, are syntactically and morphologically accusative in their alignment. Recall from Chapter 6 that this gives rise to languages which have a definite *subject* grammatical relation, and which generally also have case marking and/or verbal agreement which patterns according to the nominative/accusative alignment. Thus, accusative systems treat all subjects the same way (A plus S noun phrases), and treat objects differently (O noun phrases): S = A ≠ O.

But what about the passive in ergative/absolutive languages, which group S and O arguments (the ABSOLUTIVE NPs) in opposition to A arguments (the ERGATIVE NPs): S = O ≠ A? It will help at this point to revise the discussion in Chapter 6 concerning the different ways in which NPs group together in each system. These tables should help to refresh your memory:

Table 7.1

Accusative and ergative alignment systems

Accusative system	
A S	O
Nominative	Accusative

Ergative system	
A	S O
Ergative	Absolutive

有些具有作格/通格系统的语言是没有被动结构的。

It might seem that ergative languages would not have a passive construction, since the division between all subjects and all objects found in accusative languages is much less evident, or even absent. Indeed, not all ergative languages have passives: for instance, Dyirbal and Lezgian (see Chapter 6) do not. However, a number of ergative languages do have a passive construction, as illustrated in (9) from Inuktitut (Greenlandic), and (10)—slightly adapted—from Tzotzil. As before, the (a) sentences are active, the (b) ones passive, and the passive marker on the verb is in bold. The core grammatical relations (A, O, S) are also indicated on the NPs.

(9) a. angut-ip(A)   arnaq(O)   taku-vaa   (Inuktitut)
       man-ERG   woman.ABS   see-3SG/3SG
       'The man saw the woman.'
    b. arnaq(S)   (anguti-mit)   taku-**tau**-puq
       woman.ABS   man-by   see-PASSIVE-3SG
       'The woman was seen (by the man).'

(10) a. S-mil-ox-Ø   Xun(O)   li   Petul-e(A)   (Tzotzil)
        3SG.ERG-kill-PAST-3SG.ABS John   the   Peter-DEF
        'Peter killed John.'
     b. Mil-**bil**-Ø   ju?un   Petul   li   Xun-e(S)
        kill-PASSIVE-3SG.ABS   by   Peter   the   John-DEF
        'John was killed by Peter.'

In (9a), ergative/absolutive alignment is indicated in the active sentence via case marking on the NPs, the A argument being ergative, and the O argument absolutive: in other words, standard ergative case marking, given a transitive verb. The verb in (9a) also agrees with both its core arguments (both are third person singular). In the passive, (9b), the former ergative NP meaning 'man' is demoted, and appears in an optional *by*-phrase. Moreover, the verb is now *intransitive*, so agrees only with its remaining core argument, *arnaq*, 'the woman', which has become the S argument of the intransitive verb. So just as in accusative languages, the NP *arnaq* has undergone a change in grammatical relation in the passive, from O to S. However, in an ergative language, this doesn't change the case marking of the promoted NP: the NP *arnaq* remains absolutive, because this is the case used both for O and for S. Of course, it doesn't become ergative, since this case is reserved for the A argument of a *transitive* verb.

The Mayan language Tzotzil (spoken in Mexico) has no case marking on the NPs themselves, but has an ergative agreement system, indicated by verbal affixes. In the active sentence in (10a) we see two verbal affixes: an ergative agreement prefix, marking the A argument *Petul*, 'Peter', and an absolutive agreement suffix, marking the O argument *Xun* 'John'. The passive construction in (10b) shows that the verb has lost the ergative prefix *s-*, since there is no longer an ergative NP for the verb to agree with: the former A argument, the ergative NP *Petul*, is now demoted, again appearing in a *by*-phrase. The passive verb has become intransitive, as in the other passives we've seen, and so agrees just with the S, its one remaining core argument, the NP *Xun* 'John'. This agreement marker is still absolutive: *Xun* 'John' has changed from being an absolutive O argument in (10a) to the absolutive S in (10b)—the single argument of an intransitive verb.

Other ergative languages with a passive construction include other Mayan languages, the South Caucasian language Georgian, and the European language isolate Basque.

Since the passive construction in an ergative language doesn't change the *case* of the original O noun phrase—it's still absolutive when it becomes an S, as we've seen—then why have a passive at all? Perhaps the main effect of the passive in ergative systems is to remove focus from the original A noun phrase, in examples such as (9a) and (10a), by removing it from the core: demoting the NP to a *by*-phrase makes it less prominent. In fact, passives also have this same effect of defocussing the agent in accusative languages as well, as shown for English in (1) through (3)— the agent is either demoted or deleted entirely, and so becomes much less prominent. Cross-linguistically, then, passives have a common pragmatic effect: that of removing focus from the agent NP. This function holds for passives both in accusative systems and in ergative systems.

7.1.2 The impersonal construction

此段的内容涉及无人称被动式（impersonal passive）的问题。所谓无人称被动式是指涉及明显的动词被动屈折变化而没有词汇主语（lexical subject）的各种被动结构。在具有无人称被动式的语言中，无人称被动句最为典型的是由不及物动词转化而来的。

In this section we will see the IMPERSONAL construction. Here, the subject argument is suppressed, which also occurs in the passive; but unlike the passive, the impersonal construction does not create a new subject (Blevins 2003). The passive construction involves verbs that are transitive, as shown in Section 7.1.1 above. The impersonal construction can occur with intransitive verbs, as illustrated in (11) from German; the (a) sentence is active and the (b) sentence is the impersonal:

(11) a. Die Leute tanzten. (German)
the people dance.3PL.PAST
'The people danced.'
b. Es wurde getanzt.
it become.PAST dance.PAST PARTICIPLE
'There was dancing.'
(Literally 'It became danced.')

In (11b), no core NP has been promoted to subject. The construction is thus 'impersonal'—in fact, the verb here has no core arguments at all. However, (11b) does have what is often called a 'dummy' subject, *es* 'it'; this fills the otherwise empty subject position, but doesn't have any intrinsic meaning or semantic role. So we can still maintain that the impersonal has no true subject.

Turkish also has an impersonal construction, with no constituent in subject position. Our example sentence is formed from an ordinary transitive verb, but it is again an impersonal because—unlike the passive—it does not create a new subject. As before, the (a) sentence is active and the (b) one the impersonal:

(12) a. Hasan dün bütün gün kitap oku-du (Turkish)
Hasan yesterday whole day book read-PAST
'Hasan read books all day yesterday.'
b. Dün bütün gün kitap oku-**n**-du
yesterday whole day book read-IMPERSONAL-PAST
'Yesterday books were read all day.'
(Literally 'Book reading was done all day yesterday.')

We can tell that in Turkish the object of the active sentence, *kitap* 'book', has not been promoted to subject position in (12b) because it must remain in the standard direct object position that it occupies in (12a), which is immediately preceding the verb.

As with the passive, an important function of the impersonal is to remove focus from the former agent by demoting or deleting the subject NP. The difference is that no other NP is promoted to subject in an impersonal construction. Impersonals are quite widespread, occurring for instance in Dutch, Latin and—outside Indo-European—Turkish, Shona (Bantu) and Tarahumara (Uto-Aztecan). If a language has an impersonal construction, then it will also have an ordinary 'personal' passive construction of the type illustrated in Section 7.1.1, which does involve the creation of a new subject.

7.2 THE ANTIPASSIVE

7.2.1 Basic facts

In Section 7.1.1, we saw that both accusative and ergative languages can have a passive construction, although the passive is certainly found more commonly in accusative languages than ergative ones. However, another construction which changes grammatical relations also occurs in ergative languages. This is known as the ANTIPASSIVE, and this does not occur in accusative languages. Like the passive, the antipassive also takes a transitive clause and makes it intransitive via a process of promotion of one NP and demotion of another. I will focus first on the DEMOTION effects of the antipassive. Compare the ordinary active sentence in (13a) with the antipassive version in (13b), both from Inuktitut (Greenlandic); the antipassive marker is in bold.

反被动结构（antipassive construction）存在于作格语言之中，在功能上与使用主格/受格系统语言中的被动结构相对应。在作格语言中，主动句中的话题通常是受事，而不是施事者，而反被动就是要把施事者作为句子的话题。

(13) a. arna-p**(A)**   niqi**(O)**   niri-vaa   (Inuktitut)
        woman-ERG   meat.ABS   eat-3SG/3SG
        'The woman ate the meat.'
    b. arnaq**(S)**   niqi-mik   niri-**NNig**-puq
        woman.ABS   meat-with   eat-ANTIPASSIVE-3SG
        'The woman ate some of the meat.'

In (13a), the 'woman' NP *arnap* is the A argument of a transitive verb, and is therefore ergative, whilst the 'meat' NP *niqi* is the O argument of the transitive verb, and is therefore absolutive: this is the standard ergative case alignment discussed in Chapter 6. In the antipassive sentence in (13b), the former O argument *niqi* 'meat' is now DEMOTED. It is no longer a core argument of the verb, but is instead an oblique NP: the suffix *-mik* in fact indicates what is known as 'instrumental' case, which I've glossed as 'with'. The effect of this demotion is to give the 'meat' NP a PARTITIVE reading—the woman ate *some* of or *part* of the meat, as indicated in the translation. Since the verb in (13b) is no longer transitive (in Inuktitut), the NP *arnaq* 'woman' is the single S argument of an intransitive verb, and so takes the absolutive case. I strongly recommend re-reading this section up to this point before moving on!

The antipassive construction has a variety of functions in ergative languages, including giving rise to a partitive reading as shown above. Consider first the pair of sentences from the Siberian language Chukchee in (14); the (a) sentence is active, the (b) antipassive, with the antipassive marker in bold:

(14) a. ətləg-e(A)   keyng-ən(O)   penrə-nen   (Chukchee)
         father-ERG   bear-ABS   attack-3SG/3SG.PAST
         'Father attacked the bear.'
     b. ətləg-ən(S)   penrə-**tko**-gʔe   keyng-etə
         father-ABS   attack-ANTIPASSIVE-3SG.PAST   bear-DATIVE
         'Father ran at the bear.'

In the active sentence, (14a), the 'father' NP *ətləge* is the A argument of a transitive verb, and hence is marked with ergative case, whilst the 'bear' NP *keyngən* is an O, the object of a transitive verb, and hence is marked with absolutive case. The verb agrees with both these core arguments in (14a): it has a 3SG agreement for each of them (fused into a single marker, along with the past tense morpheme). The antipassive again has the effect of demoting the former object: the 'bear' NP *keyng* in (14b) has become dative, and we get the effect of *running at* the bear rather than attacking it. The 'father' NP *ətləgən* becomes the single argument of an intransitive verb in (14b), and hence is marked as an S—with absolutive case—and the verb now agrees with just this single core argument. In both (13) and (14), the antipassive has the clear effect of DETRANSITIVIZING the verb—making it no longer transitive—and the former object becomes in some way less affected by the action of the verb (Palmer 1994: 181).

> Detransitivize,去及物化,就是把及物动词变成不及物动词。

Next, consider the pair of sentences from Chamorro in (15). As before, the (a) sentence is active and the (b) sentence is the antipassive, and the antipassive marker is in bold:

(15) a. un-hongge   i   lahi   (Chamorro)
         2SG.ERG-believe   the   man(.ABS)
         'You(A) believe the man(O).'
     b. **man**-hongge   hao   [nu   i   lahi]
         ANTIPASSIVE-believe you.ABS OBLIQUE   the   man
         'You(S) believe in/have faith in the man.'

In the active sentence, (15a), the 'you' argument is the A, shown by the second person singular ergative verbal inflection, *un-*; there is a pronominal affix here, but no independent second person pronoun. The 'man' NP, *i lahi*, is the object of a transitive verb, and is therefore absolutive, though as is typical for languages with ergative alignment, the absolutive case doesn't receive any overt marking in (15a). The effect of the antipassive in (15b) is to demote *i lahi* and remove it from core argument status: it is no longer the O (object of a transitive verb), and now instead has an oblique marker *nu*. Since the verb doesn't have an object NP in (15b), but is now intransitive, the former ergative argument (meaning 'you') has now become an S, the single argument of an intransitive verb. So *hao*, 'you', is marked for absolutive in (15b), as is standard for the S argument in an ergative system. The verb is again detransitivized in the antipassive, and its former object demoted.

An O argument may be merely demoted in the antipassive, but it can also be deleted altogether. In this sense, the antipassive is parallel to the passive construction, where an A argument can be deleted, as in *The vases were broken*. Again, the verb is detransitivized. In (16) is an example of O deletion from an Australian language, Yidiny. As before, the (a) sentence is active and the (b) sentence is the antipassive:

(16) a. [Yinydyuu-n bunyaa-n](**A**)   [mayi](**O**)   buga-ng.   (Yidiny)
         this-ERG   woman-ERG   vegetables.ABS   eat-PRES
         'This woman is eating vegetables.'
     b. [Yinu   bunya](**S**)   bugaa-**dyi**-ng.
         this.ABS   woman.ABS   eat-ANTIPASSIVE-PRES
         'This woman is eating.'

Before going further, outline the effects of the antipassive construction in (16), using the correct grammatical terms. What effects does the antipassive have on the core arguments here? What effect does it have on the verb's valency, i.e. the number and type of core arguments associated with the verb?

The active construction in (16a) has a transitive verb, and the clause has the standard case marking in the ergative alignment: an ergative A noun phrase, *yinydyuun bunyaan* 'this woman', and an absolutive O noun phrase, *mayi* 'vegetables'. The antipassive construction in (16b) has only one argument, *yinu bunya*—the absolutive S argument of what is now an intransitive verb—and the former O noun phrase is simply deleted. The verb's valency is thus reduced: a transitive verb with both A and O arguments is intransitive in the antipassive, with only an S.

7.2.2 Primary grammatical relations and grammatical pivots

So far, we have considered antipassives in which the main effects of the construction are on the O argument of the active verb: this NP has been demoted so it's no longer a core argument of the verb, or it's been deleted entirely. However, another equally important use of the antipassive in ergative languages involves the PROMOTION of the A noun phrase—the ergative 'subject' in the transitive clause—to be an S: an absolutive 'subject' in an intransitive clause. It may surprise you to think of this as promotion. In the more familiar accusative languages, it's easy to see how the passive construction, which changes the grammatical relation of an object NP and makes it the subject, is a process of promotion—consider the difference between the active *A crocodile ate my friend* and the passive *My friend was eaten by a crocodile*. Any native speaker of English would agree that the passive focusses on what happened to the friend in a way the active does not—indeed, the active can sound truly callous!

But why is A > S a promotion? Recall from Section 6.3 that in both accusative systems and ergative systems it's the noun phrase that appears as the S argument which is the most basic in usage. Whether it's a nominative NP, as in accusative systems, or an absolutive NP, as in ergative systems, the S is generally unmarked in both form (case marking) and function (syntactic constructions). Following Palmer (1994) we can say that the S is always a PRIMARY grammatical relation. In accusative systems, of course, S groups with A to give SUBJECT as the primary grammatical relation, whilst in ergative systems, S groups with O to give ABSOLUTIVE as the primary grammatical relation.

Table 7.2

Primary grammatical relations

Primary grammatical relations	
Accusative systems	S + A = Subject NPs
Ergative systems	S + O = Absolutive NPs

The passive construction is mostly found in the accusative alignment, whilst the antipassive occurs exclusively in ergative systems. Both passive and antipassive constructions have the effect of creating a new S argument. The passive does this by promoting O > S, and the antipassive does it by promoting A > S. So both constructions have the effect of making a NONPRIMARY NP into a primary NP: the nonprimary NPs are O in accusative systems, A in ergative systems. Let's see now what sort of effects this has in ergative systems.

In the Mayan language Mam (Guatemala and Mexico), the verb is initial in the clause in the basic constituent order, but an NP can be focussed by FRONTING it to the start of the clause. However, the only NPs which can undergo fronting are the two absolutive NPs, the S and the O—the two NPs which form the primary grammatical relation in an ergative language. Examples (17) and (18) illustrate this fronting, in an intransitive and a transitive clause respectively. The fronted NP is shown in bold in each sentence. Verbal agreement markers occur in each example: you can tell which NP the ergative and absolutive markers cross-reference by the fact that 'the man' NP, *xiinaq*, is always indicated by a 3SG marker, whilst 'the horses' NP *qacheej* is 3PL. There is no ergative case-marking in this language; the ergativity is shown via verb agreement.

(17) **xiinaq**(S) s-uul (Mam)
man ASPECT.3SG.ABS-arrive.here
'**The man** arrived here.'

(18) **qa-cheej**(O)   x-hi   kub'   t-tzyuun   xiinaq(A)
PL-horse   ASPECT-3PL.ABS   DIRECTION   3SG.ERG-grab   man
'The man grabbed *the horses*.'

Examples (17) and (18) are standard active clauses for an ergative language. In an intransitive clause, the S argument is absolutive, and triggers verb agreement, which in (17) is shown by an affix *s-* on the verb. In the transitive clause in (18), the O argument meaning 'the horses' is absolutive, and triggers a verbal agreement marker *-hi*; the A argument *xiinaq* 'the man' is ergative, and triggers a verbal agreement marker *t-*. What if a speaker wants to focus on the A noun phrase in (18), *xiinaq* 'the man'? As (19) shows, it's not possible to do this by simply fronting *xiinaq* in the ordinary active sentence: the result is ungrammatical, because *xiinaq* is an A, not an S or an O, and so is not a primary grammatical relation:

(19) *****xiinaq**(A)   chi   kub'   t-tzyuun   qa-cheej(O)
man   3PL.ABS   DIRECTION   3SG.ERG-grab   PL-horse
(≠'*The man* grabbed the horses.')

Instead, the ergative NP *xiinaq* must first be promoted to be absolutive—becoming a primary NP—so it can then be fronted. This promotion from A to S is achieved by using the antipassive construction:

(20) **xiinaq**(S) x-Ø-kub'   tzyuu-n   t-e   qa-cheej
man   ASPECT-3SG.ABS-DIRECTION   grab-ANTIPASSIVE   3-OBLIQUE   PL-horse
'*The man* grabbed the horses.'

In (20) we find the grammatical version of what (19) was unable to express. The former O argument of the transitive clause, *qacheej* 'horses', is demoted in (20): it is no longer an O in the Mam sentence, but has become an oblique NP, as is indicated by the oblique marker that precedes it (like a preposition). This means that *xiinaq*, 'the man', is now the single argument of an intransitive verb, an S, and so is absolutive and can be focussed. We can tell from the verb agreement (3SG absolutive, agreeing with *xiinaq*) that the promotion has taken place. Hence, the antipassive serves here to allow an NP to be focussed where it otherwise couldn't be.

A second construction requiring the antipassive to promote an NP from ergative to absolutive can be illustrated from an Australian language, Dyirbal. This involves the CO-ORDINATION of clauses. First, some reminders of facts from a typical accusative language, English. In Section 6.5.2, we saw that a subject can undergo ellipsis (= omission) in the second of two conjoined clauses. If you need to revise this, please look back now. The subscript index $_i$ or $_j$ shows which NP in the first clause the omitted NP, designated Ø, refers back to:

(21) a.   Chris woke up and (Chris) saw Lee.
b.   Chris$_i$ disturbed Lee and Ø$_i$ complained bitterly.
c.   *Chris disturbed Lee$_i$ and Ø$_i$ complained bitterly.

  d. Chris$_i$ greeted Lee and then Ø$_i$ kissed Mel.
  e. *Chris$_i$ greeted Lee$_j$ and then Mel kissed Ø$_{i/j}$.

What these examples show is that in accusative languages like English, the ellipsis revolves around *subjects*. So for instance, (21b) can only mean that it was Chris who complained, and (21c) cannot mean that Lee complained. The grammatical sentences, (21a), (21b) and (21d), show that a subject can undergo ellipsis in the second clause, but only when it's co-referential with (= refers back to) the subject of the first clause. As for the ungrammatical sentences, (21c) shows that an omitted subject can't refer back to the object of the first clause—which is why (21c) can't mean that Lee complained; and (21e) shows that it's only a subject which is omitted in English, and not an object, so that (21e) is ungrammatical whatever the omitted NP refers back to.

  We can therefore say that accusative languages which operate as English does in (21) have a SUBJECT PIVOT, comprising the two primary NPs—those with the grammatical relations S and A. A PIVOT links noun phrases together across different clauses, for instance as seen in (21), by allowing one NP to be omitted providing it can refer back to another NP in the first clause. Some languages have no syntactic restrictions on the interpretation of NPs across clauses. This means that two clauses can be linked together and *any* NP which is repeated can be omitted. In such languages, the equivalent to any of the examples in (21) should be perfectly grammatical in the appropriate context. Languages of this kind, then, do not have a syntactic pivot. In languages that do have a syntactic pivot, it may operate as in English, revolving around the subject relation, or alternatively, in the case of some ergative languages, the pivot may revolve around *absolutive* NPs.

  If a language has a subject (or SA) pivot, we expect constructions that link NPs to revolve around the S and the A relations. This is what happens in English. First, both S and A noun phrases—that is, all subjects—undergo ellipsis, as we can see from the fact that both an intransitive verb like *complain* and a transitive verb like *see* or *kiss* allow their subject to be omitted. And second, both the S subject of an intransitive verb like *wake up* and the A subject of a transitive verb like *disturb* or *greet* can be the NP that controls an omitted subject in the second clause. Finally, if we want to indicate what (21c) attempts to do—namely that it was Lee who complained—we do it by passivizing the first clause, to give *Lee$_i$ was disturbed by Chris and Ø$_i$ complained bitterly*. This, of course, has the effect of promoting Lee to subject position, which makes it a primary grammatical relation, so that it can now control the omitted NP in the second clause.

  In a language like Dyirbal which is syntactically ergative, ellipsis revolves around absolutive NPs. So Dyirbal has an ABSOLUTIVE PIVOT: this comprises the two absolutive grammatical relations, S and O, which together form the primary relation. This means that both the NP in the first clause which controls the ellipsis and the NP which undergoes ellipsis must be one of the absolutive NPs, either S or O. Let's see how this works first when ordinary active clauses are co-ordinated, starting with (22). Before you tackle the examples that follow, here are some hints to help you.

Subject pivot, 主语支点，指把不同小句中的主语联系起来的词。

- Case is indicated in Dyirbal via a suffix on the nouns, though the absolutive is in fact unmarked (there is no absolutive inflection), whilst ergative and other cases such as dative each have a particular suffix.

- You can tell which NP refers to which other NP by looking at the subscripts, $_i$. So for instance, in (22), the NP that undergoes ellipsis in the second clause is coreferential with *nguma* 'father' in the first clause.

- Read the glosses and translations carefully and try not to let the constituent order worry you: the absolutive NP is initial in each clause, whether it's an S or an O. I've indicated the grammatical relation of the NPs here in the gloss, with a small subscript (S, O or A), and also in the translation.

- Note also that there's no actual word for 'and' in Dyirbal co-ordination. In these examples I have put each co-ordinated clause in square brackets, to help you see the start and end of the clauses.

(22) [nguma$_i$ yabu-nggu   bura-n]   [Ø$_i$ banaga-n^{y}u]   (Dyirbal)
     father.ABS$_O$ mother-ERG$_A$ see-PAST   [ ]$_S$ return-PAST
     'Mother(A) saw father(O) and [he](S) returned.'

The NP that's omitted in the second clause in (22) has to refer back to *nguma*, 'father', the absolutive O noun phrase—it can't refer back to *yabunggu*, 'mother', the ergative A noun phrase. In English, this is not a possible construction: *Mother saw father and returned* can only mean that mother returned, not that father did. The only way to get that reading in English is to use a pronoun *he* in the second clause, as I've shown in the translation of (22), but crucially, there is no pronoun in the corresponding Dyirbal sentence.

In (22), the two co-referential NPs are an O in the first clause and an S in the second clause. Both are, of course, absolutive. In (23), the first clause has an S and the second clause omits an O which refers back to that S:

(23) [nguma$_i$ banaga-n^{y}u]   [Ø$_i$ yabu-nggu   bura-n]
     father.ABS$_S$ return-PAST   [ ]$_O$ mother-ERG$_A$ see-PAST
     'Father(S) returned and mother(A) saw [him](O).'

The English translation would again be impossible without the pronoun in the second clause: we don't get *Father returned and mother saw*. But again, there is no pronoun in the corresponding Dyirbal: the O argument can be omitted when it is co-referential with the S of the first clause. Both (22) and (23) show that ellipsis in Dyirbal operates in terms of the absolutive NPs, S and O, rather than with a subject pivot as in English. Dyirbal then has an absolutive pivot.

What happens, though, if a Dyirbal speaker wants to say something that means 'Mother saw father and (mother) returned'? Example (22) does not and could not mean this. Instead, the antipassive construction is used: this promotes the ergative NP meaning 'mother' in a sentence like (22) so that it *becomes* absolutive, and as an absolutive NP it can be a pivot: it can control the ellipsis of the S in the second clause. Example (24) illustrates; the first clause is the one that's antipassive:

(24) [yabu$_i$ bural-**nga**-n^{y}u   nguma-gu]   [Ø$_i$ banaga-n^{y}u]
     mother.ABS$_S$ see-ANTIPASSIVE-PAST   father-DATIVE   [ ]$_S$ return-PAST
     'Mother(S) saw father and (S) returned.'

In the first clause of (24), what in an ordinary active clause such as (22) would be the O—the object of a transitive verb—has now been demoted to become an oblique NP: the 'father' NP *ngumagu* is now dative, and the verb is detransitivized with the antipassive suffix. The remaining core NP, *yabu* 'mother', is therefore the S argument of an intransitive verb meaning 'see'. As an S, it is absolutive, and so can be a pivot: it allows the omitted NP in the second clause to refer back to it. So the antipassive construction serves to make an NP available as a pivot; here, as the controller of ellipsis.

Second, the antipassive can make an NP into a pivot so it is available to *undergo* ellipsis. This is shown in (25), where this time the second clause has become antipassive, in order to get the reading 'Father returned and saw mother'.

(25) [nguma$_i$ banaga-n^{y}u]   [Ø$_i$ bural-**nga**-n^{y}u   yabu-gu]
     father.ABS$_S$ return-PAST   [ ]$_S$ see-ANTIPASSIVE-PAST   mother-DATIVE
     'Father(S) returned and (S) saw mother.'

In the second clause, the 'mother' NP *yabugu* is not a primary NP but has been demoted to an oblique function, as we can tell by its dative case. The antipassive verb meaning 'see' is again detransitivized: it has only one core argument, the S noun phrase—the single argument of an intransitive verb. As an S, this NP is a possible pivot, so allowed to undergo ellipsis when co-referential with another absolutive NP. So the empty S position in (25) refers back to *nguma*, 'father', in the first clause.

To summarize, the antipassive construction has the following characteristics cross-linguistically.

The antipassive construction

- Applies to a transitive clause (the active clause) and forms an intransitive clause.
- A argument (ergative) promoted > S argument (absolutive).
- O argument demoted > oblique, or is deleted.
- Changes in the morphology of the verb signal antipassivization.

Both the passive and the antipassive constructions have in common the fact that they change basic grammatical relations by promoting some NPs and demoting others. This results in changes to the valency of the verb: both constructions reduce the number and type of core arguments that a verb has, since they apply to transitive verbs and result in intransitive verbs. Thus, the passive and antipassive are both VALENCY-REDUCING processes. The following two sections introduce two other grammatical relation-changing processes: the applicative and the causative constructions. Like the passive and antipassive, these do not occur in all languages, but are widespread nonetheless.

> **Checklist for Sections 7.1 and 7.2**
>
> If you're happy about the points below, you're ready to move on. If not, I recommend revising before reading further.
>
> - What are the main effects of the passive construction, cross-linguistically?
> - What are the main effects of the antipassive construction, cross-linguistically?
> - How does each of these constructions interact with grammatical pivots?

7.3 THE APPLICATIVE CONSTRUCTION

English has an alternation between the (a) and (b) forms in sentences like (26) and (27). Let's assume that the (a) sentences are the more basic, and the (b) sentences are derived from them by processes of promotion and demotion. (One reason for taking the NP-PP constructions as in (26a) and (27a) to be the more basic is that not all verbs which take NP and *to/for*-PP complements can undergo the alternation: **I dispatched the children the presents* vs. *I dispatched the presents to the children*.)

(26) a.   My brother sold his bike to Sue.
     b.   My brother sold Sue his bike.

(27) a.   I baked a cake for Kim.
     b.   I baked Kim a cake.

This alternation occurs just with certain three-argument verbs in English. In their basic form these verbs take a direct object NP (such as *his bike*, *a cake*) plus a PP headed by *to* or *for*, such as *to Sue, for Kim*. In the (b) sentences, the NPs *Sue* and *Kim* have been PROMOTED to direct object position—immediately following the verb in English—and the original direct object is DEMOTED to become a second object: there is no longer a PP in the (b) sentences. This construction in English is often known as DATIVE MOVEMENT (although English has no actual dative case marking) because, in some languages, indirect objects such as 'to Sue' are marked dative (see Section 6.5.4).

Dative movement, 与格移位，指与格名词短语被移动到原来直接宾语的位置。

Now compare the parallel construction found in two completely unrelated languages (unrelated both to each other and to English): an Austronesian language,

Indonesian, and a Bantu language, Chichewa (the rather strange-sounding examples from this language are taken from Baker 1988). We examine below the APPLIC (standing for APPLICATIVE) affixes shown in bold type on the verb in the (b) sentences.

(28) a. Mereka mem-bawa   [daging itu] [kepada dia]. (Indonesian)
        they   TRANS-bring   meat   the   to   him
        'They brought the meat to him.'
    b. Mereka mem-bawa-**kan**   [dia] [daging itu].
       they   TRANS-bring-APPLIC him   meat   the
       'They brought him the meat.'

(29) a. Mbidzi zi-na-perek-a   msampha kwa nkhandwe. (Chichewa)
        zebras SU-PAST-hand-ASPECT   trap   to fox
        'The zebras handed the trap to the fox.'
    b. Mbidzi zi-na-perek-**er**-a   nkhandwe msampha.
       zebras SU-PAST-hand-APPLIC-ASPECT fox   trap
       'The zebras handed the fox the trap.'

These constructions involve the same changes in grammatical relations as those found in English in (26) and (27). In (28a), the NP *dia* 'him' is originally in an oblique function as part of a 'to'-PP *kepada dia*; it is promoted in (28b) to become a core NP, the direct object—as in English, this immediately follows the verb in Indonesian. The preposition disappears. The NP *daging itu* becomes a second object. In Indonesian, but not in English, there is also a special marker on the verb to indicate the promotion: the suffix *-kan*. This is glossed as APPLICATIVE, a traditional grammatical term used both for the verbal marker of promotion and for the construction as a whole.

The Chichewa applicative in (29) is exactly parallel: the 'fox' NP *nkhandwe* was an indirect object within a PP in (29a), but is promoted to direct object position in (29b). The original direct object in (29a), *msampha* 'trap', is demoted in (29b), becoming a second object, and again there's an applicative marker on the verb, the suffix *-er*.

The general properties of the applicative construction, including English dative movement, can be summarized as follows.

The applicative construction

- Oblique NP or indirect object > promoted to object.

- Former object > demoted to second object or oblique.

- Changes may occur in the morphology of the verb to signal the applicative construction.

English is fairly restrictive in the type of oblique phrase that can undergo promotion, but cross-linguistically various kinds of oblique phrases can be promoted, including locative expressions (= those involving location, such as 'on the table', 'into the water'), goals (as in *We sent the letter **to Mel*** > *We sent Mel a letter*), beneficiaries (as in *I baked a cake **for Kim*** > *I baked Kim a cake*) and instrumental phrases, such as 'with a stick', as in the Dyirbal example in (30):

(30) a. yabu   nguma-nggu   balga-n   yugu-nggu   (Dyirbal)
        mother.ABS$_O$ father-ERG$_A$ hit-PAST   stick-INSTRUMENTAL
        'Father hit mother with a stick.'
     b. yugu   nguma-nggu   balgal-**ma**-n yabu-gu
        stick.ABS$_O$ father-ERG$_A$ hit-APPLIC-PAST mother-DATIVE
        'Father used a stick to hit mother.'

Example (30a) is an ordinary transitive clause in Dyirbal, with an ergative A noun phrase, *ngumanggu*, meaning 'father', and an absolutive O noun phrase, *yabu*, meaning 'mother'. In the English translation, *stick* appears inside a PP headed by *with*—it's an oblique phrase; in Dyirbal, the 'stick' NP *yugunggu* is also oblique, and this is marked by a special INSTRUMENTAL case.[2] Instrumental NPs cannot undergo dative movement in English, whereas in Dyirbal the 'stick' NP can indeed be promoted to become a core argument: it's the O in (30b). This NP *yugu* now has absolutive case—the case of normal objects in ergative systems—whilst the former O noun phrase *yabu*, 'mother', has been demoted to a non-core position, as shown by its dative case marking: *yabugu*.

Instrumental case, 工具格, 也是名词短语的一种形式, 表示 "借助……手段" 的意思。

Finally, an NP which has been promoted by the applicative construction to become a direct object can generally undergo a second promotion by the passive construction, thus becoming a subject. In fact, we have already seen an example of this in Section 1.1.1, in the discussion comparing English and Indonesian. The examples in (31) and (32) are again from Chichewa (some English speakers may not find the translation of (31b) grammatical):

(31) a. Kalulu   a-na-gul-ir-a   mbidzi   nsapato   (Chichewa)
        hare   SU-PAST-buy-APPLIC-ASPECT   zebras   shoes
        'The hare bought shoes for the zebras.'
        (*more literally, 'The hare bought the zebras shoes.'*)
     b. Mbidzi   zi-na-gul-**ir-idw**-a   nsapato   (ndi   kalulu)
        zebras   SU-PAST-buy-APPLIC-PASSIVE-ASPECT shoes   by   hare
        'The zebras were bought shoes by the hare.'

In (31a), *mbidzi* 'zebras' has already undergone promotion by the applicative construction, and has become the direct object: as in English, the direct object immediately follows the verb. Once promoted to direct object position, the NP *mbidzi* can undergo a further promotion in the passive construction, (31b): it becomes the subject. The former subject *kalulu* 'hare' is demoted to become an oblique constituent, occurring in an optional *ndi*('by')-phrase. Crucially, the 'shoes' NP in (31a), *nsapato*, cannot undergo promotion to subject by the passive construction, because it's not the direct object but a second object. We can tell that *nsapato* is not a direct object by the fact that it doesn't immediately follow the verb.

If we try to promote the second object in the passive construction, the result is ungrammatical, as in (32):

(32) *Nsapato   zi-na-gul-ir-idw-a   mbidzi   (ndi   kalulu)
     shoes   SU-PAST-buy-APPLIC-PASSIVE-ASPECT   zebras   by   hare
     '*Shoes were bought the zebras by the hare.'

So in Chichewa—and in English—only an NP which is, *or has become*, a direct object can undergo promotion by the passive. Although this restriction is very common cross-linguistically, it's not universal: in some languages both the direct object and the second object of an applicative construction behave like a prototypical object. In Kinyarwanda—another Bantu language—for instance, either type of object can be promoted to subject by the passive construction (see Palmer 1994: Section 6.6).

Cross-linguistically, it is usual to find that the applicative (or dative movement) construction feeds into the passive construction, as illustrated for Chichewa in (31b) and for English by the translation of this example. In other words, the applicative creates new direct objects which can then be promoted to subject. However, not all languages have an applicative construction. French, for example, has no construction parallel to English dative movement; so in French (33a) cannot become (33b), with promotion of *Pierre* to direct object position:

(33) a. Marie a   donné   un cadeau à   Pierre.   (French)
        Marie has   give.PAST PARTICIPLE   a   present to Pierre
        'Marie has given a present to Pierre.'
     b. *Marie a   donné   Pierre un cadeau.
        Marie has   give.PAST.PARTICIPLE   Pierre a   present
        (≠ 'Marie has given Pierre a present.')

In turn, this means that the 'dative movement' construction in (33b) is unavailable as input to the passive construction. The passive version of (33a) is (34a), which is fine—the original direct object *un cadeau*, 'a present', has been promoted to subject position. But as *Pierre* is not a possible direct object in (33b), then we'd predict that this sentence won't be a possible input to the passive construction, since the passive in French only promotes direct objects. And, indeed, the passive version of (33b), with *Pierre* promoted to subject position, is ungrammatical in French as predicted, as in (34b):

(34) a. Un cadeau a   été   donné   à   Pierre par Marie.
        a   present has been give.PAST PARTICIPLE   to Pierre by Marie
        'A present has been given to Pierre by Marie.'
     b. *Pierre a   été   donné   un cadeau par Marie.
        Pierre has been give.PAST PARTICIPLE   a   present by Marie
        (≠ 'Pierre has been given a present by Marie.')

So cross-linguistically, we find a continuum which at one extreme allows no applicative constructions, as in French, and at the other extreme is very free in the kinds of prepositional objects and other oblique NPs that can be promoted to object position. Chichewa lies at the latter end of the spectrum, as does Dyirbal; see (30). English falls somewhere in the middle, having dative movement with a restricted set of verbs.

7.4 THE CAUSATIVE CONSTRUCTION

So far in this chapter we have examined constructions which change grammatical relations by promotion and demotion processes, but which don't introduce any new NP arguments. The passive and antipassive either have the same number of arguments as their active counterparts, or they may reduce that number; the *by*-phrases are optional in (1) through (3), for instance. And the applicative/dative movement construction generally doesn't change the number of arguments in the construction, but simply promotes one to be a core argument and demotes another. In this section I introduce the last major construction type which changes grammatical relations: the causative. This differs from the constructions seen so far in that it always increases the verb's valency by introducing a new argument—the causative agent—and it often introduces an entire new causative predicate as well. I illustrate first from English.

In English, the main way of expressing the idea of causing someone else to do something is by using a verb such as *make, let, cause* or *have*. So we get pairs of sentences like those in (35) and (36):

(35) a. The students left.
 b. We **made/let** the students leave.

(36) a. The students read the book.
 b. We **had** the students read the book.

In both examples the (a) sentences are basic, simple clauses; (35a) is intransitive, (36a) transitive. The (b) examples in each case are CAUSATIVE constructions. In both, *the students* has been DEMOTED from its original position as the subject of the simple clause, and a new subject, *we*, has been introduced. Note that this new subject hasn't been promoted from anywhere, since it doesn't exist in the (a) sentences; it arises from the causative construction. These two properties are common to causative constructions cross-linguistically: the original subject is demoted and a new subject is introduced.

The causative construction in English introduces a new subject and a new predicate—*We made/let/had* in (35) and (36)—so creating a whole new clause. This means that the causative construction turns the simple sentences (with just one clause) in (35a) and (36a) into complex sentences in (35b) and (36b).

This same kind of causative construction with a 'make' or 'cause' verb plus the basic verb also occurs in many other languages. In (37), from Korean, (37a) is the basic clause with *ku sayka* 'the bird' as subject: it has nominative case. And (37b) is the causative, with the causative verb in bold. This has a newly introduced subject, the causative agent *Yonghoka* 'Yongho', which is nominative. It also has a new predicate, glossed 'do'. (The gloss INDIC stands for INDICATIVE, a 'mood' of the verb which is used to refer to real rather than hypothetical events.)

> Indicative, 直陈式, 动词语气的一种, 与虚拟式、祈使式等语气相对应。

(37) a. ku   say-ka   cwuk-ess-ta   (Korean)
          the   bird-NOM   die-PAST-INDIC
          'The bird died.'
      b. Yongho-ka   [ku   say-lul   cwuk-key]   **hay-ss-ta**
          Yongho-NOM   the   bird-ACC   die-COMP   do-PAST-INDIC
          'Yongho caused the bird to die.'

As in English, Korean causatives are complex sentences, containing two clauses. The embedded clause is in brackets, and contains a complementizer, -*key*, '(so) that'. Since Korean is head-final, the complementizer -*key* is final in the embedded clause, and the whole complement clause precedes the verb that selects it, *hayssta*. Literally, (37b) means 'Yongho [that the bird died] caused'. The matrix clause is the 'cause' clause with the predicate *ha(y)* 'do, make, cause'.

French causatives also use a 'make' or 'do' predicate of causation, the verb *faire*. In (38), (a) is again the basic sentence and (b) the causative, with the causative verb in bold:

(38) a. Jean   a   lu   ce   livre.   (French)
          Jean   has.3SG   read.PAST PARTICIPLE this   book
          'Jean has read this book.'
      b. Nous   avons   **fait**   lire   ce livre à Jean.
          we   have.1PL   make.PAST PARTICIPLE read.INFIN   this book to Jean
          'We made Jean read this book.'

However, in French, unlike in Korean or English, the causative does not produce a biclausal construction. Although (38b) does contain two independent lexical verbs, the 'make' verb of causation and the 'read' verb, in fact the two verbs behave generally as a single verbal unit and not as predicates in separate clauses. For instance, unlike in English, the two verbs can't be separated by the NP *Jean*, as (39) shows:

(39) *Nous   avons   fait   Jean   lire   ce   livre.
       we   have.1PL   make.PAST PARTICIPLE   Jean   read.INFIN   this book
       (≠ 'We made Jean read this book.')

So *Jean* doesn't behave like the subject of an embedded clause. In the French, the two lexical verbs are actually both inside a single clause, and share a single set of arguments rather than each having their own arguments as they do in English or in Korean; this should remind you of the verb serialization discussed in Section 3.3.3.

One kind of typological variation in causatives, then, concerns whether or not the addition of a causative verb gives rise to an additional clause. However, not all causatives are formed by using an actual causative verb. In Korean, the most productive type of causative is that shown in (37b), but there is another type known as a **MORPHOLOGICAL CAUSATIVE**, illustrated in (40):

(40) Yongho-ka   ku   say-lul   cwuk-**y**-ess-ta   (Korean)
      Yongho-NOM   the   bird-ACC   die-**CAUS**-PAST-INDIC
      'Yongho killed the bird.'

> Morphological causative, 形态使役动词，即通过动词本身形态的变化（例如，词缀的使用）而形成的使役动词。

The example in (40) only contains a single clause, and instead of a separate causative verb it has causative morphology: an affix -*y* (glossed as CAUS) on the 'die' verb. If we consider this example to be derived from the intransitive clause in (37a), then the former nominative subject NP *ku saylul*, 'the bird', has been demoted to object in (40): it now has accusative case. And a new nominative NP has been introduced, increasing the valency of the verb.

Many languages (though not English) also have a causative affix on the verb rather than using a separate causative verb. This situation parallels the one discussed in Section 7.1.1 above, where we saw that some languages have a special passive affix—see (6) through (8) for instance. Other examples of languages with a morphological causative are shown in (41) and (42): the basic sentence types are shown in each (a) example, the causatives in (b), and the causative affixes are in bold:

(41) a. Mtsuko   u-na-gw-a   (Chichewa)
          waterpot   SU-PAST-fall-ASPECT
          'The waterpot fell.'
      b. Mtsikana   a-na-u-gw-**ets**-a   mtsuko
          girl   SU-PAST-OBJ-fall-CAUS-ASPECT waterpot
          'The girl made the waterpot fall.'

(42) a. Müdür   mektub-u   imzala-dı   (Turkish)
          director.NOM letter-ACC   sign-PAST
          'The director signed the letter.'
      b. Dişçi   mektub-u   müdür-e   imzala-**t**-tı
          dentist.NOM   letter-ACC   director-DATIVE sign-CAUS-PAST
          'The dentist made the director sign the letter.'

In the Chichewa examples, the causative (41b) differs from the basic sentence in various ways. Example (41a) is intransitive, whilst (41b) is transitive. The original subject, *mtsuko*, has been demoted to object in (41b): we can tell because there's an object agreement marker *u-* on the verb, agreeing with *mtsuko* 'waterpot' (in gender, though this isn't shown by the gloss). Also, the verb has a new subject agreement marker *a-* in (41b), and this agrees in gender with *mtsikana* 'girl' (rather than *mtsuko*). Finally, there's a CAUSATIVE suffix *-ets* on the verb in (41b).

In the Turkish examples, there's once again a new subject, *dişçi*, introduced into the causative construction in (42b). The former subject, *müdür*, 'director' is demoted to the position of indirect object in (42b), marked by the dative case; since there's already a direct object, *mektub* 'the letter', it can't take that position.

So far in this section we have seen two types of causative: first the 'cause'-verb plus 'effect'-verb type, and second the morphological causative, as in (41b) and (42b). Although English has no morphological causative (just as it has no morphological passive) it does illustrate a third type of causative construction, the lexical causative. For instance, some verbs can be used either intransitively, so that no causation is expressed, or transitively, so that they include a causer as their subject: *The bottle broke/I broke the bottle* (also *melt, sink, smash, dissolve, burn, spill* and many other verbs). A few intransitive verbs have a closely related causative transitive verb, such as *sit/seat* and *rise/raise*, as in *The wreck **rose** to the surface/We **raised** the wreck to the surface*. Another example of a lexical causative is shown from Greek in (43):

(43) a. pijéno   (Greek)
         go.1SG
         'I go.'
    b. pijéno   to   peðí   s   to   sxolío
         go.1SG   the   child.ACC   to   the   school.ACC
         'I take the child to school.'

Example (43b) is causative, but there's no marker of this at all—the same verb meaning 'go' is used in both (43a) and (43b). Note that the English translation here also uses a lexical causative, but of a different kind, since *go* is replaced in English with a causative verb *take* (= 'cause to go').

As the examples in this section illustrate, causatives can generally be derived from either a basic intransitive verb or a basic transitive verb. The cross-linguistic properties of the construction are as follows:

The causative construction

- Ø > subject (i.e. a new subject is introduced).

- In simple-sentence causatives of the kind shown in (41) and (42), the former subject is demoted > object; or demoted to become an oblique argument; or is deleted.

- Verb adding causation is introduced ('make', 'have' etc.), or else the main verb has causative morphology.

An example illustrating the deletion of the original subject in a causative construction is given in (44). Songhai (or Sonrai) is a Nilo-Saharan language of Mali, Burkino Faso and Niger: the basic sentence is in (44a), the causative in (44b), and the causative affix is in bold.

(44) a. Garba nga   tasu di.   (Songhai)
         Garba eat   rice the
         'Garba ate the rice.'
    b.   Ali   nga-**ndi** tasu di
         Ali   eat-CAUS   rice the
         'Ali got someone to eat the rice.'/'Ali caused the rice to be eaten.'

The original subject of the basic clause, *Garba*, is simply deleted in (44b), whilst a new subject of the causative verb is added, *Ali*.

Finally, recall from Section 7.3 that the applicative construction can feed into the passive construction by creating new object NPs, and these new objects can then be further promoted to subject. Similarly, the causative construction can create new objects by demoting the former subject, and these new objects are then available to be passivized. So the causative often feeds into the passive construction as well. Example (45) illustrates from Chichewa. In (45a) we have the causative construction, which has already made the NP *ana*, 'the children', into a direct object; in (45b) we see the passive that can then be formed, with the NP *ana* now promoted to subject:

(45) a. Buluzi   a-na-wa-sek-ets-a   ana.   (Chichewa)
         lizard   SU-PAST-OBJ-laugh-CAUS-ASPECT children
         'The lizard made the children laugh.'
    b.   Ana   a-na-sek-ets-edw-a   ndi buluzi.
         children SU-PAST-laugh-CAUS-PASSIVE-ASPECT by   lizard
         'The children were made to laugh by the lizard.'

The NP *ana* 'children' in (45a) is shown to be a direct object because it triggers object agreement on the verb, so the object marker *wa-* agrees with *ana* (in gender, though again not directly shown by the gloss). In the passive, (45b), this former object *ana* has undergone promotion to the subject position of the whole verbal complex: as in English, subjects are initial in the clause. And the object marker, *wa-*, has now disappeared from the verb, since passivized verbs are of course intransitive and hence have no object to agree with.

We can conclude, then, that it is quite common for processes that change the grammatical relations of noun phrases to interact with one another, creating further promotions and demotions.

Checklist for Sections 7.3 and 7.4

See if you need to revise these two constructions before moving on:

- What are the main properties of the applicative construction, cross-linguistically?
- What is the name generally given to the applicative construction in English? Give a couple of examples of this construction.
- What are the main properties of the causative construction, cross-linguistically? What distinct types of causatives are found in the languages of the world?

7.5 SUMMARY

'Valency' refers to the number of core arguments that a verb has. We saw in this chapter that languages typically have at least one valency-changing operation. These may increase the number of core arguments, for instance as seen in the causative constructions in Section 7.4. Or alternatively, valency-changing may involve a decrease in the number of core arguments, for instance in the passive and antipassive (Sections 7.1 and 7.2). The processes we've seen also involve promotion and demotion of core arguments, foregrounding some NPs and backgrounding others—removing them from the 'core'—for various pragmatic purposes. We have also seen that these processes interact with one another, for instance by producing a new core argument that can be further promoted.

FURTHER READING

Palmer (1994) will be very useful for many of the issues covered in this chapter, especially passives and antipassives, syntactic pivots, causatives and applicatives. See also Keenan (1985a), Foley and Van Valin (1985) on the passive, and Comrie (1989: ch. 8; 1985b) and Song (1996) on the causative. Some of the data on processes that change grammatical relations come from Baker (1988), a very advanced work which you should probably only tackle (as opposed to browsing for interesting data) after a course in theoretical syntax. Dixon and Aikhenvald (2000) is an edited collection of papers which all focus on valency-changing processes, and from which I've taken some of the data in this chapter.

EXERCISES

1. In Section 7.3 we considered the type of applicative construction known in English as DATIVE MOVEMENT, an alternation which gives rise to pairs such as *Kim gave the book to Lee/Kim gave Lee the book*. As noted earlier, not all verbs which take an NP and a *to*-PP complement can undergo the alternation. Your task is to work out what factors condition the application of dative movement. I have given a few examples, but you will need to find others, to get a fuller picture. I have also suggested grammaticality judgements which accord with my own intuitions, but you should feel free to disagree with them, and to find or make up other examples to support your case. Given that judgements may vary, the 'correct answer' here is a rather fluid concept!

   (1) a. Lee donated the prize money to her favourite charity.
       b. *Lee donated her favourite charity the prize money.

   (2) a. The shopkeeper refunded the money to me.
       b. The shopkeeper refunded me the money.

(3) a. Kim passed the ball to Lee.
    b. Kim passed Lee the ball.

(4) a. I transferred the money to Lee.
    b. *I transferred Lee the money.

(5) a. We showed/sent/forwarded/texted that message to all our friends.
    b. We showed/sent/texted/forwarded all our friends that message.

(6) a. Kim dispatched that letter to his lawyer.
    b. *Kim dispatched his lawyer that letter.

(7) a. I faxed my answer to him straight away.
    b. I faxed him my answer straight away.

(8) a. I handed/delivered the parcel to the publishers.
    b. I handed/*delivered the publishers the parcel.

(9) a. I awarded/presented fantastic prizes to the best students.
    b. I awarded/*presented the best students fantastic prizes.

(10) a. I recommended/introduced *Knowledge of Language* to the students.
     b. *I recommended/introduced the students *Knowledge of Language*.

2. Study the data in (1) through (10) from a Malayo-Polynesian language called Kambera (taken from Klamer 1994).

Task: (i) First, work out how the causative construction is formed in this language. Assume that non-causative sentences are basic, and outline exactly how the causatives are formed from these. Compare the syntax of the two clause types. (ii) Note that one crucial affix in the Kambera is left unidentified and unglossed. What is it? What would be a good gloss for this affix?

(1) Na   pakanabu-ta   weling   la   ài.
    he   fall-1PL.OBJ   move   from   tree
    'He made us fall from the tree.'

(2) Da   rara   hàmu   da   pàu.
    they   be.red   be.good   the.PL   mango
    'The mangoes are nice and ripe.'

(3) Na   lui   du ...
    it   melt   EMPHASIS
    'It should dissolve ...'

(4) Na   palui-ya   na   liling.
     he   melt-3SG.OBJ   the.SG   candle
     'He melts the candle.'

(5) Da   pakatuda-ya   na   anakeda.
     they   sleep-3SG.OBJ   the.SG   child
     'They put the child to sleep.'

(6) Napa   jàka   u   kabeli …
     later   if   you   return
     'Later, if you (*sg.*) return …'

(7) Parara-ya   na   pàu.
     be.red-3SG.OBJ   the.SG   mango
     'Let the mango ripen.'

(8) Da   kawàra   katuda.
     they   both   sleep
     'They both sleep.'

(9) Ta   pakabeli-ha   da   tentara.
     we   return-3PL.OBJ   the.PL   soldier
     'We get the soldiers to return.'

(10) Ambu   ta   kanabu.
     NEG   we   fall
     'Let's not fall.'

3. The data in this exercise are from an Australian language, Kalkatungu, and are taken from Blake (2001b).

Task: (i) Example (1) shows a basic clause. Work out what construction is illustrated by the data in (2) and (3). (ii) A crucial grammatical morpheme, *ntjama*, is left unglossed. What is its function? (iii) What other changes are seen in (2) and (3) as compared with (1)? Make sure you use the correct grammatical terminology in describing them, as far as possible.

(1) Kalpin-tu   intji-mi   nga-tji   utjan
     man-ERG   chop-FUT   me-DAT   firewood
     'The man will chop my firewood.'/'The man will chop the firewood for me.'

(2) Kalpin-tu   intji-**ntjama**-mi   ngayi   utjan
     man-ERG   chop-???-FUT   me.OBJ   firewood
     'The man will chop firewood for me.'

(3)   Kalpin-tu   intji-**ntjama**-mi-ngi   utjan
      man-ERG   chop-???-FUT-me   firewood
      'The man will chop firewood for me.'

4. Southern Tiwa, a native American language from the Tanoan family of New Mexico, has a construction which is traditionally regarded as passive, and is illustrated in the examples below. However, in Southern Tiwa this construction has an important restriction which doesn't occur in English or the other languages seen so far.

Task:

i. What is the syntactic restriction on the passive in Southern Tiwa? Make sure that your answer generalizes as much as possible over the data.

ii. Why are the examples in (4), (6) and (11) ungrammatical?

iii. Finally, do you have any ideas about why a language might have such a restriction on the passive? Think again about PERSON and about what effect the passive has on a subject: compare (3) with (4) and (5) with (6).

Hints:
- Note that in examples like (3), (5), (7), (8) and (9) there are no independent pronouns in the Southern Tiwa sources. Instead, the verb *mũ* meaning 'see' has bound pronominal prefixes showing the PERSON and NUMBER of subject and object. These prefixes occur in (3) through (10), and specify all the information that in the English translations is realized by independent pronouns (such as *You saw me*). (Southern Tiwa in fact has an ergative agreement pattern, but this isn't reflected in this exercise.)

- When the verb in Southern Tiwa has both a subject and an object, these markers are fused together to form a single prefix: see (3) and (5), where the gloss indicates these fused forms with /. In (3), for example, the prefix *bey-* means 2SG(SU) *and* 1SG(OBJ), i.e. it shows simultaneously that the subject is second person singular and the object is first person singular. In (5), the prefix *i-* means that the subject is first person singular and the object is second person singular. Obviously, the fused forms only occur if the verb has both a subject and an object. *The answer to the exercise has nothing whatever to do with the fusion of subject and object markers, or with the appearance or non-appearance of independent pronouns.*

- Read through all the data first. Then go through it step by step, and formulate a hypothesis at each stage about the restriction on the passive. Amend your hypothesis to account for new data as necessary. Be prepared to detail your hypotheses at each stage.

- I've used the notation ≠ in the English translations to indicate what the ungrammatical forms in Southern Tiwa would mean if they were grammatical.

(1) seuanide liora-mũ-ban
    man   lady-see-PAST
    'The man saw the lady.'

(2) liora mũ-che-ban   seuanide-ba
    lady   see-PASSIVE-PAST   man-by
    'The lady was seen by the man.'

(3) bey-mũ-ban
    2SG(SU)/1SG(OBJ)-see-PAST
    'You saw me.'

(4) *te-mũ-che-ban   'ĩ-ba
    1SG(SU)-see-PASSIVE-PAST   you-by
    (≠ 'I was seen by you.')

(5) i-mũ-ban
    1SG(SU)/2SG(OBJ)-see-PAST
    'I saw you.'

(6) *a-mũ-che-ban   na-ba
    2SG(SU)-see-PASSIVE-PAST   me-by
    (≠ 'You were seen by me.')

(7) Seuanide te-mũ-ban
    man   1SG(SU)-see-PAST
    'I saw the man.'

(8) te-mũ-che-ban   seuanide-ba
    1SG(SU)-see-PASSIVE-PAST   man-by
    'I was seen by the man.'

(9) a-mũ-che-ban   seuanide-ba
    2SG(SU)-see-PASSIVE-PAST   man-by
    'You were seen by the man.'

(10) a-mũ-che-ban   awa-ba
     2SG(SU)-see-PASSIVE-PAST   him-by
     'You were seen by him.'

(11) *seuanide mũ-che-ban   na-ba
     man   see-PASSIVE-PAST   me-by
     (≠ 'The man was seen by me.')

The data in this exercise are mostly from Allen and Frantz (1983)—modified slightly—with additional data courtesy of Don Frantz.

5. The data in (1) through (3) below (taken from Nedjalkov 1997) are from the Tungusic language Evenki, spoken in eastern Siberia.

   Task: (i) Examine each pair, and figure out what is the function of the verbal suffix marked in bold in each (b) sentence—I have glossed it simply as SUFFIX, rather than showing its meaning. (ii) Identify exactly what kind of construction is shown in the (b) sentences. (iii) What other grammatical changes occur in the (b) sentences? Why do they occur?

   Hints:
   - Different verbs take different forms of the suffix in question, but the function of the suffix is the same in each instance.
   - It will help to consider what arguments the verbs have in each pair of examples.
   - You will need to concentrate especially on the glosses in each example, rather than on the English translations.

   (1) a. Asatkan suru-re-n.
          girl   go.away-PAST-3SG
          'The girl went away.'
       b. Atyrkan   asatkan-me   suru-**pken**-e-n.
          old.woman girl-ACC   go.away-SUFFIX-PAST-3SG
          'The old woman made the girl go away.'

   (2) a. Beje eme-re-n.
          man   come-PAST-3SG
          'The man came.'
       b. Beje moo-l-va   eme-**v**-re-n.
          man   tree-PL-ACC   come-SUFFIX-PAST-3SG
          'The man brought firewood.'

   (3) a. Tyge d'alup-ta-n.
          cup   become.full-PAST-3SG
          'The cup became full/The cup filled.'
       b. Asatkan tyge-ve   d'alup-**ki**-ra-n.
          girl   cup-ACC   become.full-SUFFIX-PAST-3SG
          'The girl filled the cup.'

6. In Section 7.2, we introduced the idea that syntactically ergative languages can have a pivot which operates in terms of the *absolutive* NPs, whilst syntactically accusative languages can have a pivot which operates in terms of *subject* NPs. (You might like to revise Section 7.2 before tackling this exercise.) The data sets below are from two unrelated languages: A. is from Bare, an extinct language of the North Arawak family, from Brazil and Venezuela (data from Aikhenvald 1995) and B. is from Guugu Yimidhirr, a native language of Australia (data taken from Haviland 1979). Both data sets illustrate co-ordinate clauses with ellipsis of one grammatical relation in the second clause. Each clause is bracketed, and

neither language uses actual conjunctions such as 'and'. You will need to look at the index on each NP in order to see which NP in the first clause the omitted NP refers back to.

Task: Examine each data set, and figure out whether each language is syntactically ERGATIVE or syntactically ACCUSATIVE. Outline your evidence clearly and concisely, using the correct grammatical terminology.

Hints:
- I haven't labelled the NPs with A, S and O so you will need to work out for yourself which NP is the A, the S and the O in these examples.
- There is no actual case-marking on the NPs in Bare, so you won't be able to tell from the form of the noun phrases whether or not Bare is morphologically ERGATIVE.
- A language which is morphologically ergative may or may not also be syntactically ergative.

A. Bare

(1) a. [kwati$_i$ i-karuka tšinu$_j$] [Ø$_j$ i-baraka]
jaguar 3F.SG-bite dog 3F.SG-run
'A jaguar$_i$ bit the dog$_j$ and [it]$_j$ ran.'

b. [da kwati$_i$ i-d'áwika] [mawaya$_j$ a-kharuka Ø$_i$]
the jaguar 3F.SG-die snake INDEF-bite
'The jaguar$_i$ died (because) a snake$_j$ bit [it]$_i$.'

B. Guugu Yimidhirr

(2) a. [Nyulu yarrga$_i$ gada-y] [Ø$_i$ mayi$_j$ buda-y].
3SG boy.ABS come-PAST food.ABS eat-PAST
'The boy$_i$ came and [he]$_i$ ate the food$_j$.'

b. [Nyulu yarrga-a$_i$ mayi$_j$ buda-y] [Ø$_i$ gada-y]
3SG boy-ERG food.ABS eat-PAST come-PAST
'The boy$_i$ ate the food$_j$ and then [he]$_i$ came.'

7. The data in this exercise (slightly adapted from Chung 1976) are from Indonesian, a syntactically accusative language. The usual constituent order is seen in (1). You have five tasks to complete. (i) Examine the data in (1) first and state what is the unmarked order of the verb and its arguments, which are subject, object and indirect object or oblique NP.

(1) a. Monjet men-gigit saja.
monkey TRANS-bite I
'A monkey bit me.'

b. Saja mem-bawa surat itu kepada Ali.
I TRANS-bring letter the to Ali
'I brought the letter to Ali.'

c. Mereka ber-lajar ke Amerika.
   they INTRANS-sail to America
   'They sailed to America.'

The next set of data illustrates a fronting process in Indonesian. (ii) Examine the sentences in (2) and (3) and figure out what GRAMMATICAL RELATION the fronted constituent must bear. Your answer should account both for the grammatical data in (2) and the ungrammatical examples in (3). (The English translations are deliberately neutral here, so you will need to study the original Indonesian carefully.) Then (iii) say what other grammatical changes occur when the constituent is fronted.

(2) a. Ikan merah itu dia sudah tangkap.
       fish red the he PERF catch
       'He already caught the red fish.'
    b. Itu dapat kita lihat pada mata-nja.
       that can we see in eye-its
       'We can see that in its eyes.'

(3) a. *Polisi itu saja serahkan sendjata saja kepada.
       police the I surrender weapon I to
       ('I surrendered my gun to the police.')
    b. *Danau itu sedang mereka be-renang di.
       lake the PROG they INTRANS-swim in
       ('They were swimming in the lake.')

The next data set illustrates a construction in Indonesian which alters grammatical relations, changing a basic sentence such as (4a) into (4b). (iv) What syntactic processes does this involve? Discuss them in terms of PROMOTION and/or DEMOTION and state the effects of the construction on the grammatical relations.

(4) a. Saya meng-kirim surat itu kepada wanita itu.
       I TRANS-send letter the to woman the
       'I sent the letter to the woman.'
    b. Saya meng-kirim-i wanita itu surat itu.
       I TRANS-send-APPLIC woman the letter the
       'I sent the woman the letter.'

If the fronting construction you identified in connection with (2) and (3) applies to the examples in (4), the results are as follows: (5a) is ungrammatical but (5b) is grammatical. (v) In light of your answers concerning (4), account for this difference in grammaticality. You will need to say why the constituent can be fronted in (5b) but not in (5a).

(5) a. *Wanita itu saja kirim surat itu (kepada)
       woman the I send letter the to
       (≠ 'I sent the woman the letter.')

b. Wanita itu saja kirim-i surat itu.
      woman the I send-APPLIC letter the
      'I sent the woman the letter.'

8. In each of the following three data sets, A. to C., the (b)/(c) sentences show a CAUSATIVE construction derived from the corresponding (a) sentences.

   Task: State how the causative is formed in each of the three languages illustrated. Your answer should include:

   i. an explicit and concise statement of how the causative is expressed in each of the languages;

   ii. an indication of and explanation for any additional grammatical changes in each example, especially in the verbal morphology, and in the position and morphology of NP arguments of the verb, where there are any;

   iii. an attempt to explain the reason for the ungrammaticality in examples (8c) and (9c) in the Japanese data set.

   Hints:
   - Don't worry about the actual form of the verbal morphology in these examples. In some cases there are alternations or irregularities in the morphology, but these need not concern us here.
   - You will find it helpful to consider at the start whether the language in each data set is nominative/accusative or ergative/absolutive in its morphology.

   A. **K'iche'** (data from Campbell 2000)
   (1) a. š-e:-kam-ik
          ASP-3PL.ABS-die-INTRANS
          'They died.'
       b. š-e:-qa-kam-isa:-x
          ASP-3PL.ABS-1PL.ERG-die- CAUS-TRANS
          'We killed them.'

   (2) a. š-Ø-atin-ik
          ASP-3SG.ABS-bathe-INTRANS
          'He bathed.'
       b. š-Ø-r-atin-isa:-x
          ASP-3SG.ABS-3SG.ERG-bathe-CAUS-TRANS
          'She washed him.'

   B. **Amharic** (data from Amberber 2000)
   (3) a. k'ibe-w k'əllət'ə
          butter-DEF melt.PERF.3M.SU
          'The butter melted.'
       b. aster k'ibe-w-in a-k'əllət'ə-čč

     Aster(female name) butter-DEF-ACC CAUS-melt.PERF-3F.SU
     'Aster melted the butter.'

(4) a. lɨǰ-u dabbo bəlla
    child-DEF bread eat.PERF.3M.SU
    'The child ate some bread.'

  b. aster   lɨǰ-u-n dabbo a-bəlla-čč-ɨw
    Aster(female name) child-DEF-ACC bread CAUS-eat.PERF-3F.SU-3M.OBJ
    'Aster fed the child some bread.'

(5) a. aster   č'əffərə-čč
    Aster(female name) dance.PERF-3F.SU
    'Aster danced.'

  b. ləmma   aster-in as-č'əffər-at
    Lemma(male name) Aster-ACC CAUS-dance.PERF.3M.SU-3F.OBJ
    'Lemma made Aster dance.'

C. **Japanese** (data from Dixon 2000 and Tsujimura 1996)

(6) a. Taroo-ga konsaato-e it-ta
    Taro-NOM concert-to go-PAST
    'Taro went to a concert.'

  b. Ryooshin-ga Taroo-o konsaato-e ik-ase-ta
    parents-NOM Taro-ACC concert-to go-CAUS-PAST
    'His parents made Taro go to a concert.'

  c. Ryooshin-ga Taroo-ni konsaato-e ik-ase-ta
    parents-NOM Taro-DATIVE concert-to go-CAUS-PAST
    'His parents let Taro go to a concert.'

(7) a. Hanako-ga aruita
    Hanako-NOM walk.PAST
    'Hanako walked.'

  b. Taroo-ga Hanako-o aruk-ase-ta
    Taro-NOM Hanako-ACC walk-CAUS-PAST
    'Taro made Hanako walk.'

  c. Taroo-ga Hanako-ni aruk-ase-ta
    Taro-NOM Hanako-DATIVE walk-CAUS-PAST
    'Taro had/let Hanako walk.'

(8) a. Hana-ga migotoni saita
    flower-NOM beautifully bloom.PAST
    'The flowers bloomed beautifully.'

  b. Taroo-ga hana-o migotoni sak-ase-ta
    Taro-NOM flower-ACC beautifully bloom-CAUS-PAST
    'Taro made the flowers bloom beautifully.'

  c.   *Taroo-ga   hana-ni   migotoni   sak-ase-ta
     Taro-NOM   flower-DATIVE   beautifully   bloom-CAUS-PAST
     (≠ 'Taro had the flowers bloom beautifully.')

(9)   a.   Hanako-ga   kizetu-sita
     Hanako-NOM   faint.PAST
     'Hanako fainted.'
   b.   Taroo-ga   Hanako-o   kizetu-sase-ta
     Taro-NOM   Hanako-ACC   faint-CAUS-PAST
     'Taro made Hanako faint.'
   c.   *Taroo-ga   Hanako-ni   kizetu-sase-ta
     Taro-NOM   Hanako-DATIVE   faint-CAUS-PAST
     (≠ 'Taro had Hanako faint.')

NOTES

1 The abbreviation PN in (6) is for 'proper noun marker', that is, it marks names in Chamorro. Note also that the passive marker -*in*- is actually an INFIX on the verb in (6b): it's inserted into the stem of the verb itself.

2 The instrumental case in Dyirbal in fact has the same suffix as the ergative case, -*nggu*, but there are good reasons to consider the two cases to be syntactically distinct. Dixon (1994: 170, fn. 22) notes that instrumental NPs and ergative NPs have different syntactic behaviour. In the antipassive construction, an ergative NP is promoted from A to S—see (24) and (25) above—but an instrumental NP doesn't get promoted. In the applicative construction, an instrumental NP gets promoted to O whereas an ergative NP undergoes no promotion.

8

Wh-constructions: Questions and relative clauses

章节导读

通过上一章的内容看出，我们可以通过名词短语的升格与降格来改变动词的论元结构。在这一章我们将会学到，一个句子中的短语也可以在不改变语法关系的情况下在句子内部移动，这主要体现在 WH 疑问句和关系小句上。

WH 疑问句是指以 WH 语项即 what, who, whom, where, which, how 等疑问词开始的句子。在英语和许多其他的语言之中，词类句子是通过一般陈述句的 WH 语项移位而产生的。首先我们用一个适当的 WH 语项来代替原来陈述句中需要提问的部分，然后把 WH 语项向前移动。被移位的 WH 语项虽然被前置，但是并不产生新的语法关系。例如，在英语中，WH 语项总是位于句子的起始，但是并不充当句子的主语。在许多语言中，WH 语项经过移位后所处的位置都在标句短语（complementizer phrase）之前。另外，WH 移位并非仅仅存在于母句之中，从属小句中也存在这一现象。但是，母句中 WH 移位主要进行主语和助动词的倒置，而从属小句中的移位则不需要。

WH 疑问句是 WH 语项被前置的结果，但是，在英语中这并不是唯一的构成疑问句的方式，我们也可以采用反问句的形式。在许多语言中（其中包括汉语和日语），反问句的结构是主要的疑问方式。对于这些语言来说，在构成疑问句时，只需要把原来陈述句中需要提问的部分变成 WH 语项即可，而不需要再做进一步的移位。WH 移位和 WH 原位是世界上语言中两种主要的构成 WH 疑问句的方式，对于某些语言来说，它们以其中的一种方式为主，而在另外的一些语言中，两种方式都是常用的。在具有多个 WH 语项的情况下，在 WH 移位语言中，其中的一个 WH 语项会被前置，其他的则被保留在原位，而在 WH 原位语言中，所有的 WH 语项都会保留在原位。

关系小句在各种语言中的使用都比较普遍。所有包括关系小句的句子都是复杂句，因为关系小句是一个修饰母句中中心名词的从属小句。在英语中，关系小句紧随在它所修饰的名词之后，另外它和 WH 疑问句一样也是由 WH 移位而形成的。因此，许多语言学家也把关系小句看作是一种 WH 结构。但是在许多其他的语言中，关系小句往往位于它所修饰的名词之前，这种现象在中心词开头的语言中尤为常见。另外，在少数语言中，关系小句也并不是套嵌于母句之中的。

WH 疑问句和关系小句都涉及成分的移位，其实，许多语言都采用移位的方法将话语的焦点放在某个特定的短语上，这与 WH 前置具有许多相似之处。在日语和汉语中，这一过程被称为倒换。

Chapter 7 introduced processes of promotion and demotion: we looked at ways in which languages alter the argument structure of verbs by changing their grammatical relations. As we saw, this led to changes in the core arguments of verbs—for instance, objects may be promoted to become subjects, and subjects may be demoted to an oblique phrase, or even deleted. In this chapter we will see that languages also have ways of moving phrases around within the clause without changing their grammatical relations. I concentrate particularly on two types of construction: *wh*-questions (Section 8.1) and relative clauses (8.2). We also look at focus and other movement constructions (Section 8.3).

8.1 *WH*-QUESTIONS

8.1.1 Languages with *wh*-movement

Wh-questions are so called because in English they begin with *wh*-words and *wh*-phrases such as *what* and *what kind of sandwich*. Other examples are *which* or *which pickle*, *who*, *where*, *when*, *why* and also *how*. (1) and (2) illustrate:

由这两个实例我们可以看出句法学研究的一个基本思路，即一些特殊的句子结构是从更为常见的、一般的句子结构转换而来的，例如，被动句来自于主动句，疑问句来自于陈述句等。

(1) a. Lee saw [that girl with the long scarf] at the bus-stop yesterday.
 b. [Who] did Lee see ___ at the bus-stop yesterday?

(2) a. Lee saw that girl with the long scarf [at the bus-stop] yesterday.
 b. [Where] did Lee see that girl with the long scarf ___ yesterday?

Note that the sequence of words which is being questioned must be a constituent—in fact, this was one test for constituent structure in Chapter 5. I have indicated in square brackets the constituent being questioned in the (a) sentences, and also the *wh*-word which replaces it in the (b) sentences, since this is a constituent too. The gap shows the position that the questioned phrase formerly occupied. In English, and in many other languages, a *wh*-phrase is 'fronted': it occurs in a special position to the left of the clause. This is known as **wh-movement**.

Wh-questions are constructed as follows. The phrase that we're asking a question about is first replaced by a suitable *wh*-word or *wh*-phrase, such as *which girl*. What constitutes a suitable *wh*-word depends on the category and properties of our original phrase. An NP such as *that girl with the long scarf* is replaced by *who*, or *which girl*; an NP headed by an inanimate noun, such as *that wonderful hand-built bike*, or a non-human noun, such as *that dreadful dog*, would be replaced by *what*, or *which X*. The *wh*-phrase *where* replaces LOCATIVE PPs—that is, PPs expressing location; and *when* replaces TEMPORAL PPs and NPs, such as *at three o'clock, this morning, yesterday*.

Then the *wh*-word or phrase moves to its position before the left edge of the clause, leaving behind it a gap in the clause structure. As we saw in the discussion of cleft sentences in Section 5.1.2.4, displacement creates a DEPENDENCY between the moved phrase and the gap left behind. This is also true of *wh*-movement. The *wh*-phrase and the gap are, in effect, one and the same, which we can indicate by means of the subscript index notation: [Who]$_i$ did Lee see [___]$_i$ at the bus-stop yesterday?. Both the *wh*-word and its dependent gap have the same subscript $_i$, and are thus shown to refer to the same entity.

Note, then, that the fronted *wh*-phrase doesn't get a new grammatical relation when it is displaced. The *wh*-phrase moves leftwards to appear before the start of the clause in English; it doesn't, for instance, become the subject of the clause: so in (1) and (2), the subject is still *Lee*. Instead, the *wh*-phrase *replaces* the phrase it stands for. In (1), for instance, *who*—or more specifically, the gap associated with *who*—fulfils the requirement of the transitive verb *see* to have a direct object; see Section 5.1.2.4. And in (2), *where* replaces the adjunct *at the bus-stop*. The *wh*-phrase also has the same syntactic category as the phrase it replaces: this means that *who*, *what* and *which girl* are all NPs, while *where* is a PP. We can tell that the *wh*-phrase replaces the phrase it stands for by the fact that we can't put another phrase of the same type back into the gap. This is particularly clear in (1), since the verb *see* can only have one direct object NP. Trying to re-fill the gap where the object used to be is impossible, as in (3):

(3) **Who* did Lee see **that girl with a scarf** at the bus-stop yesterday?

Before reading further, consider the example in (4):

(4) [When] did Lee see that girl [at two o'clock]?

This is fully grammatical, even though there's a *wh*-phrase *when* as well as the temporal PP *at two o'clock*, yet it doesn't constitute a counter-example to the claim that we can't re-fill the gap left behind when a *wh*-phrase is moved to its pre-clause initial position. Why not?

Wh-movement, WH 移位, 有时也称作 WH 前置（WH-fronting, WH-preposing），或 WH 提升（WH-raising）。

WH 语项在被移位之后留下的空白被称为语迹（trace），语迹与被移走的 WH 语项之间存在着依附关系，具有相同的指标，因此用同样的标记。

A transitive verb can only have one direct object, so (3) is ungrammatical because both *who* and *that girl with a scarf* fulfil the function of direct object. But the same verb can have any number of adjunct PPs. Just because one of these phrases gets replaced by *when* doesn't necessarily mean that there shouldn't be other adjuncts in addition. So (4) could be derived from a statement such as this: *Lee saw that girl* [*on April 1st*] [*at two o'clock*]. This means that the structure of (4) is actually as in (5): there's a PP-gap which is connected to *when*, as well as another overtly present PP, *at two o'clock*.

(5)   When did Lee see that girl ___ [at two o'clock]?

Many other languages, including many entirely unrelated to English, also move *wh*-words and *wh*-phrases leftwards, to a similar initial position; this position is outside the main body of the clause, since it's not a position associated with any grammatical function. In other words, it's not movement to a subject position, as we've seen, or indeed an object position or any other position occupied by the arguments of a verb. Some further examples of *wh*-phrases in the same position are shown in (6), from Koromfe, a Gur or Voltaic language of Burkina Faso:

(6) a. **alama** pa   vaga   koŋ   a   mũĩ   (Koromfe)
        who.PL   give   dog   the   ART   rice
        'Who (pl.) gave the dog rice?'
    b. **sefu**   də   na   a   manɛ   hɛ̃ŋ
        when   he   see   ART   money the
        'When did he find the money?'
    c. **ase**   a   kɛ̃õ   hoŋ   panɛ   a   vaga   koŋ
        what   ART   woman   the   give.PAST ART dog   the
        'What did the woman give to the dog?'
    d. **nde**   də   na   mə   sundu koŋ
        where   he   see   my   horse the
        'Where did he see my horse?'

In languages with *wh*-movement to an initial position, the *wh*-expression precedes the material that normally occurs at the start of the clause. So for instance, in Welsh, the normal constituent order is VSO—that is, the finite verb is initial in the clause in a statement. But the *wh*-expression precedes the finite element in a *wh*-question. Examples (7) and (8) show some statements and the related *wh*-questions, with the gap corresponding to the original position of the moved expression shown as usual by an underline. The finite verb is in italics, and the *wh*-phrase is in bold type:

(7) a. *Enillodd*   y   myfyrwyr   y   wobr   ddoe.   (Welsh)
        win.PAST.3SG   the   students   the   prize   yesterday
        'The students won the prize yesterday.'
    b. **Beth** *enillodd*   y   myfyrwyr   ___   ddoe?
        wha   win.PAST.3SG   the   students   yesterday

8. Wh-constructions: Questions and relative clauses

'What did the students win yesterday?'

(8) a. *Mae* 'r castell fwyaf yng Nghymru yng Nghaerffili.
be.PRES.3SG the castle largest in Wales in Caerffili
'The largest castle in Wales is in Caerffili.'
b. **Ym mha dref** *mae* 'r castell fwyaf yng Nghymru ____?
in which town be.PRES.3SG the castle largest in Wales
'In which town is the largest castle in Wales?'

In fact, there is evidence from a variety of languages that the initial position to which the *wh*-phrase moves is the position immediately before the clause-introducing element known as a COMPLEMENTIZER (see Chapter 3, and also Section 4.1.6). (Of course, not all languages have complementizers, or may not have them in all clause types.) The data in (9) (Radford 1988) illustrate the *wh*-phrase appearing immediately before the complementizer in a variety of Arabic, (9a), and in Frisian, a Germanic language, in (9b): the *wh*-expression is in bold, and the complementizer is in italics:

(9) a. **Mᶜamn** *lli* hdarti? (Colloquial Moroccan Arabic)
with.whom that you.spoke
'Who did you speak to?'
b. **Wat** *oft* ik drinke woe? (Frisian)
what whether I drink would
'What would I drink?'

It seems, then, that there is a special initial position, immediately preceding the complementizer, which *wh*-phrases are moved to in languages that have *wh*-movement. We can consider this to be a position at the left edge of the CP, the COMPLEMENTIZER PHRASE, which was discussed in Section 4.1.6.

Finally, note that *wh*-movement doesn't just apply in root clauses, but also applies in embedded clauses too, as (10) illustrates:

(10) a. I wonder [CP **who** left the cake out in the rain].
b. I enquired [CP **which books** the students had read over the vacation].
c. We need to know [CP **where** the bus will stop].

Before reading further, please work out (i) what kind of phrase each *wh*-phrase in bold in (10) represents (i.e. NP, AP, PP or what?); (ii) where is the gap in each embedded clause, and what is the function of this phrase in each clause?; and (iii) what is the major syntactic difference in English between embedded *wh*-questions like those in (10) and *wh*-questions in root clauses, such as those in (1) and (2)?

读完此段，结合前面的内容，我们可以得到两个主要的发现：一是WH语项所处的位置不属于小句的主体部分；二是WH语项位于CP之前。理解这两点之后，读者可以进一步阅读生成语法关于疑问句结构的描述，在管辖约束理论中，一个小句被看作是一个CP，而WH语项是它的限定成分（specifier）。

Here are the answers:

i. In (10a) and (10b), the *wh*-phrases are both NPs, and in (10c), *where* represents a PP.

ii. The gaps are shown here:
    a. I wonder [**who** __ left the cake out in the rain].
    b. I enquired [**which books** the students had read __ over the vacation].
    c. We need to know [**where** the bus will stop __].

    The gap in (10a) is the subject of the embedded clause—it's parallel to a sentence like **Mel** *left the cake out in the rain*. The gap in (10b) is the object of the embedded clause—compare *The students had read* **all the books on the reading list** *over the vacation*. And the gap in (10c) is a PP adjunct to the verb *stop*, as in *The bus will stop* **at the market place**.

iii. The major syntactic difference in English between embedded *wh*-questions and *wh*-questions in root clauses is that subject/auxiliary inversion generally only applies in root clauses, as we saw first in Chapter 3. So in (1), we get *Who did Lee see?*, but in an embedded clause we'd normally get *He asked* [*who Lee saw*], rather than *He asked [*who did Lee see*] (though some dialects find this grammatical). Also, as noted in Chapter 3, if the embedded clause is taken to be a quotation of direct speech, then inversion is typically acceptable.

8.1.2 Languages with *wh*-in-situ *wh*-questions

In Section 8.1.1 we saw that one common way of forming *wh*-questions cross-linguistically is to move a *wh*-expression to a special, pre-clause initial position at the left edge of CP: this is known as *wh*-fronting. However, not all languages form *wh*-questions by moving the *wh*-expression at all. Recall from Chapter 5 the ECHO QUESTION construction, which is illustrated again in (11):

(11) a. Lee bought **how many copies** of that wonderful book?
     b. Kim took 300 pictures of **which mountain range** with her new camera?
     c. You've fallen in love with **who**?

The main characteristic of examples such as these is that the *wh*-phrase remains in the usual position occupied in the clause by the phrase that is being questioned. So for (11a), for instance, we find a related statement such as *Lee bought* **four copies** *of that wonderful book*. English generally has the option of asking a *wh*-question in this way; it typically conveys incredulity, or else is used when the addressee didn't hear a portion of the statement.

In some languages, however, the counterparts to (11) form the *only* way of asking *wh*-questions. In such languages there is no *wh*-fronting, but instead the *wh*-word simply replaces a constituent in its normal position without moving, just as in echo questions in English. The technical term for this construction when the *wh*-phrase does not move is WH-IN-SITU—the Latin phrase means that the phrase stays in position.

Chinese and Japanese are both good examples of *wh*-in-situ languages. The first example is from Chinese, with the statement in (12a), and the question, showing *wh*-in-situ, in (12b):

(12) a. Ni kanjian-le Zhangsan. (Chinese)
you see-ASPECT Zhangsan
'You saw Zhangsan.'
b. Ni kanjian-le **shei**?
you see-ASPECT who
'Who did you see __?'

The Chinese statement in (12a) has SVO order (as in English), so when the direct object is questioned, (12b), the interrogative (question) phrase remains immediately after the verb, in the normal position for the object.

In (13) and (14) we illustrate from Japanese: (13) is a statement, and (14) shows two different *wh*-questions formed from it. The *wh*-phrases are again shown in bold:

(13) Hanako-ga kinoo [tomodati-to] [susi-o] tukurimasita. (Japanese)
Hanako-NOM yesterday friend-with sushi-ACC make.PAST
'Hanako made sushi with her friends yesterday.'

(14) a. Hanako-ga kinoo [**dare-to**] [susi-o] tukurimasita ka?
Hanako-NOM yesterday who-with sushi-ACC make.PAST QU
'Who did Hanako make sushi with __ yesterday?'
b. Hanako-ga kinoo [tomodati-to] [**nani-o**] tukurimasita ka?
Hanako-NOM yesterday friend-with what-ACC make.PAST QU
'What did Hanako make __ with her friends yesterday?'

In (14a) the position questioned is the object of the postposition *to* 'with'– note that the NP object *precedes* the P in Japanese, since this is a head-final language. In (14b) the position questioned is the object of the verb *tukurimasita* 'made', and the object again precedes the verb. Note that there is also an interrogative complementizer *ka* in (14), showing that these are questions; as Japanese is head-final, the complementizer follows the clause rather than preceding it.

You should now be able to see that just as in an echo question in English, the *wh*-phrase does not move in these Chinese and Japanese examples, but always remains in the normal position of the phrase being questioned.

In some languages, ordinary questions (rather than echo questions) can be formed either by *wh*-movement or by *wh*-in-situ: in other words, it appears that such languages employ both of the available strategies. In (15) and (16) I illustrate from French: the statement is in (15), and the two methods of forming a question (in informal French) are shown in (16):

Wh-in-situ, 疑问词原位, 其中的 in-situ 来自于拉丁语, 意思是"在原位"。在疑问词原位语言中, 关于 WH 语项是否移位的问题, 是近年来句法学研究的一个焦点问题。

注意这两个汉语实例的写作方式, 这是一个标准的通用做法, 当我们在用英语写论文, 需要引用汉语句子的实例时, 也应采取这样的做法。

(15) Tu   vois   Pierre ce   soir.   (French)
     you   see.PRES.2SG   Pierre this   evening
     'You're seeing Pierre tonight.'

(16) a. **Qui** tu   vois   ___   ce   soir ?
         who   you   see.PRES.2SG   this   evening
         'Who are you seeing ___ tonight?'
     b. Tu   vois   **qui** ce   soir?
         you   see.PRES.2SG   who   this   evening
         'Who are you seeing ___ tonight?'

In (16a) we have *wh*-fronting, as in English, but in (16b), the *wh*-word *qui* 'who' is in exactly the same position—the object position—as the ordinary object NP, *Pierre*, in (15). It seems, then, that some languages are 'mixed' in terms of their methods for forming *wh*-questions.

8.1.3 Multiple *wh*-questions

Sections 8.1.1 and 8.1.2 discussed the two main alternatives available cross-linguistically for forming *wh*-questions, and also showed that some languages appear to employ both strategies. In this final section on questions, we illustrate the strategies which are employed when more than one constituent is questioned in a single clause.

English, of course, is a language with *wh*-fronting. However, if more than one constituent is questioned, then only one of the resulting *wh*-expressions can move leftwards to the initial position in CP, and the remaining *wh*-phrase(s) must remain in-situ:

(17) a. [Kim] saw [that stray dog] last night.
     b. [**Who**] saw [**what**] last night?
     c. *Who what saw last night?

In (17b) we see the only grammatical option for asking a MULTIPLE WH-QUESTION in English; (17c) shows that if we attempt to front all of the *wh*-phrases in such a question, the result is completely ungrammatical.

So what happens in other languages? In *wh*-in-situ languages, multiple *wh*-questions also occur, but since there is no *wh*-fronting, then all the questioned phrases must appear in-situ. Examples (18) and (19) illustrate from Japanese:

(18) Taroo-ga   [Yosiko-ni]   [hon-o   ni-satu]   ageta.   (Japanese)
     Taroo-NOM Yoshiko-DATIVE   book-ACC   two-CLASSIFIER give.PAST
     'Taroo gave two books to Yoshiko.'

(19) Taroo-ga   [**dare-ni**]   [**nani-o**]   ageta   no?
     Taroo-NOM who-DATIVE   what-ACC   give.PAST   QU

'Who did Taroo give what?'

In (18) we see a statement, and in (19) two of the constituents in that clause have been questioned: both the indirect object (the dative 'recipient' NP, *Yosiko-ni*) and the direct object (the accusative 'theme' NP, *hon-o ni-satu* 'two books'). The *wh*-phrases replacing these two constituents each remain in-situ, and, as (19) shows, each bear the usual case-marking appropriate for the grammatical functions which they hold in the clause.

So far, then, we have seen that multiple *wh*-questions may be formed as in English, by fronting one *wh*-phrase and leaving any others in-situ, or as in Japanese, by leaving all *wh*-phrases in-situ. There is, however, a third option, namely to front *all* the *wh*-phrases in a multiple *wh*-question. This strategy, known as MULTIPLE **wh-fronting**, occurs for instance in some of the Slavonic languages, such as Bulgarian and Serbo-Croatian. I illustrate first from Bulgarian: (20) through (23) show that all the *wh*-phrases are fronted in multiple *wh*-questions, even if this means fronting three *wh*-expressions:

Multiple *wh*-fronting, 多项疑问词前置,指在有多个WH语项的情况下,所有的WH疑问词被前置的现象。

(20) **Kogo** vižda John? (Bulgarian)
who sees John
'Who does John see?'

(21) **Koj kogo** vidjal?
who whom saw
'Who saw whom?'

(22) **Kogo kakvo** e pital Ivan?
whom what is asked Ivan
'Who did Ivan ask what?'

(23) **Koj kogo kakvo** e pital?
who whom what is asked
'Who asked whom what?'

In Bulgarian, the fronted phrases have to occur in a fixed order, as illustrated in these examples. In some languages with multiple *wh*-fronting, however, the *wh*-expressions can occur freely in any order. A closely related language, known by the cover term Serbo-Croatian (comprising Bosnian, Serbian and Croatian), allows *both* of the orders in (24), and both have the same meaning:

(24) a. **Ko koga** voli? (Serbo-Croatian)
who whom loves
'Who loves whom?'
b. **Koga ko** voli?
whom who loves
'Who loves whom?'

Since *wh*-expressions show case marking just like ordinary NPs in this language, it is possible to tell which *wh*-phrase represents the subject and which represents the object: the nominative *ko* represents the subject, and the accusative *koga*, the object. Formal English also has a relic of a parallel case marking, indicated by the *who/whom* distinction.

Finally, just as we saw in Section 8.1.2 that some languages (such as French) may employ both the *wh*-movement and the *wh*-in-situ strategies for forming ordinary *wh*-questions, there are also languages which allow different options in multiple *wh*-questions. In Malagasy, which has the basic constituent order VOS, three constructions occur as alternatives, subject to some syntactic restrictions. The three possibilities are as follows: (i) like English, one *wh*-phrase fronts to the pre-clause initial position in CP and remaining *wh*-phrases remain in-situ: this is shown in (25); or (ii), like Japanese, all *wh*-phrases remain in-situ: this is shown in (26); or (iii), like Bulgarian and Serbo-Croatian, all *wh*-phrases front to the initial position: (27) illustrates:

(25) a. **Iza** no nividy **inona**? (Malagasy)
 who PRT bought what
 'Who bought what?'
 b. **Inona** no novidin' **iza**?
 what PRT bought who
 'Who bought what?'

(26) Anasan' **iza** **inona** ny savony?
 washes who what the soap
 'Who washes what with the soap?'

(27) a. **Aiza** **iza** no mividy ny vary?
 where who PRT buys the rice
 'Where does who buy the rice?'
 b. **Aiza** **inona** no vidinao?
 where what PRT buy.2
 'Where do you buy what?'

8.2 RELATIVE CLAUSES

8.2.1 Relative clauses in English

The next major *wh*-construction is the RELATIVE CLAUSE, an extremely widespread construction, cross-linguistically. Some typical examples from English are given in (28), where the relative clauses are in brackets.

(28) a. She snarled at the **students** [who hadn't read the book].
 b. The **paper** [(which) we discuss next week] looks really interesting.
 c. I expect the **film** [(that) we're going to tonight] will be fantastic.

d. They wrote a review of that **concert** [they saw in Newcastle].

First, note that we are dealing with COMPLEX SENTENCES here (see Section 3.2 for a reminder of these). We can tell that these examples are all complex sentences because they each contain more than one main verb: *snarled* and *read* in (28a), *discuss* and *looks* in (28b), and so on.

The relative clause itself is a type of subordinate clause which modifies (= says something about) a HEAD NOUN in the matrix clause: the head nouns are in bold type in (28). As you can see right away, these embedded clauses—*who hadn't read the book* and so on—couldn't be independent clauses of English, since they are all incomplete in some way, even if we take away the *who*, *which* and so on at the start of these clauses.

The function of the relative clause is to restrict the possible set of students, papers, films and concerts to just the subset that the speaker wants to talk about.[1] For example, in (28a), she didn't snarl at *all* the students, she snarled at a specific subset of students—only the ones who hadn't read the book. Relative clauses in other languages may look very different syntactically to the English examples in (28), but they all have in common this property of restricting the set of possible items that the head noun refers to. Cross-linguistically, relative clauses often have other typical features too, as we will see.

Looking specifically at English relative clauses, there are two properties which should help you with their identification. First, we see from (28) that the relative clause in English may just follow straight after the head noun, as in (28d), or else it may begin with a word like *who*, *which* or *that*, as in (28a), (28b) and (28c) respectively. Although these words may help you to detect relative clauses, each of them also has other roles in English, so you need to be careful in using them to identify relative clauses. For example, *that* is of course a complementizer, and so can also introduce an ordinary embedded clause selected by a verb, as in *Lee believed [that they'd be back soon]*. (We can tell that this is not a relative clause because it doesn't modify a head noun, and doesn't have the property—outlined above—of referring to a subset.) And the words *who* and *which* also occur in *wh*-questions, as we saw in Section 8.1.

The second property of relative clauses in English is that, like *wh*-questions, they contain a gap, and that is why the embedded clauses could not be stand-alone clauses. More precisely, each relative clause in (28) has a 'missing' noun phrase, indicated with a dash in (29):

从关系小句的内部结构来看，每个小句都有一个句法上的空位，因此，关系小句的引导词一般被认为是移位而来，并在原处留下语迹。

(29) a. __ hadn't read the book
　　 b. we discuss __ next week
　　 c. we're going to __ tonight
　　 d. they saw __ in Newcastle

We understand the gap to refer back to the head noun that's modified by the whole relative clause. The relativized position is said to be CO-REFERENTIAL with the head noun. So in (29a), the gap is understood to refer to the students, and in (29b), the gap refers to the paper that'll be under discussion. The gap within the relative clause is known as the RELATIVIZED position, and in English, any position that could contain a noun phrase can be relativized. In (29a) the relativized position is the subject position of the relative clause; in (29b) and (29d), it's the direct object position; in (29c), the object of the preposition *to*.

It is also possible in English (though not common cross-linguistically) to have the relativized position as a POSSESSOR noun phrase: an example is shown in (30):

(30)   This is the student [CP whose name I always forget __].

There is a gap in direct object position in (30): the verb *forget* is transitive. However, the relativized position itself is actually a possessor NP: the phrase in bold in *I always forget **that student's** name*. In standard English, though, relative clauses can't simply leave a gap in the possessor position: this would give something like **This is the student (who) I always forget ___'s name*. Though I've marked this as ungrammatical, this non-standard form does sometimes occur in informal English. But the strategy used in standard English is rather different. Instead of just leaving the NP gap in the possessor position, the POSSESSED noun *name* is taken out too; this leaves a gap where the entire NP *that student's name* would have been. In (30), that position happens to be the direct object of *forget*. Then in order to form the relative clause, the relativized position *that student's* is expressed by a special possessive form *whose*, rather than by a gap. And the whole phrase *whose name* is moved to the dedicated position for *wh*-phrases which comes at the start of the CP, just as we saw in the case of *wh*-questions in Section 8.1.

Relative clauses in English are not all introduced by an overt *wh*-phrase, as we can see in (28c) and (d), but they always could be. In (28c), for instance, we could have *I expect the film **which** we're going to tonight will be fantastic*. So all relative clauses in English can contain a *wh*-word like *which* or *who*; there are also other possibilities, such as *where* as in *the place where we met __*. Since relative clauses can always utilize a *wh*-word, and since they contain a gap which indicates movement, linguists consider relative clauses to be one type of *wh*-construction. Indeed, cross-linguistically, relative clauses and *wh*-questions have a great deal in common.

Before reading further, please examine the sentences in (31), all containing relative clauses, and work out:

- what are the head nouns (the nouns being modified in the matrix clause);
- what are the relative clauses;
- where is the relativized position (the gap) in each relative clause, and what grammatical function does it have.

(31) a. That storm we experienced last night was amazing.
b. I wouldn't want the job Lee applied for the other day.
c. The application forms that arrived yesterday look quite hard.
d. Kim picked up a book Lee had left lying on the stairs.

The head nouns are shown in bold, the relative clauses are bracketed, and the relativized positions are marked with a __ gap in (32):

(32) a. That **storm** [we experienced __ last night] was amazing.
b. I wouldn't want the **job** [Lee applied for __ the other day].
c. Those application **forms** [that __ arrived yesterday] look quite hard.
d. Kim picked up a **book** [Lee had left __ lying on the stairs].

In (32a) the relativized position is the object of *experienced*; in (32b), it's the object of the preposition *for*; in (32c), it's the subject of *arrived*; and in (32d), it's the object of *left*.

8.2.2 Cross-linguistic variation in relative clauses

First, do all languages have relative clauses? While it appears that most do, it has been claimed that a few languages do not; one well-known example is an Amazonian language, Pirahã.

Second, although relative clause constructions in other languages will contain a head noun and a 'restricting' relative clause that modifies it, they don't necessarily share any of the other syntactic properties of English relative clauses. For instance, although European languages often have a counterpart to the so-called relative pronouns *who* or *which* introducing the relative clause, this is much less common in other parts of the world. Here, we'll look at some of the cross-linguistic variation.

8.2.2.1 Order of the relative clause and the head noun

One major typological distinction (= a distinction in type) is in the order of the relative clause and the head noun. In English, the relative clause follows the head noun. For example, in *the* **students** [*who hadn't read the book*], the relative clause [*who hadn't read the book*] follows *students*. This order is also found in a great many other languages. In (33) and (34) are two examples from languages unrelated to English. The relative clauses are bracketed, and the head nouns are shown in bold (SM in (33) stands for 'subject marker'):

(33) wa **mwîê** rra [nrâ sùveharru nrâ toni] nrâ truu numea (Tinrin)
the woman there 3SG like SM Tony 3SG stay Noumea
'The woman that Tony likes lives in Noumea.'

This example is from a Melanesian language, Tinrin. Just as in the English, the relativized position is the direct object position within the relative clause—the object of the verb *sùveharru* 'like'. The relative clause is not introduced by any relative pronouns or other special markers.

In the Yimas language of Papua New Guinea, the verbal prefix *m-*, glossed as RM for relative marker, 'functions much like the *wh*-word or *that* in English—to mark the whole relative clause as a definite referring expression' (Foley 1991: 413). Note, however, that this is not a relative pronoun, and does not come at the start of the relative clause—it's simply an affix on the verb:

(34) ŋaykum [irut m-naampa-nt-um] (Yimas)
women mat RM-weave-PRES-3PL
'the women who are weaving the mats'

Since it is so familiar to readers of English, it may seem natural that relative clauses follow the head noun. In verb-final languages, though, relative clauses often *precede* the head noun. Consider the Japanese examples in (35) and (36): the head nouns are shown in bold type, and the relativized position is the gap within the relative clause:

(35) [kimura-san-ga ___ katte-iru] **inu** (Japanese)
Kimura-Mr.-NOM keep-NONPAST dog
'the dog that Mr. Kimura keeps'

(36) [kimura-san-ga ___ inu-o ageta] **kodomo**
Kimura-Mr.-NOM dog-ACC give.PAST child
'the child to whom Mr. Kimura gave a dog'

In (35), the relativized position is the direct object of the verb *katte*, 'keep': recall that Japanese is an SOV language, so the 'missing' object NP immediately precedes the verb in the bracketed relative clause. And in (36), the relativized position is the indirect object of the verb *ageta* 'gave'; the basic position for an indirect object in Japanese is before the direct object, hence the position of the gap shown here. Note that there is no equivalent to the English relative pronouns *who* or *which* in Japanese, nor any other word introducing the relative clause, and that the relative clause simply comes right before the head noun.

This constituent order 'relative clause—head noun' is common in other HEAD-FINAL languages. For instance, the relative clause construction which is native to Turkish (a language with SOV constituent order) is also head-final in this way (Kornfilt 1997), and the same applies to Korean. Hungarian, however, has both types of relative clauses—the English pattern 'head noun—relative clause' as well as the head-final pattern.

8.2.2.2 *Relative clauses are complex NPs*

The examples in (35) and (36) are not full sentences, of course, but noun phrases, consisting of a head noun modified by the relative clause; the same applies to their English translations, and indeed to all head noun + relative clause constructions. These are rather special NPs, though: a noun with a clausal modifier of any kind is known as a COMPLEX NP, so 'head noun plus relative clause' is one type of complex NP. As with the term 'complex sentence', this technical term doesn't mean 'complicated', but simply indicates a construction with an embedded clause. If we put complex NPs into a sentence, we can see that—just like any other noun phrases—they can generally slot into whatever position an NP can fill. For instance, both of these complex NPs can be subjects, as in (37). The whole complex NP—head noun and the relative clause that modifies it—is bracketed:

关系从句和它所修饰的名词短语一起构成一个复杂名词短语，具有名词的属性。

(37) [The dog that Mr. Kimura keeps] has a bad cough.
[The child to whom Mr. Kimura gave a dog] has a bad cough.

Or alternatively, both complex NPs can be direct objects:

(38) I've never liked [the dog that Mr. Kimura keeps].
I've never liked [the child to whom Mr. Kimura gave a dog].

In the Japanese example in (39), and in its English translation, we see the whole complex NP used as the subject of a clause: the head noun *hon*, 'book', is again in bold:

(39) [Kinoo Ziroo-ga __ yondeita **hon**]-ga nakunatta. (Japanese)
yesterday Ziro-NOM (ACC) was.reading book-NOM missing
'[The **book** that Ziro was reading __ yesterday] is missing.'

In Japanese, the whole complex NP (bracketed) is marked as the subject of the clause by the fact that it bears nominative case, the case for subjects—the *-ga* marker at the end of the complex NP signals this. Note, though, that the gap *within* the relative clause itself is a direct object gap in (39). In both languages, the relativized position is the object of the 'read' verb. For that reason, I have marked the gap in the gloss as 'accusative', the case of direct objects in Japanese.

8.2.2.3 *Relative clauses that are not embedded*

In the examples of relativization seen so far, the relative clause is embedded *within* the main clause: the relative clause plus the head noun that it modifies form an NP that occupies a standard NP position, such as subject or object. We saw this in data such as (37) to (39), where the whole bracketed complex NP acted as subject or object of the main clause. However, in some languages the relative clause is not embedded within the main clause, as we'll now see. Our examples are from Bambara, a member of an African language family known as Mande (Niger-Congo), and have been adapted from Creissels (2000). Consider first a simple sentence, where the constituent order is SOV (Subject-Object-Verb):

(40) wùlú   yé   démísέŋ   ʹkíŋ   (Bambara)
     dog   PERF   child   bite
     'The dog bit the child.'

Next are two different relative clauses formed from (40). The way that Bambara shows that these are relative clauses is by using a relative marker (glossed RM), *miŋ*, which signals the relativized position. In (41a) this marker immediately follows *wùlú* 'dog', and the relativized position is the subject, while in (41b), *miŋ* immediately follows *démísέŋ* 'child', and the relativized position is the object:

(41) a. wùlú   ʹ**miŋ** yé   démísέŋ   ʹkíŋ
         dog   RM   PERF   child   bite
         'the dog that ___ bit the child'
     b. wùlú   yé   démísέŋ   ʹ**miŋ**   ʹkíŋ
         dog   PERF   child   RM   bite
         'the child that the dog bit ___ '

Note that all that is changed between (40) and the two examples in (41) is the presence of the relative marker in the latter examples. Now if we want to use one of these relative clauses in a sentence, we see that it is not embedded *within* the main clause, but is more like an adjunct which is tacked onto a following independent clause. The literal translation provided here gives a flavour of this. Compare the actual English translation, where the whole complex NP (bracketed) is the object of *saw* in the main clause:

(42) wùlú yé   démísέŋ   ʹmiŋ   ʹkíŋ,   n   yʹ   ó   bòlitɔʹ   ʹyé
     dog PERF child   RM   bite   I   PERF   this.one   running   see
     'I saw [the child that the dog bit] running away.'
     (Literally, 'The child that the dog bit, I saw this one running away.')

The main clause *n yʹ ó bòlit ɔʹ ʹyé* 'I saw this one running away' can indeed be a full independent clause in Bambara: nothing is missing from it. This strategy is the only relativization strategy found in most of the Northern Mande languages (Creissels 2000: 255).

8.2.2.4 *Relativization strategies*

As noted in Section 8.2.1, in English more or less any position in a clause that can contain an NP can be relativized, including the subject, direct object, and object of a preposition. We also saw that the relativized position in such examples contains a gap: here, each gap is marked and its position (grammatical function) within the clause is shown too:

(43) a. the forms [that __ arrived yesterday]   • subject
      b. the paper [(which) we discuss __ next week]   • direct object
      c. the film [(that) we're going to __ tonight]   • prepositional object

So these relative clauses use what is termed the 'gap strategy': the relativized position is simply empty.

In the case of a possessor NP, as we saw in Section 8.2.1, standard English has a special strategy. This involves using the form *whose* to form the relative clause, and moving the whole of the possessive noun phrase from its basic position to the special position in CP, at the left edge of the clause, which is reserved for *wh*-phrases: *this is the student whose name I always forget*. As we saw earlier, this strategy also leaves a gap, here in the direct object position after *forget*. However, in informal English, we often use an alternative construction, shown in (44). This has no gap following *forget*, as you can verify for yourself, but instead uses a **RESUMPTIVE PRONOUN** in the relativized position (shown in bold). This is called the 'resumptive' strategy:

(44) This is the student [who I always forget **her** name]   • possessor

Resumptive pronoun, 复述代词，指在某些类型的关系从句中重述先前一个成分的代词。

There is one more position which may be relativized in English: the object of comparative *than*:

(45) This is the guy who my cat is smarter than __/him   • object of comparison

As you can see, English doesn't much like these relative clauses: they somehow often don't sound quite right, either with a gap or with the resumptive pronoun (*him*) in the relativized position.

There are, then, around five NP positions which can potentially be relativized: subject, direct object, object of preposition/postposition, possessor NP and object of comparison. Cross-linguistically, these NP positions each take a place in what is known as the **Accessibility Hierarchy**, as shown in (46), where the subject is the highest position on the hierarchy and the object of comparison the lowest. The '>' means 'is more accessible than'—that is, more accessible to relativization. This accessibility manifests itself in various ways cross-linguistically, as we'll see.

(46) NP Accessibility Hierarchy for relative clause formation
      Su > Direct Obj > Object of adposition > Possessor > Object of comparison

Accessibility hierarchy, 可及性等级，它表示名词之间的依存关系，在这个等级序列中，每个成分要比其右边的成分在适用句法规则上更为自由。也就是说，如果我们知道除了第一项之外的其中任何一项在某种语言里可以不受限制地实现关系化，那么它左边的项也会不受限制地实现关系化。

In some languages we find a rather more fine-grained set of possible NP positions. For instance, Welsh treats the objects of finite verbs differently from the objects of non-finite verbs. Some languages also have a separate indirect object position, but in many languages, as in English, indirect objects (*Kim gave the book to her friend*) are syntactically the same as ordinary prepositional objects. So (46) shows a basic set of NP positions that are available, which may differ a bit from language to language.

In what sense, though, is (46) a hierarchy? First, every position on the hierarchy is a cut-off point for relative clause formation in some language or languages. Subjects are most accessible to relativization, and indeed, virtually all known languages can relativize subjects. But some languages don't allow relative clauses formed on any position lower down the hierarchy. Tagalog is an example of a language which only relativizes subjects. Other languages only relativize subjects and direct objects (e.g. Tongan); others only relativize the highest three positions, and so on. The prediction is that there are no languages that could relativize a position low on the hierarchy, such as the object of a preposition (e.g. *This is the film we're going to __*), but which would disallow a relative clause on some higher position, such as subject.

The hierarchy is also manifested within the grammars of individual languages. Though English has quite a lot of latitude in relative clause formation, we saw in (45) that the lowest position, object of comparison, is a bit marginal. What we expect, then, is that relative clauses formed on lower positions of the hierarchy may not sound as natural in a language. How far down the hierarchy these dispreferred 'lower' positions start will vary from language to language.

The other way in which the hierarchy is manifested is in the different strategies used for relativization. Basically, the gap strategy is expected in the highest positions, especially for relativized subjects, and very often for direct objects. This is not too surprising as these are the core NP relations. Conversely, the resumptive strategy is often used for relative clauses formed in the less accessible positions lower down the hierarchy: in other words, having a pronoun rather than a gap in the relativized position seems to make the lower positions more accessible. Once the resumptive strategy 'kicks in' at some point on the hierarchy, it's normally expected that this strategy will also be used for all lower positions that the language can relativize. So if a language starts using resumptive pronouns, say, when a prepositional object is relativized, we'd predict that it would use the resumptive strategy for any lower positions too.

English is actually unusual, cross-linguistically, in using the gap strategy when the relativized position is the object of a preposition (*the film we're going to __*). Compare the Hausa in (47) with the English translation (the Hausa word *da* at the start of the relative clause is a relative marker):

(47) wuqad [da ya kashe ta da **ita**] (Hausa)
knife RM he killed her with it
'the knife that he killed her with __'

The relativized position in the Hausa and in the English translation is the object of the preposition *da*, 'with'. English uses the gap strategy, and allows prepositions to be 'stranded' at the end of the clause; i.e. left with no prepositional object. But most languages avoid this one way or another, for instance by using the resumptive strategy as the Hausa does here.

The Accessibility Hierarchy is broadly supported by investigations of relative clause formation across many languages. If you know a language other than English, perhaps you can now test for yourself how relative clauses are formed (if at all) on each position on the hierarchy.

8.3 FOCUS MOVEMENTS AND SCRAMBLING

So far we have seen two kinds of *wh*-construction, questions and relative clauses, both of which often involve movement. Many languages use displacement of constituents in order to focus on a particular phrase, perhaps in order to emphasize it, or else to contrast it with other parts of the clause. Cross-linguistically, FOCUS constructions frequently move a particular constituent to a special position. These constructions typically have much in common with *wh*-fronting constructions. For instance, they often move a focalized constituent to a special position in CP before the left edge of the clause, and also, this movement leaves a gap in the clause that corresponds to the moved XP (that is, a 'something' phrase). This occurs in English, as we first saw in Chapter 1, as in *Beans I like __, but spinach I can't stand __*. The gap shows the position of the focalized constituent: here, it's the direct object of the verb in both these co-ordinated clauses.

Focus, 焦点, 指说话人最关注的信息。

We have already seen a number of examples of this kind of fronting from other languages. In the discussion of Mam in Section 7.2, we saw that although the basic constituent order is verb-initial, an absolutive NP can be focalized through fronting. And in exercise 6 in Chapter 5, we saw that Welsh (also verb-initial in basic constituent order) uses fronting for the same purpose. Some similar Welsh examples are given here: (48) shows the normal constituent order, (49a) has a PP fronted for focus, and (49b), a fronted VP. The basic position of these fronted phrases is shown with a gap:

(48) Mae   Caryl   yn   palu   yn   yr   ardd   heddiw.   (Welsh)
     be.PRES.3SG Caryl   PROG   dig.INFIN   in   the garden today
     'Caryl is digging in the garden today.'

(49) a. [PP Yn yr ardd]   mae   Caryl   yn   palu   __   heddiw.
            in the garden be.PRES.3SG Caryl   PROG   dig.INFIN   today
        'It's *in the garden* that Caryl is digging today.'
     b. [VP Palu   yn yr ardd]   mae   Caryl   __   heddiw.
            dig.INFIN   in the garden be.PRES.3SG Caryl   today
        '??It's *digging in the garden* that Caryl is today.'

The English translation of (49b) sounds very odd (hence prefaced with two question marks) because in English a VP constituent can't be focussed in this way—it can't simply be fronted, nor can it occur in the cleft construction. As I noted in Chapter 5, this doesn't mean that there isn't a VP constituent in English, just that not all syntactic processes necessarily apply to all constituents in a language.

In (50), (51) and (52) we see object-fronting for focus in three Oceanic languages which are normally subject-initial, i.e. SVO or SOV (data from Lynch 1998):

(50) [La paia taume], eau kama hilo-a. (Nakanai)
the dog your I not see-it
'As for your dog, I haven't seen it.'

(51) [Boroma] Morea ese e-ala-ia. (Motu)
pig Morea ERG he-kill-it
'The pig, Morea killed it.'

(52) [Nimwa aan nɨmataag-asuul] r-ɨm-atakɨn. (Lenakel)
house that wind-big it-PAST-destroy
'That house was destroyed by the cyclone.'

Although the pre-clause position is frequently used, cross-linguistically, for focussing a constituent, this is not the only option. For instance, in Hungarian, the position immediately preceding the verb is the position used for contrastive focus. The following illustrate: (53a) and (54a) each show a neutral sentence, i.e. one with no particular focus on any constituent, and the two (b) examples show a constituent moved to the pre-verbal focus position (shown in bold):

(53) a. Péter olvasta a könyvet. (Hungarian)
Peter read.DEF the book.ACC
'Peter read/was reading the book.'
b. Péter **a könyvet** olvasta.
Peter the book.ACC read.DEF
'It's *the book* that Peter read.'

(54) a. Tegnap vendégek érkeztek a szállodá-ba.
yesterday guests arrived the hotel-in
'Guests arrived at the hotel yesterday.'
b. A vendégek **tegnap** érkeztek a szállodá-ba.
the guests yesterday arrived the hotel-in
'It's *yesterday* that the guests arrived at the hotel.'

In Japanese and Korean, a leftward movement construction related to focus movement is known as SCRAMBLING. This construction results in a very free ordering of constituents, as we can see in (55), from Japanese. All of these sentences are grammatical, and the only restriction on order is that the verb must be in final position. The basic (neutral) constituent order in Japanese is SOV, as illustrated in (55a):

(55) a. Kinoo Taroo-ga Ginza-de susi-o tabeta. (Japanese)
yesterday Taro-NOM Ginza-in sushi-ACC eat.PAST
'Taro ate sushi in Ginza yesterday.'

b. Taroo-ga Ginza-de kinoo susi-o tabeta.
c. Kinoo susi-o Taroo-ga Ginza-de tabeta.
d. Susi-o kinoo Taroo-ga Ginza-de tabeta.
e. Ginza-de Taroo-ga kinoo susi-o tabeta.
f. Kinoo Ginza-de susi-o Taroo-ga tabeta.

In languages which have extensive case marking, variations in phrase order resulting from scrambling are unlikely to cause any ambiguity, because each of the nominal constituents has a case-marker showing its grammatical relation (subject, object and so on). Japanese has nominative/accusative case marking, and a fixed order is not required in order to show who is doing what. The variations are not glossed in (55), as the constituents are identical to those in (55a), but before finishing this chapter please ensure that you can see what each phrase means.

8.4 SOME CONCLUSIONS

In this chapter we have seen a variety of what are known as *wh*-constructions. Although these do not all contain an actual *wh*-word or phrase—or its equivalent in other languages—there are various properties which are common to these constructions, and this leads linguists generally to regard them as a related family of constructions. In English, two reliable signs of a *wh*-construction are the potential presence of a *wh*-expression (as in *The animals (which) I was filming __ yesterday*), plus the existence of a gap within the clause from which some phrase has moved. These same indications of *wh*-movement also occur in the constructions seen in (56) and (57):

(56) What a strong swimmer Kim is ___ !
How tired I feel __ these days!

(57) Kim is stronger than Lee is ___ .
Wrens are smaller than robins are ___ .

The examples in (56) are known as EXCLAMATIVES (something that you exclaim), and are reasonably transparently seen as *wh*-constructions with a fronted *wh*-phrase and a gap. These are related to statements like *Kim is such a strong swimmer*, or *I feel so tired these days*.

The examples in (57), on the other hand, are less obviously *wh*-constructions, even though they do contain a gap, since there's no *wh*-word or phrase. Note, though, that these COMPARATIVE constructions may indeed contain an overt *wh*-word in non-standard English, as in *Kim is stronger than **what** Lee is*. Such evidence is regarded as a legitimate sign of a *wh*-construction.

We have seen that not all languages have what is known as *wh*-movement, either in interrogative clauses, or within a relative clause. However, despite the existence of superficial differences cross-linguistically, all these constructions are nonetheless regarded as closely related to the more familiar *wh*-constructions which do display movement, including the ones seen in this short section.

We have also looked briefly at focus constructions and scrambling, generally considered to be related to *wh*-constructions cross-linguistically. All of these movements differ from those discussed in Chapter 7 in that they specifically do *not* cause any change in the grammatical function of the moved phrase. Although most languages exploit the possibility of at least some movements of this type, there is a great deal of variation in terms of the freedom or the immobility of phrases.

Checklist for Chapter 8

If you're uncertain about any of these points, I recommend revising before moving on to the exercises and the final chapter.

- Cross-linguistically, what are the two major alternative ways in which languages form *wh*-questions?
- What are the alternative strategies employed for handling multiple *wh*-questions?
- What are the main properties of relative clauses, cross-linguistically?
- What kinds of strategies are in use, cross-linguistically, to form relative clauses?
- Can you name any other *wh*-constructions?

FURTHER READING

On relative clauses, central readings are Keenan and Comrie (1977, 1979), Comrie and Keenan (1979), Comrie (1989: ch. 7) and Keenan (1985b). On *wh*-questions and the idea that they leave a gap in the extraction site, see Radford (1988: ch. 9). A seminal reading from the generative grammar tradition on *wh*-constructions and their general properties—though one which you will almost certainly find very challenging—is Chomsky (1977).

EXERCISES

1. Consider the Turkish *wh*-questions illustrated in (1) through (6), taken from Kornfilt (1997).

   Task: (i) What is the basic constituent order in Turkish? (ii) Explain concisely and accurately how *wh*-questions are formed in Turkish. Generalize across all the examples shown.

(1) bu   kitab-ı   kim   oku-du?
    this   book-ACC   who   read-PAST
    'Who read this book?'

(2) Hasan   kitab-ı   kim-e   ver-di?
    Hasan   book-ACC   who-DATIVE   give-PAST
    'To whom did Hasan give the book?'

(3) Mehmet   tarafından   kim   öl-dür-ül-dü?
    Mehmet   by   who   die-CAUS-PASSIVE-PAST
    'Who was killed by Mehmet?'

(4) Hasan   ne-yi   oku-du?
    Hasan   what-ACC   read-PAST
    'What did Hasan read?'

(5) Hasan   [sinema-ya   kim   git-ta]   san-ıyor?
    Hasan   cinema-DATIVE   who   go-PAST   believe-PROG
    'Who does Hasan think went to the cinema?'

(6) Hasan   dün   hangi   kız-la   dans-et-ti?
    Hasan   yesterday   which   girl-with   dance-do-PAST
    'Which girl did Hasan dance with yesterday?'

2. The data in this exercise are from Malayalam, a Dravidian language of India, and are taken from Asher and Kumari (1997). The examples show two kinds of data. There are seven examples that illustrate some basic, unmarked sentences, and the remaining eight are examples with various different constituents contrastively focussed: the italics in the English translation enable you to work out which constituent in the Malayalam is being focalized.

Task: (i) Indicate precisely how focus is achieved in Malayalam. (ii) State exactly which part of the clause is being focussed in each example that has it: give it in Malayalam and say what its function is.

Hints:
- I have jumbled up the data illustrating neutral sentences and the sentences with focus, but you will probably find it helpful to sort the sentences out into an A set (neutral) and a B set (those with focus) before you start, and to group similar examples. You have enough data here to work out the essential facts concerning how focus is achieved in Malayalam.
- There are a few minor morphological (i.e. not syntactic) irregularities in the data; I have not ironed these out, but left them as examples of the natural, untidy nature of linguistic data. Comment on any that you find.

(1) ɲaan   innale   vannu
    I   yesterday   come.PAST
    'I came yesterday.'

(2) nii   pooyee   tiiruu
    you   go   must
    'You really must *go*.'

(3) avan   atə   ceytilla
    he   it   do.PAST.NEG
    'He didn't do it.'

(4) kuʈʈi   viiʈʈil   illa
    child   at.home   NEG
    'The child is not at home.'

(5) ɲaanee   varaam
    I   come.FUT
    '*I* shall come.'

(6) avan   varum
    he   come.FUT
    'He will come.'

(7) ɲaan   paṛayaan   marannu
    I   talk.INFIN   forget.PAST
    'I forgot to say.'

(8) nii   pookaanee   paaʈilla
    you   go.INFIN   prohibition
    'You should not *go*.'

(9) avan   eɻutanee   paṛaɲɲuḷḷuu
    he   write.INFIN   tell.PAST
    'He only told me to *write*.'

(10) avan   pookaan   paaʈilla
     he   go.INFIN   prohibition
     'He mustn't go.'

(11) paṛayaanee   paaʈilla
     talk.INFIN   prohibition
     '(You) should not *talk*.'

(12) poostʈ saadhaaraṇa raṇʈə maṇikkə varunnu
post usually two hour.DATIVE come.PRES
'The post usually comes at two o'clock.'

(13) avanee varum
he come.FUT
'*He alone* will come.'

(14) naaḷe paṭʈə maṇikkee varuu
tomorrow ten hour.DATIVE come.IMPERATIVE
'Come at *ten o'clock* tomorrow.'

(15) avan atə ceyteeyilla
he it do.PAST.NEG
'He *didn't* do it.'

3. This exercise is on relative clauses in Standard Arabic (data from Aoun et al. 2010 and Alotaibi and Borsley 2013).

Task: (i) First, organize the data according to the position relativized in each example, grouping together parallel examples (Section 8.2.2.4). You can use the English translations as a rough guide, but make sure you are looking for the relativized position in the Arabic data, rather than the English translations: the two languages may differ in some instances. (ii) Then examine the patterns of gaps vs. resumptive pronouns in the relativized positions. **NB** gaps are not directly indicated, so you will have to work out their occurrence from the glosses. Where do gaps occur? Where do optional resumptive pronouns occur? Where do obligatory resumptive pronouns occur? Organize your answers systematically. (iii) What general properties of relative clause formation cross-linguistically do these patterns relate to?

Hints:
- Assume that the only options for either a gap or a resumptive pronoun in the relativized positions are the ones shown. A gap will have no resumptive; an optional resumptive is shown in parentheses; an obligatory resumptive is marked as such, using the standard linguistic notation.
- Assume the judgements given. Some native speakers may not agree with all judgements, and dialects of Arabic will differ in various ways.

(1) al-kitaabu allaði sayaštari(-hu) saami mawžudun fi-l-maktabati
the-book that buy.FUT.3M.SG-(it) Sami exist.M.SG in-the-bookshop
'The book that Sami will buy is found at the bookshop.'

(2) Turida l-waladu allaði mazzaqa l-kitaaba
expelled.3M.SG the-child that tore.3M.SG the-book
'The boy who tore up the book was expelled.'

(3) ʔaʕrifu   l-mumaθilata   allati   sayuqabilu(-ha)   saami
    know.1SG   the-actress   that   FUT.meet(-her)   Sami
    'I know the actress that Sami will meet.'

(4) qaabaltu   r-rajula   allaðii   ʔaʕrifu(-hu)
    met.1M.SG   the-man   that   knew.1SG(-him)
    'I met the man that I knew.'

(5) qaabaltu   rajulan   ʔaʕrifu-*(hu)
    met.1M.SG   man   knew.1SG-him
    'I met a man that I knew.'

(6) ʔufattišu   ʕan   kitaabin   ʔaDaʕtu-*(hu)   l-yawma
    look.1SG   for   book   lost.1SG-it   the-day
    'I am looking for a book that I lost today.'

(7) Taradat   l-muʕallimatu   bintan   Darabat   tilmiiðan   fi   S-Saffi
    expelled.3F.SG the-teacher.F.SG girl   hit.3F.SG student   in   the-class
    'The teacher expelled a girl who hit a student in the class.'

(8) qaraʔna   l-kutuba   allati   ʔaxbarana   ʕan-*(ha)   kariimun
    read.1PL   the-books   that   told.3M.SG   about-them   Karim
    'We read the books that Karim told us about.'

(9) wajadtu   kitaaban   ʔaxbarat-ni   ʕan-*(hu)   laila
    found.1SG   book   told.3F.SG-me about-it   Laila
    'I found a book that Laila told me about.'

(10) taʕarrafnaa   ʕala   muxrijin   taʕrifu   ʔibnu-*(hu)   laila
     met.1PL   on   director   know.3F.SG   son-his   Laila
     'We met a director whose son Laila knows.'

4. The data in this exercise (taken from Hualde et al. 1994) are from the Lekeitio dialect of Basque. In each example, one constituent is focalized. The focalized constituents are indicated for you via the italics in the English translations; you will need to work out where they are in the Basque.

Task: How exactly is a constituent focalized in Basque? Give a generalization which covers all the data. (Allative in (5) is a case marker, and gives the meaning expressed by the preposition *to* in English.)

(1) lagunak   txakurra   ekarri-dau   gaur   goixian
    friend.ERG   dog.ABS   bring-AUX   today   morning
    'The friend brought *the dog* this morning.'

(2) txakurra   lagunak   ekarri-dau   gaur   goixian
    dog.ABS   friend.ERG   bring-AUX   today   morning
    'The friend brought the dog this morning.'

(3) txakurra   gaur   goixian   ekarri-dau   lagunak
    dog.ABS   today   morning   bring-AUX   friend.ERG
    'The friend brought the dog *this morning.*'

(4) gaur goixian   aitta   etorri-da
    today morning   father   come-AUX
    'This morning, *father* arrived.'

(5) estau   nai   Bilbora   žun
    NEG.AUX   want   Bilbao.ALLATIVE   go
    'S/he doesn't want to go *to Bilbao.*'

(6) etxe   barriža   ikusi-dot,   es   subi   barriža
    house   new.ABS   see-AUX   no   bridge   new.ABS
    'I saw *the new house,* not the new bridge.'

(7) Péruk   esan   dau   bižar   etorríko   dala
    Peru.ERG   say   AUX   tomorrow   come   AUX
    'Peru has said that he'll arrive *tomorrow.*'

5. This exercise is about RESPONSIVES in Colloquial Welsh—answers to yes/no questions. These are questions which in many languages can simply be answered 'yes' or 'no'. As you will see, Welsh is more complex.

Task: Study the data below, and describe as accurately and concisely as possible the main principles that regulate the choice of the correct responsive. Your answers should take the form 'If the question …, then the responsive …'. You should generalize where possible across similar data types. It is not necessary (nor, in fact, helpful) to address the data in the order in which examples are given. It will help you to provide (or make for personal use) a flow chart, so that you can figure out what order the relevant information occurs in.

Hints:
- The finite element (either verb or auxiliary) is clause-initial in Welsh in the unmarked word order. Other, marked orders also occur; for instance, mild contrastive focus is indicated by fronting a constituent in some examples. Your answer must reflect the fact that the responsives in such examples differ from all the remaining data.
- You will especially need to consider the (morpho)syntax of the finite verbs and auxiliaries in these data, which will mean examining the glosses very carefully. In some examples, you'll also need to consider the post-verbal

syntax. Don't worry unduly about remaining syntactic features of the clause, which are generally not relevant to your answer.

- The form of *bod* 'be' in the third-person singular present tense differs according to whether the subject is definite (*ydy*) or indefinite (*oes*).
- You don't need to attempt to account for the distinctions between the *affirmative* forms and the *negative* forms of the responsives in (8b), (9b) and (10b) (e.g. *gwnaf* vs. *Na wnaf*); this is not relevant to your answer. The distinction between the responsives themselves in (8), (9) and (10), however, *is* relevant.

(1)   a.   Welaist ti 'r ffilm?
              see.PAST.2SG you the film
              'Did you see the film?'
      b.   Do / Naddo.
              yes / no
              'Yes / No.'

(2)   a.   Gysgodd hi 'n dda?
              sleep.PAST.3SG she PRED good
              'Did she sleep well?'
      b.   Do / Naddo.
              yes / no
              'Yes / No.'

(3)   a.   Wnaeth Mair weld y ffilm?
              do.PAST.3SG Mair see.INFIN the film
              'Did Mair see the film?'
      b.   Do / Naddo.
              yes / no
              'Yes / No.'

(4)   a.   Ydyn nhw 'n ateb y ffôn?
              be.PRES.3PL they PROG answer.INFIN the phone
              'Are they answering the phone?'
      b.   Ydyn / Nac ydyn.
              be.PRES.3PL / NEG be.PRES.3PL
              'Yes / No.'

(5)   a.   Wyt ti 'n mynd?
              be.PRES.2SG you PROG go.INFIN
              'Are you going?'
      b.   Ydw / Nac ydw.
              be.PRES.1SG / NEG be.PRES.1SG
              'Yes / No.'

(6) a. Ydy   'r   dŵr   yn   berwi?
       be.PRES.3SG the water PROG boil.INFIN
       'Is the water boiling?'
   b. Ydy   / Nac   ydy.
      be.PRES.3SG / NEG be.PRES.3SG
      'Yes / No.'

(7) a. Oes   'na   goffi   yn   y   gegin?
       be.PRES.3SG there coffee   in   the kitchen
       'Is there coffee in the kitchen?'
   b. Oes   /   Nac   oes.
      be.PRES.3SG / NEG be.PRES.3SG
      'Yes / No.'

(8) a. Helpith   y   ferch   heno?
       help.FUT.3SG the girl   tonight
       'Will the girl help tonight?'
   b. Gwneith   /   Na   wneith.
      do.FUT.3SG / NEG   do.FUT.3SG
      'Yes / No.'

(9) a. Gwnei   di   agor   y   ffenest?
       do.FUT.2SG   you   open.INFIN   the window
       'Will you open the window?'
   b. Gwnaf   /   Na   wnaf.
      do.FUT.1SG / NEG do.FUT.1SG
      'Yes / No.'

(10) a. Fyddi   di   'n   dod   i   'r   ffilm   heno?
        be.FUT.2SG   you   PROG   come.INFIN   to   the   film   tonight
        'Will you be coming to the film tonight?'
    b. Byddaf   /   Na   fyddaf.
       be.FUT.1SG /   NEG be.FUT.1SG
       'Yes / No.'

(11) a. Cyngerdd   welaist   ti?
        concert   see.PAST.2SG   you
        'Was it *a concert* that you saw?'
    b. Ie   / Nage.
       yes / no
       'Yes / No.'

(12) a. I   'r   ffilm   wyt   ti   'n   mynd?
        to   the   film   be.PRES.2SG you   PROG   go.INFIN
        'Are you going *to the film*?'

b. Ie / Nage.
yes / no
'Yes / No.'

6. The data in this exercise are from Kurdish, specifically the northern variety known as Kurmanji (or Kurmanci), and are taken from Creissels (2008a, b), citing data from Blau and Barak (1999), with additional data courtesy of Jawzal Nechirvan. You should re-read Section 6.3 before starting the exercise.

Hints:
- Two distinct case markings occur on NPs in these data, which are termed 'direct' case and 'oblique' case here (it's not unusual for language-specific terms to be used in the specialist literature on a language). In (1) and (2), for instance, the subject is in the 'direct' case. This case is formally and functionally unmarked; it has no inflection, and is the 'bare' citation form used for nouns. The nouns *mirov* in (7) and *Sînem* in (4) and (8) are also in the direct case. In fact, all NPs and pronouns that are not specifically marked in the gloss as oblique should be regarded as having direct case. All the oblique NPs and pronouns are specifically marked as such, as the glosses show (OBL): for NPs this involves a suffix -*ê* (feminine singular) or -*î* (masculine singular), and for pronouns, a distinct oblique form is used (compare English *she* vs. *her* etc.). Your task below, however, will be to work out the case/agreement alignment patterns in these data, using the standard notation set out in Chapter 6.
- In the data in (3) through (14), two different verb tenses occur. You will find it helpful to group examples together according to tense.
- If you would find it easier to answer these questions with a continuous narrative, rather than point by point, you may do so, but your answer must be clear and concise, and must cover all the issues raised.

Task:
- First, consider the verb agreement in intransitive clauses, (1) to (3). (i) Which argument does the verb agree with: A, S or O?

(1) Ez dikev-im
1SG fall.PRES-1SG
'I'm falling.'

(2) Mirov dikev-e
man fall.PRES-3SG
'The man is falling.'

(3) Ez ket-im
1SG fall.PERFCTV-1SG
'I fell.'

- Next, consider transitive clauses, here shown in two distinct tenses, present and perfective, in (4) to (14). (ii) Which argument(s) does the verb agree with in (4) through (14)? Answer in terms of the A, S and O relations. (iii) Now relate the patterns found in the transitive clauses to those in the intransitive clauses in (1) to (3). Indicate the alignment pattern or patterns that you find, using the standard terminology and notation, and say why each pattern occurs. In other words, what conditioning factors do you find for each pattern? (iv) What is the technical term for this pattern of data?

(4) Ez Sînem-ê dibîn-im
    1SG Sinem-OBL.F.SG see.PRES-1SG
    'I see Sinem.'

(5) Min Sînem dît-Ø
    1SG.OBL Sinem see.PERFCTV-3SG
    'I saw Sinem.'

(6) Tu Sînem-ê dibîn-î
    2SG Sinem-OBL.F.SG see.PRES-2SG
    'You see Sinem.'

(7) Ez mirov-î dibîn-im
    1SG man-OBL.M.SG see.PRES-1SG
    'I see the man.'

(8) Min mirov dît-Ø
    1SG.OBL man see.PERFCTV-3SG
    'I saw the man.'

(9) Te Sînem dît-Ø
    2SG.OBL Sinem see.PERFCTV-3SG
    'You saw Sinem.'

(10) Sînem min dibîn-e
     Sinem 1SG.OBL see.PRES-3SG
     'Sinem sees me.'

(11) Sînem-ê ez dît-im
     Sinem-OBL.F.SG 1SG see.PERFCTV-1SG
     'Sinem saw me.'

(12) Sînem te dibîn-e
     Sinem 2SG.OBL see.PRES-3SG
     'Sinem sees you.'

(13) Mirov-î ez dît-im
     man-OBL.M.SG 1SG see.PERFCTV-1SG
     'The man saw me.'

(14) Sînem-ê   tu   dît-î
       Sinem-OBL.F.SG   2SG   see.PERFCTV-2SG
       'Sinem saw you.'

NOTE

1 Some languages distinguish RESTRICTIVE relative clauses from NON-RESTRICTIVE ones, which don't serve to delimit a subset of items but are more like parenthetical comments. Examples of the latter from English are *Kim, who you met last night, is my sister's friend* or *Students—who never have any money—often take poorly paid work*. English non-restrictive relative clauses have a special intonation, as the commas or dashes indicate in the written form.

9

Asking questions about syntax

章节导读

　　本章是全书的最后一章，我们将在前面几章学习的基础上，从总体上来看句法学需要研究的一些主要问题。在对一种语言进行句法描述时，我们需要回答以下问题：（1）该语言是否存在基本的语序？如果有，是什么？如果没有，就要描述该语言中词汇排列的主要原则。（2）是否存在其他的基本语序？如果有，它的标记程度如何？（3）母句与从属小句的语序是否相同？如果不同，就需要细致地描述它们的差异之处。（4）该语言的主要词类有哪些？有什么特性？在划分词类时要从词的形态特性以及句法分布两个方面进行。（5）该语言是中心词开始还是中心词结尾的？（6）该语言是如何表达小句否定的？（7）该语言中构成复杂句的方式有哪些？补语的类型有哪些？它是否存在小句主语？如果有，它们是定式的还是不定式的？它是否存在名词化的套嵌结构？（8）该语言是如何标记中心词和它的依附成分之间的关系的？（9）在该语言中，我们是否容易识别成分？如果可以，我们需要采用至少两种以上的成分检验方法来识别成分，而且要同时采用合乎语法和不合乎语法的实例。（10）描述该语言中语法功能的识别方法：该语言是主要依靠词序、一致还是格的标记？这种语言采用的是受格还是作格系统？具体情况如何？（11）该语言如何改变动词与名词之间的语法关系，增加或减少动词论元的数量？是否存在被动、反被动、无人称、应用语态或者使役结构？（12）WH 疑问句是如何构成的？是否存在 WH 前置，还是 WH 保留原位？该语言中形成关系从句的主要方式是什么？是否存在其他的 WH 结构？是否存在焦点移位？如果有，它与 WH 疑问句的形成是否相似？（13）是否存在上述问题没有涵盖的句法结构？

　　另外，在本章中，作者也讨论了与句法学相关的且有争议的三个问题：（1）为什么成年人学习一门新的语言如此困难？（2）世界上所有的语言都同样复杂吗？是否有的语言要比其他语言难学？（3）是否所有的语言都具有同样的句法特性？

The title of this chapter is deliberately rather ambiguous. I am hopeful that by this point, you will be able to construct a basic syntactic description of a language, either a language that you speak well yourself, or one for which you can find a native speaker consultant. Section 9.1 outlines the kinds of questions that you will need to investigate. Section 9.2 provides a short case study of Welsh, illustrating how these questions could be answered. These sections, then, refer to asking questions about syntax in the most literal way. However, I also hope that the discussion in the previous chapters has ignited some curiosity about the human language faculty more generally. In Section 9.3, I briefly outline some issues and questions surrounding our syntactic abilities that are currently widely debated within linguistics. Section 9.4 looks at possible further directions to pursue in your study of syntax.

9.1 SYNTACTIC DESCRIPTION: WHAT QUESTIONS TO INVESTIGATE

This section aims to give you a framework with which to write a basic syntactic description of a language that you know well, or for which you can access data readily. If appropriate, you can ask one or more native speakers to act as language consultant(s). Make sure you give the source(s) of your data, including attributions to the literature (i.e. cite your sources). Acknowledge any help given by language consultants.

- Give the name by which the language is known to its native speakers, plus its English name, if any. State its language family and the principal locations in which it is spoken. You will probably find two online resources very helpful indeed: the *Ethnologue*, www.ethnologue.com (Lewis et al. 2013) and *WALS online*, http://wals.info (Dryer and Haspelmath 2013).

- Your description should include *some or all* of the questions outlined in (1) to (13) below, depending on what features of the language you consider to be most interesting from a syntactic, morphosyntactic and typological point of view. Give enough information on (and illustration of) any feature to make it comprehensible to someone who has no prior knowledge of the language.

- *All* parts of the discussion must be illustrated with appropriate and sufficient data, glossed and translated. Number each example, following the conventions used in this textbook. If your language uses a writing system other than the Roman alphabet, cite data using whatever standard system of transliteration is used for this language.

- Give a list of abbreviations used in the gloss where these differ from those found in this textbook.

- You won't need to discuss syntactic properties that are not manifested in your language. For instance (question (8) below), not all languages mark morphologically the relationship between a head and its dependents; see Section 4.3.7. If you were discussing Chinese, question (8) wouldn't be relevant. In such cases you can simply state that your language does not, for instance, display head- or dependent-marking. Similarly, you don't need to mention the antipassive construction unless your language has an ergative alignment (Chapter 7).
- You can collapse questions together where this makes sense for your language. For instance, questions (8) and (10) touch on the same kinds of data, and for some languages it would be appropriate to discuss them together.
- Make sure, when answering each question, that you provide adequate explanations: do not leave the reader to work out for themselves what your data show.

Some basic questions to consider:

(1) What is the neutral, or unmarked, constituent order (sometimes termed 'word order') in the clause, if there is one? (Chapter 1, Chapter 6). If there is no neutral constituent order, describe the main principles of linearization. You should at least illustrate a transitive clause with two full NP arguments, and an intransitive clause. Are the orders the same in both these clause types?

(2) What alternative neutral constituent orders are possible, if any? How marked are these?

(3) Are the constituent orders occurring in subordinate clauses the same as those in root clauses, or different? If different, describe the differences carefully (Chapter 3). Are there any (other) noteworthy differences between root and embedded clauses?

(4) What are the main word classes (or syntactic categories) in your language? Discuss any that have especially interesting properties. Focus on the main LEXICAL classes N, V and A. You can expect any language to have a distinct class of nouns and verbs. Most languages will also have a distinct class of adjectives. Most will also have at least one or two (and maybe dozens of) adpositions. Justify all word classes that you posit: in other words, give evidence from its morphosyntactic properties and syntactic distribution to demonstrate that each proposed class should be regarded as distinct (Chapter 2, Chapter 4). Include some of the main FUNCTIONAL CATEGORIES that your language distinguishes.

(5) Is your language predominantly head-initial or predominantly head-final? Illustrate with data from more than one word class of heads. Are there any

difficulties in establishing a predominant linearization? (Chapter 4). Remember that you are looking at the ordering of heads and their complements here, rather than the position of adjuncts with relation to heads.

(6) How does your language express clausal negation? (Chapter 3)

(7) Describe the main strategies for joining clauses together that are found in your language. What kinds of complementation occur? For instance, does the language have both finite and non-finite complement clauses? Does it have clausal subjects? If so, can they be both finite and non-finite? Does your language rely largely on subordination, as is the case for typical European languages? Does it have nominalized embeddings? Or does it, for instance, use co-ordination or verb serialization? (Chapter 3)

(8) How, *if at all*, does your language mark morphosyntactically the relationship between heads and dependents? (Chapter 4) In other words, is your language largely head-marking or largely dependent-marking? Does it display a mix of both strategies? Illustrate at least with reference to the verb and its arguments.

(9) Does your language readily identify distinct constituents? (Chapter 5) If so, give at least two tests for constituency, illustrating with contrasting grammatical and ungrammatical data. Are there distinctive DISPLACEMENT processes for constituents in your language? Perhaps alternatively your language has free word order of the type found in Warlpiri (Chapter 6); if so, illustrate.

(10) Describe the way(s) in which the grammatical functions A, O and S are identified in your language (Chapter 6). Does this rely predominantly on constituent order, on agreement or cross-referencing, or on case marking? Does your language exemplify an accusative or an ergative alignment? Make sure you give enough data to illustrate this. If your language has ergative alignment, is this purely morphological, or is it also (a much rarer possibility) syntactic? In other words, is there a clear SUBJECT relation in your language? Is it possible to identify a syntactic pivot?

(11) Your language almost certainly has some readily identifiable ways to change the grammatical functions or relations, either increasing or decreasing the valency of a verb (Chapter 7). Does it have a passive? If ergative, an antipassive? An impersonal construction? An applicative? A causative?

(12) Describe how *wh*-questions, also known as constituent questions, are formulated (Chapter 8). Does the language have *wh*-fronting or *wh*-in-situ, or perhaps both? Discuss the main strategies for forming relative clauses in your language. Are there other *wh*-constructions in your language; for instance, is focus movement found, and if so, is it similar to *wh*-question formation?

(13) Are there any other interesting syntactic constructions that are not covered by the questions above? If so, explain and illustrate them.

You may be wondering why it's worthwhile to investigate the grammars of languages. I hope that the preceding chapters have answered this question, but in case not, you should consider the fact that every week, languages are becoming extinct. Today there are perhaps 6,000 or so languages in the world; we don't know the exact number, and to some extent the answer depends on what counts as a distinct 'language' rather than a 'dialect'. As is the case with sciences such as palaeontology, scholars broadly divide into two camps: lumpers and splitters. Lumpers will often suggest that related dialects form a single language, even if they are not completely mutually comprehensible, whereas splitters will regard such dialects as separate languages. Most of the world's languages, perhaps as many as 90 per cent of the total, are endangered. A language that has only a handful of speakers, even a few hundred or a few thousand speakers, is unlikely to survive to the end of this century. Many languages will become extinct by the end of this decade (see Crystal 2000; Dixon 1997).

When a language dies out because its speakers have chosen to speak (or been browbeaten into speaking) one of the large 'global' languages, much of the culture of that society is likely to die out too (see Nettle and Romaine 2000). Just as biological diversity is endangered by the relentless march of westernized societies, so linguistic diversity is threatened by domination from the world's major languages, including English. Every time another language becomes extinct, we lose the opportunity to discover something more about the human language faculty; every language investigated to date has fascinating constructions and patterns that we may never know about unless linguists (including native speaker linguists) uncover them. If you decide that you want to undertake linguistic fieldwork, you will need professional training in all its aspects, which includes handling often complex socio-political situations.

For more information about how to describe and document the syntax and morphosyntax of a language, see T. Payne (1997, 2006). For an entertaining first-hand perspective on linguistic fieldwork, see Everett (2008).

9.2 A CASE STUDY: GRAMMATICAL SKETCH OF COLLOQUIAL WELSH

This section provides a necessarily brief grammatical sketch of Colloquial Welsh, illustrating the kinds of answers that could be given to questions in the previous section. The term 'Colloquial Welsh' is used by linguists to indicate, broadly speaking, the modern spoken language.

Colloquial Welsh is spoken in many, though not all parts of Wales, where it has around half a million native speakers. Welsh speakers are also scattered throughout Britain, and there is a Welsh-speaking community in Argentina. The language is known as *Cymraeg* to its native speakers. Welsh is a member of the Celtic language family, a branch of Indo-European, and is thus related ultimately to English.

Let's now turn to the syntactic properties. In the examples that follow, I have deliberately left in place the 'messy' morphological details that characterize natural languages. See if you can spot some of these. If you'd like further information, please contact me.

In neutral constituent order, a finite element (either a main verb or an auxiliary) is in clause-initial position. The subject immediately follows. With an inflected main verb, this gives VS(O) order, as in (14) and (15); no other neutral word orders occur. Many VSO languages allow an alternative SVO order, but Welsh does not, as (16) shows:

(14) Gwerthodd   Elin   y   delyn.
     sell.PAST.3SG Elin   the   harp
     'Elin sold the harp.'

(15) Diflannodd   y   delyn.
     disappear.PAST.3SG the   harp
     'The harp disappeared.'

(16) *Elin gwerthodd   y   delyn.
      Elin sell.PAST.3SG the   harp
      ('Elin sold the harp.')

A fixed constituent order identifies the grammatical functions, A, S and O. Welsh has accusative alignment, and a clear subject relation. S and A are identical; both immediately follow the finite verb or auxiliary, and, in a VSO clause, O immediately follows S. This is seen in (14). Both the S and A relations trigger subject agreement on a finite verb, under restricted conditions, as is illustrated below.

A finite auxiliary (in bold) occurs in clause-initial position in both (17) and (18); again, the subject immediately follows, and there is also a non-finite lexical verb lower down in the clause:

(17) **Gwnaeth**   Elin   werthu   'r   delyn.
     do.PAST.3SG   Elin   sell.INFIN the   harp
     'Elin sold the harp.'

(18) **Mae**   Elin   wedi/yn   gwerthu   'r   delyn.
     be.PRES.3SG   Elin   PERF/PROG   sell.INFIN the   harp
     'Elin has sold/is selling the harp.'

The main difference between these two clauses, apart from the different auxiliaries, is that (18) is an overtly aspectual clause. Aspectual particles, including *wedi* (PERFECT) and *yn* (PROGRESSIVE) co-occur with a part of the auxiliary *bod*, 'be', as shown in (18). *Bod* is the only aspectual auxiliary; there is no 'have' auxiliary in Welsh. (The auxiliary *bod* 'be' has suppletive (= unpredictable and irregular) morphology, as you can see from (18).)

Welsh is a strongly head-initial language. A verb precedes its direct object, as in *gwerthu'r delyn*, 'sell the harp', just seen in (18). All adpositions are prepositions, as in *wrth y drws* 'at the door'. Nouns precede their possessors, as in *ci Elin* (dog Elin), 'Elin's dog'. Across all categories, in fact, heads precede complements.

Negation is a particularly complex area of Welsh syntax. Here, I illustrate clausal negation in finite clauses:

(19) Ddiflannodd   y   delyn **ddim**.
     disappear.PAST.3SG the   harp   NEG
     'The harp didn't disappear.'

(20) Wnaeth   Elin **ddim** gwerthu   'r   delyn.
     do.PAST.3SG   Elin NEG   sell.INFIN the   harp
     'Elin didn't sell the harp.'

(21) Dydy   Elin **ddim** wedi/yn   gwerthu   'r   delyn.
     NEG.be.PRES.3SG   Elin NEG   PERF/PROG   sell.INFIN the   harp
     'Elin hasn't sold/isn't selling the harp.'

(22) Werthodd   Elin **mo** 'r   delyn/*ddim y   delyn.
     sell.PAST.3SG Elin NEG   the   harp   NEG   the   harp
     'Elin didn't sell the harp.'

As the first three examples show, clausal negation involves a negative adverb, *ddim*, which occurs in post-subject position. However, the adverb *ddim* can't appear before a direct object, as (22) shows; instead, a form *mo* is used, which literally means 'nothing of'. There are also changes to the finite verbs and auxiliaries in initial position in (19) through (22), as you'll see if you compare them with the affirmative clauses seen earlier; these changes occur because the clause is negative.

The lexical categories N, V and A are clearly distinct in Welsh, as they are in other European languages. The morphosyntactic categories that these word classes inflect for are very familiar from European languages, so I will not illustrate these specifically; examples occur in the data below. The inflectional categories include: for nouns, number and gender (masculine/feminine); for verbs, tense and subject agreement; and for adjectives, comparison. Welsh has a large class of prepositions, and these are more interesting, since most of them inflect to agree with their pronominal objects (see Section 4.3.2.2). Table 9.1 illustrates a characteristic paradigm. The bare citation form of the preposition is *wrth*.

Table 9.1
Inflectional paradigm for the Welsh preposition *wrth* 'at'

	singular			plural		
first person	wrth-a	i		wrth-on	ni	
	at-1SG	me	'at me'	at-1PL	us	'at us'

				(Continued)
second person	wrth-at	ti	wrth-och	chi
	at-2SG	you 'at you'	at-2PL	you 'at you (PL)'
third person	wrth-o	fo / wrth-i hi	wrth-yn	nhw
	at-3SG.M	him / at-3SG.F her	at-3PL	them
	'at him' / 'at her'		'at them'	

As the occurrence of an inflectional paradigm for prepositions indicates, Welsh is head-marking rather than dependent-marking. Unlike in English, there is no case-marking whatever on either pronouns or nouns. Welsh has extensive agreement morphology. Heads agree with a following pronominal argument for person, number and, in the third person singular forms only, gender (excluding finite verbs, which display no gender agreement). In all instances, agreement crucially co-occurs *only* with a following pronominal argument, and *never* with a lexical noun phrase. When the argument is a full lexical NP, the head doesn't display the agreement, but instead generally occurs in its bare citation form. This is illustrated in (23) through (25). Agreement occurs on six distinct categories of head, of which three are illustrated here: finite verbs agree with a pronominal subject: (23); non-finite verbs agree with their pronominal object: (24); prepositions also agree with their pronominal object: (25). In each case, the agreeing head and the following pronominal that it agrees with are underlined:

(23) a. Cerddon   nhw   i   'r   dre.
        walk.PAST.3PL   they   to   the   town
        'They walked to town.'
    b. Cerddodd   / *Cerddon   y   genod   i   'r   dre.
        walk.PAST.3SG / walk.PAST.3PL   the   girls   to   the   town
        'The girls walked to town.'

(24) a. Gwnaeth   Meic   eu   gweld   nhw.
        do.PAST.3SG   Meic   3PL   see.INFIN   them
        'Mike saw them.'
    b. Gwnaeth   Meic   (*eu)   weld   y   genod.
        do.PAST.3SG   Meic   3PL   see.INFIN   the   girls
        'Meic saw the girls.'

(25) a. arni   hi   b. arnyn   nhw
        on.3SG.F her   on.3PL   them
        'on her'   'on them'
    c. ar   yr   eneth / *arni   'r   eneth
        on   the   girl / on 3SG.F   the   girl
        'on the girl'
    d. ar   y   genod / *arnyn   y   genod
        on   the   girls / on.3PL   the   girls
        'on the girls'

Example (23a) shows a verb agreeing with a plural pronominal subject in person and number. However, when the verb has a lexical noun phrase subject, as in (23b), this agreeing form is ungrammatical. For finite verbs, there is no 'bare' citation form; instead, the third-person singular is the default form, as (23b) shows.

For non-finite verbs, such as *gweld*, 'see', in (24a), the agreement element is not a verbal inflection, but rather a preverbal marker (here, *eu*) which agrees with the pronominal object—here, in person and number. As (24b) shows, the agreement marker cannot occur with a lexical noun phrase object.

Examples (25a) and (25b) show an inflecting preposition, *ar* 'on', agreeing with a pronominal object. In (25c) and (25d) we see once again that when the preposition has a lexical noun phrase object, there is no agreement, and instead, the preposition occurs in its 'bare' citation form, *ar*.

Unlike more canonical head-marking languages, Welsh does not have true pronominal affixes; in other words, person and number cannot be reliably identified solely from the verbal or prepositional inflections. Table 9.2 illustrates this with the past tense paradigm for a regular verb, *gweld*, 'see' (giving 'I saw', 'you (SG) saw' etc.). Note that there are only three distinct forms of the verb, namely *gwelis*, *gwelodd* and *gwelso*: the pronouns that follow are therefore essential to identify the participant. Colloquial Welsh is, then, not what is termed a 'pro-drop' language: the subject pronouns cannot generally be omitted.

Table 9.2

Inflectional paradigm for the past tense of the Welsh verb *gweld* 'see'

	singular		plural	
first person	gwelis see.PAST.SG	i I	gwelso see.PAST.PL	ni we
second person	gwelis see.PAST.SG	ti you	gwelso see.PAST.PL	chi you(PL)
third person	gwelodd see.PAST.3SG	o/hi he/she	gwelso see.PAST.PL	nhw they

There are two remaining inflectional paradigms for lexical verbs in Colloquial Welsh, namely the future tense and the conditional. Both of these have parallel properties to the past tense in terms of verbal agreement.

As is typical for a European language, Welsh makes extensive use of subordination. Constituent order is the same both in finite root and embedded clauses: (26) illustrates a finite embedded VSO clause, bracketed:

(26) Dywedodd Aled [darllenith Elin y papur].
say.PAST.3SG Aled read.FUT.3SG Elin the paper
'Aled said that Elin will read the paper.'

As well as finite complement clauses, as in (26), Welsh has infinitival complement clauses. The syntax of the latter is actually rather complex, since some of these are interpreted as finite, others as non-finite. Examples (27) and (28) illustrate these two types: both are introduced by a small functional element, *i*, which I've glossed as 'to' since it looks identical to the preposition *i* 'to'. The complement clauses in these examples are superficially identical, but have very different meanings and properties:

(27) Dywedodd Aled [i Elin ddarllen y papur].
say.PAST.3SG Aled to Elin read.INFIN the paper
'Aled said that Elin had read the paper.'

(28) Disgwyliodd Aled [i Elin ddarllen y papur].
expect.PAST.3SG Aled to Elin read.INFIN the paper
'Aled expected Elin to read the paper.'
(i.e. *not* 'Aled expected that Elin had read the paper.')

The difference between the two clause types stems from the kind of verb that occurs in the matrix clause. When the 'upstairs' predicate is a verb like *dweud*, 'say', as in (27), or *meddwl*, 'think', the infinitival clause is interpreted as finite. In fact, there is good evidence that these clauses really are finite, including the fact that they have the same interpretation as ordinary tensed clauses. Conversely, when the 'upstairs' predicate is a verb like *disgwyl* 'expect' or *dymuno*, 'wish/want', the infinitival clause is not interpreted as finite; instead, very like its English translation, it tends to refer to future events that have not yet happened. Syntactically, the embedded clause in (28) does not behave like a finite clause, either. For instance, it is negated with a distinct negator that occurs in non-finite clauses, not at all like the negation seen in (19) to (22), and shown here in bold:

(29) Disgwyliodd Aled [i Elin **beidio â** darllen y papur].
expect.PAST.3SG Aled to Elin NEG with read.INFIN the paper
'Aled expected Elin not to read the paper.'

Clausal subjects are another form of subordination in Welsh, but these can only be non-finite, as in the bracketed clause in (30), and not finite, as in (31):

(30) Mae [**mynd i 'r cyfandir**] yn gyffrous.
be.PRES.3SG go.INFIN to the continent PRED exciting
'Going to the continent is exciting.'

(31) *Mae [bydd Aled yn mynd] yn gyffrous.
be.PRES.3SG be.FUT.3SG Aled PROG go.INFIN PRED exciting
('That Aled will be going is exciting.')

Various valency-changing operations occur in Welsh. The main valency-reducing process is the passive, illustrated in (33), which is formed from the active construction in (32):

(32) Mae   'r   plismon   wedi dal   y   lladron.
     be.PRES.3SG   the   policeman PERF catch.INFIN   the   thieves
     'The policeman has caught the thieves.'

(33) Mae   'r   lladron wedi cael   eu   dal   (gan y   plismon).
     be.PRES.3SG   the   thieves PERF get.INFIN   3PL   catch.INFIN   by   the policeman
     'The thieves have been caught (by the policeman).'

As in passives generally, the subject of the active sentence in (32)—*y plismon*, 'the policeman'—is demoted or deleted in the passive; in (33) there is an optional *gan* 'by' phrase, containing the agent. And the direct object of the active construction (*y lladron* 'the thieves') is promoted to subject position in the passive. These changes can be seen from the constituent order: as always, the subject immediately follows the finite verbal element in Welsh. Like many other languages, Welsh has an auxiliary-plus-main-verb passive construction: the added auxiliary is *cael* 'get' in (33). The lexical verb, *dal* 'catch', also has an agreement marker in the passive, which agrees with the promoted subject in (33): here, it is *eu*, third person plural, agreeing with the plural subject (*y lladron* 'the thieves'). Literally, the passive reads 'The thieves have got their catching by the policeman'. There is no morphological passive in Welsh. (Note also that in keeping with the usual restrictions on agreement in Welsh, the finite auxiliary does not agree with a lexical subject NP in (33), and is therefore singular, *mae*, rather than plural, **maent*, be.PRES.3PL.)

Welsh also has a causative construction, which uses a causative verb such as *gwneud*, 'make', or *peri*, 'cause'; there is no morphological causative. This is a valency-increasing construction.

There is also an impersonal construction (Section 7.1.2), indicated by a morphological change in the verbal inflection (we translate this using a passive in the English, since we have no corresponding impersonal construction):

(34) **Torrwyd**   y   ffenest   (gan y   bachgen).
     break.PAST.IMPERSONAL   the   window   by   the boy
     'The window was broken by the boy.'

Unlike the passive, the impersonal construction does not involve the promotion of an object to subject position: *y ffenest* 'the window' remains the object of the finite verb, and there is no subject at all in (34). The impersonal verb is marked for tense only, and never agrees with the post-verbal argument, even if this is a pronoun. This confirms that the post-verbal element is indeed the object, and not the subject.

Turning finally to *wh*-constructions, Welsh has a *wh*-fronting construction as shown in (35); more examples can be seen in Chapter 8:

(35) [Pa ferch] welaist ti ___ neithiwr?
    which girl see.PAST.2SG you last.night
    'Which girl did you see ___ last night?'

This construction leaves a gap in the position from which the *wh*-phrase has moved, which in this case is the direct object position. A relative clause formed on the direct object position of a finite verb is exactly parallel:

(36) y ferch welaist ti ___ neithiwr
    the girl see.PAST.2SG you last.night
    'the girl you saw ___ last night'

For both *wh*-fronting and relative clause formation, the subject and object of finite verbs in Welsh behave in a similar way: in both cases, there is a gap in the clause. Further down the Accessibility Hierarchy (see Chapter 8), a resumptive strategy either may or must be used, under rather complex conditions. Here, I will simply illustrate one such construction, a *wh*-question formed on the object of a preposition. Note that the preposition inflects and that a resumptive pronoun is optional:

(37) Pwy gest ti 'r anrheg ganddo (fo)?
    who get.PAST.2SG you the present with.3SG.M him
    'Who did you get the present from ___ ?'

Compare here the English translation, which has a gap in the position of prepositional object.

Focus constructions in Welsh are structurally parallel to *wh*-questions, and also involve the fronting of a constituent; some examples can be seen in exercise 4 in Chapter 5.

There are many more fascinating features of Welsh syntax (see Borsley, Tallerman and Willis 2007); the above provides a brief sketch and illustrates the major typological properties of the language.

9.3 SOME QUESTIONS CONCERNING SYNTAX

In this section I briefly address some questions and controversies that have been widely debated in recent linguistic research. Some central readings are provided to whet your appetite.

- Why is it so hard for adults to learn a new language?

Many of us have *attempted to learn* at least one language, in other words by making a conscious effort. And we mostly find it very difficult, even if we're immersed in the new culture. As adults, we can only envy the effortless, naturalistic way in which children learn the ambient language(s) of their culture without any instruction. Moreover, across the world, it's totally normal for children to learn—natively—more than one language; it's English-speaking cultures that are abnormal in being so overwhelmingly monolingual. So children have a head-start in language learning, and adult language learners are always at a grave disadvantage compared to children. As we approach puberty, our language-learning ability declines; beyond puberty, it largely atrophies. After that we may, with persistence, become fluent speakers of a new language, but we won't become native speakers—and we won't have the same intuitions about grammaticality as someone who learnt the language as a child. Language, in common with many other acquired skills, such as musical ability, has what is called a critical period (or a sensitive period) for learning. If learning takes place beyond that period, it is no longer effortless, and acquisition will probably be less than native-like.

In biological terms, none of this is terribly surprising. Many other animals exhibit **sensitive periods** for various systems, including motor systems (involving movement), sensory systems, and behaviour. An example often cited is birdsong. Some (though not all) species of songbirds have to learn their songs by hearing an adult model, inevitably inviting comparisons with language. If they don't have an appropriate adult model (for instance, if they are reared without a singing adult male bird), their song fails to develop properly. Some aspects of song are therefore genetically determined, but input from the environment is crucial. What is important in both birdsong and language, then (and indeed, in many other biological systems) is the interaction between genes and environment. Humans have a language faculty which is genetically specified. This does not mean that there is *in any sense* a single 'language gene', or, most likely, even a dedicated group of language genes. It means that in normal situations, we all acquire at least one language as children: that is hard-wired in our species. The interaction of many genes is almost certainly involved. And input from the environment is needed before the child's brain can get to work building a language. No other species has a language faculty, and no other species can acquire a human language, even under intensive instruction. But for the genetic predisposition to learn language to be triggered, cultural input is required. Language-learning in children relies on normal human interaction, including exposure to language data: this is the environment.

Sensitive periods, 敏感期，又称关键期，指在个体发展过程中，受环境影响最大并最适宜于学习某种行为的时期。在关键期，在适宜的环境影响下，行为习得特别容易，发展特别迅速，机体对来自环境的影响也极为敏感。这时如果正常的发展受到阻碍，将会在以后的发展中产生障碍。这一现象被运用于儿童语言习得领域，被称为"关键期假说"（Critical Period Hypothesis）。

How much of our linguistic ability is pre-specified by our genes, and how much is down to the influence of our environment, is currently a hot topic of debate within linguistics. If all languages have some feature in common, is it inbuilt, part of the genetic recipe for being human? Or can it be attributed to the fact that we are all exposed to human cultures, which present children with certain uniform experiences of the world? Frankly, we don't really know.

When adults do try to learn another language, we typically find it easier to learn languages that are closely related to our own, or that are similar typologically—in other words, languages which have similar characteristics, such as sharing the same word order. As in other spheres of life, the familiar is easier to grasp than the radically new. But this brings us to the next question.

- Are all languages equally complex? And are some languages harder to learn than others?

Impressionistically, few people (including professional linguists) are in any doubt that some languages are harder for each of us to learn as adults. But can languages be intrinsically hard, or intrinsically easy? It used to be generally considered that all languages were, essentially, equally complex, and that complexity in one area of the grammar would be balanced out by simplicity in another area. Recently, that view—which was more ideological than evidence-based—has been challenged from many quarters, and it now seems indefensible. The collection of papers in Sampson et al. (2009) provides much interesting discussion. One of the authors (Guy Deutscher) calls the claim that 'all languages are equally complex' nothing more than an urban legend!

It also now seems that the demographic properties of a language—including the number of speakers it has and the extent of its spread around the world—directly correlate with the linguistic complexity of the language (Lupyan and Dale 2010). At least in terms of their morphosyntax, large global languages which have many millions of speakers, such as English, have been found to be massively simpler than languages with small populations (less than 100,000 people) which are spoken only in one region of the world. One of the main factors seems to be that the large global languages are under pressure to become simpler over time because they are learned by adult learners—who, as we saw above, are not very good at learning the complexities of language when compared with child learners. Conversely, 'esoteric' languages—the small languages of remote communities—may maintain their linguistic complexity exactly because it facilitates learning by infants; complex morphosyntax seems to provide cues to language structure, and since children are so good at learning such complexities, there is no pressure for it to decrease within a small, closed community. For instance, Levinson (2006) discusses a language called Yélî Dnye, spoken by fewer than 4,000 people on a remote island (Rossel Island) several hundred kilometres off the coast of New Guinea. This language, Levinson suggests, is so complex that it lies at 'the boundaries of learnability': adult incomers to the community cannot learn it, and children seem to need an entire community of speakers to learn it successfully, so that if their parents migrate, the offspring may fail to acquire the language fully. It seems, then, that some languages genuinely are more complex than others.

Having reached the end of this book, you should be clear that complexity lies in differing areas of the grammar from language to language. But in standard circumstances (living within a normal linguistic community) children seem to learn each language *as a system* with equal ease, as far as is known. Certainly, there are no languages which are so hard that their speakers don't become fluent until they're eighteen years old. So we can say that whatever complexities a language throws at children, they can cope. Does that mean that all languages are 'the same' in terms of their inherent difficulty for children? I leave this as an open question.

- Do all languages manifest broadly the same syntactic properties?

From reading this book, you will know that on the face of things, there is a great deal of syntactic and morphosyntactic diversity between languages. Does that mean that languages can vary from each other at random, differing in essentially any way? Recently, some eminent linguists have suggested that this is the case (Evans and Levinson 2009). These authors reject the idea that languages are built to a universal pattern, citing many examples of 'esoteric' data that are not common to all languages. They claim that languages can differ in fundamental ways, resulting in a 'jungle' of linguistic complexity. Equally, there is, in their view, no language faculty—no innate template for language-learning that is shared by all members of our species. But this seems to hugely overstate the case. Since all normal children are able to learn a language or several languages very quickly indeed, and without any instruction, and since no other species can achieve anything remotely similar, it seems wrong to deny that we are biologically pre-programmed for language learning.

A very different view to that of Evans and Levinson is outlined by linguists Ray Jackendoff and Peter Culicover (Jackendoff 2002; Culicover and Jackendoff 2005). These linguists suggest that what is often termed 'universal grammar'—the biological endowment for language-learning in our species—provides a 'toolkit': a set of basic principles for building languages, which each language customizes in its own unique ways. There is no reason to expect that everything the toolkit can build will be found in all languages, and this is clearly correct. But the toolkit constrains what *can* be built; when properly investigated, languages do *not* vary from each other at random, but rather, look extremely similar. For instance, Morcom (2009) investigated whether languages all have distinct lexical classes of nouns and verbs, a property which has been denied by certain linguists. She looked at the most controversial languages, and discovered that in each case, there was indeed a distinct noun word class and a distinct verb word class. Careful investigation of this nature by trained linguists often uncovers patterns that are not obvious on the surface.

Having finished revising this book for the fourth edition, I personally am left with the impression that despite the very evident cross-linguistic diversity in syntax and morphology, the languages of the world are similar in many crucial ways. All distinguish several word classes (Chapter 2) and, amongst these word classes, it seems that all languages have a class of nouns and a separate class of verbs. All languages have predicates and all have participants in the event denoted by the predication. All languages have ways of negating clauses, of asking questions, of giving commands. Most languages (perhaps all) distinguish between simple sentences and complex sentences, although not all languages make use of the kind of subordination that is familiar from European languages, as we saw in Chapter 3. All languages have heads which, together with their dependents, form phrases—the constituents of sentences; these were the topics of Chapters 4, 5 and 6. Although languages do not share the same set of constituents, the same sorts of tests for constituent structure can be applied in all languages. These tests rely on harnessing the native-speaker intuitions which we all have about our native language(s), by calling on us to make grammaticality judgements. Hierarchical constituent structure is a universal linguistic feature, though it is clearly exploited far more in some languages than others; free word order languages, such as those discussed in Chapter 6, make less use of constituency. All languages exhibit dependencies between elements in a sentence, such as those examined in Chapters 4, 5 and 8. All languages have at least one method of encoding grammatical relations—via constituent order, morphological case or verbal agreement—as we saw in Chapter 6. All languages appear to exploit variations in constituent order or word order to foreground or background elements, to add focus and emphasis, or to show the topic of a sentence. The vast majority of languages have at least some valency-changing processes, and processes of promotion and demotion which change the basic grammatical relations borne by noun phrases (Chapter 7). The remarkable unity among totally unrelated languages is nicely illustrated in Chapter 7 by the applicative construction, which turns up again and again across the world, and which has much the same grammatical effects in each case. And though not all languages have *wh*-movement, all languages have a way of forming *wh*-questions, and the vast majority have relative clauses too (Chapter 8).

My overall impression, then, is that the syntactic diversity amongst languages from different families and different regions of the world is not trivial, but that the overwhelming homogeneity which exists between languages is far more impressive. In particular, when we look at language isolates (languages with no known relatives) and find that they too utilize the same 'toolkit', it seems safe to say that languages are, unmistakably, amazingly similar in design.

9.4 LAST WORDS: MORE SYNTAX AHEAD

My feeling when I started writing the first edition of this book (published by Arnold/OUP in 1998) was that there is an awful lot of syntax out there in the world, much of it rather daunting. This is a view that students of syntax often appear to share! I hope that by now you are familiar with many of the basic concepts needed in order to understand the ways in which syntax operates in the natural languages of the world, and feel less daunted by its complexities. There is certainly much more syntax out there than a short book can cover, but my intention has been to introduce you to the major syntactic constructions found in the world's languages, and to the main ideas, terms, concepts and scientific argumentation used by linguists to discuss syntax.

Of course, the syntax part of the grammar of a language doesn't exist in isolation. We have seen in nearly every chapter how it interacts both with form (morphology) and meaning (semantics). Not all languages have much morphology, as I've often noted, in the sense of having variations in the form of words. However, many languages use morphology to signal the kinds of syntactic processes that I've talked about in this book, such as the formation of passives or of causatives. Many languages use morphology—case marking, verbal agreement or both—to distinguish between the core participants in a clause, although some languages rely almost entirely on word order to do this. Matters morphological have arisen over and over throughout this book, and if these have interested you, you may wish to move on to a specialized book on the topic, such as Lieber (2010).

Although the topics of semantics, pragmatics and discourse are beyond the scope of this book, all of these areas also critically interact with syntax in all languages. For instance, there are important discourse factors involved in the selection of syntactic constructions; as an example, we saw in Chapter 7 how the need to allow noun phrases to be co-referential with previous noun phrases within the sentence can give rise to constructions such as the passive and the antipassive.

Having completed this introduction, you are now ready to further your study of syntax. There are various (overlapping) paths your study might take. One is to look at descriptions of languages, studying grammars written by linguists. In a good grammar, the chapters on syntax and morphology should be very prominent, and should ideally cover (at least) all the areas we've seen in this book: word classes, grammatical categories (Chapter 2); simple sentences and complex sentences (Chapter 3); heads and their dependents, head-initial or head-final syntax, head-marking or dependent-marking morphology (Chapter 4); constituent structure (Chapter 5); case, agreement, constituent order and grammatical relations (Chapter 6); syntactic processes which change grammatical relations, such as passives and/or antipassives, causatives and applicatives (Chapter 7); and *wh*-questions, relative clauses and focus constructions (Chapter 8). A fascinating overview of the typological variation in the structures of the world's languages is available online: *The world atlas of language structures online* (Dryer and Haspelmath, eds, 2013) is available at http://wals.info.

You might also take a course in linguistic fieldwork, which will build on the knowledge gained throughout this text, and might ultimately lead you to investigate the grammar of languages as yet undescribed (of which there are many).

A further way your study might proceed is by looking at syntactic theory. In order to explain the syntactic differences and similarities between languages, linguists need first to know how alike (and unalike) the world's languages are. This requires good descriptions of the sort mentioned above. Most linguists want not merely to describe languages in isolation, however, but to discover the ways in which their structures are related, even when there are no genetic relationships between the languages. For instance, the morphology and syntax in the majority of languages operates on the basis of either the nominative/accusative system or the ergative/absolutive system, with the former predominating cross-linguistically, as we saw in Chapter 6. Why do languages generally 'choose' one system or the other as their major system, in spite of the existence of several other logical possibilities? The likelihood is, as I suggested in Chapter 6, that the most economical way of, say, distinguishing between grammatical relations is to use one or other of these major systems.

Such economies in the grammar of a language are of interest to theoretical linguists, in part because we hope they will ultimately tell us something about how children can learn their native languages so quickly, regardless of all the complexities that exist. Linguists are also interested in language as a faculty unique to one species, *Homo sapiens*, and in addition, through the study of the human language faculty, we seek to discover more about the remarkable properties of the brain and of human cognition.

Sources of data used in examples

Data sources for the exercises are given in the exercise section of each chapter. Data not listed below are taken from personal knowledge or research or have been obtained from language consultants.

Chapter 1

Indonesian: Foley and Van Valin (1985).
Japanese: Kuno (1978); also in Chapters 2, 3 and 4.
Kwamera: Lindstrom and Lynch (1994); also in Chapter 2.
Rapa Nui: Chapin (1978).

Chapter 2

Akan: Schachter (1985).
Breton: Press (1986); also in Chapter 3.
Chadian Arabic: Abu-Absi (1995); also in Chapters 3 and 4.
ChiBemba: Chung and Timberlake (1985).
Chichewa: Baker (1988); also Chapter 7.
Chinese: Li and Thompson (1978); also in Chapters 4 and 6.
Chinook: Silverstein (1974).
Gunin: McGregor (1993).
Irish: Ó Siadhail (1989); also in Chapters 3, 5 and 6.
Jarawara: Dixon (2004b).
Mbalanhu: Fourie (1993).
Northern Sotho: Louwrens et al. (1995); also in Chapter 6.
Saliba: Mosel (1994); also in Chapter 4.
Yimas: Foley (1991); also in Chapter 8.

Chapter 3

Bare: Aikhenvald (1995); also in Chapters 4 and 7.
Chinese: Thompson (1973), cited in Foley and Van Valin (1984).
Comanche: Charney (1993), cited in Whaley (1997).
Evenki: J. Payne (1985a).
Greek: Horrocks (1983); Terzi (1992) cited in Baker (1996).
Irish: McCloskey (1979).
Japanese: Tsujimura (1996); also in Chapter 8.
Kambera: Klamer (1994); also in Chapters 4 and 6.

Ndyuka: Huttar and Huttar (1994); also in Chapter 4.
Nupe: Thompson and Longacre (1985).
Portuguese: Raposo (1987).
Swedish: Börjars (1991).
Ukrainian: Danylenko and Vakulenko (1995).
Vagala: Pike (1967), cited in Foley and Van Valin (1984).
Yoruba: Bamgbose (1974), cited in Foley and Van Valin (1984).
Wappo: T. Payne (1997).

Chapter 4

Ayacucho: Adelaar (2004).
Chechen: Nichols (1986).
Evenki: Nedjalkov (1997).
Mangga Buang: T. Payne (1997).
Marathi: Pandharipande (1997).
Southern Tiwa: Allen and Frantz (1978, 1983); Allen et al. (1984).
Tinrin: Osumi (1995); also in Chapter 8.
Turkish: Kornfilt (1997); also in Chapter 7.
Tzutujil: Dayley (1981) cited in Nichols (1986).

Chapter 5

Basque: Rebuschi (1989); Hualde et al. (1994); also in Chapter 6.
Malagasy: Keenan (1978).
Persian: J. Payne (1985b).

Chapter 6

Abaza: Allen (1956) cited in Dixon (1994).
Ancient Greek: Blake (2001a).
Apalai: Koehn and Koehn (1986).
Apurinã: Derbyshire and Pullum (1981).
Biri: Beale (1974) cited in Dixon (2002).
Dyirbal: Dixon (1994); also in Chapter 7.
Gilbertese: Keenan (1978).
Icelandic: Andrews (1985); Platzack (1987); Sigurðsson (1991); Zaenen et al. (1985).
Irish: Stenson (1981).
Kalkatungu: Blake (2001b).
Lezgian: Haspelmath (1993).
Malagasy: Keenan (1976).
Pitta-Pitta: Blake (1979).
Tagalog: Andrews (1985); Foley and Van Valin (1984); Schachter (1976).
Turkish: Comrie (1985a).
Warlpiri: Hale (1973, 1983); Austin and Bresnan (1996).

Chapter 7

Chamorro: Gibson (1980) cited in Baker (1988); Cooreman (1988) cited in Palmer (1994).
Chukchee: Kozinsky et al. (1988) cited in Palmer (1994).
Gilbertese: Keenan (1985a).
Greek: Joseph and Philippaki-Warburton (1987) cited in Song (1996).
Indonesian: Chung (1976/1983).
Inuktitut (Greenlandic): Woodbury (1977).
Japanese: Iwasaki (2002); also in Chapter 8.
Korean: Sohn (1999).
Mam: England (1983a, b) cited in Manning (1996) and Palmer (1994).
Songhai: Comrie (1985a).
Tzotzil: Foley and Van Valin (1985).
Yidiny: Dixon (1977).

Chapter 8

Bambera: Creissels (2000).
Bulgarian: Boeckx and Grohmann (2003).
Chinese: Boeckx and Grohmann (2003).
Frisian: Radford (1988).
Hausa: Abraham (1959) cited in Keenan and Comrie (1977).
Hungarian: Kenesei et al. (1998).
Koromfe: Rennison (1997).
Lenakel: Lynch (1998).
Malagasy: Sabel (2003).
Moroccan Arabic: Radford (1988).
Motu: Lynch (1998).
Nakanai: Lynch (1998).
Serbo-Croatian: Stjepanovič (2003); Boeckx and Grohmann (2003).

Chapter 9

Welsh: Additional data can be found in Borsley, Tallerman and Willis (2007).

Glossary

This glossary contains brief definitions of some of the most important (and most difficult) terms and concepts used in the text. The definitions are intended to be a reminder rather than the last word on any given concept, and are thus largely based on examples from English where possible. More extensive cross-linguistic discussion, with data, can be found by looking up the terms in the subject index. For a more comprehensive listing, I recommend that the reader obtains a good dictionary of linguistics, such as Crystal (2008) 6th edition or Matthews (2007), or a more detailed text such as Hurford (1994).

absolutive case: The case of the two CORE ARGUMENTS S and O in an ERGATIVE/ABSOLUTIVE language. If overtly marked, may be indicated via case-marking or by cross-referencing (AGREEMENT) on the verb.

accusative case: The case of the CORE ARGUMENT O in NOMINATIVE/ACCUSATIVE languages. Centrally, the case assigned to DIRECT OBJECTS in languages such as Latin, Russian and German. May be used for other ARGUMENTS of verbs or ADPOSITIONS.

adjunct: A function represented by optional modifying phrases of various classes, e.g. *The post arrived **promptly*** (Adverb Phrase)/***in good time*** (PP)/***this morning*** (NP). Adjuncts are optional modifiers to a HEAD, i.e. not selected by a head, and typically have a rather loose relationship with the head that they modify.

adposition: A cover term for POSTPOSITION and PREPOSITION.

adverb: Typically, an optional modifier to a verb, an adjective, or another adverb. In English, a member of the word class whose central members are recognized by the *-ly* suffix (e.g. *gently, slowly, happily*). Note that not all adverbs have this suffix (e.g. *soon*), and that not all *-ly* words are adverbs (e.g. *friendly, ungodly*). Some adverbs are not optional, but are part of a verb's ARGUMENT structure, e.g. *badly* in *Kim treats Lee **badly***.

adverbial: The traditional term for ADJUNCT, i.e. an optional modifying phrase. The term adverbial refers to a function which may be filled by phrases of various classes. Thus, not all adverbials are ADVERBS, and nor do all adverbs necessarily fulfil the adverbial function.

agreement: The marking of various morphosyntactic properties of a HEAD (such as person, number and gender) on the dependents of that head. For instance, within an NP, DETERMINERS and attributive adjectives often agree with the number and gender of the head noun. An example from French, illustrating agreement in gender, is *le livre vert* (the.M book(.M) green.M 'the green book') vs. *la porte verte* (the.F door(.F) green.F 'the green door'). In English, demonstratives such as *this* vs. *these* agree with the head noun in number: *this book, these books*.

agreement, verb *(see also* CROSS-REFERENCING*)*: The occurrence of inflections or other morphological changes in the verb which reflect the morphosyntactic properties (such as person, number, gender) of some or all of the ARGUMENTS of the verb. For instance, many European languages have verbs which agree with their SUBJECTS, particularly in person and number. In English, a small amount of subject/verb agreement occurs in the third person singular, present tense only: *She sings*.

antipassive: A syntactic process which occurs only in ERGATIVE languages, and which changes the basic GRAMMATICAL RELATIONS borne by CORE ARGUMENTS in the following way: demotes or deletes an O, and promotes an A to an S.

applicative: A construction which creates two OBJECTS, a primary and a secondary object, from an NP-PP construction. In English, refers to the dative movement construction, which relates *Kim sent the parcel to Sue* with *Kim sent Sue the parcel*.

argument: A phrase selected by a HEAD verb, adposition or other class of head. Typically refers to the set of obligatory dependents of a verb. INTRANSITIVE verbs have one argument; TRANSITIVE verbs have two, and so on.

auxiliary: Sometimes termed a 'helping verb'. An element occurring in many, though not all, languages, and which represents the same type of grammatical information as is represented on verbs, e.g. tense, aspect, person/number etc. In English, two major classes: modals (*can*, *must*, *will* etc.) and aspectual auxiliaries (*have*, *be*).

bound form: a morpheme that cannot stand alone, but which is part of a larger word; pronominal affixes are a typical example, as are affixes marking tense.

case-marking: The appearance of morphology on the NP ARGUMENTS of a HEAD (verb, adposition etc.) which marks the relationship each NP has with that head. Two major systems occur cross-linguistically: NOMINATIVE/ACCUSATIVE and ERGATIVE/ABSOLUTIVE.

causative: A verb denoting a meaning such as to 'cause' or 'make' someone do something. May be represented by a lexical verb or via verbal morphology. A causative agent is added to the verb's ARGUMENT structure.

clause: The central unit of syntax: a 'sentence'. Contains a single PREDICATE.

clause, embedded *or* subordinate: In a COMPLEX SENTENCE, any clause which is not the ROOT CLAUSE. In English, recognized by characteristics which include the inability to take SUBJECT/AUXILIARY INVERSION, and the ability to take a COMPLEMENTIZER such as *that*, *whether*.

clause, matrix: A clause which contains a subordinate clause embedded within it.

cleft: A type of focus construction which in English takes the form *It is/was* [***phrase***] *that Y*, e.g. *It was* [*last night*] *that we celebrated the happy event*. The portion bracketed is also shown to be a constituent.

complement: A phrase which is selected by a HEAD, and is often obligatory. Complements typically have a close relationship with the head they modify. In English, the complements to heads generally immediately follow the head in neutral constituent order. However, the ARGUMENT of the verb which is the SUBJECT is also often considered a complement.

complementizer: A word from a small class of grammatical items which introduce a CLAUSE, such as English *that* or *whether*. May indicate the tense or FINITEness of the clause. In HEAD-FINAL languages, a complementizer often follows the clause.

complex sentence: A sentence containing more than one CLAUSE. Includes co-ordinated clauses, but is more generally used to refer to clausal subordination.

copula: A linking word with relatively little semantic content, such as the verb *be*, linking the SUBJECT and the PREDICATE. An English example, where the subject is *that huge dog*: *That huge dog **is** horribly wet and muddy.*

core arguments: The SUBJECT of an INTRANSITIVE verb (S), and the subject (A) and DIRECT OBJECT (O) of a TRANSITIVE verb.

cross referencing (*see also* AGREEMENT): In many languages, verbs are morphologically marked with pronominal affixes which encode information about the verb's arguments. This phenomenon is known as cross-referencing. The term cross-referencing often indicates that the verb alone can constitute a sentence, and is thus sometimes distinguished from verbal agreement, a term indicating that the verb has independent arguments with which the head agrees. Extensive cross-referencing is found in HEAD-MARKING languages. Some linguists regard cross-referencing as part of agreement.

dative: A case often used to mark the indirect object in a language with extensive CASE-MARKING; also often used for experiencer SUBJECTS.

dependent-marking: A language or construction which shows the relationship between a HEAD and its dependents by marking the dependents, rather than by marking the head. Classic dependent-marking is CASE-MARKING on the CORE ARGUMENTS of a verb or the COMPLEMENT of an ADPOSITION. *See* also HEAD-MARKING.

determiner: A member of a small, closed class of words which co-occur with a HEAD noun, and form a noun phrase. English examples include *the, a, this, that, these, those*. Considered by some linguists to constitute the head of the nominal phrase (hence, forming a 'determiner phrase') rather than a dependent to a head noun.

direct object *or* object: The O ARGUMENT of a TRANSITIVE verb is known as the (direct) object. The COMPLEMENT of an ADPOSITION is also known as its object.

ditransitive verb: A verb of the *give, send, take* type, which has three ARGUMENTS: [*Mel*] sent [*the cake*] [*to her auntie*].

echo question: In English, a construction of the type: *She saw **who** at the ice-rink last night?*

ellipsis: A construction in which some portion is omitted when it can be understood from the context. Can often be used as a test for constituency.

ergative language: *see* ERGATIVE/ABSOLUTIVE.

ergative/absolutive: A language which indicates via CASE-MARKING and/or verb AGREEMENT the pairing of the S and O ARGUMENTS (known as ABSOLUTIVE) as opposed to the A argument (known as ERGATIVE) of the verb. Such languages are often termed simply 'ergative'.

ergative case: The case of the CORE ARGUMENT A in an ERGATIVE language. May be indicated via case-marking or by cross-referencing (AGREEMENT) on the verb.

finite verb *and* finite auxiliary: One marked for such grammatical categories as tense, aspect, AGREEMENT with the verb's ARGUMENTS. May not necessarily bear overt inflections, e.g. in English *I/you/we/they **sing**; We **must** leave.* English requires a finite verb or auxiliary in ROOT CLAUSES.

free form: a morpheme which can stand alone; independent pronouns, for example, are free forms.

grammatical relations (*or* grammatical functions): The functions fulfilled by the ARGUMENTS of a verb or ADPOSITION, or other HEAD. Examples are SUBJECT, OBJECT, indirect object.

head: The word which gives a phrase its word class; for instance, the verb in the VP, the PREPOSITION in the PP, the noun in the NP, and so on. Determines the meaning and grammatical properties of the phrase it heads. May require its dependents to agree with it in terms of grammatical categories such as number and gender. It may sometimes be necessary to distinguish between the syntactic head, which determines the word class of the phrase, and the semantic head, which determines its central meaning.

head-final: A phrase in which the HEAD follows its COMPLEMENT(s). For instance, in a POSTPOSITION phrase such as Japanese *sanfuranshisuko made* (literally, *San Francisco to*), the P follows the postpositional object NP. Typically, languages are either predominantly head-final, meaning that the head follows the complement in all major phrase types, or else predominantly HEAD-INITIAL.

head-initial: A phrase in which the HEAD precedes its COMPLEMENT(s). For instance, the head verb precedes the direct object, and the head preposition precedes the prepositional object. Typically, languages are either predominantly head-initial, meaning that the head precedes the complement in all major phrase types, or else predominantly HEAD-FINAL.

head-marking: A language or construction which shows the relationship between a HEAD and its dependents by marking the head, rather than by marking the dependents. Classic head-marking gives rise to extensive verbal CROSS-REFERENCING: the verb is morphologically marked to reflect the grammatical categories of its dependents. *See also* DEPENDENT-MARKING.

infinitive: A NON-FINITE verb form. In English, the bare (uninflected) form of the verb which is used in the frames *Kim must __ (that)* and *He needs to __ (that)*. May have a special marker in some languages, such as French *-er, -ir, -re*.

intransitive verb: A verb taking just one ARGUMENT, namely its SUBJECT. Examples in English are *expire, disappear*. May have optional modifiers, e.g. *The permit expires **in two days***.

inversion, subject/auxiliary: The construction used in English to ask yes/no questions, e.g. ***Will Kim** be there later?*, in which an AUXILIARY moves to the left of the SUBJECT. Also occurs in *wh*-questions in English, e.g. *Where **will Kim** be then?*.

matrix: *see* CLAUSE, MATRIX.

nominalization: A grammatical process which turns a word of a different word class into a noun. Typically, refers to the process by which verbs are turned into nouns, e.g. *approve/approval*; *announce/announcement*.

nominative/accusative language: A language which indicates via CASE-MARKING and/or verb AGREEMENT the pairing of the S and A ARGUMENTS (i.e. all SUBJECTS) as opposed to the O argument (the OBJECT) of the verb. Also refers to languages with little or no overt marking (e.g. English, Chinese) which organize aspects of their syntax along the same alignment, i.e. SA vs. O.

nominative case: The case of the CORE ARGUMENTS S and A ('SUBJECTS') in NOMINATIVE/ ACCUSATIVE languages. Is not necessarily shown overtly by any morphological CASE-MARKING.

non-finite verb: Centrally, one which is not marked either for tense or person/number/gender contrasts. A non-finite clause contains only non-finite verbs or non-finite AUXILIARIES.

object: *see* DIRECT OBJECT.

participle: A term used for certain NON-FINITE verb forms, but excluding the INFINITIVE. In English, refers to the *-ing* form of the verb in *Kim is **sleeping*** and the *-ed/-en* form of the verb (the past participle) in *Kim has **taken/finished*** *the cheese.*

passive: A construction which changes the GRAMMATICAL RELATIONS of CORE ARGUMENTS in the following way: the original SUBJECT of an active sentence is demoted or deleted, and the object of the verb is promoted to the GRAMMATICAL RELATION of subject. The valency of a transitive verb is reduced, since it now contains a subject but no object. The change in grammatical relations is marked by changes to the verbal morphology. An example in English would be *Kim stole the cheese* (active) and *The cheese **was stolen*** *by Kim* (passive).

postposition: *see* PREPOSITION.

predicate: Used in two different senses. May refer just to the verbal element in a CLAUSE, or to the verb and all its modifiers (a VP). There are also non-verbal predicates, for instance those headed by a noun or adjective.

preposition *and* postposition: Typically, small words indicating location in time and space, such as in English *on, in, at, under, over, through, beside* etc. May be transitive or intransitive, i.e. may or may not have an OBJECT.

proform: A word which stands for a full phrase. For instance, a pronoun replaces a full noun phrase. The existence of a proform for a given phrase can be used as a test for constituency.

relative clause: An optional subordinate CLAUSE used to modify a HEAD noun. Restricts the possible referents of that noun to just the subset which the speaker wishes to refer to. For instance, in *Kim liked the dentist who she saw the other day*, there may be other dentists that Kim does not like.

root clause: Root clauses are not embedded within any other clause. The highest MATRIX clause in a COMPLEX SENTENCE is one type; independent clauses are another. In English, root clauses are recognized by characteristics which include the ability to take SUBJECT/AUXILIARY INVERSION.

semantic roles: Roles such as agent, theme or patient, goal and experiencer which are taken by NP ARGUMENTS of a HEAD, especially a head verb. Specific semantic roles are determined by lexical properties of the verb.

subject: A GRAMMATICAL RELATION which refers to the grouping of the A and S ARGUMENTS of a verb. In English, subject pronouns have a special CASE-MARKING in the first and third person, i.e. *I, we, he/she, they*. Cross-linguistically, prototypical subjects are agents, but subjects may bear numerous other SEMANTIC ROLES.

transitive verb: A verb taking two ARGUMENTS, typically referred to as the SUBJECT and (DIRECT) OBJECT. Examples of verbs in English which must be transitive are *assassinate, uncover*.

References

Aarts, Bas (2013). *English syntax and argumentation*, 4th edition. Basingstoke: Palgrave Macmillan.
Abraham, Roy C. (1959). *The language of the Hausa people*. London: University of London Press.
Abu-Absi, Samir (1995). *Chadian Arabic*. Languages of the world/Materials 21. Munich and Newcastle: Lincom Europa.
Adelaar, Willem F. H. (2004). *The languages of the Andes*. Cambridge: Cambridge University Press.
Aikhenvald, Alexandra (1995). *Bare*. Languages of the world/Materials 100. Munich and Newcastle: Lincom Europa.
Aikhenvald, Alexandra, Dixon, R. M. W. and Onishi, Masayuki (eds) (2001). *Non-canonical marking of subjects and objects*. Amsterdam: John Benjamins.
Allen, Barbara J. and Frantz, Donald G. (1978). Verb agreement in Southern Tiwa. *Proceedings of the Fourth Annual Meeting of the Berkeley Linguistics Society*, 11–17.
Allen, Barbara J. and Frantz, Donald G. (1983). Advancements and verb agreement in Southern Tiwa. In David Perlmutter (ed.) *Studies in relational grammar* 1. Chicago, IL and London: University of Chicago Press, 303–314.
Allen, Barbara J., Gardiner, Donna and Frantz, Donald G. (1984). Noun incorporation in Southern Tiwa. *International Journal of American Linguistics* 50, 292–311.
Allen, W. Sidney (1956). Structure and system in the Abaza verbal complex. *Transactions of the Philological Society (1956)*, 127–176.
Alotaibi, Mansour and Borsley, Robert D. (2013). Gaps and resumptive pronouns in Modern Standard Arabic. In Stefan Müller (ed.), *Proceedings of the 20th International Conference on Head-Driven Phrase Structure Grammar, Freie Universität Berlin*. Stanford, CA: CSLI Publications, 6–26.
Amberber, Mengistu (2000). Valency-changing and valency-encoding devices in Amharic. In Dixon and Aikhenvald (eds), 312–322.
Anderson, Stephen (1976). On the notion of subject in ergative languages. In Li (ed.), 1–23.
Anderson, Stephen (1985). Inflectional morphology. In Shopen (ed.), Volume III, 150–201.
Andrews, Avery (1985). The major functions of the noun phrase. In Shopen (ed.), Volume I, 62–154.
Aoun, Joseph, Benmamoun, Elabbas and Choueiri, Lina (2010). *The syntax of Arabic*. Cambridge: Cambridge University Press.
Asher, R. E. and Kumari, T. C. 1997. *Malayalam*. London and New York: Routledge.

Austin, Peter and Bresnan, Joan (1996). Non-configurationality in Australian aboriginal languages. *Natural Language and Linguistic Theory* 14, 215–268.
Baker, Mark (1988). *Incorporation: A theory of grammatical function changing.* Chicago, IL and London: University of Chicago Press.
Baker, Mark (1996). *The polysynthesis parameter.* Oxford and New York: Oxford University Press.
Baker, Mark (2001). *The atoms of language: The mind's hidden rules of grammar.* New York: Basic Books.
Baker, Mark (2003). *Lexical categories: Verbs, nouns, and adjectives.* Cambridge: Cambridge University Press.
Baker, Mark and Kandybowicz, Jason (2003). Verb phrase structure and directionality in Nupe. In John M. Mugane (ed.), *Linguistic typology and representation of African languages: Trends in African linguistics* 5. Trenton, NJ: Africa World Press, 1–22.
Bamgbose, Ayo (1974). On serial verbs and verbal status. *Journal of West African Languages* 9, 17–48.
Beale, Anthony (1974). A grammar of the Biri language of North Queensland. Ms. Australian National University.
Blake, Barry J. (1977). *Case marking in Australian languages.* Canberra: Australian Institute of Aboriginal Studies.
Blake, Barry J. (1979). Pitta-Pitta. In Dixon and Blake (eds), 182–342.
Blake, Barry J. (2001a). *Case*, 2nd edition. Cambridge: Cambridge University Press.
Blake, Barry J. (2001b). The noun phrase in Australian languages. In Simpson et al. (eds), 415–425.
Blau, Joyce and Barak, Veysi (1999). *Manuel de kurde (kurmanji).* Paris: L'Harmattan.
Blevins, James (2003). Passives and impersonals. *Journal of Linguistics* 39, 473–520.
Boeckx, Cedric and Grohmann, Kleanthes K. (2003). Introduction. In Boeckx and Grohmann (eds), 1–15.
Boeckx, Cedric and Grohmann, Kleanthes K. (eds) (2003). *Multiple* wh-*fronting.* Amsterdam and Philadelphia, PA: John Benjamins.
Börjars, Kersti (1991). Complementation in the Scandinavian languages. In Nigel Vincent and Kersti Börjars (eds), *Complement structures in the languages of Europe— more preliminary surveys.* EUROTP Working Papers (European Science Foundation, Programme in Language Typology) III: 2, 65–91.
Börjars, Kersti and Burridge, Kate (2010). *Introducing English grammar*, 2nd edition. London: Routledge.
Borsley, Robert D., Tallerman, Maggie and Willis, David (2007). *The syntax of Welsh.* Cambridge: Cambridge University Press.
Burton-Roberts, Noël (2010). *Analysing sentences: An introduction to English syntax*, 3rd edition. Harlow: Longman.
Campbell, Lyle (2000). Valency-changing derivations in K'iche'. In Dixon and Aikhenvald (eds), 223–281.
Chapin, Paul G. (1978). Easter Island: A characteristic VSO language. In Lehmann (ed.), 139–168.
Charney, Jean O. (1993). *A grammar of Comanche.* Lincoln, NE: University of Nebraska.

Chomsky, Noam (1977). On *wh*-movement. In Peter Culicover, Thomas Wasow and Adrian Akamajian (eds), *Formal syntax*. New York: Academic Press, 77–132.

Chomsky, Noam (1986). *Knowledge of language: Its nature, origin and use*. New York: Praeger.

Chomsky, Noam (2012). *The science of language: Interviews with James McGilvray*. Cambridge: Cambridge University Press.

Chung, Sandra (1976). An object-creating rule in Bahasa Indonesia. *Linguistic Inquiry* 7, 1–37. Reprinted in David Perlmutter (ed.), *Studies in relational grammar* 1 (1983). Chicago and London: University of Chicago Press, 219–271.

Chung, Sandra and Timberlake, Alan (1985). Tense, aspect and mood. In Shopen (ed.), Volume III, 202–258.

Clamons, Robbin, Mulkern, Ann E., Sanders, Gerald and Stenson, Nancy (1999). The limits of formal analysis: Pragmatic motivation in Oromo grammar. In Michael Darnell, Edith Moravcsik, Frederick J. Newmeyer, Michael Noonan and Kathleen Wheatley (eds), *Functionalism and formalism in linguistics. Volume II: Case studies*. Amsterdam: John Benjamins, 59–76.

Comrie, Bernard (1976). *Aspect*. Cambridge: Cambridge University Press.

Comrie, Bernard (1985a). *Tense*. Cambridge: Cambridge University Press.

Comrie, Bernard (1985b). Causative verb formation and other verb-deriving morphology. In Shopen (ed.), Volume III, 309–348.

Comrie, Bernard (1989). *Language universals and linguistic typology*, 2nd edition. Oxford: Basil Blackwell.

Comrie, Bernard and Keenan, Edward L. (1979). Noun phrase accessibility revisited. *Language* 55, 649–664.

Cook, Anthony (1988). Participle sentences in Wakiman. In Peter Austin (ed.), *Complex sentence constructions in Australian languages*. Amsterdam and Philadelphia, PA: John Benjamins, 69–95.

Cooreman, Ann (1988). The antipassive in Chamorro; variations on a theme of transitivity. In Shibatani (ed.), 561–593.

Corbett, Greville (1991). *Gender*. Cambridge: Cambridge University Press.

Corbett, Greville (2000). *Number*. Cambridge: Cambridge University Press.

Corbett, Greville (2006). *Agreement*. Cambridge: Cambridge University Press.

Creissels, Denis (2000). Typology. In Heine and Nurse (eds), 231–258.

Creissels, Denis (2008a). Remarks on split intransitivity and fluid intransitivity. In Olivier Bonami and P. Cabredo Hofherr (eds), *Empirical issues in syntax and semantics* 7. Paris: Colloque de Syntaxe et Sémantique à Paris, 139–168.

Creissels, Denis (2008b). Direct and indirect explanations of typological regularities: The case of alignment variations. *Folia Linguistica* 42, 1–38.

Croft, William A. (2001). *Radical construction grammar: Syntactic theory in typological perspective*. New York and Oxford: Oxford University Press.

Crystal, David (2000). *Language death*. Cambridge: Cambridge University Press.

Crystal, David (2008). *A dictionary of linguistics and phonetics*, 6th edition. Oxford: Wiley Blackwell.

Culicover, Peter W. and Jackendoff, Ray (2005). *Simpler syntax*. Oxford: Oxford University Press.

Danylenko, Andrii and Serhii Vakulenko (1995). *Ukrainian*. Languages of the world/ Materials 5. Munich and Newcastle: Lincom Europa.

Davenport, Mike and Hannahs, S. J. (2010). *Introducing phonetics and phonology*, 3rd edition. London: Routledge.

Dayley, Jon P. (1981). *A Tzutujil grammar*. Unpublished PhD dissertation, University of California, Berkeley, CA.

Deering, Nora and Delisle, Helga (1976). *Mohawk: A teaching grammar*. Kahnawake, Quebec: Thunderbird Press.

Derbyshire, Desmond C. and Pullum, Geoffrey K. (1981). Object initial languages. *International Journal of American Linguistics* 47, 192–214.

Dixon, R. M. W. (1972). *The Dyirbal language of North Queensland*. Cambridge: Cambridge University Press.

Dixon, R. M. W. (1977). *A grammar of Yidiny*. Cambridge: Cambridge University Press.

Dixon, R. M. W. (1979). Ergativity. *Language* 55, 59–138.

Dixon, R. M. W. (1994). *Ergativity*. Cambridge: Cambridge University Press.

Dixon, R. M. W. (1995). Complement clauses and complementation strategies. In F. R. Palmer (ed.), *Grammar and meaning: Essays in honour of Sir John Lyons*. Cambridge: Cambridge University Press, 175–220.

Dixon, R. M. W. (1997). *The rise and fall of languages*. Cambridge: Cambridge University Press.

Dixon, R. M. W. (2000). A typology of causatives: Form, syntax and meaning. In Dixon and Aikhenvald (eds), 30–83.

Dixon, R. M. W. (2002). *Australian languages: Their nature and development*. Cambridge: Cambridge University Press.

Dixon, R. M. W. (2004a). Adjective classes in typological perspective. In R. M. W. Dixon and Alexandra Y. Aikhenvald (eds), *Adjective classes: A crosslinguistic typology*. Oxford: Oxford University Press, 1–49.

Dixon, R. M. W. (2004b). *The Jarawara language of Southern Amazonia*. Oxford: Oxford University Press.

Dixon, R. M. W. and Aikhenvald, Alexandra (eds) (2000). *Changing valency: Case studies in transitivity*. Cambridge: Cambridge University Press.

Dixon, R. M. W. and Blake, Barry J. (eds) (1979). *Handbook of Australian languages* 1. Canberra: Australian National University and Amsterdam: John Benjamins.

Donohue, Mark and Brown, Lea (1999). Ergativity: Some additions from Indonesia. *Australian Journal of Linguistics* 19, 57–76.

Dryer, Matthew S. (1991). SVO languages and the OV: VO typology. *Journal of Linguistics* 27, 443–482.

Dryer, Matthew S. (1997). Are grammatical relations universal? In Joan Bybee, John Haiman and Sandra A. Thompson (eds), *Essays on language function and language type. Dedicated to T. Givón*. Amsterdam: John Benjamins, 115–143.

Dryer, Matthew S. and Haspelmath, Martin (eds) (2013). *The world atlas of language structures online*. Leipzig: Max Planck Institute for Evolutionary Anthropology. (Available online at http://wals.info)

Emonds, Joseph E. (1986). Parts of speech in generative grammar. *Linguistic Analysis* 16, 247–285.

England, Nora (1983a). Ergativity in Mamean (Mayan) languages. *International Journal of American Linguistics* 49, 1–19.

England, Nora (1983b). *A grammar of Mam, a Mayan language.* Austin, TX: University of Texas Press.

Evans, Nicholas and Levinson, Stephen C. (2009). The myth of language universals: Language diversity and its importance for cognitive science. *Behavioral and Brain Sciences* 32, 429–492.

Everett, Daniel. (2008). *Don't sleep, there are snakes. Life and language in the Amazonian jungle.* London: Profile Books.

Everett, Daniel and Kern, Barbara (1997). *Wari'.* London and New York: Routledge.

Foley, William A. (1991). *The Yimas language of New Guinea.* Stanford, CA: Stanford University Press.

Foley, William A. and Van Valin, Robert D. Jr. (1984). *Functional syntax and universal grammar.* Cambridge: Cambridge University Press.

Foley, William A. and Van Valin, Robert D. Jr. (1985). Information packaging in the clause. In Shopen (ed.), Volume I, 282–364.

Fourie, David J. (1993). *Mbalanhu.* Languages of the world/Materials 3. Munich and Newcastle: Lincom Europa.

Frajzyngier, Zygmunt (2002). *A grammar of Hdi.* Berlin and New York: Mouton de Gruyter.

Fromkin, Victoria, Rodman, Robert and Hyams, Nina (2007). *An introduction to language*, 8th edition. Boston, MA: Thomson Wadsworth.

Gazdar, Gerald, Klein, Ewan and Pullum, Geoffrey K. (eds) (1983). *Order, concord and constituency.* Dordrecht: Foris.

Gibson, Jeanne D. (1980). *Clause union in Chamorro and in universal grammar.* Unpublished PhD dissertation, University of California, San Diego, CA.

Greenberg, Joseph (1966). Some universals of grammar with particular reference to the order of meaningful elements. In Joseph Greenberg (ed.), *Universals of language*, 2nd edition. Cambridge, MA: MIT Press, 73–113.

Hale, Kenneth L. (1973). Person marking in Walbiri. In Stephen R. Anderson and Paul Kiparsky (eds), *A festschrift for Morris Halle.* New York: Holt, Rinehart, and Winston, 308–344.

Hale, Kenneth L. (1983). Warlpiri and the grammar of non-configurational languages. *Natural Language and Linguistic Theory* 1, 5–47.

Haspelmath, Martin (1993). *A grammar of Lezgian.* Berlin and New York: Mouton de Gruyter.

Haspelmath, Martin (2007). Pre-established categories don't exist: Consequences for language description and typology. *Linguistic Typology* 11, 119–132.

Haviland, John (1979). Guugu Yimidhirr. In Dixon and Blake (eds), 26–180.

Hawkins, John A. (1983). *Word order universals.* New York: Academic Press.

Heine, Bernd and Nurse, Derek (eds) (2000). *African languages: An introduction.* Cambridge: Cambridge University Press.

Horrocks, Geoffrey (1983). The order of constituents in Modern Greek. In Gazdar et al. (eds), 95–111.

Hualde, José Ignacio, Elordieta, Gorka and Elordieta, Arantzazu (1994). *The Basque dialect of Lekeitio*. Bilbao: University of the Basque Country.
Huddleston, Rodney and Pullum, Geoffrey K. (2002). *The Cambridge grammar of the English language*. Cambridge: Cambridge University Press.
Huddleston, Rodney and Pullum, Geoffrey K. (2005). *A student's introduction to English grammar*. Cambridge: Cambridge University Press.
Hudson, Richard A. (1984). *Word grammar*. Oxford: Basil Blackwell.
Hudson, Richard A. (1987). Zwicky on heads. *Journal of Linguistics* 23, 109–132.
Hudson, Richard A. (1990). *English word grammar*. Oxford: Basil Blackwell.
Hudson, Richard A. (2007). *Language networks: The new word grammar*. Oxford: Oxford University Press.
Hurford, James R. (1994). *Grammar: A student's guide*. Cambridge: Cambridge University Press.
Huttar, George L. and Huttar, Mary L. (1994). *Ndyuka*. London and New York: Routledge.
Jackendoff, Ray (1993). *Patterns in the mind: Language and human nature*. New York and London: Harvester Wheatsheaf.
Jackendoff, Ray (2002). *Foundations of language: Brain, meaning, grammar, evolution*. Oxford: Oxford University Press.
Iwasaki, Shoichi I. (2002). *Japanese*. Amsterdam and Philadelphia, PA: John Benjamins.
Jones, B. M. and Thomas, Alan R. (1977). *The Welsh language: Studies in its syntax and semantics*. Cardiff: University of Wales Press.
Joseph, Brian D. and Philippaki-Warburton, Irene (1987). *Modern Greek*. London: Croom Helm.
Keenan, Edward L. (1976). Towards a universal definition of 'subject'. In Li (ed.), 303–333.
Keenan, Edward L. (1978). The syntax of subject-final languages. In Lehmann (ed.), 267–327.
Keenan, Edward L. (1985a). Passive in the world's languages. In Shopen (ed.), Volume I, 243–281.
Keenan, Edward L. (1985b). Relative clauses. In Shopen (ed.), Volume II, 141–170.
Keenan, Edward L. and Comrie, Bernard (1977). Noun phrase accessibility and universal grammar. *Linguistic Inquiry* 8, 63–99.
Keenan, Edward L. and Comrie, Bernard (1979). Data on the noun phrase accessibility hierarchy. *Language* 55, 333–352.
Kenesei, István, Vago, Robert M. and Fenyvesi, Anna (1998). *Hungarian*. London and New York: Routledge.
Klamer, Marian (1994). *Kambera: A language of Eastern Indonesia*. Amsterdam: Holland Institute of Generative Linguistics.
Koehn, Edward and Koehn, Sally (1986). Apalai. In Desmond C. Derbyshire and Geoffrey K. Pullum (eds), *Handbook of the Amazonian languages* 1. Berlin: Mouton de Gruyter, 32–127.
Kornfilt, Jaklin (1997). *Turkish*. London and New York: Routledge.
Kozinsky, I. Sv., Nedjalkov, V. P. and Polinskaya, M. S. (1988). Antipassive in Chukchee: Oblique object, object incorporation, zero object. In Shibatani (ed.), 651–706.

Kuno, Susumo (1978). Japanese: A characteristic OV language. In Lehmann (ed.), 57–138.

Lehmann, Winfred P. (ed.) (1978). *Syntactic typology: Studies in the phenomenology of language*. Sussex: Harvester Press.

Levinson, Stephen C. (2006). Introduction: The evolution of culture in a microcosm. In Stephen C. Levinson and Pierre Jaisson (eds), *Evolution and culture*. Cambridge, MA: The MIT Press, 1–41.

Lewis, M. Paul, Simons, Gary F. and Fennig, Charles D. (eds) (2013). *Ethnologue: Languages of the world*, 17th edition. Dallas, TX: SIL International. Online version: www.ethnologue.com.

Li, Charles N. (ed.) (1976). *Subject and topic*. New York: Academic Press.

Li, Charles N. and Thompson, Sandra A. (1978). An exploration of Mandarin Chinese. In Lehmann (ed.), 223–266.

Lieber, Rochelle (2010). *Introducing morphology*. Cambridge: Cambridge University Press.

Lindstrom, Lamont and Lynch, John (1994). *Kwamera*. Languages of the world/Materials 2. Munich and Newcastle: Lincom Europa.

Lobeck, Anne (2000). *Discovering grammar: An introduction to English sentence structure*. New York and Oxford: Oxford University Press.

Louwrens, Louis J., Kosch, Ingeborg M. and Kotzé, Albert E. (1995). *Northern Sotho*. Languages of the world/Materials 30. Munich and Newcastle: Lincom Europa.

Lupyan, Gary and Dale, Rick (2010). Language structure is partly determined by social structure. *PLoS ONE* 5(1): e8559. doi:10.1371/journal.pone.0008559.

Lynch, John (1998). *Pacific languages: An introduction*. Honolulu, HI: University of Hawai'i Press.

Lyons, John (1966). Towards a 'notional' theory of the 'parts of speech'. *Journal of Linguistics* 2, 209–236.

McCloskey, James (1979). *Transformational syntax and model-theoretic semantics: A case study in Modern Irish*. Dordrecht and Boston: D. Reidel Publishing Company.

McCloskey, James (2000). Quantifier float and *wh*-movement in an Irish English. *Linguistic Inquiry* 31, 57–84.

McGregor, William B. (1993). *Gunin/Kwini*. Languages of the world/Materials 11. Munich and Newcastle: Lincom Europa.

McMahon, April M. S. (1994). *Understanding language change*. Cambridge: Cambridge University Press.

McWhorter, John H. (2011). *Linguistic simplicity and complexity: Why do languages undress?* Berlin: de Gruyter.

Manning, Christopher D. (1996). *Ergativity: Argument structure and grammatical relations*. Stanford, CA: CSLI Publications.

Matras, Yaron (2002). *Romani: A linguistic introduction*. Cambridge: Cambridge University Press.

Matthews, Peter (2014). *The concise Oxford dictionary of linguistics*, 3rd edition. Oxford and New York: Oxford University Press.

Millar, Robert McColl (2007). *Trask's historical linguistics*, 2nd edition. London: Routledge.

Morcom, Lindsay (2009). *The universality and demarcation of lexical categories cross-linguistically*. Unpublished DPhil. thesis, University of Oxford.
Mosel, Ulrike (1994). *Saliba*. Languages of the world/Materials 31. Munich and Newcastle: Lincom Europa.
Nedjalkov, Igor (1997). *Evenki*. London and New York: Routledge.
Nettle, Daniel and Romaine, Suzanne (2000). *Vanishing voices: The extinction of the world's languages*. Oxford and New York: Oxford University Press.
Nichols, Johanna (1986). Head-marking and dependent-marking grammar. *Language* 62, 56–119.
Noonan, Michael (1985). Complementation. In Shopen (ed.), Volume III, 42–140.
Ó Siadhail, Mícheál (1989). *Modern Irish: Grammatical structure and dialectal variation*. Cambridge: Cambridge University Press.
Osumi, Midori (1995). *Tinrin grammar*. Honolulu, HI: University of Hawai'i Press.
Otsuka, Yuko (2005). Two derivations of VSO: A comparative study of Niuean and Tongan. In Andrew Carnie, Heidi Harley and Sheila Ann Dooley (eds), *Verb first: On the syntax of verb-initial languages*. Amsterdam and Philadelphia, PA: John Benjamins, 65–90.
Palmer, F. R. (1994). *Grammatical roles and relations*. Cambridge: Cambridge University Press.
Pandharipande, Rajeswari V. (1997). *Marathi*. London and New York: Routledge.
Payne, John (1985a). Negation. In Shopen (ed.), Volume I, 197–242.
Payne, John (1985b). Complex phrases and complex sentences. In Shopen (ed.), Volume II, 3–41.
Payne, Thomas E. (1997). *Describing morphosyntax: A guide for field linguists*. Cambridge: Cambridge University Press.
Payne, Thomas E. (2006). *Exploring language structure: A student's guide*. Cambridge: Cambridge University Press.
Pike, Kenneth (1967). *Grammar as wave*. Georgetown University Monographs on Language and Linguistics 20. Washington, DC: Georgetown University Press, 1–14.
Pinker, Steven (1994). *The language instinct*. London: Penguin Books.
Platzack, Christer (1987). The Scandinavian languages and the null-subject parameter. *Natural Language and Linguistic Theory* 5, 377–401.
Poole, Geoffrey (2011). *Syntactic theory*, 2nd edition. Basingstoke: Palgrave Macmillan.
Press, Ian (1986). *A grammar of Modern Breton*. Berlin: Mouton de Gruyter.
Pullum, Geoffrey K. and Ladusaw, William A. (1996). *Phonetic symbol guide*, 2nd edition. Chicago, IL and London: University of Chicago Press.
Radford, Andrew (1988). *Transformational grammar: A first course*. Cambridge: Cambridge University Press.
Raposo, Eduardo (1987). Case theory and Infl-to-Comp: The inflected infinitive in European Portuguese. *Linguistic Inquiry* 18, 85–109.
Rebuschi, Georges (1989). Is there a VP in Basque? In László Marácz and Pieter Muysken (eds), *Configurationality: The typology of asymmetries*. Dordrecht: Foris, 85–116.
Rennison, John R. (1997). *Koromfe*. London and New York: Routledge.
Sabel, Joachim (2003). Malagasy as an optional *wh*-fronting language. In Boeckx and Grohmann (eds), 229–254.

Sampson, Geoffrey, Gil, David and Trudgill, Peter (eds) (2009). *Language complexity as an evolving variable*. Oxford: Oxford University Press.

Schachter, Paul (1976). The subject in Philippine languages: Topic, actor, actor-topic or none of the above. In Li (ed.), 491–518.

Schachter, Paul (1985). Parts-of-speech systems. In Shopen (ed.), Volume I, 3–61.

Shibatani, Masayoshi (ed.) (1988). *Passive and voice*. Amsterdam and Philadelphia, PA: John Benjamins.

Shopen, Timothy (ed.) (1985). *Language typology and syntactic description*. Volume I: *Clause structure*; Volume II: *Complex constructions*; Volume III: *Grammatical categories and the lexicon*. Cambridge: Cambridge University Press.

Shopen, Tim (2001). Explaining typological differences between languages. In Simpson et al. (eds), 187–197.

Siewierska, Anna (2004). *Person*. Cambridge: Cambridge University Press.

Sigurðsson, Halldór Ármann (1991). Icelandic case-marked PRO and the licensing of lexical arguments. *Natural Language and Linguistic Theory* 9, 327–363.

Sigurðsson, Halldór Ármann (2006). The Icelandic noun phrase: Central traits. *Arkiv för nordisk filologi* 121, 193–236.

Silverstein, Michael (1974). Dialectal developments in Chinookan tense–aspect systems: an areal-historical analysis. *International Journal of American Linguistics*, Memoir 29, 44–99.

Simpson, Jane, Nash, David, Laughren, Mary, Austin, Peter and Alpher, Barry (eds) (2001). *Forty years on: Ken Hale and Australian languages*. Canberra: Pacific Linguistics.

Sohn, Ho-Min (1999). *The Korean language*. Cambridge: Cambridge University Press.

Song, Jae Jung (1996). *Causatives and causation: A universal-typological perspective*. London and New York: Longman.

Song, Jae Jung (2001). *Linguistic typology: Morphology and syntax*. London: Longman.

Stenson, Nancy (1981). *Studies in Irish syntax*. Tübingen: Gunter Narr Verlag.

Stjepanović, Sandra (2003). Multiple wh-fronting in Serbo-Croatian matrix questions and the matrix sluicing construction. In Boeckx and Grohmann (eds), 255–284.

Stucky, Susan (1983). Verb phrase constituency and linear order in Makua. In Gazdar et al. (eds), 75–94.

Terzi, Arhonto (1992). *PRO in finite clauses: A study of the inflectional heads of the Balkan languages*. Unpublished PhD dissertation, City University of New York.

Thompson, Sandra A. (1973). Resultative verb compounds in Mandarin: A case for lexical rules. *Language* 49, 361–379.

Thompson, Sandra A. and Longacre, Robert E. (1985). Adverbial clauses. In Shopen (ed.), Volume II, 171–234.

Tomlin, Russell (1986). *Basic word order: Functional principles*. London: Croom Helm.

Tsujimura, Natsuko (1996). *An introduction to Japanese linguistics*. Oxford: Blackwell Publishers.

van der Wal, Jenneke (2009). *Word order and information structure in Makhuwa-Enahara*. Utrecht: LOT.

Van Valin, Robert D., Jr. (1985). Case marking and the structure of the Lakhota clause. In Johanna Nichols and Anthony C. Woodbury (eds), *Grammar inside and outside the clause: Some views of theory from the field*. Cambridge: Cambridge University Press, 363–413.

Watters, John R. (2000). Syntax. In Heine and Nurse (eds), 194–230.

Whaley, Lindsay J. (1997). *Introduction to typology: The unity and diversity of language*. Thousand Oaks, CA and London: Sage Publications.

Woodbury, Anthony (1977). Greenlandic Eskimo: Ergativity and relational grammar. In Peter Cole and Jerry Sadock (eds), *Grammatical relations* (Syntax and Semantics 8), 307–336.

Zaenen, Annie, Maling, Joan and Thráinsson, Höskuldur (1985). Case and grammatical functions: The Icelandic passive. *Natural Language and Linguistic Theory* 3, 441–483.

Zwicky, Arnold M. (1985). Heads. *Journal of Linguistics* 21, 1–29.